D0219900

BEYOND AUSCHWITZ

Beyond

940.5318
M849b

Post-Holocaust Jewish Thought in America

MICHAEL L. MORGAN

OXFORD

UNIVERSITY PRESS

2001

OXFORD
UNIVERSITY PRESS

Oxford   New York

Athens   Auckland   Bangkok   Bogotá   Buenos Aires   Cape Town
Chennai   Dar es Salaam   Delhi   Florence   Hong Kong   Istanbul   Karachi
Kolkata   Kuala Lumpur   Madrid   Melbourne   Mexico City   Mumbai
Nairobi   Paris   São Paulo   Shanghai   Singapore   Taipei   Tokyo   Toronto   Warsaw

and associated companies in
Berlin   Ibadan

Copyright © 2001 by Michael L. Morgan

Published by Oxford University Press, Inc.
198 Madison Avenue, New York, New York 10016

Oxford is a registered trademark of Oxford University Press.

All rights reserved. No part of this publication may be reproduced,
stored in a retrieval system, or transmitted, in any form or by any means,
electronic, mechanical, photocopying, recording, or otherwise,
without the prior permission of Oxford University Press.

Library of Congress Cataloging-in-Publication Data
Morgan, Michael L., 1944–
Beyond Auschwitz : post-Holocaust Jewish thought in America / Michael L. Morgan.
p.   cm.
ISBN 0-19-514589-5; 0-19-514862-2 (pbk.)
1. Holocaust, Jewish (1939–1945)—Influence.   2. Holocaust (Jewish theology)
3. Philosophy, Jewish.   4. Judaism—United States.   I. Title
D804.3 .M657 2001
940.53'18—dc21   00-067751

1 3 5 7 9 8 6 4 2

Printed in the United States of America
on acid-free paper

TO AUD

In the late sixties and early seventies, for American Jews, especially at the time of the Six Day War and thereafter, the memory of Auschwitz "flashed up" on the screen of consciousness. That memory was seized by the American Jewish world and by a small number of Jewish thinkers or theologians. It was a threatening memory, but at the same time it incorporated resources for the present and the future. These thinkers were not alone. Others before them had also struggled with that memory—Hannah Arendt, Raul Hilberg, Elie Wiesel and Primo Levi among them, as did others during the same period and after. So many they were, pressed by urgency and despair to wrestle with madness and to win a small victory for hope in the face of danger. Theirs was no small achievement, to have forced themselves to face honestly and deeply the most disturbing horrors, atrocities beyond imagination but not beyond actuality, and then to have found a way to recovery, to the past, and then, in the end, back to the present. Our debt to them, to these custodians of memory and laborers of recovery, is great; by telling their story we begin to repay it.[1]

Today many Jews in America face the future with a sense of uncertainty and suspicion. As they try to understand the world and their place in it, they turn to the past—to the world of eastern European Jewry, the period of Emancipation, the period of messianic fervor in seventeenth century Europe, the golden age in Spain, and beyond. They turn to tradition and texts, to Bible, midrash, halakhah, and poetry, and to commentaries, liturgy, homilies, and law. But this vast resource is mediated to the present by recent events of transforming significance—the destruction of European Jewry, the creation and use of nuclear weapons, the reestablishment of the Jewish state, the emergence of the civil rights movement, the student rebellions of the sixties, the wars in Israel—the Six Day War, the Yom Kippur War, the Lebanon War, and now the fragmentation of the Soviet empire and the resurgent nationalism throughout the world. The Nazi Holocaust plays a special role among these events; at a particular point, Jewish theologians found the courage to confront it and to recover a Jewish world in terms of that encounter. This book is about that encounter and how those thinkers performed it.

This book, then, is about recovering the past as part of identity and self-understanding, and it is about challenges to that project, when a past event is both undeniable and threatening. It is a book of philosophy and religious thought that involves an interpretive encounter with an episode in recent Jewish thought and life.

My focus, moreover, has not been theological, in a narrow sense, but rather philosophical; some may call it theoretical. The novelty and significance of post-Holocaust Jewish thought, I argue, concerns the relation between history and identity and not the particular theological results—the doctrines of God, covenant, providence, and messianism—that these thinkers develop. Some may find this misguided of me; I try to defend it as I go along. This means that there are dimensions of American Jewish thought that I do not discuss fully and that others might usefully examine. Indeed, even my discussion of these figures and issues is very selective.

I have been working on this project for nearly twenty years, and its roots for me go back about thirty years. On countless occasions I discussed these themes with classes of students, groups of colleagues, and congregational audiences, both Jewish and Christian. Many colleagues and friends have contributed to my thinking about these matters, at one time or another. These include Roy Eckardt, Irving Greenberg, Ken Seeskin, Michael Stroh, Arnie Eisen, Zev Harvey, David Biale, David Ellenson, Paul Mendes-Flohr, David Myers, David Finkelstein, Paul Franks, Jim Tully, Michael Meyer, John Efron, Jeff Isaac, John Bodnar, Robert Willis, Clark Williamson, Saul Friedlander, Michael André Bernstein, David Stern, Aron Rodrigue, David Tracy, Steven Aschheim, Michael Marmur, and Charles Taylor. Of special importance were long conversations with Chuck Taylor in Montreal, Saul Friedlander in Bloomington, and correspondence with Michael Bernstein. For years, Sam Westfall and I discussed these and other matters; he is deeply missed— his wonderful qualities of mind and spirit and his sensitivity to the benefits and the burdens of science to the religious sensibility. I also want to thank Joshua Shaw for assistance with the proofs and index and Indiana University for several grants and for the wonderful opportunity I have had to teach and work. The Library at the Hebrew Union College was extremely helpful as I studied periodicals and source material from the postwar period. I also thank the Hebrew Union College in Cincinnati for the opportunity to conduct a class for rabbinic students on post-Holocaust Jewish thought in the fall of 1997. Debbie and Sara were always polite in their questions about how the book was developing and when it might be completed. Audrey, as always, was more than tolerant; without her patience and her love, I would accomplish little and have no reason for even that.

When I was an undergraduate, I first read an essay by Emil Fackenheim and then, when I entered rabbinical seminary, my classmate Shelly Zimmerman gave me a mimeographed collection of Fackenheim's essays that he had used in Toronto. Shelly has become a lifelong friend; Emil has become more than my teacher. From the moment we met, a special bond has existed and grown between us. This book would not exist but for him, his unqualified fidelity to philosophical integrity and Jewish life, his seriousness and probity, his humor and friendship.

Contents

BEYOND AUSCHWITZ

To articulate the past historically does not mean to recognize it "the way it really was." It means to seize hold of a memory as it flashes up at a moment of danger. . . . The danger affects both the content of the tradition and its receivers. The same threat hangs over both. . . . *[E]ven the dead* will not be safe from the enemy if he wins.

— Walter Benjamin,
"Theses on the Philosophy of History" (*Illuminations*)

Introduction

What has been the impact of the Holocaust on Jewish theology in North America? What questions has the Holocaust raised for Jewish religious thinkers as they have tried to reflect on the character of Judaism and Jewish experience in the decades following World War II? What problems has it posed for them? Have religious thinkers been able to cope with Auschwitz, to confront it openly and seriously and yet to go on? Has their work been appreciated, read, understood; has it been influential, marginal, or significant?

Questions like these need to be addressed and answered. For at least two decades, from the mid-1960s through the 1980s, Jewish religious thought—what was once called "Jewish theology"—was dominated by the demands of Auschwitz and what seemed to follow from those demands. To be sure, Jewish thought of this period was not exclusively concerned with the Holocaust and what it meant for Judaism, Jewish concepts, belief, principles, and practice.[1] There were other styles and interests that arose in the 1970s and 1980s—textual hermeneutics, for example, feminist theology, a renewed interest in mysticism and spirituality, and a return to Maimonides. But the most prominent and persistent trend in Jewish thought involved an encounter with the death camps and an effort to identify the implications of such an encounter for Jewish belief and Jewish life. Often these implications seemed to coalesce around the themes of God, the covenant, messianism, Israel, and such matters fundamental to Judaism. Hence, post-Holocaust Jewish theology determined an agenda for Jewish theological discussion, for historical interest, and for Jewish life. It legitimated a widespread desire to examine and discuss Nazism, the victims of Nazism, and the history of the Nazi destruction of European Jewry. It grounded in principle the deeply felt need to keep the memory of the Holocaust alive, through liturgical innovation and cultural creation—in films, poetry, fiction, monuments, and museums.[2] And it authorized the centrality of the Holocaust in American Jewish self-consciousness and hence in Jewish identity.

3

There has been a good deal of debate about the role and influence of the Holo-caust on American Jewish identity since the late 1960s.[3] The debate has many di-mensions—psychological, historical, and theological. Is it healthy or appropriate or authentic to shape Jewish self-understanding in terms of an event that is so nega-tive, so extraordinary in its horror, and so alien? Perhaps some will find these issues immediate and pressing. However, I do not think that they can be honestly and re-sponsibly addressed until we understand better what the American Jewish response to Auschwitz has been and, more important, what the American Jewish theologi-cal response was. In one sense, that response has already taken place, and to debate whether it should have is beside the point. In another sense, of course, we should be concerned about whether we should continue it and what we can and should learn from it. At a minimum, these latter issues make demands on us; they are unavoid-able. What, in other words, should we learn from the reflections of the post-Holo-caust Jewish thinkers? What do they teach us about our approach to the future and our approach to the past? These writings stand between us and the vast resources of the Jewish past, between us and the writings of Martin Buber and Franz Rosen-zweig, of Hermann Cohen and Moses Mendelssohn, of Maimonides and Rashi, and on and on. Our stance toward the past ought to be defined by our understand-ing of our total situation, and one important feature of that situation is the Holo-caust and recent theological responses to it.

With whose writings am I concerned? I concentrate on certain works by just a few authors—Richard Rubenstein, Emil Fackenheim, Irving Greenberg, Eliezer Berkovits, and Arthur Cohen. Each one, in the 1960s and 1970s, began to treat the Holocaust as a central and determining feature of his Jewish thinking. I want to understand how each thinker proceeded, what role or roles the Holocaust played for him, and how his thinking developed in terms of it.

Why have I chosen just these five figures? The major reason is that each con-ceived of his theological task as understanding Judaism in terms of an act of com-ing to grips with Auschwitz. Each saw the Holocaust as an unavoidable phenom-enon; to each Jewish theology could not proceed ahead and perform its tasks without also facing up to the Shoah. The five, to be sure, came to different conclu-sions about what the Holocaust means for Judaism and Jewish beliefs. They use different methods of thinking, have different styles and different orientations, and have had distinctive influence of varying kinds and on various constituencies. There may be very little that unifies them. But if I am right, the five shared a com-mon subjective attitude: that no authentic Jewish thought could take any step into the future without first exposing itself to Auschwitz. For each, then, the Holocaust had to be confronted seriously and with integrity.

These five, then, are not the only post-Holocaust Jewish thinkers, if a "post-Holocaust" theologian is one who has thought about the religious character of Ju-daism *after* the Holocaust. For them, "post" means "in terms of" and not merely "after." Others have also written *after* 1945 about Judaism and its religious character, and others have written about Jewish life in America *after* 1945. But only these five, I believe, have written about American Jewish life and what it ought to be like *in terms of* the Holocaust and what it was. Furthermore, they are the only ones to have done so in ways that are original or nonderivative and deep. All other theologians who have agreed that Judaism today must be understood in terms of Auschwitz derive their basic orientation from one or more of these five. I am speaking here of theologians, not literary figures, poets, rabbis, and other nontheological interpreters. These five, once they have accepted the responsibility of confronting the Holocaust, do not without reason set it aside; it becomes central and determinative for them, in one sense or another. And what they think and say is novel; they do not simply repeat what others have said or agree with others. Rather others quote, repeat, debate, and agree with them. They are the focal figures, and their writings the ones that constitute the literary content of post-Holocaust Jewish thought.

For a variety of reasons, moreover, these five have been influential in different ways and for different constituencies. They wrote their most important post-Holocaust essays and books at different times, as early as the mid-1960s and as late as the mid-1970s and 1980s. Nonetheless, a careful reading of these essays and books shows that they express positions that were developed independently; there is little indication that one position was worked out in response to another. They are largely five separate views or at least five separately developed positions. In print, Rubenstein's account is presented first; *After Auschwitz,* a collection of fifteen essays, was published in 1966, but the earliest essay dealing with the Holocaust dates from 1960 or so.[4] Arthur Cohen's book *The Tremendum* appeared in 1981, but the first chapter, "Thinking the Tremendum," was delivered as a Leo Baeck Memorial Lecture in 1974. Emil Fackenheim's first published statement on the Holocaust was in 1967, and his most systematic and deepest discussion, *To Mend the World,* appeared in 1982 (reissued with a new introduction in 1989 and then again, with a further introduction, in 1994); in between he published several books and dozens of articles. Irving Greenberg's major statement is a long article, published in 1977 but based on a lecture given in 1974, and Eliezer Berkovits's book, *Faith after the Holocaust,* written in 1967, was published in 1973. Fackenheim, Greenberg, and Rubenstein have been perhaps the most widely quoted, Cohen the least so. Because of his association with the "Death of God" movement that flashed across the sky of Christian theology so briefly and episodically in the 1960s, Rubenstein has become well known as a secularist, but he is rarely read. The same can doubtless be said of Fackenheim, whose voluminous and often technical writings are commonly cited but virtually never examined and whose famous formulation of a 614th commandment ("Thou shalt give Hitler no posthumous victories") became a virtual slogan for the general Holocaust-oriented sensibility of American Jewry. Berkovits and Greenberg are both orthodox theologians and rabbis; if post-Holocaust thinking has touched the liberal orthodox in America, it is through these two.[5] Fackenheim has probably had the widest influence among Reform and Conservative Jews but for what is taken to be his general position and not for the details of his thought. That general position, including an unconditional respect for the Holocaust and its victims and a commitment to Jewish survival, Israel, and more, has also appealed to some Jewish intellectuals. To others, neither Fackenheim's view nor any that gives the Holocaust primacy has had any appeal.[6]

My goal is to examine the writings of these five theologians. I want to show that a close study of their books and essays, and of the historical and cultural contexts in which they were written and read, will reveal some important lessons for Jewish religious thought.

Almost naturally, given the unimaginable atrocities and suffering that the Holocaust incorporated, a confrontation with that event should lead us to rethink our views about God, human nature, morality, and similar themes. The thinkers I want to focus on do not avoid these issues. But, I believe, their thinking is deeper than this. Their attempts to grapple honestly and profoundly with the Holocaust lead them to consider at a fundamental level the very nature of religious thought in general and Jewish belief in particular. That is, they are led to reconsider, in the light of this event, the relationship between Jewish belief and Jewish life on the one hand and history and experience on the other. In their own way, then, they are made to deal with issues about philosophy, religious belief, interpretation, truth, and relativism that have been widely discussed in recent decades. Moreover, these thinkers are driven to consider such issues not by theoretical debate or intellectual controversy; rather they are driven by a sense of utter honesty and genuineness that will not allow them to avoid, distort, or belittle the Holocaust or its victims.

Nor is this realization of a fundamental problem about the status of religious belief the end of the matter for these thinkers. They do not agree on its solution. But in the course of their thinking, they do come to recognize the most serious issues that are raised by the problem. In their own terms, they recognize that an honest encounter with the Holocaust demands a sense of discontinuity or rupture with the past and yet, at the very same time, a sense of continuity or accessibility. The Holocaust raises for them the question of the roles of history in religious self-identity. This question, the relation between present and past, between identity and memory, is an important dimension of the meaning of this movement, and it is one that has not been well appreciated, if appreciated at all. In short, these thinkers confront a threefold challenge: (1) to encounter the death camps and the destruction of European Jewry honestly and seriously; (2) to oppose unconditionally the evil and negativity of that event and all the evil it represents; and (3) to go on as a Jew, to continue to live Jewishly in the contemporary world.

In the early chapters I examine postwar Jewish theology and especially the growth of Jewish existentialism, its debates with Jewish naturalism, and early postwar treatments of the death camps and Nazi totalitarianism. These developments and encounters were especially influential on post-Holocaust Jewish thought. They constitute significant dimensions of the broad world in which the five figures lived, studied, wrote, and have been read.

In chapter 4 I examine the way in which post-Holocaust Jewish thought began to emerge in the sixties and its role within Jewish religious thought, and in chapter 5 I consider the impact of the Six Day War of June 1967 on American Jewish life and especially on the way American Jews perceived Israel and the Holocaust. The events of that summer and the changing character of American life shaped the constituencies for the post-Holocaust Jewish thinkers; they also helped to shape them and their work. In chapters 6 to 10 I engage in analysis and examination of the writings of the major Jewish thinkers. I try to capitalize on my earlier efforts at situating their work in order to explore the theme of history and identity as it occurs in their work. It will turn out that these figures struggled with very deep and pressing problems not only about God and the Jewish people and about human nature and moral purpose but also about the very nature of Jewish belief and its understanding of the world, history, God, and much else. They realized the dangers that accompanied their sensitivity to Auschwitz and their unconditional commitment to an honest and probing encounter with the death camps. At the same time, they refused to abandon Judaism. In some ways, they appear like other intellectuals of our era, who realize that we cannot transcend history nor can we be overwhelmed by it. In other ways, they appear unlike them, for their sense of value and purpose arises out of the horror of the death camps and all they incorporated and not out of an intellectual need, a philosophical argument, or general social pressures. Their commitments to fidelity and honesty are especially powerful, in ways that should remind us how deep are the moral and religious roots that nourish Jews and hold us firm.

In chapter 11 I examine some responses to the work of these figures, and then, in chapter 12, I consider the legacy of this movement for Judaism and Jewish self-understanding today. For various reasons, the primacy of the Holocaust has been seen by many as opposed to many recent developments in Jewish life, especially the return to texts, the renewal of ritual celebration, and the commitment to "liberal" values. Often the motives for this exclusionary attitude are political and psychological. I encourage us to appreciate the realism and yet the idealism of the post-Holocaust thinkers and to see how their goal, like all of ours, is to find a way to return to the past in order to live into the future—with integrity and hope.

The themes of this book are broad ones about religion, politics, history, morality, and identity in recent decades. I am a historian of philosophy and religious thought; I seek to understand texts in the historical contexts out of which they arise, which they address, and in which they are read and recalled. Rich understanding of who we are, I believe, requires attentiveness to a variety of types of writings and all kinds of history, political and social as well as intellectual and popular. It requires reflection on the ways that religious thought, institutions and practices, philosophy, literature, and much else have interacted in the past four decades and what this means for our understanding of Judaism and Jewish life. This book is, in one sense or another, about all of these matters, viewed through the prism of one theological movement—its rise, its significance, and its role in contemporary Jewish self-understanding.

Chapter One

The Holocaust and the Intellectuals
of the Fifties and Sixties

From 1945 to 1965 the Holocaust and the Nazi destruction of European Jewry were coming to occupy the attention of a small number of intellectuals whose work would have a significant impact on post-Holocaust Jewish thought. One of the most important, Raul Hilberg, was a political scientist by training, but his work was primarily historical. *The Destruction of the European Jews*, which appeared in 1961, meticulously examined the destruction process and, now available in a vastly expanded edition, remains a classic.[1] But this massive, detailed work was rarely read. The most influential books were those of Hannah Arendt, Elie Wiesel, and Primo Levi. They provided powerful, important views of the death camps and the Nazi horrors; they also introduced modes of discourse for describing and discussing the crimes perpetrated, the criminals, and the victims. Post-Holocaust Jewish theology would not have emerged as it did if it were not for these three figures and their work.[2]

Arendt's examination of Nazism and totalitarianism, published in articles in the 1940s and culminating in her tremendously important book, *The Origins of Totalitarianism* (OT) of 1951, framed postwar intellectual discussion of the Holocaust. In order to appreciate her impact, we need to look at Arendt's early essays and then especially at sections of part 3 of OT. This material dates from 1945 and 1948–51; it provides not only an account of totalitarianism and its relation to the death camps but also brilliant portraits of the agents and the victims of totalitarian domination. In addition, Arendt's account of the radical evil of the totalitarian extermination camps provides an important background for understanding her portrayal of Eichmann and evil in her later work.

Arendt's article "Organized Guilt and Universal Responsibility" appeared in the *Jewish Frontier* in January 1945. The time and place were appropriate. In 1942 Hayim Greenberg, editor of the *Jewish Frontier*, had been one of the first to report on the atrocities then occurring in eastern Europe. And in the years after 1942,

Arendt had lectured on the need to act in the face of the suffering and mass exter-
minations of Jews in Europe.[3] By early 1943, she had sketched, with her husband
Heinrich Blücher, a major work on totalitarianism and modernity that was conceived in an atmosphere of shock and disbelief. Years later, Arendt would recall
that "at first we did not believe it. Even though my husband had always said we
should put nothing past [the Nazis]. . . . This couldn't be. This should never have
been allowed to happen. I don't mean the number of victims, but the method, the
fabrication of corpses."[4] By late 1944 or early 1945, the first outline was complete,
and the book had a tentative title: *The Elements of Shame: Anti-Semitism — Imperialism — Racism*. At the war's end, and stimulated by a conversation with Paul
Tillich, Arendt published "Organized Guilt," in which she denied the notion of collective guilt and characterized the new type of criminal agency implicated in the
Nazi atrocities.[5]

Arendt's account in this article of the "characteristic personality" of the "systematic mass-murderer," the agent of the "mass-murder machine,"[6] found its way
into OT and forms the background for Arendt's report of Adolf Eichmann's character and the banality of his evil. Here she calls this figure "the mob man" and "the
great criminal of the century" and describes him as a normal jobholder and family
man.[7]

Arendt warns that "the true problem" is not the cognitive one of determining
who the real Nazi was, of clarifying how Nazism was present in Germany, or of
identifying its place in the history of German beliefs. "It is rather to consider how to
conduct oneselves and how to bear the trial of confronting a people among whom
the boundaries dividing criminals from normal persons, the guilty from the innocent, have been so completely effaced that nobody will be able to tell in Germany
whether in any case he is dealing with a secret hero or with a former mass mur-
derer."[8] The real problem is not one of definition, identification, or even explanation; it is not a matter of terminology or belief. Rather it is a problem of living with
or at least dealing with a people in which all are somehow implicated in the organization of mass murder.[9] "That is the horrible thing," Arendt continues, "that
everyone, whether or not he is directly active in a murder camp, is forced to take
part in one way or another in the workings of this machine of mass murder.
. . . For systematic mass-murder . . . strains not only the imagination of human beings, but also the framework and categories of our political thought and action."[10]
This is the gist of Arendt's thinking, that our capacity to think and act politically
(meaning also morally and existentially) is tested by the Nazi mass murders because
all were implicated, because all Germans were criminals. The boundary between
the innocent and the guilty had been obliterated.

At one level this conclusion, that the problem is one of political breakdown that
follows from an immobilization of "the framework and categories of our political
thought and action," seems obvious. We know how to deal with someone who is innocent, with comfort, support, or even neglect, and we know how to deal with a

criminal, with prosecution and ultimately with punishment. But how do we deal with a group when all members are both guilty and innocent or when there are no standards for distinguishing one from the other? In what sense are we still dealing with a human community?

This is a plausible reading of Arendt's reasoning but not, I think, an accurate one. A few lines later she gives her conclusion in these words: "There is no political method for dealing with German mass crimes," recalling the word "political," which she had used earlier.[11] She then adds to this conclusion another: "Just as there is no political solution within human capacity for the crime of administrative mass murder, so the human need for justice can find no satisfactory reply to the total mobilization of a people for that purpose. Where all are guilty, nobody in the last analysis can be judged."[12] In other words, the earlier argument cannot be about a moral or judicial response to Germany, for she only here introduces such an issue. Rather that argument must deal with our political response and how the special way that individuals are participants in the mass murder machine sabotages our normal political thoughts and actions. But what is that mode of criminality? Who are the criminals, and what effect does such criminality and such crimes have on the categories that organize our political thinking and action?

Arendt asks the question this way: "what were the real motives that caused people to act as cogs in the mass-murder machine?" In using the language of motivation, causality, and action Arendt is being very precise, as I will show. She suggests that the answer to this question will come from an examination of the characteristic personality of the agent of the murder machine, and this is Heinrich Himmler, the "organizing spirit of the murder." Arendt's contention is that the typical member of Himmler's organization, unlike the earlier units of the SS and Gestapo, were like Himmler himself, and that an investigation of the Himmler personality type will reveal the real motivation of such a person, his real character, goals, and virtues. What is at issue here is a general view of human nature and character. Since our political frameworks are tied to such views, it is possible that the view of human nature and character integral to Nazi mass murder might be utterly dissonant with that integral to our rational, liberal, post-Enlightenment political world. The central question Arendt raises, then, is what type of character and identity do Himmler and his subordinates have.[13]

Himmler was neither an eccentric Bohemian like Joseph Goebbels nor a "sex criminal" like Julius Streicher nor a "perverted fanatic" like Hitler nor an adventurer like Hermann Goering. He was a typical "bourgeois," a jobholder and family-man, with a

> kind concern and earnest concentration on the welfare of his family . . . worried
> about nothing so much as his security . . . who for all his industry and care could
> never be certain what the next day would bring. . . . [F]or the sake of his pension,
> his life insurance, the security of his wife and children, such a man was ready to

sacrifice his beliefs, his honor, and his human dignity. . . . [A]fter such degradation he was entirely prepared to do literally anything when the ante was raised
and the bare existence of his family was threatened. The only condition he put
was that he should be fully exempted from responsibility for his acts.[14]

This normal jobholder and new functionary—we might call him a typical bureaucrat—is "the new criminal of the century." Arendt gives us a well-known portrait,
detailed for her own purposes. This Nazi functionary is descendant from Hobbes's
vision of the state of nature as a total war of self-interested and isolated individuals; to be sure, perhaps a bit like Locke and even Rousseau, Arendt's family-men do
care for their wives and children, but they are the acquisitive and alienated population of the new, urban, technocratic metropolis so fully described by Georg Sim-
mel and Georg Lukács.[15] When threatened with doubts and insecurities, however,
they will sacrifice all sense of principle—belief, honor, and dignity—and do anything that will secure peace, now and in the future, for their families and themselves. Moreover, this

> transformation of the family man from a responsible member of society, inter-
> ested in all public affairs, to a "bourgeois" concerned only with his private exis-
> tence and knowing no civic virtue, is an international modern phenomenon. . . .
> [But it] enjoyed particularly favorable conditions in Germany . . . [which is] so lit-
> tle imbued with the classic virtues of civic behavior . . . [and where] private life
> and private calculations play[ed] so great a role.[16]

The mob-man, then, the Nazi criminal, is a function of modernity, and his key
feature is the separation, as we might describe it, between his desires and his actions. There is a sense in which there is no unity in him between what he does and
what he wants. Arendt puts this separation in these terms:

> He has driven the dichotomy of private and public functions, of family and oc-
> cupation, so far that he can no longer find in his own person any connection be-
> tween the two. When his occupation forces him to murder people, he does not
> regard himself as a murderer because he has not done it out of inclination but in
> his professional capacity. Out of sheer passion he would never do harm to a fly.[17]

Hence such an agent cannot be held accountable for what he did, since, for him,
what he did was to do his job well enough to gain peace and security. He never intended to kill others, nor did he choose to kill others, but only to do his job well and
to secure his future.

Arendt has in mind an ideal of political thinking and political conduct, the
model of civic virtue that arises from Plato and Aristotle, in which the polity is
shaped to facilitate a certain conception of the good life and in which members
seek to cultivate characteristics that make the polity best possible and that
make their lives as good as can be.[18] In such a view, the public and private spheres
form a unity; they and their goals and virtues are continuous. Hence members dis-

cuss with each other what the good life should be like, how the state should be ordered to facilitate it for its members, and what kind of people they should aspire to
be. When they deliberate, they attempt to determine what they should do, in terms
of these public, common ideals. In the modern world, however, and particularly in
Germany, this ideal has been smashed and replaced by another, in which the state
serves as a framework for constraining individual desire and interest in order to
maximize the security and gains of its competing members. Arendt's point is that
individuals who function like this can be easily directed to do anything in order
to achieve their own goals—even to participate in systematic mass murder, as long
as they can be enabled to live with themselves and feel no regret, guilt, or shame.
In their occupational lives, such agents are schizophrenic: they intend one thing,
accepting what they do as described in one way and motivated by self-interest, and
they do something that *we* but not *they* would describe as systematic mass murder.
From our point of view, there is one action described two ways; from their point of
view, there is one action described in one way. Hence, as we see it, their thoughts,
deliberation, action, and even choice are *detached* from what they do, as we might
describe it. In terms that Arendt will later employ, these functionaries are utterly
thoughtless, that is, their actions and their deliberative, intentional thinking are utterly detached.[19]

For this reason, then, we are incapable of a genuine *political* response to Germany. If our conception of the self and of the human condition is that of the civic
ideal, then our conception of political action will malfunction when it confronts a
nation of these bourgeois.[20]

This conception of the Nazi mass murderers is used and developed in Arendt's
masterpiece, OT. In the final section of chapter 10, which deals with totalitarian
leaders and their followers, Arendt repeats almost verbatim her description of the
mob man, the new criminal of the twentieth century.[21] Although she calls him both
a member of the *bourgeois*, an outcome of the growth of the masses, and a philistine
but not a mob man, her description is a briefer version of the account I have just
examined.

Arendt's great work, the result of nearly a decade's labor, was published in 1951
and contained a comprehensive account of the novelty and the destructiveness of
totalitarianism. In the 1950s it was tremendously influential among liberal intellectuals, many of them ex-communists and socialists, who found in it a brilliant and
useful critique of European fascisms and Stalinist communism.[22] Later, the post-
Holocaust theologians, among others, were moved not by its general thesis but
rather by its powerful description of the world of the extermination camps, of
Planet Auschwitz. Brilliantly Arendt identified and probed those features of domination and extremity that led her to claim that the death camps were the most
characteristic and essential totalitarian institution. In these pages, near the end of
the work, her general thesis about modernity and totalitarianism becomes dramatically particular.

The crucial text is the original final chapter of the book, and especially its last section, "Total Domination."[23] Drawing on her research on the concentration camps and their unique role in totalitarian regimes and specifically on her 1948 article in *Partisan Review*, Arendt examines a phenomenon she sees as the ultimate device of domination, of the unrestricted expansiveness that seeks to outstrip every conception of evil we possess. The camps are the venue for radical or absolute evil; in these pages Arendt tries to explain why and how this is so.

Arendt's account is a series of episodic, penetrating, suggestive insights into the workings of these camps, their goals, and their role as totalitarian institutions. These comments culminate in a crescendo of more and more profound readings of the totalitarian goal: to alter human nature, to make human beings superfluous, and ultimately to realize radical evil, an expression of unconditional totalization, and hence to transcend every human limit. The order of Arendt's insights is less important than what they tell us about the camps and how their existence challenges all our relevant concepts, principles, and frameworks. Here is a review of some of these observations and interpretations.

First, Arendt claims (1) that the fundamental belief of totalitarianism, its ideology, is that everything is possible;[24] (2) that the regime seeks to verify this belief through total domination in the concentration camps;[25] (3) that "these camps are the true central institution of totalitarian organizational power";[26] and (4) that such total domination is a "radical evil, previously unknown to us"[27] and hence historically unprecedented. The burden of Arendt's reasoning is that if claim 2 is true, then so are claims 3 and 4. But claim 2 can be shown to be true only if we understand first what total domination involves and what the central belief means. Clarifying these things should help us to see why Arendt calls the camps vehicles of "radical evil."[28]

What, then, does the central belief of totalitarianism mean? Arendt suggests that the belief that everything is possible involves the transcending of traditional limits and boundaries; it involves something "that should never be involved in politics as we used to understand it, namely all or nothing."[29] This is not very helpful until we know what limit is being eclipsed. Totalitarianism is the commitment to unqualified expansiveness, unrestricted domination. Hence it is committed to the belief that what it does and dominates cannot limit it in any way. Its predecessors presumably would have thought that some things were not possible; some actions could not be performed. But why not? What restriction or limit a priori narrowed the domain of the possible?

Prior to the twentieth-century totalitarian regimes, there had been, Arendt notes, wars of aggression, the massacre of victims, the extermination of native peoples during colonization, and enslavement. There had even been concentration camps, invented during the Boer War and used in South Africa and in India. These phenomena may point to total domination, but they do not yet exemplify it.

[A]ll these are elements they utilize, develop, and crystallize on the basis of the nihilistic principle that "everything is permitted," which they inherited and already take for granted. But wherever these new forms of domination assume their authentically totalitarian structure they transcend this principle, which is still tied to the utilitarian motives and self-interest of the rulers, and try their hand in a realm that up to now has been completely unknown to us: the realm where "everything is possible." . . . What runs counter to common sense is not the nihilistic principle that "everything is permitted," which was already contained in the nineteenth-century utilitarian conception of common sense. What common sense and "normal people" refuse to believe is that everything is possible.[30]

Prior atrocities, whether in war, massacre, or slavery, were permitted in a sense because they were employed as means to certain ends, what Arendt calls the "utilitarian motives and self-interest of the rulers." What was permitted was any action or policy that would serve some political goal. As long as practical reasoning was instrumental, then the permissible and the preferable were functions of the desirable. This may be nihilistic by some standards, but it is reasonable and compatible with common sense. Hence, by such a principle, not everything is possible, for possibility is restricted by the permissible, and the permissible is limited to whatever serves the ruler's needs or desires or goals. The right is the servant of the good.

Totalitarian regimes, however, have no such goals; they aim to dominate without restriction. They have no external desires, like happiness or prestige or wealth. Their only desires are internal, that is, to totalize or, in other terms, to implement and not merely to achieve unlimited power. Hence everything, whether permissible by the old utilitarian standards or not, is possible. But is this belief true? Can it be verified? Only if the most extreme things, actions beyond any former standards, occur. If so, then the principle is confirmed, even verified. On the old scheme, an evil action or practice or policy was one that did not facilitate the desired result. On the new one, the totalitarian scheme, the evil is a denial of all standards; it is the commitment to and verification of unrestricted domination, and this means pointless but total annihilation of people.

This annihilation in fact is what total domination involves. It seeks to transform the human species into a subhuman species, to alter human nature itself. "What totalitarian ideologies therefore aim at is not the transformation of the outside world or the revolutionizing transmutation of society, but the transformation of human nature itself. The concentration camps are the laboratories where changes in human nature are tested."[31] As Elie Wiesel later put it, in the death camps not only man died but also the idea of man.[32] In a sense, totalitarianism sought to dominate and alter our concepts and categories, our world, and indeed nature itself. "The camps are meant not only to exterminate people and degrade human beings, but also serve the ghastly experiment of eliminating, under scientifically controlled conditions, spontaneity itself as an expression of human behavior and of transforming the human personality into a mere thing, into something that even animals are not."[33] These Arendt later calls "inanimate men, i.e., men who can no longer be psychologically understood, whose return to the psychologically or otherwise intelligibly human world closely resembles the resurrection of Lazarus."[34]

If the camps sought to implement this policy of total domination, and succeeded, then their existence confirms the totalitarian belief in unrestricted expansion and exemplified an unprecedented radical evil in history. Moreover, the camps would then challenge our conceptual and imaginative capacities. It would be a feat for us or even for the surviving victims to describe their operations and what they were about. Here too Arendt is explicit about our limitations when it comes to dealing with the camps.[35] "There are no parallels to the life in the concentration camps. Its horror can never be fully embraced by the imagination. . . . It can never be fully reported for the very reason that the survivor returns to the world of the living, which makes it impossible for him to believe fully in his own past experiences. It is as though he had a story to tell of another planet."[36]

Hence comparisons provide no help; they even misdirect our understanding or confuse. In the camps the inmate is made superfluous, a term that Arendt uses often to indicate the way in which the victim is stripped of all role, utility, character, function, and even individuality; the camp creates "superfluous human material," wholly unnecessary, without purpose or use, and disposable. Here the superfluity created by the development of the assembly line and the division of labor, hallmarks of modern, industrial culture, is exaggerated; not only is any specific individual made superfluous and replaceable but also the individual's very humanity. Hence, "forced labor in prisons and penal colonies, banishment, slavery, all seem for a moment to offer helpful comparisons, but on closer examination lead nowhere."[37] For in each case the victim has some value, some role to play, some function to perform, whereas to Arendt this is not true of the concentration camp inmates. For reasons like this, we should not say that the camps were an explicable development of existing institutions; they were rather a dramatic break with the past and with our traditional conceptual and cultural resources. In a deep way, the camps make no sense; they are dark and obscure, contrary to all categories and logic.

These are bold claims that will be taken up later by others and debated often. But they are complicated by Arendt's coordinate claim, that "in comparison with the insane end-result—concentration-camp society—the process by which men are prepared for this end, and the methods by which individuals are adapted to these conditions, are transparent and logical. The insane mass manufacture of corpses is preceded by the historically and politically intelligible preparation of living corpses."[38] Many would agree and even confirm the bureaucratic rigor of the camps and the complex, diabolical logic of Nazi persecution and terror.[39] Arendt pursues this point through a threefold account of the total domination whereby the juridical character, moral personality, and unique identity of each inmate are systematically murdered. In the case of the inmates' moral personality, for example, this is done "by making martyrdom, for the first time in history, impossible,"[40] for in the camps death was anonymous and without dignity and gestures had no social meaning, no witnesses, no purpose. The result was a systematic dehumanization that displayed organization and order, as susceptible to analysis and comprehension as the result itself defied both.

One of Arendt's conclusions is (claim 3) that the camps were the central institutions of totalitarianism. We can now see exactly why she thought this was so. The camps epitomized the kind of regime to which totalitarianism aspired; they also confirmed that such a regime was possible by verifying its fundamental affirmation and aided in creating such a regime through "the undefined fear they inspire and the very well-defined training they offer in total domination."[41] They were, in sum, both symbol and instrument of that "unlimited power" that totalitarianism desires. Arendt distinguishes such a goal from others, even the goal of despotic rule. The point of totalitarian domination is not control or use; rather it is the alteration of human nature, the creation of what Arendt calls superfluity or uselessness. "Total power can be achieved and safeguarded only in a world of conditioned reflexes, of marionettes without the slightest trace of spontaneity."[42] This process involves the destruction of character and the nullification of individuality; all must be made equally and utterly superfluous. In such a world, on such a planet, there is nothing—the perfunctory disposal of such superfluous human material—that is impossible.

In the final pages of the original edition of OT Arendt adds to the words of her earlier article a discussion of what makes this evil radical.[43] This is a theme that will play an important role in the work of Fackenheim and others and in the controversy over the Holocaust's uniqueness and special significance. Here Arendt turns away from the issue of historical situatedness, which concerned her earlier, to the nature of the evil itself. This task leads her to treat the evil as crime and action and to consider how it is motivated, described, explained, and responded to. The camps involved actions on the part of the SS and others, and these are the locus of the evil of the camps and the regime itself. But what makes the actions unconditionally evil?

> When the impossible was made possible it became the unpunishable, unforgivable absolute evil which could no longer be understood and explained by the evil motives of self-interest, greed, covetousness, resentment, lust for power, and cowardice; and which therefore anger could not revenge, love could not endure, friendship could not forgive.... It is inherent in our entire philosophical tradition that we cannot conceive of a "radical evil," and this is true both for Christian theology, which conceded even to the Devil himself a celestial origin, as well as for Kant, the only philosopher who, in the word he coined for it, at least must have suspected the existence of this evil even though he immediately rationalized it in the concept of a "perverted ill will" that could be explained by comprehensible

motives. Therefore, we actually have nothing to fall back on in order to understand a phenomenon that nevertheless confronts us with its overpowering reality and breaks down all standards we know. There is only one thing that seems to be discernible: we may say that radical evil has emerged in connection with a system in which all men have become equally superfluous.[44]

It may be that Arendt never successfully surpasses the points about radical evil that she makes in this extraordinary passage. First, it is the actions that are radically evil and this in part because they simply are beyond understanding and explanation; that is, they cannot be explained by reference to the agent's normal motives—greed, anger, lust for power, and so forth. In other words, a particular SS guard did not beat an inmate because he hated him or wanted something from him. Hence, since there is in a sense no motive, we could not punish the agent in any normal sense of punishing someone; nor could one forgive, endure, or even requite the act and the agent in any normal sense. But, and this is Arendt's second point, if the action is evil and yet radically so, surely "radical" means more than "in a way we do not comprehend." Or does it? For if we investigate the Western religious and philosophical tradition, do we find persuasive accounts of radical evil, of an evil that is wholly and unconditionally so? No; we do not. Here, in the Nazi crimes, we have instances of something that is beyond our categories and beyond our understanding. In Christianity, even the devil, the agency of the most extreme evils, is of divine origin and hence inherently good; in Kantian moral philosophy, even a radically evil will is basically good.[45] That is, even Kant rationalized and mitigated the worst intentions we have by explaining them as perversions of something that is fundamentally good and hence redeemable. Radical evil, for Kant, is a propensity or tendency that human beings have, prior to the adoption of a good or evil maxim, to prefer inclination over duty.

> The propensity to radical evil in human nature therefore does not mean that men necessarily adopt evil maxims, or that they are incapable of moral goodness in general. Rather it only means that in our moral strivings we do not begin from a "natural innocence," but must presuppose a "wickedness of the will" in the form of a propensity to evil, and must therefore "begin with the incessant counteraction against it."[46]

Nowhere do we find a conception of an evil that is total, unconditional, and radical. Because of what Nazism achieved, then, it realized more than the possible; in the camps, indeed, more was actual than was possible.[47]

Ten years after the publication of *The Origins of Totalitarianism*, the trial of Adolf Eichmann, who had been captured in Argentina on May 24, 1960, by Israeli agents, began in Jerusalem. Two years later, in February and March 1963, Hannah Arendt's articles on the trial appeared in the *New Yorker* and subsequently in a book, *Eichmann in Jerusalem: A Report on the Banality of Evil*.[48] A storm of controversy ensued, both within the American Jewish community and without. The two issues raised by the book and the two issues most debated in subsequent discussion are the ones most relevant here: first, Eichmann's character and the concept of the banality of evil; second, the complicity and cooperation of the Jewish leadership and the existence of resistance to the Nazis.[49]

Our discussion of Arendt's essay "Organized Guilt" and the final chapters of OT anticipate her portrait of Eichmann and her brief but controversial reflections on the banality of evil. We have examined her earlier description of the "new criminal of the century," the modern philistine. What does she say about Eichmann?

Eichmann in Jerusalem (EJ) offers the results of Arendt's lengthy but narrow observations of Eichmann. For although the trial lasted a long time and Eichmann spoke a good deal, Arendt only saw him in restricted terms, as a defendant giving testimony.[50] Furthermore, she had a conception of the typical Nazi criminal worked out and either expected Eichmann to exemplify and confirm that conception or came to see him in terms of it. Finally, in characterizing what was evil about Eichmann, Arendt abandoned the terminology of radical or absolute evil employed in OT;[51] she also abandoned any attention to the historically unprecedented character of the death camps and the nature and victims of the crimes.[52] Rather she focused solely on Eichmann's motivations. She found that they were like those of her philistine in OT, and she called Eichmann's evil banal; the character of Nazi domination, its diabolical integration of unboundedness, senselessness, and structure, and its horrifying outcomes, "superfluous human material"—all this she ignored. Why?

Arendt summarizes her understanding of Eichmann in a postscript written in 1964:

> When I speak of the banality of evil, I do so only on the strictly factual level, pointing to a phenomenon which stared one in the face at the trial. Eichmann was not Iago and not Macbeth, and nothing would have been further from his mind than to determine with Richard III "to prove a villain." Except for an extraordinary diligence in looking out for his general advancement, he had no motives at all. . . . He *merely*, to put the matter colloquially, *never realized what he was doing*. . . . In principle he knew quite well what it was all about, and in his final statement to the court he spoke of the "revaluation of values prescribed by the [Nazi] government." He was not stupid. It was sheer thoughtlessness—something by no means identical with stupidity—that predisposed him to become one of the greatest criminals of that period. And if this is "banal" and even funny, if with the best will in the world one cannot extract any diabolical or demonic profundity from Eichmann, that is still far from calling it commonplace. . . . That such remoteness from reality and such thoughtlessness can wreak more havoc than all the evil instincts taken together which, perhaps, are inherent in man— that was, in fact, the lesson one could learn in Jerusalem. But it was a lesson, neither an explanation of the phenomenon nor a theory about it.[53]

This passage begins and ends with a proviso—to see that Eichmann's evil was banal is only to describe it and not to explain or understand it. Hence recognizing the phenomenon is to be able to identify or pick it out; it is not to grasp it and its causal context and assimilate it to our understanding of social and political life. Further, Eichmann's evil rested on his lack of motivation and lack of grasping what he was doing. Strictly speaking, of course, he did have a motivation, his advancement, and he did grasp what he was doing, as advancing his career, but he had, with regard to the process of mass murder, no motivation and no conception of what he was contributing to it. Arendt calls this "thoughtlessness" and glosses it as a "remoteness from reality." What does it mean?

What I am asking, of course, is not whether Arendt was right about Eichmann or about Himmler or in general about the agents of Nazi destruction. There is every reason to think that Arendt saw only part of the story and that the motivations and thinking of the Nazis were much more complicated, especially as one attends to the many levels of agency that stretch from Hitler himself to Goebbels, Reinhard Heydrich, and on, to a private in the reserves called up to perform acts of extermination in an ad hoc situation.[54] But even if Arendt is wrong about Nazi criminality in general and even about Eichmann, what is she saying about him? What is the evil she has in mind, and what does she mean by calling it "banal?"[55]

One might suggest that Arendt concluded that Eichmann was unaware of his own wickedness. In a sense, this is correct but not deep enough, for his lack of self-awareness is a consequence of his condition, and it is this condition that makes him evil. Clearly, as the passage just quoted shows, for Arendt the evil has something to do with Eichmann's actions, his intentions, his understanding of what he was doing, and his motives. Elisabeth Young-Bruehl uses the notion of a base motive to clarify Arendt's point:

> Three characteristics of radical evil had recurred in Hannah Arendt's discussions in *The Origins of Totalitarianism*, *The Human Condition*, and *On Revolution*. It is unpunishable in the sense that no punishment can be adequate or commensurate; it is unforgivable; and it is rooted in motives so base as to be beyond human comprehension. The last characteristic was the one Eichmann's trial brought into question. . . . In *Eichmann in Jerusalem*, she attributed superfluity to motives: when motives become superfluous, evil is banal.[56]

While correct in a sense, this interpretation does not do complete justice to what Arendt says on the last page of OT, which I examined earlier. When she says that the Nazi crimes are absolute evil that cannot be understood and explained by evil motives like greed and lust for power, this need not mean that the crimes *do* have other motives, just not these. This is Young-Bruehl's reading, but it is a reading wholly at odds with Arendt's earlier account of the bourgeois or new philistine. Such a person did have motives: private and familial security; but he "was ready to sacrifice everything—belief, honor, dignity—on the slightest provocation."[57] That is, in certain circumstances, the bourgeois became detached from his actions so that these actions, for example, deporting hundreds of thousands to their deaths, can be viewed by us and were viewed by him as having no motives, intentions, and decisions at all. In the end, these crimes or actions were thought-less, that is, performed without thought or plan or intention or even without the agent's conception of what they amounted to. This is the account of the Nazi agents in the essay "Organized Guilt" and in the section on the elite and the mob in OT; it is also, I think, the account that lies behind Arendt's portrait of Eichmann, who appears to her as similarly acting without thought, that is, without the deliberation and judgment that would tie his motives to his conduct, described in a certain way. If I am right, however, then we cannot accept Young-Bruehl's interpretation of the shift from OT to EJ. The shift is one of terminology and not one of doctrine or substance. But then we should ask, what in fact is the point of the change from radical or absolute evil to evil that is banal?[58]

Earlier in the section "Total Domination" Arendt had called the creation of "superfluous human material" a manifestation of "all or nothing," implying thereby that it was what verified the principle of limitless expansion and total domination. "It was the appearance of some radical evil, previously unknown to us."[59] Later, on the last page of OT, she alludes to this reference when she says that "absolute evil" comes about when the "impossible becomes possible."[60] That absolute evil is unpunishable, unforgivable, beyond understanding and explanation. But what is the evil, the "it," that has these features? Is it the crimes or actions, the results of those crimes, or the agents? Arendt seems to have the totality in mind—the entire phenomenon of victims and agents that are beyond the pale of human solidarity and the incomprehensible crimes that tie them together. This totality is absolute or radical evil for a variety of reasons: because it is unprecedented and hence beyond the actual; because it is a verification of unbounded expansiveness and of the principle that everything is possible; because it transcends our categories of understanding and explanation; and because it is unqualifiedly and unconditionally evil—there is no good in it. One feature of this constellation that makes these crimes and criminals distinctively evil is the fact that they cannot be explained by motives or goals that would, to one degree or another, mitigate their extremity, while they make them comprehensible. They do not serve another purpose, produce some beneficial outcome, or arise out of necessity. In *Eichmann in Jerusalem* Arendt focuses on *just this one feature* of Eichmann and his actions. While there is nothing—no motive or purpose, for example—that could mitigate what Eichmann did, there is also a sense in which his actions and his deliberations were *detached*. He is not, in a sense, the reflective agent of his crimes; they have no such agency and hence they are free-floating, as it were, riding on the surface of history without roots in real, rationally reflective, active persons and their intentions. In this sense, these crimes are banal or superficial. This does not mean that all evil is banal; clearly much is not. Nor does it mean that Eichmann's evil is *only* banal; it is also unforgivable, unpunishable, and so forth. But Arendt seems to have narrowed the meaning of "radical" by the time that she wrote EJ; for now it means "extreme and with positive content," and since Eichmann's crime is evil but thought-less and hence without positive content, his crime cannot be "radical evil."

In a famous letter to Gershom Scholem, dated July 24, 1963, responding to his objections, Arendt says just this:

> You are quite right: I changed my mind and do no longer speak of "radical evil." . . .
> It is indeed my opinion now that evil is never "radical," that it is only extreme, and
> that it possesses neither depth nor any demonic dimension. It can overgrow and lay
> waste the whole world precisely because it spreads like a fungus on the surface. It is
> "thought-defying," as I said, because thought tries to reach some depth, to go to the
> roots, and the moment it concerns itself with evil, it is frustrated because there is
> nothing. That is its "banality." Only the good has depth and can be radical.[61]

Arendt here uses the word "extreme" to capture all those features that had played a role in her earlier account of evil. Hence, Eichmann's crimes are extreme and yet banal. But surely Arendt exaggerates, for she provides no reason for thinking that all evil or even all extreme evil is banal. Indeed, it is not even clear why, in examining Nazism and the death camps, it is more illuminating and more important to identify the crimes that are banal than to identify those that are extreme but not banal, those, for example, of Goebbels, of Heydrich, and of Hitler himself. In her early work, Arendt had pointed to an evil beyond that of the functionaries, the new philistines; in her later years, she did not; such evil was all there was.

Arendt's reasons for focusing so narrowly on thought-less evil, extreme and banal, have to do with her conception of the human ideal. That conception, which is Aristotelian and Kantian, involves the primacy of freedom and rationality in articulating the best life for human beings as a life of civic virtue. It is a life of rational discussion, of deliberation and judgment on moral and political matters, and of the active, political self. Arendt's shift in terminology, from "radical" to "banal" evil, and her sensitivity to a phenomenon that eschews rational thought and disengages thought from action are deeply rooted in her ongoing inquiry into the human condition, an inquiry that proceeded to the day of her death on the evening of December 4, 1975.[62]

This account of the human condition and the centrality of rational thought and political action is also the core of Arendt's understanding of Jewish history and Zionism. And it was her views on all these matters that lay behind the ten pages in which she discusses the cooperation of Jewish leaders in the destruction process.[63] This question of complicity, even more than the account of the banality of Eichmann's evil, provoked severe critique and widespread controversy, especially within the community of Jewish leaders and intellectuals.[64]

In a series of essays, many written in the 1940s, Arendt sketched the rudiments of an interpretation of Jewish history, Zionism, and anti-Semitism. Indebted to her friend Kurt Blumenfeld, the interpretation is heavily Zionist. Its central concept was that of political action, of rational self-determination of the Jewish people in a political context. In "The Jewish State: Fifty Years After," published in *Commentary* in May 1946, she claimed that "during the twenty centuries of their Diaspora the Jews have made only two attempts to change their condition by direct political action," one the aborted messianic movement around Shabbatai Zevi in 1665–66, the other modern Zionism.[65] The essential feature of the latter was that it treated the Jewish problem as a political problem and hence urged autonomous, self-determined political action as the vehicle to recover Jewish identify. Arendt's account urges realism and action and understands action as self-determined. The distinction between active and passive, rational and passional, extends back through Kant and Spinoza to the Stoics and beyond. In her own way, Arendt appropriates this dichotomy and associates the goal of Jewish history and the ground of Jewish dignity with genuine political *action* that is both free and rational. Moreover, she opposes such action to both the traditional style of Jewish leadership that sought security by pandering to Gentile rulers and the modern type of Zionist leadership that sought to establish and defend statehood by catering to non-Jewish powers, the great powers.[66] If one were to work out the details of this view of Jewish history and politics, eventually it would be rooted in Arendt's ideal of rational, free political conduct and civic virtue, the primacy of political discussion and of local councils. Its result, in the context of the Eichmann trial, was her negative treatment of the cooperation of Jewish leadership.

Much of the controversy concerning Arendt's report centered on this portrait, which was narrow, often erroneous, demeaning, and even offensive.[67] For my purposes, the controversy's most important feature was one of its outcomes, an intense and long-term interest on the part of historians and others in the complex modalities of the victims' reactions to each and every stage of the Final Solution.[68] After Arendt's work was published, a keen interest developed in the modes and degrees of resistance to the Nazi persecution, and in a variety of ways the results of these inquiries entered the thought of the post-Holocaust theologians. These were among the tangible results of the controversy, at least for the historians, theologians, and other intellectuals, and indeed much of the controversy was carried out in journals and magazines of an intellectual kind.[69]

But there were heated public discussions too, at City College in New York and Columbia University, at a meeting of the Bergen-Belsen Survivors Association in New York, at the University of Chicago, and at a public forum sponsored by *Dissent*. These and the untold effects of her brashness and insensitivity on Jews and non-Jews throughout the country did more than generate intellectual results; they raised the Holocaust to a new level of consciousness in the awareness of American Jews. In Israel there were those who may have sought, in the trial, some kind of catharsis, a vehicle for facing and perhaps even overcoming the guilt and trauma that lay beneath the surface. In America, the trial and its aftermath, including the controversy over Arendt's account of Eichmann, were neither orchestrated for a purpose nor cathartic. Rather they occurred at a time of tremendous turmoil and conflict in American life, adding one more ingredient to the uncertainties and anxieties of American Jewish life in the early 1960s.

Indeed, the controversy over Arendt's book on Eichmann provides an excellent indication of the impact of the Holocaust on American Jewish intellectuals. For my purposes, the issue is not whether Arendt was right or wrong, whether her critics persuasively refuted her or her advocates adequately defended her.[70] Just as what is most interesting about Arendt's reportage is what it reveals about her, her political and moral views, and her relationship to Jews, Judaism, and Zionism, so what is most significant about the controversy is what it shows about her critics and their views about Judaism, the camps, and so forth. Among the most revealing contributions to the debate are those of Lionel Abel and Daniel Bell.

Lionel Abel's critique, "The Aesthetics of Evil: Hannah Arendt on Eichmann and the Jews," appeared in *Partisan Review* in the summer of 1963.[71] Abel focuses on two assertions that he believes Arendt makes. The first is that the Jewish Councils, set up by the Nazis, were their "irreplaceable" necessary instruments for destroying European Jewry, and the second is that Eichmann was merely a replaceable cog in the machine.[72] He argues vigorously that Arendt, by omitting and misinterpreting evidence available to her, failed to make either case. Furthermore, he claims that Arendt's "accusations . . . are never political, never moral. . . . Her judgment [of the leaders of the Councils and of Eichmann] is, I think, fundamentally an aesthetic one."[73] In the case of the *Judenrate*, he argues, this aestheticism has to do with Arendt's failure to consider their moral and political alternatives. Indeed, Abel believes that they did make moral and political judgments, even though Arendt did not think that they did—or could have. His view in fact is that they chose to guarantee and even to secure Jewish survival, a purpose Arendt even denies them.

This clarification, however, is not very helpful in explaining why Arendt's judgment of the leaders is aesthetic. Presumably Abel does not mean that Arendt judges the *Judenrate* to be aesthetic or that they made aesthetic decisions. Clearly, they made political, tactical, and prudential decisions. What Abel must mean is that Arendt does not treat these choices and actions as moral or political ones. She *treats them aesthetically*. But is this so? Surely she is critical of the leaders and their actions; she takes them to have pandered to the Nazi command, to have obeyed, cooperated, and aided the extermination of millions of Jews. Is this to be aesthetic rather than moral? Is this to withhold moral censure?

Abel's discussion of Arendt's aesthetic treatment of Eichmann is more illuminating. "Instead of depicting Eichmann as ideological, Miss Arendt insists on describing the man as a comical, mediocre, and dutiful servant of Hitler."[74] That is, Arendt, according to Abel, does not perceive Eichmann as a moral or political agent; she portrays him as a low-level bureaucrat who makes no significant moral choices or decisions of preference in his life. She denies ascribing an ideology to him, for that would imply that he made decisions based on principle or that he made rational choices based on a large-scale view of things. In Arendt's eyes, Abel says, Eichmann is "finally inexplicable" but "commonplace, without humor, comical."[75] Abel replies that in fact Eichmann was a "moral monster" who had said that he would jump laughing into his grave out of satisfaction for having sent to their death millions of Jews. Arendt had called this mere "bragging," but Abel takes her response to be obtuse.[76] Ultimately, Arendt conceives of Eichmann as a victim of totalitarianism, for the latter can do anything, even exploit mediocre bureaucrats to exterminate an entire people. But, Abel believes, she is wrong; the Jewish leaders were more heroic and Eichmann more monstrous than she thinks.

We can see clearly why Abel thinks Arendt's judgment of Eichmann to be aesthetic. It is because that is all the assessment that remains once ideology, intention, choice, and genuine action are stripped away. Earlier I examined Arendt's account of the Nazi criminals in her essay "Organized Guilt," in *The Origins of Totalitarianism*, and in *Eichmann in Jerusalem*, and if I was correct, then Arendt does not strip Eichmann of all intentions or motives; she detaches his choices and actions from real thought, that is, rational deliberation, but they are still actions that can be applauded or despised. Abel was mistaken, then, about what Arendt had done, but his error is revealing.

Abel's real concern with Arendt is not about any injustice to the victims or to the Jewish people. Rather it is about a fundamental failure concerning morality that is closely associated with an error about theory and life. Abel is deeply disturbed that Arendt has not seen Eichmann correctly, that theory has distorted her account of him, and that she has, as a result of these failures, avoided the proper moral judgment, especially of the Nazi criminals. The outcome of her report, that Eichmann is "aesthetically palatable" while "his victims are aesthetically repulsive" encourages moral confusion, and this twin result is the outcome of an inability to see Eichmann clearly.

Abel reveals this deep worry about theory and observation in the very best passage in his critique.[77] Simone de Beauvoir, making a point about trial and justice, called attention to a fact about Pierre Laval, who was tried after the war in 1946 for crimes performed between 1940 and 1945. This fact is that "the criminal in the dock can never be the same person that he was when he committed his crimes. Would that he could be punished when glorying in his deeds, with his guilt full-blown upon him! But he can only be tried when he is caught and already defeated. And it is only then that you can punish him. The man you really wanted to punish has, in a way, escaped."[78] Abel calls this "one of the best things in existentialist literature" and expects that Arendt is as aware of it as he is. Yet, he believes, Arendt ignores this Sartrian caution; she treats the Eichmann in the dock and the Eichmann who sent millions to their deaths as the same Eichmann, and this is simply an error. The benign, defeated bureaucrat standing before her was not, in a sense, the monster who glorified in the death of millions. Arendt's is a failure to take perspective, time, and context seriously; it is a willingness, indeed a desire, to make observation fit one's theory rather than to allow theory to follow observation.

In the subsequent issue of the *Partisan Review*, in the fall of 1963, Daniel Bell published his interpretation of Arendt's book and incidentally his criticism of Abel's attack.[79] It was entitled "The Alphabet of Justice: Reflections on 'Eichmann in Jerusalem,'" indicating with the word "justice" that he disagreed with Abel about the moral character of Arendt's report. Bell believes that Arendt is committed to a "single standard of universal order," an objective, uncompromising standard of justice that eliminates questions of motivation and conscience and is not tied to any parochial identity. In short, Bell uses a distinction between moral objectivism and moral relativism to interpret Arendt and claims that it was Arendt's emphasis on a universal, abstract concept of justice that misled critics like Abel into thinking that her judgments are not moral at all.[80] Although this is, I think, a misunderstanding of both Abel and Arendt, it does lead Bell to ask how fair Arendt has been to "the Israelis, to the judgment of Eichmann, to the memory of the Jews murdered in Europe."[81] Here Bell is ambivalent. On the one hand, he believes that Arendt is completely fair, for she wants to show how "the Nazi crimes, the rationalized murder of entire populations, is the beginning of a new set of fearful possibilities in human history" and hence are crimes against humanity, not just Israel.[82] The error was one of being "parochial at a time when the problem of mass murder had become universal."[83] But, on the other hand, Bell thinks that Arendt has failed to deal with the "existential person" and "one's identity as a Jew, as well as a *philosophe*." As he puts it, she has reduced "a tragic drama to a philosophical perplexity"; sometimes, as the Midrash puts it, abstract justice is too "strong" a yardstick to judge the world.[84] To Bell, then, Arendt is largely right but insensitive.[85] In a way, Bell agrees with Abel, that Arendt has failed to appreciate features of context and perspective, but Bell does not think, as Abel does, that these errors mitigate the overall moral character of her work. Both, ultimately, are torn by the need to apply moral standards and yet to take the historical, existential context seriously. They want to universalize the event but at the same time cannot allow themselves to do so.

This exchange between Abel and Bell suggests that the most important issue concerning the intellectual debate over Arendt's book on Eichmann was not whether they supported it or criticized it.[86] Indeed, no general answer on that matter is forthcoming. Abel was critical, as was Podhoretz, who charged Arendt with applying a double standard to Jews and everyone else.[87] Dwight Macdonald and Bruno Bettelheim produced laudatory reviews.[88] Marie Syrkin and Gershom Scholem were severely critical, while Bell was mixed. The real issue lies elsewhere. It is that the debate raised to consciousness a whole set of convictions about universal principles and the particularity of historical situation. In a sense Arendt's strategy was to confront the death camps through the mediation of theory and preconception. From Howe to Abel, Bell to Podhoretz, there were those who wondered whether one's initial responsibility was not to confront Auschwitz first and only then to seek some response to it. From one point of view, it is this shift of strategy that is a hallmark of post-Holocaust Jewish thought. But it was not to arise vividly and powerfully for American Jewry until the late sixties and early seventies after the Six Day War and with the shift in America to greater cultural diversity and the politics of identification.

Chapter Two

Responses to Auschwitz and
the Literary Imagination

In an epilogue to his autobiographical memoir *Starting Out in the Thirties*, Alfred Kazin, the literary critic, recorded this experience:

> One day in the spring of 1945, when the war against Hitler was almost won, I sat in a newsreel theater in Picadilly looking at the first films of newly liberated Belsen. On the screen, sticks in black-and-white prison garb leaned on a wire, staring dreamily at the camera; other sticks shuffled about, or sat vaguely on the ground, next to an enormous pile of bodies, piled up like cordwood, from which protruded legs, arms, heads. A few guards were collected sullenly in a corner, and for a moment a British Army bulldozer was shown digging an enormous hole in the ground. Then the sticks would come back on the screen, hanging on the wire, looking at us.
>
> It was unbearable. People coughed in embarrassment, and in embarrassment many laughed.[1]

The films that circulated after the war, taken of the camp at Bergen-Belsen by the liberating Allied forces, do not of course portray the camps as they were when fully operating. They do not depict the camps as Elie Wiesel, Primo Levi, and Jean Améry experienced them and wrote about them. Rather they picture the aftermath, what remained after the chaos of retreat and abandonment, the residue, a view that was, as Arendt noted, even itself misleading.[2]

Still, to the sensitive, the films are horrifying and unsettling, unbearable and embarrassing, as Kazin recalled, to the degree that the audience's response mechanisms are sabotaged. The images of the sticks, the human skeletons, dead and alive, were indelibly etched into memory, and in the years after 1945 much intellectual activity in America was influenced by those images and the deep worries they came to represent.[3]

These liberal intellectuals in postwar America did not thematically explore the death camps, except of course for Arendt's monumental work, but they were aware of the atrocities, and there is every reason to think that they were deeply moved, indeed to the point where they had little to say but much to feel. They took the camps, where more was actual than was possible, somehow to immobilize the mind. Theodor Adorno, the critical theorist and immigrant intellectual, claimed that when confronted with the "real hell" of the camps, our metaphysical capacity is paralyzed.[4] Lionel Trilling, perhaps the foremost literary critic among the postwar New York intellectuals, developed the same theme but in his own way.

In his important work *The Liberal Imagination*, published in 1950, Trilling included an essay on the novel that originally appeared in *Partisan Review* in 1948.[5] Its theme was "whether or not the novel is still a living form";[6] Trilling's belief was that it is, but the gist of the essay involved not a defense of this position but rather an attempt "to understand under what conditions the novel may live," to explore, that is, the relationship between the literary form of the novel and the historical world in which it occurs.[7] As a problem about the rise of the novel in eighteenth-century England and hence about the social and intellectual conditions that encouraged the development of a narrative form closely tied to characterization and time, this relationship has been brilliantly discussed by critics such as Ian Watt.[8] Trilling's problem is somewhat different, not what conditions gave rise to the novel but rather what accounts for its continued existence or, counterfactually, what would account for its demise.

Trilling proposed three possible explanations for the death of the novel. Either the genre is totally exhausted or the circumstances to which it has been a response no longer exist or such circumstances continue to exist but somehow the novel is no longer adequate to deal with them.[9] In the end, what he recommended, however, is a hybrid; he believed that circumstances changed but that the novel could and should be a device for coping with them. Trilling put it in terms of will, claiming that "the will of our society is dying of its own excess . . . [and that] the great work of our time is the restoration and the reconstitution of the will."[10] The novel both reflects the current deterioration of our society and culture and yet must be revived to counter it. In the course of developing his view and defending it, Trilling introduced the death camps as a reality that confounds the intellect totally and hence as a partial explanation of "the general deterioration of our intellectual life."[11] His reasoning went this way: a main intellectual preoccupation of the modern period, from at least Swift or Shakespeare or Montaigne to Freud, has been the "representation of man's depravity and weakness."[12] No matter how great the depravity, moreover, the mind's discovery of an account of it brought joy and sometimes hope; there was delight in this discovery and optimism too. There was an uncertainty that was stimulating and provocative to the mind, for what depravity existed could not be the end of the matter, yet clearly it was present. But, Trilling adjured, all this ended with the death camps.

> The simple eye of the camera shows us, at Belsen and Buchenwald, horrors that
> quite surpass Swift's powers, a vision of life turned back to its corrupted elements

which is more disgusting than any that Shakespeare could contrive, a cannibalism more literal and fantastic than that which Montaigne ascribed to organized society. . . . [B]efore what we now know the mind stops; the great psychological fact of our time which we all observe with baffled wonder and shame is that there is no possible way of responding to Belsen and Buchenwald. The activity of mind fails before the incommunicability of man's suffering.[13]

Here, Trilling declared, is a depravity that resists representation and explanation, in fact that defies any intellectual response. Here are realities that outstrip all our literary models. "Before what we now know," the reality depicted in these photographs and films, "the mind stops."[14] For Trilling, no imaginative or intellectual response is appropriate, presumably because none seems possible.

There is, in Trilling's view, no systematic reflection on the camps, nor is there a thematic encounter with them. Either response would be beyond what Trilling thinks is possible. What response there is instead suggests ambivalence and an unappreciated inner conflict. For Trilling acknowledged that the death camps cannot be ignored; they reflect the deterioration of our society and of our intellectual life. To acknowledge them is to acknowledge too the impotence of the mind. But if the intellectual and the literary imagination are immobilized, then how can we go on? How can the novelistic intelligence seek to meet the task of restoring the will? Can it both face Auschwitz and produce novels simultaneously?

In general, the impact of the Holocaust on the work of postwar American intellectuals was neither direct nor overwhelming. Trilling's explicit acknowledgment was unusual, and even it is not central to his essay. He does not, nor would we expect him to, ask the general question, can one write novels after the death camps? In this regard he is not alone. Still, the awareness of the camps was present in the intellectual world of the 1950s and early 1960s, often as part of the violent opposition to totalitarianism, often too as an underlying guilt.[15]

During the postwar decades, more and more testimonies by survivors appeared. Elie Wiesel and Primo Levi were two figures whose work later came to be among the most widely read and whose writings most powerfully captured the thought and imagination of the post-Holocaust Jewish thinkers and indeed of North American Jews in general. Both are literary figures, authors of memoirs, fiction, and essays. Both are European, survivors of Auschwitz, one a person deeply immersed in the traditional Jewish, Hasidic life of central Europe, the other a trained Italian chemist and a secular intellectual. In both cases their earliest, most influential literary memoirs of their experiences at Auschwitz appeared in 1958, one in French, the other in Italian.[16] Within two years both had been translated into English, and while neither work was widely read until later in the 1960s, it can be said that these two, *Night* and *Survival at Auschwitz* (originally *If This Be a Man*, accurately from the Italian), forever changed North American consciousness of the extermination camps. Once these works came to the attention of American Jews, the perception of the horrors of Auschwitz came to be shaped by Wiesel's and Levi's memories and the images so brilliantly forged by their literary imaginations.[17] Indeed, by the late 1960s, Wiesel had come to perform more than a literary function; he represented the very capacity of Judaism to expose itself to Auschwitz and yet to survive.

Wiesel's *Night,* the terse distillation of a much longer manuscript, is, according to Lawrence Langer, "the terminus a quo for any investigation of the implications of the Holocaust, no matter what the terminus ad quem; on its final page a world lies dead at our feet, a world we have come to know as our own as well as Wiesel's, and whatever civilization may be rebuilt from its ruins, the silhouette of its visage will never look the same."[18] In this fictional-autobiographical memoir, Wiesel reports on his own journey from his youth in Sighet, a small village in Transylvania, where he was intimately entwined with family life and the religious life of Hasidic Judaism, to his maturity in Auschwitz, a domain of horror, pain, loneliness, death, and hopelessness. His narrative, then, is a kind of *Bildungsroman* in reverse; he is educated and initiated into adult life, but it is a negative life and the process is one of deeducation and destruction.[19] What Wiesel accomplishes in the work is multiple: to portray episodes that give the reader some access to the reality of Auschwitz in a vivid, memorable way; to expose the stages by which the most fundamental human relationships, principles, and concepts were eroded and destroyed; to portray but not to try to explain the atrocities so that the events remain beyond comprehension and understanding; to raise the questions of Jewish faith, about God, covenant, providence, prayer, and redemption as they arose for the victims and as they were raised by their experiences; to raise the question of the extent to which Auschwitz destroyed the world of its victims and, more, the world as it was known to Western culture and civilization.[20] In order to appreciate how Wiesel accomplishes these tasks, it is useful to compare his authorship with that of Arendt.

According to Arendt, the crimes performed in the death camps, the type of criminal agency implicated in the crimes, and the results of the camps—unbounded superfluity, all this made the phenomenon of totalitarian domination unprecedented historically. It also stretched to the limits our moral concepts, our legal categories, and our understanding of human nature, and indeed it was intended to do so. But for Arendt, who examined life in concentration camps through the testimony of others, the camps tested our conceptual schemes insofar as they were understood and interpreted by others. That is, Arendt engaged in an analysis of the camps and arrived at an interpretation of what happened in them. It was the camps so interpreted that were incommensurable with our conceptual frameworks; one view could not be assimilated to another set of views.

Like Arendt, Wiesel believes that Nazism could not be understood with our traditional, liberal concepts—of good and evil, of human nature, and of dignity. But in a sense Wiesel went beyond this belief. Not only can we not explain what happened; indeed, we cannot understand Nazi persecution at all. Nazism did succeed in falsifying much that we believed about human capacity and more. But it also raised the question of whether our moral and religious principles, concepts, goals, and assumptions are adequate at all. For Wiesel, they simply do not apply to Planet Auschwitz. Hence, unlike Arendt, Wiesel believed and tried to show that we really cannot understand what went on; we can try to describe what happened—tersely, simply, and graphically, but we cannot understand what happened.

If this is so, then the ways the camps challenge and stretch to the limits our concepts and principles are different for Arendt and Wiesel. For Arendt, it is our understanding of the camps that tests our conceptual scheme; for Wiesel, what shattered our concepts and principles were the events themselves, and they did this for people who themselves were victims and witnesses of these horrors. It was experience and not interpretation that destroyed thought and language. For these people, the result of living in Auschwitz and experiencing these horrors was an inability to use certain ideas, to hold certain beliefs, or to adhere to certain principles. For Wiesel, the conflict is not a cognitive one; rather it is an existential one.[21] The victim, and the reader through the victim or witness, cannot believe principles about human solidarity, compassion, and goodness and at the same time be honest to his or her experiences. The threat is one of personal disintegration, a kind of schizophrenia or self-detachedness, and the issue one of integrity. If Wiesel is right, then persons who experienced what the inmates of Auschwitz experienced must subsequently live in new conceptual worlds.

For this reason, Wiesel's account of the implications of Auschwitz for our beliefs, concepts, and frameworks is episodic and not systematic. Since the type of conflict is not cognitive but rather experiential, the connections between various ideas and principles that are challenged are not inferential or otherwise conceptual or systematic. Experienced events test the limits of concepts and principles one by one, in particular contexts, and in particular ways.

All of this, in Wiesel's early novels and especially in *Night*, is new, and in its own way it had an important influence on the post-Holocaust theologians.[22] Equally important are the themes that Wiesel addresses, themes of a profoundly Jewish nature. Wiesel wrote memoirs and fiction, works of imagination. He was not a theologian but a deeply religious and informed Jew. What he shows in vividly memorable pictures are the ways that Auschwitz tested and destroyed a religious Jew's beliefs about God, trust, providence, redemption, hope, covenant, and sanctity. Wiesel does not articulate religious beliefs and principles and then ask how particular events or types of events can be understood in these terms. Rather he portrays his own experiences and how they stretched to the breaking point his Jewish assumptions and understandings. For Wiesel, believing in divine protection, for example, was part of his way of experiencing what happened to him; as he testifies to his sufferings in Auschwitz, he testifies as well to the complex ways in which that believing trust is strained, doubted, twisted, and ultimately torn apart. This is not theology, in any normal sense, nor is it philosophy. But it does focus the reader's attention powerfully on Jewish ideas and beliefs and what the reality of Auschwitz might do to a person's commitment to them.[23] It is not surprising that the post-

Holocaust theologians so often cite Wiesel's words and recall his literary portraits as they try to understand what the death camps should mean to our understanding of Judaism and the Jewish people.

Perhaps the most memorable example of Wiesel's religious concerns and of his literary method involves the question of God's role in the atrocities, of divine redemptive or providential power, and of divine responsibility. In a justifiably famous passage from *Night*, Wiesel describes a moment when his relationship with God is tested to the limits. A young boy, "with a refined and beautiful face," the servant of a giant Dutch guard or Oberkapo, was sentenced to death for an act of sabotage; this "little servant, the sad-eyed angel," was to be hanged with two other prisoners. The whole camp was made to watch the spectacle. There were three gallows:

> The three necks were placed at the same moment within the nooses. "Long live liberty!" cried the two adults. But the child was silent. "Where is God? Where is He?" someone behind me asked. At a sign from the head of the camp, the three chairs tipped over. Total silence throughout the camp. On the horizon, the sun was setting . . . Then the march past began. The two adults were no longer alive. . . . But the third rope was still moving: being so light, the child was still alive. . . . Behind me, I heard the same man asking: "Where is God now?" And I heard a voice within me answer him. "Where is He? Here He is. He is hanging here on the gallows. . . ." That night the soup tasted of corpses.[24]

Wiesel does not engage in theological reflection. He records the event, the response of the spectators asking about divine protection and divine presence, and his own complex answer. What does it mean, that God is hanging on the gallows? That what goodness there still is in Auschwitz lies in that boy? That once the boy is hanged, then any God worth anything must be hanged with him? That after experiencing the death of the angel, surely one can no longer believe and trust in divine salvation? That nothing is the same any longer, even God and one's relationship to him? Wiesel gives us a picture that means all of this and more; it is an emblem, as it were, of the rupture between past and future, between one's inheritance and one's life yet to be. It is probably the most recalled and cited episode in all Holocaust literature; for in it is raised the idea that the death camps were a radical break in life and thought, not for the victims alone but for all of us, and that to go on requires going on in a different way.[25]

This motif of rupture is present in the extreme in Wiesel's writings when one considers whether Auschwitz does not defy all linguistic representation, whether silence or fractured language is not all that is possible. Wiesel, among others, reflects on this question about language, art, representation, and Auschwitz, and in works like *Night* he achieves something remarkable.[26] As Robert Alter puts it,

> he has managed to realize the terrible past imaginatively with growing artistic strength in a narrative form that is consecutive, coherent, and, at least on the surface, realistic, in a taut prose that is a model of lucidity and precision. Yet by the

very nature of his subject, what we might want to describe as the "realism" of his technique constantly transcends itself, as we are made to feel the pitiful inadequacy of all our commonsense categories of reality.[27]

Wiesel's writing is "factually precise"; yet it has a "hallucinated more-than-realism."[28] The challenge to our traditional categories is expressed by Wiesel's seemingly realistic accounts of events that did indeed happen; as the young boy Eliezer he sees things clearly and experiences them deeply and powerfully. Yet, in a sense, what he experiences is beyond our imagination. Wiesel's language, which becomes almost a parable, expresses the complexity of this witness. The events did in fact happen; Wiesel did experience them, and his beliefs, his understanding, even his imagination were changed by them. Yet to recall them and to take them seriously one must be mad, in a sense, misshapen, altered beyond the normal, for that is the way the events registered.

Wiesel exhibits this combination of realistic description and mad response in an episode that took place upon his arrival at Auschwitz, once the prisoners had disembarked from the train. As he clung to his father, they were secretly told of the reality of the crematoria and their destination: "Do you see that chimney over there? See it? Do you see those flames? . . . Haven't you realized it yet? You dumb bastards, don't you understand anything? You're going to be burned. Frizzled away. Turned into ashes."[29] The imagery of flames, of Hell, permeates Wiesel's narrative:

> Not far from us, flames were leaping up from a ditch, gigantic flames. They were burning something. A lorry drew up at the pit and delivered its load— little children. Babies! Yes, I saw it—saw it with my own eyes . . . those children in the flames. . . . I pinched my face. Was I still alive? Was I awake? I could not believe it. How could it be possible for them to burn people, children, and for the world to keep silent? No, none of this could be true. It was a nightmare.

A moment later someone starts to recite the kaddish, the prayer for the dead, and Wiesel takes it to be extraordinary, people uttering this prayer for themselves. He recoils. "For the first time, I felt revolt rise up in me. Why should I bless His name? The Eternal, Lord of the Universe, the All-Powerful and Terrible, was silent. What had I to thank him for?"[30] The erosion of trust, of faith, began here. Wiesel returns to the present and adds a moving reflection on these first moments in the camp and their effect on him: "Never shall I forget that night, the first night in camp, which has turned my life into one long night, seven times cursed and seven times sealed. Never shall I forget that smoke. Never shall I forget the little faces of the children, whose bodies I saw turned into wreaths of smoke beneath a silent blue sky. Never shall I forget those flames which consumed my faith forever. Never shall I forget that nocturnal silence which deprived me, for all eternity, of the desire to live. Never shall I forget those moments which murdered my God and my soul and

turned my dreams to dust. Never shall I forget these things, even if I am condemned to live as long as God Himself. Never."[31]

The flames that burned the children "consumed his faith," but not forever. In
subsequent novels and works—*The Gates of the Forest, Messengers of God, Souls on
Fire*—Wiesel seeks to recover his faith, his relationship with God, not as an easy
faith but as a troubled one, filled with anger, recrimination, and reprimand. Later
I will show that Irving Greenberg and Emil Fackenheim recall in their own way
the very same practices, the burning of the children, and they will be moved to treat
the unspeakable deaths of innocent children in those burning pits as exemplary of
the evil of Auschwitz. What Wiesel recalls may be mad, a nightmare, but it did
occur, and it burned into his soul the questions, what can one believe and imagine,
how can one live, in such a world?

Primo Levi was a chemist from Turin, Italy. His memoirs *Survival in Auschwitz*
(1958) and *The Reawakening* (1963) record his experiences in Auschwitz from 1944
to January 1945 and, after the liberation of the camps, his journey of return through
eastern Europe to Italy and civilization. In 1977 Levi retired as manager of a chem-
ical factory in Turin to devote himself exclusively to his writing. He committed suicide in April 1987.[32]

Earlier, in contrasting Wiesel with Arendt, I raised the issue of perspective.
Arendt took a detached point of view, engaged in an interpretive analysis of the
camps, and assessed the ways the camps, so interpreted, exceeded the limits of our
concepts, principles, and frameworks. Wiesel, on the other hand, occupied the engaged perspective of a victim, shifting back and forth from a direct experience of
the events themselves to the point of view of the author, at the time of writing, recalling those events and reflecting on them. For Wiesel, then, his own experiences
as a victim, when they occurred or later, challenged his beliefs and convictions. For
example, Wiesel the author, at the time of writing, proclaims that he shall never
forget his first night in the camp, the smoke, and the little faces of the children
thrown into the burning pits. "Never shall I forget," he writes, "those flames which
consumed my faith forever." As author, Wiesel tells us that he will never forget the
flames he saw as a fifteen-year-old boy. But who is it who thinks that the flames
consumed Wiesel's faith forever? Certainly not the boy, although Wiesel writes that
as a boy he had been revolted enough by the sight of the ditch, filled with burning
babies, to want to refuse to say the kaddish and to thank God. Still, it is Wiesel the
author and not the boy who says, at the time of writing, that that early experience
of the flames shattered his faith from then on.

Levi, in *Survival in Auschwitz*, differs from both Arendt and Wiesel. First, unlike Wiesel, he does not confront the camps as a religious Jew. His framework is
that of a scientist and a secular humanist.[33] The questions Levi raises are, as in
Arendt's case, largely about social and moral matters. Second, in one sense, Levi's
perspective is that of the engaged victim. But this is not the whole story. In a later
work, he remarks that his point of view was detached as well as engaged,[34] not

merely, as in Wiesel's case, because he as author was separated in time from his earlier self but also because he as victim occupied a special role in the camps that enabled him to be both engaged and detached simultaneously. That Levi realizes that one's perspective was vital to one's encounter with the camps is already important; that he takes his peculiar perspective to have afforded him in particular a special opportunity and a special duty is quite remarkable.

At a certain point during his imprisonment Levi, as a chemist, became what he calls a privileged inmate; all of his memoir, written later, is the recollection of a privileged victim, even the early stages when he was yet to be privileged. His understanding of what happened to him and to others, then, is not bound by his early engaged and totally embedded perspective; rather it is enriched by the later privileged standpoint he occupied, which was, as I will show, partially engaged and partially detached. Levi warns us that the memories of the survivors, while naturally "the most substantial material for the reconstruction of truth about the camps," "should be read with a critical eye." "The Lagers themselves were not," he said,

> always a good observation post: in the inhuman conditions to which they were subjected, the prisoners could barely acquire an overall vision of their universe. ... Surrounded by death, the deportee was often in no position to evaluate the extent of the slaughter unfolding before his eyes. ... In short the prisoner felt overwhelmed by a massive edifice of violence and menace but could not form for himself a representation of it because his eyes were fixed to the ground by every single minute's needs.

If Levi is right, then normal prisoners were not in the best position to report on the camps. Moreover, they were a majority of the inmates but a minority among the survivors, so that, as Levi remarks, the history of the camps has in fact been written not by these normal victims but rather by those, like him, who had some privileged role or other.[35]

Nonetheless, while the privileged had a better vantage point, their view "was to a greater or lesser degree also falsified by the privilege itself." In the case of the "privileged par excellence, that is, those who acquired privilege for themselves by becoming subservient to the camp authorities," this falsification was extreme; those like the Kapos and Sonderkommandos are totally unreliable witnesses.

> Therefore the best historians of the Lagers emerged from among the very few who had the ability and luck to obtain a privileged observatory without bowing to compromises, and the skill to tell what they saw, suffered, and did with the humility of a good chronicler, that is, taking into account the complexity of the Lager phenomenon and the variety of human destinies being played out in it.[36]

Levi, then, distinguishes three groups—the normal prisoners, the privileged, and the privileged par excellence. Only the second group give us a good understanding of the camps, and Levi is a member of that second group. Yet even their reports are biased and imperfect, if only because these privileged ones cannot tell—except in a detached and hence distorted way—the story of the drowned, of "the destruction brought to an end, the job completed."[37]

What does privilege provide that is relevant to the task of understanding the camp? Privilege brings with it more food, better working conditions, more time, and greater information. All of this facilitates a larger and more informed view of what was going on; it also enables reflective assessment concerning what was happening and what it meant. In *Survival in Auschwitz* we see these advantages at work in the hands of a skillful artist with keen insight and a wholly economical literary style. Again and again, Levi with lucid precision records episodes and then reflects on their meaning, their implications for human solidarity, for our moral life, and for language itself. Never trite, never sensationalist, never overly abstract, Levi's reflective observations register the impact of what he experiences, as he understands it, on the intellectual world of liberal, secular humanism and the world of Western civilization as it was informed by that tradition.

One of the most important of Levi's results is a picture of the paradigmatic victim, the camp's ideal product, the so-called *Musselmänner*, the doomed or the drowned. Levi calls this "lying on the bottom" or being "crushed against the bottom." The process that results in such a state, a short time for some, a permanent one for others, he calls "the demolition of a man." It is a state of total deprivation in which the prisoner is stripped of possessions, clothes, name, and even speech and the capacity to communicate: "if we speak, they will not listen to us, and if they listen, they will not understand."[38] Levi gives two accounts of what this state is like. The first occurs in his initial chapter, in which he describes his entrance into the camp and begins to realize what the camp procedures seek to produce:

> Imagine now a man who is deprived of everyone he loves, and at the same time
> of his house, his habits, his clothes, in short everything he possesses: he will be a
> hollow man, reduced to suffering and needs, forgetful of dignity and restraint,
> for he who loses all often easily loses himself. He will be a man whose life or
> death can be lightly decided with no sense of human affinity, in the most fortu-
> nate of cases, on the basis of a pure judgment of utility. It is in this way that one
> can understand the double sense of the term "extermination camp," and it is now
> clear what we seek to express with the phrase: "to lie on the bottom."[39]

Arendt described a process whereby the individual was systematically destroyed, until human beings were converted into "superfluous human material." Levi here sees the same process as an order of deprivations, until the human being is only "suffering and needs," subhuman, without the self-respect and sense of human solidarity with others that invokes "dignity and restraint." Not all yield to this process, but those who do last only a short time:

> one knows that they are only here on a visit, that in a few weeks nothing will re-
> main of them but a handful of ashes in some near-by field and a crossed-out

number on a register. Although engulfed and swept along without rest by the innumerable crowd of those similar to them, they suffer and drag themselves along
in an opaque, intimate solitude, and in solitude they die or disappear, without
leaving a trace in anyone's memory.[40]

Levi's description of this state, lying on the bottom, uses simple terms, psychological and moral; it fosters the image of some isolated bit of useless stuff whose career
means nothing to anyone. Even the agents in Hobbes's state of nature, bundles of
needs and desires, capable of pleasure and pain, engaged in active, rational competition; even they mattered to each other—their solitude was not opaque. Levi's
drowned are below this state.[41]

Levi's second description of them occurs in a chapter entitled "The Drowned
and the Saved."

All the musselmans who finished in the gas chambers have the same story, or
more exactly, have no story; they followed the slope down to the bottom, like
streams that run down to the sea. On their entry into the camp, through basic incapacity, or by misfortune, or through some banal incident, they are overcome
before they can adapt themselves; they are beaten by time, they do not begin to
learn German, to disentangle the infernal knot of laws and prohibitions until
their body is already in decay, and nothing can save them from selections or from
death by exhaustion. Their life is short, but their number is endless; they, the
Muselmänner, the drowned, form the backbone of the camp, an anonymous
mass, continually renewed and always identical, of non-men who march and
labour in silence, the divine spark dead within them, already too empty to really
suffer. One hesitates to call them living: one hesitates to call their death death, in
the face of which they have no fear, as they are too tired to understand.

They crowd my memory with their faceless presences, and if I could enclose
all the evil of our time in one image, I would choose this image which is familiar to me: an emaciated man, with head dropped and shoulders curved, one
whose face and in whose eyes not a trace of a thought is to be seen.[42]

I know of no more compelling, grim portrait of the product of Nazi dehumanization.[43] Later, Emil Fackenheim will use this passage to call attention to one of the
unprecedented features of Nazism, this new kind of human being, without self-
determination or spontaneity, thing-like, anonymous nonmen whose lives fill a
blank between life and death. Here, Levi proposes, is the epitome of Nazi evil.

But while the drowned are the "backbone" of the camp, they are not its exclusive inmates. There are others, whom Levi carefully and patiently recalls, who ne-
gotiate the intricate, diabolical structure of the camps and "fight merely with their
own strength to survive."[44] Often this was a struggle for survival at all costs, but at
times it was a struggle for survival without renouncing one's moral world or even
a struggle for the survival *of* one's moral world. In a variety of ways, the camp challenged the moral vocabulary and sensibility that the prisoner brought with him or
her.

Levi does not simplify the complexity of the camp's relation to our normal moral world. There are too many types of victims and too many types of perpetrators to allow any facile judgment about morality and the extermination camps. But he does not ignore the issue, for he sees the camp as "a gigantic biological and social experiment" one element of which is the role of morality in the human being's struggle for life. For the musselmänner, of course, morality has been completely obliterated; they have no sense of self, no dignity, nothing but unreflective, thoughtless need. For others too, who learn to exploit the camp for their own survival, moral principles and ideals also play no role:

> Theft in Buna, punished by the civilian direction, is authorized and encouraged by the SS; theft in camp, severely repressed by the SS, is considered by the civilians as a normal exchange operation; theft among Haftlinge [prisoners] is generally punished, but the punishment strikes the thief and the victim with equal gravity. We now invite the reader to contemplate the possible meaning in the Lager of the words "good" and "evil," "just" and "unjust"; let everybody judge . . . how much of our ordinary moral world could survive on this side of the barbed wire.[45]

This is not to say that in the camps conduct was normally criminal, that there our normal moral principles applied but were regularly broken. It is to say, rather, that neither our concepts, in their normal meanings, nor our principles, for example, do not steal, applied at all. It was not that theft was bad but a common practice or that theft was good. It was that theft, that is, the concept of theft, did not apply in the camp world as it does in ours. Taking the possessions of others was both good and bad, in one place but not in another, for some but not for others. Theft entails property, which itself requires a sense of ownership, rights, and hence selfhood; none of this had a grip in the kingdom of darkness.

Still, in this morally eccentric, disorienting context, there were those, Levi recalls, "saints or martyrs," who struggled for survival without renouncing any part of their moral world.[46] Indeed, there were some who saw their task not merely to be one of surviving but also to be one of salvaging their moral character. Levi was initiated into this task and the strategies for moral survival early by his friend Steinlauf. What Levi learned from Steinlauf concerned washing, which originally seemed a waste of energy, and the camp rules about personal hygiene that initially struck Levi as bad humor: "In this place it is practically pointless to wash every day in the turbid water of the filthy washbasins for purposes of cleanliness and health; but it is most important as a symptom of remaining vitality, and necessary as an instrument of moral survival."[47]

This was the lesson that Levi learned, that cleanliness was necessary for his moral survival; Steinlauf, as Levi recalled, taught him the lesson in these words:

> that precisely because the Lager was a great machine to reduce us to beasts, we must not become beasts; that even in this place one can survive, and therefore one must want to survive, to tell the story, to bear witness; and that to survive one

must force ourselves to save at least the skeleton, the scaffolding, the form of civilization. We are slaves, deprived of every right, exposed to every insult, condemned to certain death, but we still possess one power, and we must defend it
with all our strength for it is the last—the power to refuse our consent. So we
must certainly wash our faces without soap in dirty water and dry ourselves on
our jackets. We must polish our shoes, not because the regulation states it, but for
dignity and propriety. We must walk erect, without dragging our feet, not in
homage to Prussian discipline but to remain alive, not to begin to die.[48]

Levi recalls that he was not fully persuaded, that in part he could agree with Steinlauf
only because Levi, at that moment, refused to accept a system imposed by others.
Nonetheless, Steinlauf's point indicates a possibility within the concentration camp
universe. It was possible to develop modes of resistance that would serve the purposes
of moral survival and to do so by recognizing the goal of the process, to reduce the
victims to beasts, and by willfully, deliberately opposing that process. One could wash
and maintain a ritual of personal hygiene in order to retain a sense of self-worth and
dignity. One could do this because one felt duty-bound to live and not to die.[49]

In the end, then, Levi recalls that the camps challenged our normal moral principles, concepts, and models in a variety of ways. In one way, the camps were a new
moral universe, utterly incommensurable with our own; in another, they were an
extreme opportunity for moral resilience and extraordinary moral commitment.
Interpreted and understood from Levi's unusual standpoint, the camps could be
seen to conflict with our ideas, beliefs, and even with our language. By using Levi's
accounts, his descriptions, his memories, and his reflections, we can see why others
would agree with him that the camps were a distinctive, unprecedented phenomenon that altered decisively our moral and social landscape.

One of the essays in Primo Levi's final book, *The Drowned and the Saved*, called
"The Intellectual in Auschwitz,"[50] is a critique of an essay by Jean Améry, born
Hans Meyer, an assimilated Viennese Jew, philosopher-journalist, and disciple of
Jean Paul Sartre, a member of the Belgian resistance, and prisoner in Auschwitz
during Levi's period of incarceration.[51] In 1966 Améry published a collection of five
essays on his experiences of the death camps (originally *Jenseits von Schuld und
Suhne* (*Beyond Guilt and Atonement*, an allusion to Nietzsche); translated into English as *At the Mind's Limits: Contemplations by a Survivor on Auschwitz and Its
Realities* (1980). On October 17, 1978, Améry committed suicide. Written in
1964, the first of his five essays on Auschwitz, how he came to be an inmate, and
what followed his imprisonment, deals with the situation of the intellectual in the
camp.

Levi calls his essay "a summary, a paraphrase, a discussion, and critique" of
Améry's essay, which has two titles, "The Intellectual in Auschwitz" and "At the
Limits of the Spirit." This is an accurate description; Levi does paraphrase, endorse,
and corroborate much of what Améry contends: that the intellectual was, for example, ill equipped to deal with the chaos of the camps and the sheer physical de-

mands of the work. He also paraphrases and modifies many of Améry's observations. He claims that for him, at least, his intellectual, that is, scientific, attitude encouraged him to observe others, enabled him to classify people and experiences, in a somewhat detached way, and to seek understanding and explanation; his intellect, that is, was not for Levi an unqualified disadvantage.[52] In addition, Levi's attachment to culture, especially literary culture — most important, his memories of Dante — moved him to recover the past, "saving it from oblivion and reinforcing my identity."[53] Améry is relentless in finding ways that the mind and demeanor of the intellectual either were useful or harmful in the camp; Levi mitigates this extremism, initially by widening the category of the intellectual to include those, like himself, who are mathematicians and scientists and not philosophers or artists but who nonetheless are involved in intellectual pursuits, have advanced education, are cultured, and are intellectually curious.[54] He then qualifies one after another of Améry's indictments of the intellect's role in the camps.

There is another way of treating Améry's observations about the intellectual in Auschwitz. By describing how features of the intellectual life — its tendency to abstract thinking, to rational analysis, to an aesthetic attitude toward death and dying,[55] and so forth — were dissonant with the demands of camp life and even disadvantaged the inmate in his struggle for survival, Améry was, at the same time, showing how Auschwitz was discontinuous with the world of Western philosophical, rational culture, that is, with the world of the Enlightenment. Its concepts, principles, assumptions, style, and framework simply did not apply in the camp. Hence, their universality is compromised; a world exists that does not fit this intellectual culture.

> Long practice in questioning the phenomena of everyday reality prevented [the intellectual] from simply adjusting to the realities of the camp, because these stood in all-too-sharp a contrast to everything that he had regarded until then as possible and humanly acceptable. . . . [T]he SS was employing a logic of destruction that in itself operated just as consistently as the logic of life preservation did in the outside world. You always had to be clean-shaven, but it was strictly forbidden to possess razor or scissors, and you went to the barber only once every two weeks. . . . The intellect revolted against [these circumstances] in the impotency of abstract thought.[56]

Just as Arendt and Levi showed how the camps refuted, indeed made meaningless our moral concepts and our understanding of human nature, and just as Wiesel showed the tension between his Jewish belief and his experience of atrocity, so Améry exposed the limitations of reason, the language of Western intellectual culture, and liberalism. If this is the aspiration to spiritual transcendence, then Améry sought to show that "nowhere else in the world did reality have as much effective power as in the camp, nowhere else was reality so real. In no other place did the attempt to transcend it prove so hopeless and so shoddy."[57]

Levi's most important disagreement with Améry concerns what we might call the response to assault and the requirements of dignity; Levi calls it Améry's "returning the blow" morality.[58] The difference between the two is extreme and significant. It involves the capacity to respond to evil with a blow, the moral necessity of such an act of opposition, and the role of this act in Améry's sense of Jewish identification. Levi associates the trading of blows with the question of dignity and where it lies, with the notions of political response and courage, with the role of justice and forgiveness, and with ultimate defeat—indeed with Améry's own suicide. He admires Améry's choice to descend from the ivory tower to the battlefield and return the blow, defining in this way his post-Holocaust existence. But Levi cannot make that choice; Améry could and did. What kind of Judaism emerged from it? What was this Judaism that for Améry was necessary and not impossible?

"If being a Jew implies having a cultural heritage or religious ties, then I was not one and can never become one."[59] Améry claims that he had no Jewish memories, no links with Jewish tradition, and hence could not become a Jew. He recognized nonetheless that the Nuremberg Laws of 1935 concretized an undeniable reality, that he was a Jew because the world took him to be one and that meant to be the object of bias, hatred, and ultimately threat. These observations both read like versions of Jean Paul Sartre's famous account of the Jewish situation, that what constitutes Judaism is not race or religion or history but rather the hatred of others, anti-Semitism.[60] In this way, Améry locates the core of his post-Holocaust Jewish identity; he is the object of this death threat; he is one whose human dignity is and has been denied; he is a target of ridicule, degradation, and disdain. In Sartre's terms, this is the central feature of the Jewish situation, and the only question to be asked of the Jew is how he or she shall respond to it. How shall one authentically respond to this assault on one's dignity that is thereby an assault on all humankind's dignity? How does the victim do what he or she can to regain the dignity that is being attacked? In *Anti-Semite and Jew*, the only example Sartre gives of an authentic Jew is a journal editor who does what he believes is right in defiance of the charges of nepotism and favoritism made against him. Améry's post-Holocaust Jewish existence goes beyond Sartre's example; his Judaism is shaped as a historically sensitive understanding of what is required of him to be an authentic, post-Holocaust Jew, and it is based on and a continuation of the Jewish existence he chose for himself in 1935.

That initial decision arose out of Améry's understanding of dignity and what it required. If dignity is restricted to the recognition of one's worth by others, then degradation and living under the death threat would be "an inescapable fate," as he puts it.[61] "It is certainly true that dignity can be bestowed only by society. . . . Still, the degraded person, threatened with death, is able . . . to convince society of his dignity by taking his fate upon himself and at the same time rising in revolt against it." Once Améry had recognized his position, the hatred of him and of all Jews, he could respond in a variety of ways, among them through defense mechanisms or other vehicles of escape. Even then, he says, he felt the need to avoid these evasions if he could and to choose "to overcome [the world's judgment] through revolt,"[62] not in any glamorous way but simply through commitment to resistance and through the decision to do what was not natural, in a way, that is, to strike back.

To illustrate such a decision Améry recalls a minor incident in Auschwitz when he strikes back at the Polish guard who had hit him in the face. This is the episode that Levi reports and from which he recoils, because as he says it is not in him. But the truth is that it was not in Améry either; he created it because he needed it, for it was his view that such an action of rebellion, no matter what the physical cost, was required for recovering his dignity and hence for acting authentically in his situation. "In situations like mine," he writes, "physical violence is the sole means for restoring a disjointed personality. . . . I became a person not by subjectively appealing to my abstract humanity but by discovering myself within the given social reality as a rebelling Jew and by realizing myself as one."[63] Moreover, as Améry recounts, the episode was not the end of this rebellion. It was the beginning of a process that went on after the liberation of the camps and in the years that followed. Hence, Améry's Judaism—not everyone's, as he is careful to caution—is a Judaism of threat, of lack of trust, and of rebellion. It is what he calls "Catastrophe Judaism."[64]

There is a sense, however, in which Améry's Judaism is only accidentally Jewish. It is solely constituted by the choice to resist, to return blow for blow, to be active and not to be passive; it is the choice to choose, which is simply another way of saying that it is a Sartrian act of self-awareness, self-lucidity. Levi, we recall, admitted that culture was useful to him precisely because his memories of Dante, for example, "made it possible for [him] to reestablish a link with the past, saving it from oblivion and reinforcing [his] identity."[65] To be sure, both he and Améry agreed that religious belief was beyond them, and neither, for different reasons, admits the importance or even the accessibility of Jewish tradition, its conduct, texts, images, and memories. But Levi at least realizes that identity is somehow enhanced by continuity with some past or other. For Améry, all identity is swallowed up by the present, by choosing, the choosing to be active, to return blow for blow. There is reason to think that this is too little content even for Catastrophe Judaism, that is, for a post-Holocaust Jewish existence that is genuinely Jewish, although it points to one ineliminable dimension of it, albeit a secular dimension. It is, what Améry calls, a "Jewish identity without positive determinants" and "being a Jew [without] positive identification."[66]

But if Améry's Judaism, a necessity for him, is wholly individual, wholly tied to his freedom and his decision, wholly active and personally defined by his situation, then how is he a Jew, a member of the Jewish people? At the conclusion of his essay, Améry asks and answers this question.[67] In part, there is no relationship between Améry and the Jewish people. "With Jews as Jews I share practically nothing: no language, no cultural tradition, no childhood memories."[68] The very Judaism that is impossible for Améry can provide no bridge between him and other Jews. The only Judaism that can serve as such a bridge is the Judaism that arises out of their common situation, the Judaism of threat and retaliation, of fear and anger; what produces Améry's "solidarity with every threatened Jew in this world," then, is the threat itself. His relationship with other Jews arises out of that threat; it is his "solidarity with every Jew whose freedom, equal rights, or perhaps even physical existence is threatened. . . . This solidarity is part of [his] person and a weapon in the battle to regain [his] dignity. . . . Solidarity in the face of threat is all that links [Améry] with [his] Jewish contemporaries, the believers as well as the nonbelievers, the national-minded as well as those ready to assimilate."[69]

Améry is a far cry from Arendt, as are Wiesel and Levi. They, together with other memoirists, novelists, and poets, begin and end their reflections with an unrelenting, uncompromised focus on Auschwitz. Never do these three lapse into abstractions about totalitarianism in general, hatred and cruelty in general, or evil in general. When cracks open in the standard vocabularies of morality, liberal humanism, and rationality, they do so because of the intense pressure of particular episodes, experiences, and persons. In the postwar years, Jewish theologians resisted this particularity, just as they resisted dealing with the death camps in any direct way. But they were not alone in avoiding Auschwitz while nonetheless reacting to the global impression of a wartime filled with evil and horror. Post-Holocaust Jewish thought arises only when this resistance dissipates and when some thinkers, albeit only a few, expose their thinking and themselves to Auschwitz in all of its particularity.

Jewish Theology in Postwar America

When Emil Fackenheim began doctoral study in philosophy in Toronto, Canada — having escaped from Berlin, begun his studies with a year in Aberdeen, Scotland, and spent several months in detention camps, both in England and Canada — there hardly existed anything that one could call Jewish theology in America. In those years, the early 1940s, the war preoccupied people's attention, and what Jewish theology there was derived from the revival of Protestant theology in the 1940s. Largely this was the work of Reinhold Niebuhr, whose own thinking was a blend of liberal moral thought and religious neoorthodoxy.[1] Translations of the great European theologians, from Søren Kierkegaard and Karl Barth to Paul Tillich, Rudolf Bultmann, and Martin Buber were becoming available;[2] older forms of rationalism and Kantian idealism were present, and religious naturalism, in part through the work of Mordecai Kaplan, had its adherents.[3] But all in all, in the early 1940s Jewish theology still languished. Fackenheim and others with an appreciation for German philosophy and theology doubtless found America a barren venue, a theological desert.[4]

The influence of Milton Steinberg and Niebuhr on Will Herberg was salutary. Herberg had been a Marxist and was a sociologist by trade; Steinberg was a rabbi, theologian, and novelist. By the late 1940s Herberg had taken up the challenge of welding features of religious existentialism and Jewish commitment into a new theological conception. The secular Marxist had become a Jewish theologian. For Herberg, who had been a Marxist until 1937, when the Stalinist purges destroyed forever his Marxist faith, Niebuhr's *Moral Man and Immoral Society* converted him to religion and God, and, associated with the Jewish Theological Seminary, Milton Steinberg shepherded his early steps as a Jewish theologian.[5]

While Niebuhr and other Christian theologians provided the seeds and Herberg began to plant them, it was a new generation of Jewish theologians that cultivated and nourished them as they grew into talks, articles, and books of a new Jewish theology. Along with Kierkegaard and other Christian thinkers, Martin Buber and Franz Rosenzweig were the most powerful modern resources of this new generation.[6] The most fundamental traditional resources were the Bible and the Midrashic literature. Joseph Soloveitchik was the central Orthodox figure, his *halakhic* and Maimonidean orientation coordinated with a deep commitment to an almost Kierkegaardian sense of religious faith. Abraham Joshua Heschel became the most influential Conservative theologian, with his unique blend of phenomenology, Biblical theology, and Hasidism.[7] Among Reform theologians, who struggled to impress upon rabbis and religious leaders the importance of theology and the seriousness of theological issues, Emil Fackenheim was probably the most penetrating and eloquent, but he was joined by many others, Steven Schwarzschild, Jakob Petuchowski, Lou Silberman, Bernard Martin, and Eugene Borowitz among them.[8]

The articles, reviews, and debates of the 1950s of these theologians, published in journals and periodicals such as *Commentary*, the *CCAR Journal*, *Tradition*, the *Reconstructionist*, and *Judaism*, exhibit a strange and complex irony. Certainly, to many of the protagonists, the debate was not about the propriety of theology per se for Judaism. If theological reflection involves articulating Jewish belief and understanding Judaism, then both advocates and critics of the new theology favored theological thinking. What distinguished them were their attitudes toward existentialism.[9] To some, existentialist thought was antirational, anarchic, romantic, pessimistic, dehumanizing, and Christian. To others, it was marked by a deep sense of realism, of the extent as well as the limits of human reason and human freedom, of the role of God in human experience and history, and of the human experience of a Jewish relationship with God.[10] Some saw the existentialist's recognition of human frailty and submissiveness as Christian, a philosophical version of the doctrine of original sin; others saw it as an indigenously Jewish way of relating to God in a rich and meaningful way. Ironically, the advocates were convinced that the rationalist, liberal interpretation of Judaism and the naturalism of Kaplan and his followers were both rooted outside of Judaism, just as the critics believed that existentialism was grounded in Christianity. Moreover, just as the critics were certain that human will and conduct, expressed in the advances in technology and the achievements of modern culture and society, deserved real appreciation, so the advocates of the new theology demanded a realistic acknowledgment of human failures and the consequences of finitude. Both, that is, took themselves to be genuinely Jewish and genuinely realistic and their opponents to be neither.[11]

The debate of these years over the propriety of existential thought for Jewish theology had deeper features than those most frequently discussed by the participants, features that post-Holocaust Jewish thought would bring to the surface. In his own terms, Franz Rosenzweig, earlier in the century, had raised some of these deeper issues when he distinguished between the old and the new thinking and then sought a convincing rescue and *refutation* of the old. The deepest issue of the

1950s was not whether existentialism was less Jewish and more Christian than naturalism or rationalism and not whether modern culture, science, technology, and
society are beneficial or destructive of the self. It was whether we can detach ourselves or our principles from the complexities of our personal, historical situation,
and if not, how we can nonetheless avoid relativism or skepticism in the face of
whatever our world gives us.[12]

In the 1950s and the 1960s the new Jewish theologians—the existentialists
among them—worked on two levels simultaneously. On the one hand, they attempted to clarify their understanding of a genuine Jewish theology in a polemical
context. They tried to persuade the uninitiated that theological reflection was important for Jewish life and especially for Jewish leadership. They attempted too to
defend themselves against the opponents of existential theology, who rejected the
notion of a living, personal God. On the other hand, these theologians met with
each other and probed their theological commitments together, posing problems,
exploring difficulties, and debating the content of an authentic Jewish theology.
Often, pieces of these debates were published, although the full script of the discussions and meetings is retained, if at all, only in the memories of the participants.
When these bits and pieces were published, moreover, they were doubtlessly redesigned for the wider audience that would read them, an audience of a vast uninitiated and a host of opponents, both of whom required that positions and arguments be clothed differently from the way they were for the debates among
colleagues and friends. Still, we can read the essays and talks for what they reveal
about the most pressing issues that faced the new theology, and when we do, we see
that these were the issues of faith and autonomy, revelation and *halakhah*.

The problem of faith was how to understand religious experience and God in
such a way that one could defend both against their detractors. The problem of autonomy was how to give proper credit to human freedom as the core of human selfhood and yet to incorporate the role of tradition, authority, and the divine will in
Jewish experience and Jewish life. Both problems arose for the new theologian
from within. They were real problems, because one had to face them; one could not
avoid them by claiming that their sources, the respectability of rational critique and
of divine or traditional authority, were alien to the believer. For to the existentialist theologian, they were not alien; indeed, they were part of who the believer really
was. In the end, then, faith and autonomy were not artificially generated as problems by an avoidable context; rather they were authentically generated by the believer's own situation.

Of the organized movements in American Judaism, Reform was more interested in and more receptive to theology than the more traditional types of Judaism.
Yet even in Reform circles, especially among rabbis, theological discussion was
marginal and controversial. On March 20–22, 1950, an Institute on Reform Jewish Theology was convened at the Hebrew Union College in Cincinnati. Eugene
Borowitz, recently ordained and a young assistant rabbi in St. Louis, attended the

Institute and reported in *Commentary* on its themes, debates, character, and tone.[13] The editors introduced Borowitz's report this way:

> During the past two decades, many thoughtful observers have commented on the almost total lack of concern, on the part of the American synagogue, with theological issues and thinking. The announcement of the convening of an Institute of Reform Jewish Theology was received, accordingly, with the keenest attention, being taken as evidence of a reawakening of interest in the spiritual problem of our day.[14]

Commenting on Levi Olan's presentation "Theology Today," Borowitz identified this "spiritual problem" or "religious crisis," as he called it, with general features of American religious life: people's resistance to old answers, their lack of orientation, and "a deep, if hidden, fear of the future." Olan had accurately appreciated the depth of this crisis: Western culture and civilization seemed without meaning and direction; modern society — the society of Camus, Kafka, and Dostoyevsky perhaps — was threatening and chaotic. Human resources alone could not bring order and security; some faith was needed, and the question for these Reform rabbis was whether Judaism could provide it.

Borowitz then itemized "four basic religious questions" confronting liberal Judaism. These questions concerned the belief in God as an independent reality, the possibility of believing in divine action in the world, the nature of authority in Reform Judaism, and the belief in progress as salvation.[15] But if Borowitz has accurately conveyed the atmosphere of the meeting, these issues, fundamental as they are, took a back seat to more practical considerations, especially the discussion of a "guide for Reform practice which," he claimed, "at the moment . . . is the most hotly debated issue in Reform Judaism, both in the rabbinate and among the laity." It was an issue debated at a practical level and not in theological terms. As Borowitz put it, "while there was no agreement as to the meaning of revelation in modern Judaism, its practical consequences — ritual ceremonial, law — were almost unanimously desired."[16]

This avoidance or neglect of theology was a well-established feature of the Reform rabbinate, as Borowitz made clear, but the times demanded theological renewal and creativity. As Borowitz reported, Leo Baeck, the revered survivor of Theriesenstadt, theologian, and leader of German liberal Judaism, gave the opening talk at the Institute, and in his address, Baeck highlighted the historical context, the type of crisis that calls for theological reflection, and the way that theology arises when an old problem grips a person, who resolves to struggle with the problem at a moment of crisis. What Borowitz concluded from Baeck's exhortation was a sense of urgency, the need for "bold theological thinking to make clear the relevance of Judaism today."[17] As the meetings ended, the participants too seemed to sense that need, for they voted unanimously to recommend to the Central Conference of American Rabbis (CCAR) the permanent establishment of an Institute on Theology to meet annually.

One of the essays was by Emil Fackenheim. According to Borowitz, he gave an "Existentialist interpretation of Judaism," calling attention to the evidence for human finitude in recent history, the belief in a transcendent God who gives meaning to human existence, and the inadequacies of old-fashioned notions of progress. "Existentialism came as a profound philosophical shock to the assembled rabbis."[18]

It is clear from Borowitz's report that the 1950 Institute was an event of significance. It exposed the lack of theological sensibility and orientation among even the most interested and committed of Reform rabbis. It also showed their ignorance of theological literature and strategies. At the same time, the issues were presented to them: God, the relationship with the divine, history and action, revelation and conduct, authority and self-determination, and more. Slowly, these issues and the demand for theological sophistication had their effects. In 1951, at the convention of the CCAR, two essays were presented on authority in Judaism, one by a rabbi with theological interests, Bernhard Heller, the other by a historian, Ellis Rivkin. Two years later, in 1953, the convention included a symposium on Jewish theology with papers by Samuel Cohon, Abraham Joshua Heschel, and David Polish. Then, in 1956, the CCAR established its Commission on Jewish Theology, chaired by Heller and including as members Jakob Petuchowski, Emil Fackenheim, Eugene Borowitz, Lou Silberman, Steven Schwarzschild, Levi Olan, Henry Slonimsky, Balfour Brickner, and Samuel Cohon. As the years passed, in the 1950s and 1960s, the convention programs were punctuated with essays on theological subjects, often by the members of the commission, who represented the chief theologians of the Reform movement.[19] By 1958, however, it became clear that the commission was given little support and less financial resources by the CCAR; Heller's annual reports are marked by frustration and disappointment.

Nonetheless, there were some developments. The *CCAR Journal*, founded in 1953, frequently published articles in Jewish theology. From 1958 to 1964, Emil Fackenheim served as its periodicals editor, publishing periodical reviews concerning theological and philosophical topics. In 1960, the *Journal* contained a set of four essays, a "Quest of a Reform Jewish Theology," dealing with issues such as autonomy, authority, and Reform practice.[20] The *Journal* also published controversies; Fackenheim and Ira Eisenstein, for example, engaged in a debate about naturalism and Reconstructionist theology in 1960 and 1961,[21] and Roland Gittelson published a brief critique of existentialist trends in Reform theology in 1962.[22] Later in the decade, in 1968, the *Journal* published the proceedings of the CCAR Colloquium on Ethics, with essays by James Gustafson, Hans Jonas, and others,[23] and later the same year six articles on Jewish survival, including a long essay by Steven Schwarzschild on a theology of Jewish survival.[24] In general, then, the *CCAR Journal* became, in the 1950s and 1960s, a forum for theological discussion among Reform rabbis and theologians.

By 1961, the Commission on Jewish Theology began to discuss the possibility of publishing a volume of essays on theological subjects. In 1963, the commission was reconstituted as a special interest group, and the same year the convention heard an address by Lou Silberman and three seminar essays on theology, by Samuel Karff, Steven Schwarzschild, and Eugene Borowitz.[25] By 1967 the plans for a collection of essays had materialized, and in 1968 *Contemporary Reform Jewish Thought* was published. Edited by Bernard Martin, it included twelve essays by rabbis and academics, most of which had already appeared in the *CCAR Journal* or *Yearbook*. In addition to methodological articles and a survey of Reform theology, the essays dealt with God, *halakhah*, Israel, and the mission of Israel.

Clearly, from 1950 and through the 1960s, there was theological interest and activity among the Reform rabbinate and among more traditional rabbis and thinkers as well. Some of it—especially the work of Fackenheim, Schwarzschild, and Silberman—was of high quality. Occasionally there were formal colloquia at meetings of the CCAR or at the Hebrew Union College. In addition, there were informal meetings, in the early 1960s at Oconomawac, Wisconsin, and in the mid-1960s in Quebec at the I. Meyer Segal Institutes. Often these meetings resulted in published essays—in *Judaism*, established in 1952 and a major vehicle for Jewish theological discussion, *Commentary*, the *Reconstructionist*, and *Tradition*, founded in 1958. Frequently too, these essays and gatherings resulted in books and collections of essays: *Rediscovering Judaism*, edited by Arnold Wolf; Jakob Petuchowski's books *Ever Since Sinai* and *Heirs of the Pharisees*; Eugene Borowitz's books *How Can a Jew Speak of Faith Today?* and *A New Jewish Theology in the Making*; Arthur Cohen's books *The Natural and Supernatural Jew* and *Arguments and Doctrines*; and Emil Fackenheim's book *Quest for Past and Future*. Much of this work, of course, was not liberal Jewish theology; it and its authors knew no denominational boundaries. They were expressions of a common impulse, to grasp the authentic character of Jewish faith for the postwar world in a way that was intellectually responsible and genuinely Jewish. Together with the work of Heschel, Soloveitchik, and Herberg, these writings constitute the corpus of Jewish theology in postwar America.[26]

In a survey of Jewish theology in North America in the decade 1958–68, Lou Silberman gave an account of the "dominant themes, the crucial tensions, the significant developments" of these works.[27] We can learn something about the central issues of postwar Jewish theology by considering what Silberman said and comparing it with two self-assessments: Fackenheim's account of his own thinking in chapter 1 of *Quest for Past and Future*, "These Twenty Years: A Reappraisal," and Eugene Borowitz's comments in *A New Jewish Theology in the Making*.[28] All of these works date from 1968 and in one way or another review the discussions of the 1950s and 1960s.[29]

Silberman began by emphasizing the growing theological need to articulate the religious basis of Jewish existence in the diaspora. First, for Christian intellectuals, this need arose from the same historical situation—the rise of totalitarianism, the war, and the development of nuclear weapons—that challenged the optimism of liberal thinking. "This recognition [of having been thrust out of Eden] gave rise to an intense preoccupation with theological questions . . . and the emergence of positions resolutely critical, and often less than understanding, of the liberalism of the past."[30] But the same need was not immediately felt by Jewish intellectuals and Jews in general, who were involved in rescue and care of the survivors, enthusiasm for Israel, domestic prosperity, and a new sense of identification with America. According to Silberman, the two major Jewish theologians of the 1950s, Herberg and Heschel, both of whom were influenced by Buber and continental thought, were ignored or denounced, while much American Judaism appreciated or affirmed the very liberalism that Christian neoorthodoxy was disparaging.

At some point, however, Jewish intellectuals did turn to the religious questions, and Silberman surveys their responses. First, many were influenced—perhaps even liberated—by the thinking of Martin Buber. His doctrine of I–Thou encounter made it possible to transcend naturalism and to affirm the reality of revelation as a dialogical event; it was left to coopt Franz Rosenzweig's strategy for recovering Torah and deed in their relation to revelation.[31] Buber provided access to transcendence and legitimated it; Rosenzweig enabled the "existentially-oriented Reform wing of the non-traditionalists" and "the similarly-directed Conservative group" to find an understanding of *halakhah* that each could accept. For Rosenzweig, "*halakhah* . . . was already a human response to, or comment on, [the] content" of revelation, the event of revelation itself. Here, "the non-traditionalist finds . . . the mode of relating his existentialist understanding of revelation to his existence within a historical community . . . possessing a complex structure of deed that includes all, from ritualistic behavior patterns to decisions made in the face of the exigencies of politic[al], economic, social, and personal (intimate as well as external) life."[32] It was Silberman's testimony, therefore, that central to the new theological discussion were the twin problems of God and faith, on the one hand, and autonomy, authority, and *halakhah*, on the other.

Not all, however, found Buber and Rosenzweig appealing. Silberman discussed Eliezer Berkovits's rejection of Buber from the Orthodox side and Mordecai Kaplan's naturalist critique. He then turned to Berkovits's criticism of Reconstructionism, Fackenheim's development of that critique, and the responses by Ira Eisenstein and Jack Cohen. The gist of this debate was the conflict between immanentism and supernaturalism, as Fackenheim put it, and the issue on which the conflict turned was the place of value in the scheme; is value something that is brought to nature, or is it already present in nature? Fackenheim argued "realistically [for] the clash of *two* orders—the world of amoral fact of which we are a part, and the world of moral values which commands our loyalty."[33] Once again, we encounter a crucial point, where optimism and realism part company and where authority for value and purpose is taken to demand a source external to human nature and needs and indeed external to nature itself.[34]

Silberman then turned to Richard Rubenstein and Joseph Soloveitchik and concluded with a discussion of the "so-called New Theology" and especially of Emil

Fackenheim.[35] He noted these features, first that the New Theology has at its core a "self-conscious standing within the tradition" and second that it arises out of "a sense of urgency" that emerges "from the particularly Jewish" situation.[36] Clearly, these twin commitments both point to the situatedness of existential Jewish theology, the fact that it starts from a self-conscious acknowledgment of the Jewish situation of the contemporary Jew, recognizes the role that the Jewish writings and ideas of the past play in shaping that situation, and finally senses the demand to recover that past for the present and the future.

This task is a quest for past and future, and its articulation points us in the direction of the collection of Fackenheim's essays that bears that title. These essays were published during the two decades from 1948 to 1967, essays that challenge the limitations of naturalism and rationalism, that defend the centrality of faith and revelation for Judaism, that argue for a living God who, in the spirit of Buber and Rosenzweig, enters into dialogical encounter with human beings, that show how Jewish faith and Jewish law incorporate both divine power and human freedom, and that challenge secularism and the denial of transcendence.[37] In his new introduction, Fackenheim assessed his past and took some preliminary steps into the future. These steps were in many ways decisive; later I will examine them in detail, for they point to and first formulate how the Holocaust came to determine Fackenheim's subsequent Jewish thought. For now, I am concerned with Fackenheim's theological past and the themes of his essays of the two decades between 1948 and 1967. Fackenheim called this his "reappraisal" of these twenty years.[38]

Fackenheim began by emphasizing his commitment to existential, situated thinking: "a Jew can be a faithful witness to his universal God only in his particular, singled-out Jewish condition, not through some manner of flight from it."[39] In 1968, that singled-out condition, for Fackenheim, is importantly defined by Auschwitz and Jerusalem, but this is something I will consider later. For now, what is critical is the general style of thinking and the issues it addresses. These issues are faith and Jewish life, and in these matters Fackenheim acknowledged his great debt to his predecessors, that is, to Buber and Rosenzweig, just as Silberman did in the survey I have already examined.

Unlike Silberman's treatment, Fackenheim's return to Buber and Rosenzweig dealt exclusively with faith and not Torah. For him, this debt is the first step in an account of the strengths, weaknesses, and changes in his two decades of Jewish theological work. His two predecessors, while not without their own deficiencies for the contemporary Jewish thinker, accorded a secure foundation for confronting challenges to the heart of Jewish experience. They provided an account of revelation, of the divine–human encounter, that honestly responds to the challenges yet recognizes the compelling truths of modernity.[40] Minimally, the Buber-Rosenzweig conception of the divine–human encounter meets and rejects the epistemological framework that recommends reducing revelation to a psychological experience or abandons God to an inaccessible role in natural philosophy. At the same time, it appreciates how the event of encounter and its impact must incorporate both divine power and human freedom. In this way, the concept of revelation responds to the ways that the human situation, to be genuinely appreciated, must be taken to include what is given to us and the interpretive ordering of it by the self. Fackenheim acknowledged Buber and Rosenzweig as having bequeathed to us an understanding of these matters that is compelling and decisive.

In part, the value Fackenheim found in this inheritance is a by-product of his philosophical scruples. As a philosopher, he recognized exactly how faith has been embattled, and he saw the new view of faith as rationally compelling precisely because it cut to the heart of the critique. The new view, because it doubts the universality of the post-Cartesian epistemology on which the critique is based, can be persuasive. If situated personal experience and agency are undeniable as the posture for any legitimate epistemology, then new possibilities for faith become available.[41] This, Fackenheim affirmed, is the real novelty and power in the Buber-Rosenzweig critique of modernity and their conception of man, God, and their encounters. But Fackenheim's philosophical and impersonal posture, which so often impressed his readers,[42] had its disadvantages too, and he was candid in admitting them.

Fackenheim had perceived the advantages of the Buber-Rosenzweig concept of revelation and faith from the philosopher's impartial point of view. He had also taken up his polemical task against the background of that standpoint. But, as he then tells us, a "liberation occurs when the Jewish theologian takes his stand *within* the Jewish faith, and understands it as committed openness to the voice of God."[43] The shift is one from philosophical detachment to theological commitment and engaged, situational thinking, and the gain involves what can be seen only from the standpoint of a committed Jew situated in the modern world. In part, for example, the gain is an appreciation of the strengths in liberalism, "the refusal to despair in an age rife with despair," and the need for classical Judaism and especially the Midrash "to come to terms with the modern world," from the Enlightenment to totalitarianism.[44] What Fackenheim had yet to argue is *why* the shift of standpoint from philosophical detachment to committed affirmation is *necessary* and not just preferable.[45] Nonetheless, once the shift is made, deficiencies of philosophy and theology are exposed, in part concerning the very nature and content of faith itself.[46]

But there is more to be gained by the move to situated thinking and agency. No longer is modern philosophy, so critical of religion and revelation, simply accepted as accurate, decisive, and true. Rather the posture, presuppositions, and arguments of philosophy are themselves exposed to a religious critique. Hence the confrontation is mutual, Fackenheim claimed, and "[w]hen there is mutual self-exposure in an encounter between Judaism and modern philosophy, only one thing is known in advance — that light will be shed on both."[47] Such an encounter cannot be known a priori to yield refutation, because neither standpoint is held a priori to be superior and hence determinative. The epistemological framework of some modern empiricism, for example, cannot be treated a priori as superior to a religious epistemology that acknowledges the reality of revelation. Fackenheim will have more to say about such an encounter elsewhere,[48] but the general point is clear: by starting from a standpoint of particular religious commitment, the thinker makes both theology and philosophy forego what is seen to be an ad hoc and arbitrary supremacy and exclusivity.

Furthermore, the shift makes a genuine Jewish philosophy possible — what Fackenheim calls "'philosophical thinking, or something akin to it' within Judaism."[49] What does Fackenheim have in mind? What is this philosophy within Judaism? First, it is "an inquiry into religious meaning, structure, essence, which is in principle abstractable from a commitment to religious truth, and which thus ought to qualify as uncommitted, impartial, and therefore philosophical."[50] In the case of prayer, for example, it is "a reflection on the meaning and structure of Jewish prayer emerging from the immediacy of Jewish prayer itself, and undertaken with a view to what Kierkegaard calls 'immediacy after reflection.'" Jewish philosophy, according to Fackenheim at this time, is a philosophical account of structure or meaning, that is, of universal features, that arises from a particular religious episode and is conducted in order to understand and legitimate subsequent episodes of a similar kind. For example, the thinker qua Jew engages in prayer and then, qua philosopher, reflects on the roles and nature of prayer, the attempts to reduce it to a pure psychological event, and the potential refutations of such experiences altogether. The purpose of the reflection is to make possible by the thinker qua Jew, subject to the demands of probity, a further experience of prayer, a further "immediacy" but this time "after reflection." Jewish philosophical thinking has a detached and universal quality, but it always occurs within the historical flow of the thinker-believer's experience.

Second, Fackenheim referred to his essay on revealed morality and Kantian ethics as an example of such Jewish philosophy and to its preface for a defense of the method.[51] There he had asked the question, "Can there be a Jewish philosophy . . . which is at once genuinely philosophical [i.e., objective and universal] and yet essentially Jewish?"[52] It is a question that, in the modern period, resonates only when the autonomy and exclusivity of reason does not overwhelm Jewishness to begin with, making any Jewish philosophy only Jewish by accident. For, as Fackenheim saw it, the question only makes sense if revelation and a receptivity to it are taken to be possible. If so, "then religious thinking — at least Jewish religious thinking vis á vis revelation — is from beginning to end *committed* thinking, which stands in dialogical relation to the God of Israel." Yet philosophical thinking is detached and impartial. The very possibility of a genuine Jewish thinking that is also genuinely philosophical seems undercut. But not to Fackenheim, who claimed to "assume that revelation is not *wholly* inaccessible to philosophic reason" and tried to show how this is so.[53] To begin, the philosopher qua Jew may experience or seek to experience revelation but qua philosopher "suspend[s] judgment as to the actuality of revelation." Then, the philosopher qua philosopher seeks to understand the nature of such a revelation or, as in the case of Fackenheim's essay, the nature of revealed morality. Just as a nonbeliever can understand what the believer means when the believer describes his or her belief, so the thinker can understand what any religious believer would experience;[54] the thinker can examine, attack, defend, and interpret revelation—as if he or she had never experienced it, or indeed, whether he or she had experienced it or not. There can be, then, Jewish philosophical reflection.

Indirectly, Fackenheim's defense of a genuine Jewish philosophy, a much more subtle account than that found elsewhere,[55] is a gloss on his defense of Rosenzweig's argument for how the "new thinking," that is, personal or existential thinking, can be "objective," that is, can yield universal, philosophical truth.[56] It is also, in a way, an attempt to legitimate the Buber-Rosenzweig conception of faith and the divine–human encounter by showing how it makes the harmony between Jewish experience and philosophical inquiry intelligible. Clearly, then, it supports Silberman's judgment that faith and revelation were central preoccupations of postwar Jewish theology and especially of the recovery of Buber and Rosenzweig in that period.

But Silberman had distinguished the contribution of Rosenzweig by focusing on Torah and deed. Fackenheim's most complete discussion of this issue is in "The Revealed Morality of Judaism and Modern Thought."[57] There he gives an account of the role of autonomy in Kantian ethics, develops a Kantian critique of moral theories in which authority is grounded in revelation or divine command, and uses Buber and especially Rosenzweig to show how Judaism and Kant differ concerning the very nature of morality and its foundations.[58] In this essay, then, Fackenheim attempts to show what Torah and law mean to Rosenzweig and hence to Jewish moral and religious life.

In the introductory appraisal in *Quest for Past and Future*, however, Fackenheim raised this issue of Torah or law in a different way. He suggested that the notion of a genuine Jewish philosophy, as an investigation of meaning and structure "abstractable from a commitment to truth," seems to be a recommendation for "the 19th century essence-approach to religion, despite 20th century existentialist protests."[59] But in fact Buber and Rosenzweig do recognize the appeal of the essence approach. As Fackenheim put it, "their own existential affirmations are by no means devoid of structure," for "an existential commitment open to any content would raise the spectre of anarchism,"[60] as well as relativism and nihilism. The issue is a crucial one: the role of Torah in a Judaism that is modern enough to admit human freedom and existential enough to arise out of particular divine–human encounters. How did Fackenheim locate the ground of *structure* or order that prevents revelation from lapsing into anarchism?

In an especially subtle and important stretch, Fackenheim identified the nature and ground of limitation in the experience of and response to revelation. He cited

Rosenzweig's famous statement, which he himself often quotes, that "He came down" is still revelation, whereas "He spoke" is already human interpretation.[61] But he added his own proviso, that it is not so easy to distinguish "event and content" and hence that a receptivity to revelation is itself already a "structured openness, not an empty one, if only because it is an openness which listens and responds, works and waits."[62] Fackenheim's point was that revelation may be an event, but it is expected, anticipated, and engaged by someone who lives in an ongoing tradition, who thinks, speaks, and hopes within a domain of discourse, and whose experience and response is situated and not ungrounded and unbounded. The religious agent lives in a tradition, the Jew in Judaism, "a dynamic whole" that can assimilate some novel experiences and may be transformed by others. For my purposes, Fackenheim's term "a dynamic essence" is what we call a tradition, and his conception of a structure that is part of the Jewish experience of revelation is what we call the "halakhic tradition." Moreover, this notion of essence or tradition cannot be a notion wedded to some timeless ahistorical structure. Fackenheim showed why this is so by considering the existential critique of Hegel, whose account is essentialist and historical in a way that must be avoided.

For the Jewish philosopher and for the Jew, then, one's character and identity are partially shaped by the Jewish past, by the tradition in which one lives. "He is not a man-in-general, an impartial spectator who may choose between religious options in an existential vacuum. He already exists as a Jew, and is singled out as a Jew, and he cannot make an authentic commitment unless he relates it to his singled-out Jewish condition."[63] The Torah or the Jewish tradition structures the Jew's beliefs and actions, hopes and fears; there are no choices from nowhere but only situated, structured choices. Torah is not externally imposed rules; Torah is the living identity of each Jew, some of which is present as law, some as custom, some as the very way in which the world and others present themselves to the Jew. Torah is the Jewish perspective of each Jew, and neither revelation nor any other event is confronted without it.[64]

Torah is not, however, a rigid structure; in advance, nothing identifies it as true or false, and nothing guarantees its continuity or requires its abandonment. Fackenheim's realization that this structure, and the Jewish theological thought that articulates it, are open and not closed is novel and marks the single, most decisive change in his thinking.[65] I will return to this change to discuss it later. For now it is sufficient to recognize what it means, that this "openness is necessary if history is to be serious"[66] and that "[t]oday, vulnerability is no mere theoretical possibility. For the Jewish theologian of today cannot continue to believe, or continue to engage in theological thought, as though the events associated with the dread name of Auschwitz had not occurred."[67]

At this point, Fackenheim's reappraisal moved in a new direction, one that transcends his earlier thought. I will discuss that direction and the remainder of the reappraisal later. Thus far I have shown that his assessment confirms Silberman's account, that the main themes of postwar Jewish theology were faith and Torah, revelation and *halakhah*, and that the crucial influences were Buber and Rosenzweig.

In 1968, Eugene Borowitz collected a number of his earlier essays into a kind of preface to Jewish theological thinking, *A New Jewish Theology in the Making*.[68] Many of the essays had been published earlier in the decade, from 1961 to 1968, and in one especially he recounted features of the itinerary of postwar Jewish theology.

Chapter 3, "Definition by Negation: Against Christian Neo-Orthodoxy," was originally published in *Commentary* in July 1961 as "Crisis Theology and the Jewish Community." Borowitz began by remarking on the failure of the new Jewish theology. Fackenheim and Herberg, he claimed, had taken up the challenge, proffered by Irving Kristol in a famous critique of Milton Steinberg's *Basic Judaism*,[69] that "Jewish thought in America was powerless to answer the great questions— questions about man and his condition, about destiny and the meaning of history—that the war had raised in the troubled minds of so many intellectuals in the West." "For a time," Borowitz reflected, "it seemed that a new Jewish theology— a theology concerned with the crisis of the age—was in process of being born. But the effort miscarried," and Borowitz asked, two decades later, "why this new Jewish theology failed to develop."[70] The issue concerned human finitude and the human capacity, even inclination, for doing evil, a reality that optimistic thinkers such as Steinberg could not face and that intellectuals like Irving Kristol took to be the core of "the ordeal of Western culture." The question posed by the war and its aftermath was how religion could help us to understand and cope with the human condition once that condition had been revealed in all its stark horror and threat. According to Borowitz, a theology dealing fully with these issues never developed.

The Jewish response to this reality was clear and unsatisfying. In Borowitz's words, "the prevalent mood of the Jewish community since World War II has not been one of concern with human sinfulness. . . . It has not been characterized by resignation or despair. On the contrary . . . the dominant accent of [the American Jew's] life is still his faith in the Great Deed."[71] In the 1950s Jews were not riddled with doubts or anxiety; rather they focused on marriage, children, jobs, homes, and building new communities.

> Without even having to think about it, the masses of American Jewry emerged from World War II not with a sense of man's helplessness before the evil consequences of his well-intentioned behavior or of the powerlessness of his will before his own evil inclinations, but rather with what can legitimately be called an implacable faith in man's capacity to know the righteous act and accomplish it successfully.[72]

Borowitz interpreted this not just as a response to prosperity and the opportunity for success; it is rooted in the Jewish "conviction that a man is capable both of knowing and doing the good. . . . [This conviction] has continued to dominate the

life of American Jewry in our day, despite wars, crises, and intellectual disillu-
sion."[73] The upshot is that American Jews have rejected Kristol's challenge in favor
of another, a desire for a rationale for Jewish life as a life of *mitzvah*. Hence,
Borowitz posed the problem that faced Jewish life: to begin either with the problem
of sin or with the value of *mitzvah*. And he answered that contemporary Jewish
thought in America chose the latter starting point, the one traditionally characteristic of Judaism. It recognized sin and human limitation but went on to focus on
mitzvah, action, the righteous life. The younger Jewish theologians paid increasing
attention, Borowitz claimed, to this concern with conduct, with *mitzvah*; in the
case of Emil Fackenheim, for example, his articles "have moved from the consideration of human limitations to the possibility in liberal Judaism for authoritative
guidance of Jewish living. Fackenheim's intellectual odyssey is similar to that of
most postwar Jewish theologians."[74] Borowitz called this movement "Covenant
Theology" and defined it as the effort "to explore and understand the implications
of defining religion as a covenant relation, and specifically to make manifest the nature and meaning of the Jewish Covenant with God."[75] In these terms, Judaism "is
a way of living one's life based on a relationship with God," a relationship between
God and the whole people of Israel, and "the central task of modern Judaism . . . is
to win the conscious, willed loyalty of the modern Jew to the Covenant."[76] Borowitz
emphasized the voluntaristic element in this modern stage of covenantal Jewish existence, the primacy of freedom and of personal commitment. He also noted the diversity of the interpretations of Torah and "God's law," "the specific ways through
which the Covenant shall be made manifest in life."[77] Like Fackenheim, however,
he warned against anarchy, especially within liberal Judaism, but his solution to the
problem of structure was simply to argue that covenantal faith is a communal and
not a personal religion.[78]

Finally, Borowitz claimed that "understanding Judaism as Covenant can also explain why modern Jews believe in the continuing worth of righteousness despite the
ambiguity of sin."[79] Since Judaism involves both the human and the divine, it calls for
realism about what is actual and possible. Human beings can never neglect the responsibility to act, and no human act is sufficient to warrant either total despair or
total satisfaction. "This sure faith that God stands with him in history can give the individual Jew the patience, the holy obstinacy, to endure and to act."[80] For Borowitz,
then, the covenant is permanent and unconditional; nothing can "nullify the relationship between God and man," neither human sin nor divine abandonment. The
covenant is a priori and irrefutable, and it underwrites liberal hope and optimism.

Like Silberman and Fackenheim, then, Borowitz saw that the major problems
for postwar Jewish theology involved Jewish conduct, *mitzvah* in his terminology,
and the rationale or ground for that conduct, the Jewish way of life. He called that
rationale the covenantal relationship between God and the Jewish people and located the individual within that relationship. Hence, for Borowitz, the central theological category is the life of faith, and this focus would naturally lead to theolog-

ical reflection on God, revelation, freedom, *halakhah*, and tradition. If we were to examine Will Herberg's *Judaism and Modern Man* (1951), Abraham Joshua Heschel's *God in Search of Man* (1955), Jakob Petuchowski's book *Ever Since Sinai* (1961), and Arthur Cohen's *The Natural and Supernatural Jew* (1962), we would find that these issues were precisely the central ones in each of these works, which are the foremost Jewish theological books of the postwar years.[81]

What has my consideration of the postwar Jewish theology shown about the motivation, character, themes, and approach of the period? First, the influence of religious existentialism—with its themes and method—led to ongoing debates about the role of reason, liberalism, naturalism, and so forth. Second, the central themes for the new theologians were God, faith and revelation, autonomy and tradition, and Torah or *halakhah*. In part, these themes arose as part of the attempt to meet the challenges of religious naturalism and rationalism; in part they arose as the desiderata of any authentic account of Jewish life in the modern world. Third, there was discussion about the propriety and desirability of Jewish theology and, for some, about the possibility and nature of a genuine, modern Jewish philosophy. Finally, various features of postwar Jewish theology were motivated as responses to the postwar situation, for some by the prosperity and flourishing of Jewish life in America, for others by the anxiety and trauma of the crisis of Western culture and of the atrocities of Nazi totalitarianism.

If we recognize the role of the Nazi atrocities and the awareness of them in warning some postwar Jewish theologians away from an unquestioned liberalism and optimism, then we should accept a modest view about the influence of those events—what would later, after 1959 or so, be called the Holocaust and the Shoah and what was then often called the Churban—on Jewish theology. There are, however, dramatic differences between the ways these thinkers confronted Auschwitz in these postwar decades and the ways they and others would do so in the mid- to late 1960s. At this earlier time, many would recount features of the Nazi destructions but without acknowledging for it a central role in their theological thinking.[82] Indeed, in Borowitz's essay, discussed earlier, he treated Kristol's preoccupation with the crisis of Western culture and the reality of evil, neither of which yet appreciates the particularity of Auschwitz in terms of either its perpetrators or its victims, as something that postwar Jewish theology had superseded and should supersede. This commitment that it should do so is underlined by Borowitz's claim that for Judaism the covenantal relationship is unconditional, irrevocable, unbreakable. Nonetheless, in his thinking and that of many others, there was a recoiling from any facile optimism, and surely this caution arose from an awareness of and a confrontation with the Nazi atrocities. It is false to say, therefore, that during these years Auschwitz had no impact of any kind on Jewish theology.[83] What is true is that it played no central, determinative role; it was not thematically primary. When it was mentioned, it was at the margins of theological discussion or was treated universally, swept up into the large categories of the crisis, despair, and evil of modernity.

Chapter Four

The Early Stage: The Sixties

From 1945 to 1960, anticommunism and the Cold War, the specter of nuclear weapons, individualism and conformity, alienation and self-fulfillment, prosperity and the problems of access, the black migration to the North and the nascent civil rights struggle—all of these issues seethed on and below the surface of the seemingly placid American life.[1] In the sixties, American political and cultural life exploded, and by 1965 the disenchantment, frustration, and anger were registering in polarization and fragmentation. By the seventies, anxiety and fear had congealed into caution, worry, defensiveness, and embattled, if not shattered hopes.

Judaism and Jewish life in postwar America saw new opportunities deteriorate into alienation, disenchantment, frustration, and even anger. By the late sixties, flourishing Jewish life was, like the culture and society at large, undergoing strain and division. There were worries about survival and ambivalence about the social and moral projects that had occupied the center of Jewish commitment and conduct in the early years of the decade. After the Eichmann trial, the furor over Arendt's articles, the episodic reactions to the plays of Rolf Hochhuth (*The Deputy*) and Peter Weiss (*The Investigation*), and the growing concern over the plight of Soviet Jews, attention to the Holocaust and the Final Solution began to grow. Emil Fackenheim and Richard Rubenstein began their work prior to the Six Day War, and Wiesel had already become a visible spokesperson for honesty, memory, and even heroism in the face of a horrifying, unspeakable past. With the war in June 1967, Israel and Auschwitz took center stage, one an image of hope and one of suffering and pain. Some understood the war and the threat in terms of Auschwitz. Others responded to the war by interpreting Israel and Israeli military success in terms of the suffering in the death camps. To some, a focus on the Holocaust became central to their Judaism; others resisted, or at least wanted to resist, allowing something so negative to dominate their religious identity.

A central conceptual nexus in these years concerned the past, history, memory, and identity. On the one hand, many argued for the historicity of the human condition, situatedness in a particular time and place, in a society, a culture, a world, and a narrative, indeed a set of narratives. On the other hand, the subtle, dialectical interaction that constituted selfhood and its relation to the traditions people inherited was threatened by radically negative events, and the Nazi atrocities, the death camps, were certainly this. Informed by tradition, Jews turned to tradition but only in terms of an encounter with a rupture that threatened to cut them off totally from what was once true, acceptable, and good. Once one confronted the abyss, the task was to recover and to be recovered.

The post-Holocaust Jewish thinkers did not constitute a school. They shared no institutional affiliations, nor did they influence a common set of disciples or have common views, except in some fairly general ways. To be sure, all confronted Auschwitz and took it seriously; they did not simply assimilate it to existing categories or explain away its distinctive power. In one way or other these five — Rubenstein, Berkovits, Greenberg, Cohen, and Fackenheim — did not believe that responsible and honest Jewish self-understanding could proceed and yet ignore, or even minimize, the camps, the crimes, and the horror. Each was so moved by those events that he came to view them as *somehow* central. But how they were central differed for each. Their differences are illuminating and important, but only if they are properly understood. One can compare and distinguish the five in many ways. It is especially helpful to distinguish them in terms of their awareness and appreciation of history, historicity, and the demands facing those who are historical beings, at once religious persons and reflective thinkers.[2]

Richard Rubenstein was the Jewish theologian to write earliest about the importance of the death camps for Jewish faith. His collection of essays, *After Auschwitz: Radical Theology and Contemporary Judaism*, appeared in 1966, but the earliest of the essays was written in 1955, when Rubenstein was a graduate student at Harvard and influenced by Paul Tillich.[3] In that essay, "The Symbols of Judaism and the Death of God" (1955), Rubenstein attempted to provide a "new rationale" or "new justification" for Jewish belief and Jewish practice.[4] On its very first page, he referred to the death camps: "For many, the problem of finding a new rationale [for their theological commitments] has been aggravated by the death of their personal God. After Auschwitz many Jews did not need Nietzsche to tell them that the old God of Jewish patriarchal monotheism was dead beyond all hope of resurrection."[5] A page later he used the language of Paul Tillich as a partial gloss on this "death of God" proposal: "we live in an age of 'broken symbols.' The problem of the symbolic content of Judaism in our time is to find a viable basis for continuing to maintain Jewish religious practice after its traditional validations have been altogether transparent to us."[6] "The most fruitful path for a contemporary rationale for Jewish belief and practice" is a psychological justification. If we give an account of the human condition in terms of needs, anxiety, and desires, based on Freud, Tillich, and other sources, we find that Jewish myth and ritual are devices for articulating and responding to these psychological demands of the human condition. Bar *Mitzvah*, for example, is a "puberty rite" that enables the child to pass on to another stage of life and to achieve sexual identity.[7] "In the time of the death of God, I suspect we need rituals to dramatize and celebrate the crises of life more than ever."[8] Moreover, Rubenstein argued, the literature, myths, and rituals of Judaism must have a foundation in life that gives them relevance, and this is the synagogue, the center of the "shared life of a community," where people congregate for "the existential crises of birth, death, growth, joy, sorrow, pain and mutual support."[9]

Having acknowledged the religious crisis of the postwar situation, in which the credibility and authority of religion is challenged by biblical scholarship, Auschwitz, and other features of modernity, and having argued for the continued justification of Jewish community, belief, and practice, Rubenstein turned to God, "the problem of God after the death of God."[10] His solution was that the God that remains is both ground of being and the focus of ultimate concern, "the infinite measure against which we can see our own limited finite lives in proper perspective."[11] Such a conception of God enables us to avoid idolatry, "to acknowledge our temporality and mortality without illusion," and to avoid assigning absolute status to limited things around us; it challenges us to be what we can be without self-deception and illusion.[12] God as ultimate concern is not the traditional theistic God; the problems of human freedom and human evil refute belief in such a God. Once again, Rubenstein recalled the death camps: "Even the existentialist leap of faith cannot resurrect this dead God after Auschwitz."[13] But there is a God still, not a personal God but a standard or principle that reminds us of our finitude and focuses our conduct and convictions on ourselves, our condition, our needs, and the means for dealing with life's crises.

There is much that is derivative in this essay. It is heavily indebted to existentialism and especially to Tillich, and it does not so much argue for the "death of God," for rejecting one concept of God in favor of another, as hint in the direction of such an argument or arguments. Freedom and evil are the phenomena to which Rubenstein points, more specifically to Auschwitz, but he does not specify what the term *Auschwitz* signifies, nor does he clarify exactly how these phenomena lead to the unacceptability of the theistic, patriarchal God.[14]

Much of the essay is an attempt to provide a new rationale or justification for Jewish myth, ritual, and institutions. Rubenstein's basic line of reasoning is transparent: the old justification is no longer acceptable; a new, psychological one is possible; it is compatible with a new concept of God, and the result is still a religion, albeit a new form of paganism or naturalism. Auschwitz is introduced twice in the essay but only at the earliest stage, as one way of showing that the old justification is unacceptable.[15] But Rubenstein never shows exactly how this is so.

Furthermore, while Rubenstein's thinking in this essay is broadly an attempt to understand Jewish practice and its relation to a modern liberal conception of the self, Rubenstein does not explore what freedom is or requires, nor does he explain exactly how his solution reconciles freedom and necessity, if indeed it does. One possibility is that Rubenstein has simply replaced legal or political authority with social-psychological necessity and then assumed that the latter is compatible with freedom, however it is conceived. More likely, Rubenstein takes ritual, myth, and so forth as the results of free responses to the human condition, so that the problem of freedom and authority is simply assimilated to an account of the human condition, which includes those factors that are given in the human situation and the process of choosing by which the self shapes its world and itself. But none of this is articulate in the paper; at best it is assumed, at worst simply ignored.

Even from this early essay, we can see that Rubenstein was moved at least in part by Auschwitz to doubt the viability of a certain concept of God. Of equal importance, the camps raised doubts for him about human beings and about evil; Rubenstein's abiding pessimism and realism are in part a response to Auschwitz, and both encouraged his differences with Reform or liberal Judaism, on the one hand, and with Reconstructionist naturalism, on the other.[16] In an autobiographical memoir, published in 1965, he recalled that

> reports of the capture of the camp at Madjanek, Poland, with its huge piles of ownerless shoes, left an indelible impression on me. . . . The revelation of the death camps caused me to reject the whole optimistic theology of liberal religion. People weren't getting any better, nor did I believe they ever would. The evil rooted in human nature could never entirely disappear. . . . [The camps and Nazism] revealed the full potentiality of the demonic as a permanent aspect of human nature."[17]

In 1959, in an essay published in the *Reconstructionist*, Rubenstein criticized Reconstructionism in a similar way. "Man has proven capable of irredeemable evil. . . . Guilt, ambivalence, human evil, and human aggressiveness are as inescapable as human love, affection, and self-sacrifice."[18] Rubenstein corrects the Reconstructionists for not being realistic enough about these features of human life. Human beings are tragic creatures; nature is not adapted to human purposes. It is there to be coped with and endured. One must make "the very best one can of a limited and tragic existence."[19] Existentialism, he argued, is right in its acceptance of the world as it is and in its recognition of the role of freedom and will; Reconstructionism is to be applauded for its focus on peoplehood, identity, and the nonprivileged status of Judaism. But, especially in view of Auschwitz, the teachings of Freud, and much else, one should accept reality for what it is and guard against a false optimism.

In August 1960 Rubenstein visited Germany for the first time; he returned a year later, in August 1961, and then again in February 1963.[20] Each visit is associated with writings that reveal an increasingly intense preoccupation with the death camps and their significance for Judaism. After his initial visit, a brief trip to Dusseldorf, Cologne, and Bonn during a vacation on Holland's North Sea coast, Rubenstein wrote a memoir that appeared in the *Reconstructionist*.[21] Perhaps the two most important themes of the report are his impressions of the Germans and the lesson that the Holocaust bears. First, he "was utterly convinced that the vast majority of the German people had been behind Hitler in *everything*, including the smell of Dachau's burning flesh only thirteen kilometers from cultured and charming Munich."[22] Rubenstein left Germany believing that the Germans wanted and supported Hitler and even the camps, but they did so "as someone in a trance."[23] But even though he came away convinced of German complicity, he said, he also no longer hated the Germans; he came to realize too that the desire to do away with the Jews was not restricted to them. "What terrified me most about the Germans," Rubenstein wrote, "was the extent to which they reminded us of every man's demonic. . . . The sick souls who wish to emulate [Hitler] are by no means all German; nor are they as few as we would like to believe." Finally, Rubenstein raised a problem for himself: the Holocaust is part of human history; "what now matters is what we do with this unspeakable heritage." It would be easy to say that the problem is a German one and that the Germans are to be despised or hated for what they did. However, they "have committed a terrible crime, but they have by no means exhausted criminality. . . . Only those who can honestly acknowledge the power of evil in their own heart can effectively overcome its temptation."[24] Like Améry, Rubenstein had come to see authentic response as oppositional; realizing that the evil of the Nazis does not exhaust the evil now possible, he urged that all people be sensitive and opposed to the evil in themselves and in others. The lesson of the Holocaust lies in the need for resistance.

Convinced that all Germans were either active criminals or cooperative bystanders, Rubenstein, shortly after the Eichmann trial, turned to a question that Arendt had asked, why did they do it?[25] Arendt had given a sociological-political answer; Rubenstein gives a religio-psychoanalytic one. What he tries to show is that we can explain the Nazi behavior but not with normal, sociological or psychological explanations. Only a quasi-religious one will do. The Nazis "were satanic anti-Christians, saying no to much that Christianity affirmed and saying yes to much that was absolutely forbidden in Christianity."[26] Seeking to celebrate the devil, they sought to destroy in others, the Jews, what they most feared in themselves. The camps, the central institution of Nazism, were an attempt to turn the Jews into feces, the devil's food.[27] "The people of the Devil were turned into the ultimate element of the Devil." There is no need to evaluate this speculative synthesis of modern social criticism, Freudian psychoanalysis, and history of anti-Semitism. What is important is Rubenstein's assumption that an adequate explanation of the kind he proposes is possible. Nazism, the crimes and the criminals, for Rubenstein can be understood—as regression, displacement, or whatever. It may be unprecedented, but it is nonetheless comprehensible.

This assumption underpins Rubenstein's important reflection on his meeting with Heinrich Gruber, dean of the Evangelical Church of East and West Berlin, in August 1961.[28] It was this interview, Rubenstein later notes, that brought him to a "theological point of no return—If I believed in God as the omnipotent author of the historical drama and Israel as His Chosen People, I had to accept Dean Gruber's conclusion that it was God's will that Hitler committed six million Jews to slaughter. I could not possibly believe in such a God nor could I believe in Israel as the chosen people of God after Auschwitz."[29] I have shown that in his essay of 1955 Rubenstein had hinted at this line of thinking. His memory associates this turning point with an especially significant event, the interview with Gruber, but there is reason to think that Rubenstein's theological career had for years been shaped by a cluster of influences: Reconstructionist themes of peoplehood, the realism and pessimism of existentialism, Tillich's theology, Freud, and Auschwitz. Possibly it was only after 1961 that these elements cohered in a way that Rubenstein found compelling. Or perhaps it was only in the interview with Gruber that Rubenstein found a convergence of context and content that registered as an especially memorable formulation of the impact of Auschwitz on the conception of God and Judaism.

As we read Rubenstein's account, we should remember that Tillich's concept of God as the focus of our ultimate concern, together with the general problems of human freedom and of evil,[30] had already given Rubenstein reason to reject the God of history, the "theistic God of Jewish patriarchal monotheism."[31] Reconstructionism's attraction all along had been its attention to peoplehood and its willingness to accept the Jewish people's nonprivileged status. "Perhaps the most significant contribution to Jewish self-respect made by Reconstructionism has been its insistence that it is not wrong, impious, or irreligious for Jews to insist that there is no special preeminence possessed by Judaism which justifies Jewish existence."[32] It was Tillich, then, and not naturalism that first led Rubenstein to reject the concept of a God of history. Hence what occurred in the interview with Gruber was that a strategy revealed itself to Rubenstein for starting with Auschwitz, newly branded into Rubenstein's intellectual and Jewish soul, and moving to two denials, of the chosen people doctrine and of the concept of a historical God. The result would be a clear line of thinking that began with Auschwitz and led to the existential, psychological defense of Judaism already adumbrated in the 1955 essay. Throughout this effort, Rubenstein assumed that there is a way of understanding Auschwitz and the death camps within a set of conceptual schemes or frameworks. The problem, which Rubenstein probably did not set for himself but rather was solved by the Gruber interview, was how to organize, with Auschwitz as the starting point, the conceptual materials Rubenstein was using, gathered from Tillich, Freud, Sartre, Arendt, and others. In a sense, then, what the Gruber interview provided was both a way of framing the relationship among God, the Jewish people, and Auschwitz and a context that contributed to the argument and made it memorable; together these led to Rubenstein's reorganizing his thinking in a way that became foundational for him.

Gruber had testified against Eichmann in Jerusalem and was devoted to German-Jewish reconciliation, and to Israel. But, while an opponent of anti-Semitism, Gruber was critical of German Jews and entrepreneurs and insensitive to the need

to combat hatred. Rubenstein noted Gruber's biblical standard for making demands on contemporary Jews: "Israel as the chosen people of God was under a very
special obligation to behave in a way which was spiritually consistent with Divine
ordinance."[33] Gruber was committed to a relationship between the Jewish people
and God in history. But if so, Rubenstein said, then "the Nazi slaughter of the Jews
was somehow God's will, that God really wanted the Jewish People to be exterminated."[34] Gruber answered with a reference to Psalm 44:22, "for Thy sake are we
slaughtered every day," and with the words: "For some reason, it was part of God's
plan that the Jews died."[35] Rubenstein recalled what this meant to him, "that Hitler
was simply [a] rod [of God's] anger . . . an instrument of God . . . [and] that God had
been instrumental in the holocaust."[36] This is what made his meeting so memorable
and interesting, he claimed, that this Christian who had nearly died helping Jews
nonetheless viewed them in biblical, mythic categories and not as normal human
beings.[37] As long as Jews continue to believe in the doctrine of the chosen people,
they encourage Gruber's understanding of the Jewish people. Rather than do this,
we should accept Reconstructionism's view that Jews are just like others, sharing
the human condition and bound to its challenges and difficulties. There is no special status to being a Jew.[38]

Two years later, in an essay delivered as a lecture during a return trip to Germany in 1963, Rubenstein recalled this episode, an "unforgettable conversation
with one of Germany's religious leaders," and its content: that "this gentleman . . .
asserted that it was God's will that Hitler had exterminated the Jews."[39] Rubenstein
took the inference to be inevitable that if "God is the ultimate actor in the historical drama, no other theological interpretation of the death of six million Jews is ten-
able."[40] It is a virtually automatic step in logic to deny the antecedent of this conditional, and this is precisely what Rubenstein does. Faced with pain and suffering
that cannot be seen as evidence of divine justice, Rubenstein chooses to accept "an
absurd and ultimately tragic cosmos." He then rejects the God of history: "after the
experiences of our times, we can neither affirm the myth of the omnipotent God of
history nor can we maintain its corollary, the election of Israel."[41] But this act of "demythologizing" Judaism has sobering rather than destructive results concerning
God and religious community. What these mean has been altered. Religious community is needed more than ever once one realizes that human existence, tragic and
without meaning, challenges and threatens us. It is the community in which people
share the experience of birth, death, sexuality, and more and learn to cope with natural existence. At the same time, Rubenstein rejects the atheism of someone like
Camus in favor of a paganism, an acceptance of a God that is the ground of being
and the object of ultimate concern.[42] Rubenstein defends this view of a Judaism
without myth against both traditional Jewish piety and atheistic, secular Judaism.[43]
It is the first major result of this early stage of his thinking.

By 1963, then, in part in response to the interview with Gruber, Rubenstein was
able to organize his thinking about existentialism, Judaism, Reconstructionism,

Tillich, and Freud. A summary would begin with Auschwitz and the death camps. The general Christian view is that history, especially the history of Israel, is providential, *Heilsgeschichte*. Hence Hitler was a divine instrument and the extermination of European Jewry a divine act. Rubenstein finds it unnecessary and impractical to accept such an account; it is "a difficult pill to swallow"; later he will call it obscene. Practically speaking, by adhering to this view of the chosen people, divine election, and of the God who acts in history, one encourages Christians to view the Jewish people in this way. One should therefore oppose and not support such a mythic rather than realistic view. Moreover, life or existence itself is tragic and meaningless; hence we should reject the God of history in favor of a God of nature, the ground of being, and reinterpret Judaism as a community of shared ritual and mutual concern rather than a mythic people with a historical destiny. In all of this, the central idea that Rubenstein takes Auschwitz to refute is that of the chosen people, of Jewish existence as privileged and justified. Moreover, Rubenstein has a number of reasons for rejecting this concept, reasons connected with Christian attitudes to Jews, with the death camps and how to understand them, and ultimately with how to interpret Judaism, Jewish ritual, and Jewish communal life.

There is something simplistic about Rubenstein's line of thinking here. For all its affinities with the traditional problem of theodicy, it is not formulated as a version of that problem. In one of its versions, that problem is about consistency between a theory and the realities it is intended to explain. Rubenstein sees God, history, providence, the doctrine of election, and Auschwitz as, in a sense, features of a whole theory and hence as posing a problem of consistency. But he does not simply and exclusively draw a conclusion about God from the reality of suffering in the death camps. What he balks at initially is a Christian's interpretation of the Jews as the chosen people and all this implies. Hence, we cannot fault Rubenstein for not considering alternative solutions to the problem of theodicy. At the same time, he *does* assume that a Jew is *required* to reject the notions of the chosen people and of the God of history in order to avoid the results, supporting Christian *heilsgeschichte* and calling Hitler God's instrument. But this is a non sequitur. There are many alternative ways of blocking such an inference and avoiding these results.

Moreover, Rubenstein's leap to a God of nature, the ground of being, is just that, a leap, and one that seems to be anticipated by his earlier commitment to Tillich's theology. Rubenstein is right that his thinking—á la Camus—does not demand a denial or atheism, but he is too quick to produce an alternative. Nothing prevents him from retaining belief in God, but it is not necessary that he reject a personal God; the God of Buber and Rosenzweig is as possible as the God of Tillich.

Despite these and other shortcomings, Rubenstein's thinking in these early essays is rich and certainly courageous, the expression of a strong sense of integrity and realism about Jewish experience and Jewish life. In terms of sensitivity to Auschwitz, Rubenstein was a unique figure on the Jewish theological scene in the early 1960s. This distinctiveness is revealed by looking at the well-known symposium conducted by the editors of *Commentary* in 1966, "The State of Jewish Belief."[44] In his introduction to the symposium Milton Himmelfarb suggested that what motivated the survey was the question of Jewish faith, the belief in and role of God in Judaism, and the significance of the notion of the "death of God" in Jewish thinking.[45] Five questions—three about revelation, chosenness, and the death of God—were submitted to fifty-five rabbis; thirty-eight responded. None of the five questions was about the Holocaust, none about Israel.

The first question was about the existence and nature of divine revelation and the human experience of it. It ties the symposium to one of the central issues of postwar Jewish theology. As one might expect, the answers vary, from, for example, Eliezer Berkovits's commitment to the mystery of literal revelation and the interpretation according to the oral tradition and its principles[46] to Emil Fackenheim's Rosenzweigian view that "the Torah reflects *actual events* of divine revelation, or incursions into human history. . . . But it is a *human* reflection of these events of incursion; the reception is shot through with appropriation and interpretation."[47] There are dissenters too, who believe that the Torah is sacred and vital but who do not accept any notion of revelation or divine–human encounter.[48] Other questions focus attention on the tensions between particularity and universality, between religion and politics, and between religion and ethics; these are old problems and staples of post-Enlightenment religious thought. Once again, the answers vary. Finally, the last question is the topical one about the movement in Christian theology then current, which was associated with Thomas Altizer and William Hamilton, Paul Van Buren, and Gabriel Vahanian and which developed from Nietzsche; it was called "death of God" theology. Here, if at all, the role of the death camps might arise. But did it?

Among thirty-eight responses, only a half-dozen or so even mention the death camps; two or three do more than this. One is Rubenstein, who calls himself a "religious existentialist after Nietzsche and after Auschwitz" and accepts the title "death of God theologian." He articulates the thinking I have already discussed except that here, perhaps because the central issues concern God and faith, he focuses on the relation between Auschwitz and God and the implication for Torah and Judaism. After Auschwitz, he says, "the thread uniting God and man, heaven and earth has been broken. We stand in a cold, silent, unfeeling cosmos, unaided by any purposeful power beyond our own resources." How, then, shall we cope? "[I]n a world devoid of God we need Torah, tradition, and the religious community far more than in a world where God's presence was meaningfully experienced."[49] Emphatically, Rubenstein claims that the question of God and the death camps is the single most pressing challenge to modern Judaism; yet there is silence on the issue by contemporary theologians.

In the symposium, a few others agree that Auschwitz is *a*, if not *the* central problem for contemporary theology.[50] Now, as we look back on this symposium, we can see that in only two cases, however, did a suggestion in 1966 later flourish. The first is Eliezer Berkovits, who at the time taught philosophy at the Hebrew Theological College in Skokie, Illinois. In responding to the question about the relevance of the "death of God" theology to Judaism, he argued that "the murder of six million Jews in the heart of Christian Europe" proves something about Christianity, that the Christian God who promised redemption through Jesus, his death and resurrection, is dead. There is no such redemption and no absolution of human guilt. Hence the Holocaust shows that the Christian promise and plan is undermined but not the Jewish plan, in which man always was destined to play a role. For Jews, the issue raised by Auschwitz is one of human, not divine responsibility. Berkovits elaborates these very themes in his important book *Faith after the Holocaust*.

The second thinker who refers to Auschwitz is Emil Fackenheim. As I have shown, Fackenheim was a central Jewish theological voice during the fifties and sixties. In his succinct response to the symposium question about the death of God theologians, he summarizes the contents of a long essay on the same theme, "On the Self-Exposure of Faith to the Modern-Secular World: Philosophical Reflections in the Light of Jewish Experience," which would be published the next year.[51] In the symposium, Fackenheim explores the meaning of the expression "the death of God" and even suggests a Buberian interpretation, that we live in the time of the "eclipse of God" when "modern man is *incapable* of hearing the word of God *even if he listens*."[52] Then, at the end of the answer, Fackenheim turns, if only in a highly condensed way, to the death camps. What, he asks, does this human incapacity show? Something about God or rather something about man? Does it not signify a "great religious demand . . . [for] a radical *t'shuvah*—a turning and listening to the God who can speak even though He is silent?"[53] Fackenheim does not ask whence this *demand* comes; nor does he ask why one should, after Auschwitz, still expect divine speech. Rather he assimilates this demand to old patterns—Abraham, Jeremiah, and Job: "the Jew of the generation of Auschwitz [is] required to do what . . . Jews have always done in times of darkness—contend with the silent God, and bear witness to Him by this very contention."[54]

We should appreciate three things about Fackenheim's almost cryptic formulation. First, it should be read as Fackenheim's attempt, which he will later reject, at appropriating Buber's doctrine of the "eclipse of God" as a strategy for understanding Jewish faith after Auschwitz. In "The Dialogue between Heaven and Earth," the last of three addresses, published in 1952 as *At the Turning*, Buber asks, "how is a Jewish life still possible after Auschwitz? . . . [H]ow is a life with God still possible in a time in which there is an Auschwitz?"[55] Buber answers: "One can still 'believe' in the God who allowed those things to happen, but can one still speak to Him? . . . Dare we recommend to the survivors of Auschwitz, the Job of the gas chambers: 'Give thanks unto the Lord, for He is good; for His mercy endureth forever'?" Buber then explains that for Job, the charge of divine injustice received as its response God's address, His presence, nothing more. Buber turns to us—"all those who have not got over what happened and will not get over it. How is it with us?"

His answer: "we contend, we too, with God . . . whom we once, we here, chose for our Lord . . . we struggle for [the] redemption [of earthly being], and struggling we appeal to the help of our Lord, who is again and still a hiding one."[56] Fackenheim is trying to appropriate Buber's proposal—that Jewish life goes on by contending, like Job, even though God is silent or, as Buber says, hiding. For Fackenheim, however, the contending is a struggle with God that is simultaneously a witness to him; for Buber, the contending with God is part of a struggle for the redemption of the world, and it seems that if Buber sees a witness in this act, it is through the redemptive effort. Nonetheless, this minor difference aside, Fackenheim's terse formulation looks very much like a Buberian strategy.

Second, what Fackenheim says in this passage is already, if only proleptically, superseded in the long essay "On the Self-Exposure of Faith." There he acknowledges the importance of Auschwitz for all Jewish thought:

> The events that are associated with the dread name of Auschwitz still pass human comprehension. But they have shaken Jewish existence to the core, even when they are uncomprehended. They call everything into question: for the believing Jew, for the unbelieving Jew, for the Jew who is neither believer nor unbeliever but merely asks unanswered or unanswerable questions. Only one thing is as yet clear. The Jew may not authentically think about religion, or its modern crisis, or the goods and ills of the modern-secular world as though Auschwitz had not happened.[57]

Auschwitz is beyond our understanding; yet it is an undeniable, transforming event, for all Jews. How, then, can the Jews go on? Near the end of the essay Fackenheim warns that whatever "trust and joy" the modern world provides must come with "radical distrust and profound sorrow." For this reason, "the authentic Jewish religious witness in this age must both face up to Auschwitz and yet refuse a despair of this world." Such a Jew must "reopen the quest of Jeremiah and Job, who for all their agony refused to despair either of God or the world."[58] In this passage the Buberian language is abandoned, but some of the themes are still present: facing up to despair, commitment to redeeming the world, and "a quest, a listening, indeed, an interrogating of God which, born of faith, may itself bespeak a Presence while as yet no voice is heard."[59] Fackenheim asks for a model of such authentic Jewish existence and finds one not in a philosopher nor in a theologian but rather in a novelist, Elie Wiesel. He notes that *Night* is not a speculation or fiction but an "eye-witness account of the most terrible actual darkness"; he then quotes the passage of the angel on the gallows and three further texts, from *The Accident*, *The Town Beyond the Wall*, and *The Gates of the Forest*, all of which evidence a contending with God and extreme transformation of Jewish hope. Fackenheim here begins to reach beyond his appropriation of Buber; the lineaments of an authentic post-Holocaust Judaism arise out of the complex response to Auschwitz, out of the mystery, the paradox, and the silence.[60]

Finally, Fackenheim's reply in the symposium and even his brief discussion at the conclusion of the longer essay, "On the Self-Exposure of Faith," point ahead to his first thematic discussion of Auschwitz and post-Holocaust Judaism. The occasion was a symposium organized by *Judaism* and its editor Steven Schwarzschild on Purim, March 26, 1967.[61] The invited participants were Fackenheim, Wiesel, George Steiner, and Richard Popkin. Each was asked to speak on the theme "Jewish Values in the Post-Holocaust Future"; a discussion followed. This extremely important event was preceded by a similar occasion a year earlier that prepared, as it were, for the importance of Auschwitz for Jewish theology in the midsixties.

During the winter of 1965–66, the journal *Judaism* and its editor Steven Schwarzschild sponsored a symposium on "Jewish Religious Unity." It was held in New York City to coincide with the meeting of the board of directors of the journal from the sponsoring organization, the American Jewish Congress. The speakers, one from each of the American Jewish groups, were Irving Greenberg, Mordecai Kaplan, Seymour Siegel, and Jakob Petuchowski (who was not present; his paper was presented by Eugene Borowitz).[62] Amid discussion of the explicit theme of the meeting, a few remarks are significant for the emergence of post-Holocaust Jewish thought.

Irving Greenberg, in his statement, refers to "three watershed experiences" of modern Jewish history. Westernization "created the denominational, ideological and institutional lines that divide us." The Holocaust, while it has not altered these divisions, should have: "Surely the implications of Holocaust have shattered every conventional position in the Jewish community from left to right and demonstrated, by and in affliction, that we are deeply united in faith and destiny."[63] The third event, the rebirth of the state of Israel, has also "overtaxed our capacity to understand and respond"; specifically it has been interpreted as a natural, political event rather than a religious one. These points, made almost in passing here, will later become central to Greenberg's thinking, that is, that the Holocaust marks a decisive break with the past and should underscore a new unity of faith and purpose. In the course of the four papers, Greenberg was the only participant to refer either to Auschwitz or to Israel in any significant way. But the thread was not dropped.

Mordecai Kaplan picked it up when he referred to his argument, in *The Future of the American Jew* (1947), that the doctrine of the chosen people must be abandoned precisely because, after Nazism and Auschwitz, we see to what purposes it has been put.[64] I have shown Rubenstein, in his reflection on meeting with Dean Gruber, arguing in a similar fashion. For Kaplan, an idea can be refuted by how it functions, pragmatically.[65] Moreover, Greenberg too returns to Auschwitz when, in discussion, he exhorts that any consideration of the implications of *halakhah* for contemporary life "must certainly take place in the light of Auschwitz [*sic*]. . . . [A]nybody who is a Jew today—in fact, possibly the rest of the world today—all of us are survivors of Auschwitz." But then Greenberg turns from this utterly general point to something more specific, the kind of faith one can have in a post-

Holocaust world, and he hints in a direction that sounds like the Buber, Fackenheim, and Wiesel we have already heard: "Perhaps on occasion we would band together against God. . . . Perhaps we would stop conventional religion—because who can recite blessings unless he has profound enough a love for a controversy with God?"[66] Later Greenberg will elaborate on this too, the troubled, contesting and contested faith of post-Holocaust Judaism. He will also elaborate on his concern, shared by others, about divorce, marriage, and in general the physical survival of the people, an issue the urgency of which was obviously rooted in a sensitivity to Auschwitz.[67]

Finally, Steven Schwarzschild too acknowledges Auschwitz; he refers

> to an experience which many of us here shared last summer. . . . It was a gathering in the Canadian province of Quebec, north of Montreal, where a number of us, from all over the spectrum of Jewish life and thought, gathered for a week's intensive study and conversation. . . . We discovered something at the end of the week which has just now been put on record here again, namely, that the one man who spoke and protested and stormed the heavens and implicated Israel most tellingly for our generation and for our hearts, and for our hopes, and for our tragedy, was not a theologian, nor a professor, nor even a rabbi. The de facto High Priest of our generation turned out to be Elie Wiesel.[68]

Schwarzschild here reiterated what we saw at the conclusion of Fackenheim's essay "On the Self-Exposure of Faith," the recognition in 1966 by members of the new generation of Jewish theologians of Elie Wiesel's memoirs and novels and his personal presence as a model of a first-person struggle with God in Auschwitz. Wiesel's role, his presence, in part facilitated the emergence of public theological discussion and intellectual reflection on a post-Holocaust Judaism. Already at this meeting, during the winter of 1965–66, Auschwitz had begun to grip the theological understanding of many. Doubtless in response to this sense that the time had come to confront these issues directly, *Judaism*'s next symposium was organized around these themes.

The *Judaism* symposium "Jewish Values in the Post-Holocaust Future" was a momentous intellectual event.[69] It occurred on Sunday, March 26, 1967, prior to the rising tensions in the Middle East and the Six Day War, and this, together with the evidence I have been discussing, shows that Jewish theology oriented around the reality of Auschwitz had already begun to develop, at least from 1965 or so, when the Six Day War took place. The meeting brought together Wiesel, whose role as the central figure in recollection of Auschwitz had recently been reinforced by the publication of his report on his visit to the Soviet Union, *The Jews of Silence*; Fackenheim; George Steiner, whose collection of essays *Language and Silence* had just appeared in 1967;[70] and the distinguished historian of skepticism, Richard Popkin. In retrospect the symposium's most important feature concerned Fackenheim. It was the occasion for Fackenheim's first major public statement on Auschwitz and in particular for his first statement of the now famous 614th commandment. But in its own context the real importance of the event was more general: here an audience of Jewish intellectuals, leaders, and theologians came together to hear and discuss brief talks on the centrality of Auschwitz and the death camps for Jewish life in the 1960s. Nothing of this sort had occurred before.[71]

Before I turn to Fackenheim's important statement, I will look at the other statements and the general discussion to see what issues were most prominent and generated the most interest. Of these Wiesel's is especially important. Among the features of Wiesel's writing and his posture that appealed to others were his ambivalence and his uncertainty in the face of Auschwitz. The same attitude was present here; he begins by admiring the "conviction and affirmation" of his colleagues, but, he says, he cannot share them.[72] He then retold a midrash on Purim and Hannukah and acknowledged the covenant that both holidays presupposed, a covenant of divine and human responsibility. But he suggested "for the first time in our history, this very covenant was broken."[73] How? There was idolatry; there was indifference and abandonment. "Hitler was convinced that he faced no enemy, no resistance." Culture was compatible with killing children. Our concept of evil changed. And American Jews did not come to the aid of the victims; even their own people abandoned them. Wiesel's thought then burst itself with doubts, questions: why care? How have faith in Jews, in the Jewish community? Why remember? How remember? Yet, he reflected, there is remembering or at least the effort. But can it succeed? "Language is poor and inadequate. The moment it is told, the experience turns into betrayal."[74] Here Wiesel ends: with the fear of the utter impotence of language, to portray the past or to recommend the future.[75]

Provoked by this worry, that we might be totally cut off from Auschwitz and that the only appropriate way to encounter it and to respond to it is silence, the discussion turned to a variety of themes: the uniqueness of the death camps; the relation among Auschwitz, Hiroshima, Vietnam, and Selma; the actions that would be authentic responses to the event; what is demanded of a Jew after Auschwitz; and the particularity of Jewish history. Appropriately, the final comment was made by Wiesel, and it ended with a call to respond to insanity with reason, to fight murder and absurdity and bring meaning to the world. At that moment, Wiesel was the center of attention and respect, perhaps even of reverence; his response, his witness, his imaginative suggestions, and his Jewish soul — these were the central presence at the symposium.

At the same time, Fackenheim had used the opportunity to bring himself to a new, dramatic stage in his theological development. Later he would recall his reluctance to speak publicly about Auschwitz and Nazism but also his sense of the moral imperative associated with Schwarzschild's invitation. This sense of moral responsibility had been burning within him, but it crystallized with that invitation. During this period and the years prior to 1967, that necessity was becoming more and more intense for Fackenheim; the Six Day War only increased the intensity, which issued in the reappraisal of his work in chapter 1 of *Quest for Past and Future*, the *Commentary* essay, the Charles F. Deems Lectures, the core of which had been given in Quebec at the I. Meier Segals Center for the Study and Advancement of Judaism and which were delivered at New York University in 1968, and an essay of 1968, "Idolatry as a Modern Religious Possibility." From 1966 to 1968, then, Fackenheim's thinking about Auschwitz and post-Holocaust Judaism took shape; in a preliminary way, I must discuss what that shape was.

In his contribution to the *Commentary* symposium of 1966 and the essay of 1967, "On the Self-Exposure of Faith," Fackenheim had appropriated Buber's doctrine of the eclipse of God and pointed ahead, by calling on the testimony of Elie Wiesel. In 1967, in his contribution to the *Judaism* symposium, he took one further step. Fackenheim himself has reflected on this step, and we do well to begin by attending to what he says.[76]

In addition to sketching Fackenheim's line of thinking in the *Judaism* piece, I want to call attention to three features of his account. First, Fackenheim, who had spent the decade from 1957 to 1967 working on the role of religion in Hegel's thought, employs the Buber-Rosenzweig account of revelation, viewed against the Hegelian and post-Hegelian background, in order to understand the status of the demand that exists in a post-Holocaust world. Second, the most dramatic shift in his thinking, which I shall try to clarify, enables him to confront Auschwitz and to take it seriously; in a sense, it is also *motivated* by his sense of responsibility about so doing. Finally, he discovers, in the 614th commandment and its formulation, a strategy for interpreting the demand for post-Holocaust Judaism and giving it content. I will start with the second and third points; they are the ones to which Fackenheim himself later calls attention.

First, a sketch of Fackenheim's reasoning in the *Judaism* essay:

1. Contemporary Jews face a crisis marked by three contradictions: universalism and particularism, secularism and religiosity, security and catastrophe.
2. Jews have responded to this crisis with a commitment to Jewish survival and a commitment to Jewish unity.
3. The commitment to survival is not "the tribal response-mechanism of a fossil but rather . . . a profound, albeit as yet fragmentary, act of faith, in an age of crisis to which the response might well have been either flight in total disarray or complete despair."[77]
4. An authentic response would confront the Holocaust and not despair.
5. "From this beginning confrontation there emerges what I will boldly term a 614th commandment: the authentic Jew of today is forbidden to hand Hitler yet another, posthumous victory."[78]
6. The authentic Jewish nonbeliever hears this commandment alone; the authentic Jewish believer hears the voice of the commander in the commandment.
7. The 614th commandment implies four imperatives or has four parts, that is, Jews are "first commanded to survive, lest the Jewish people perish . . . commanded, second, to remember . . . the martyrs of the Holocaust, lest their memory perish . . . forbidden, thirdly, to deny or despair of God, however

much we may have to contend with Him or with belief in Him, lest Judaism perish . . . forbidden, finally, to despair of the world as the place which is to become the kingdom of God, lest we help make it a meaningless place in which God is dead or irrelevant and everything is permitted."[79]

The basic structure of this reasoning is this: the articulation of features of the Jewish situation (1), acknowledgment of a response already made (2,3), the need for the prescription for authentic response (4), the emergence of that prescription (5), the distinction for secular and religious Jews (6), and the elaboration of the prescription (7).[80] This argument is further developed in the *Commentary* essay, in *God's Presence in History*, in various essays, and finally in *To Mend the World*. It is a line of thinking that has largely remained with Fackenheim for three decades.

Although it is not as explicit here as it will become in later formulations, for Fackenheim the unique, unprecedented character of the Holocaust threatens a radical break with the Jewish past and a total destruction of all Jewish belief. The thinking outlined here depends on the willingness to accept this threat as serious and genuine, only in the end not to succumb to it. But the threat must be real, and it can be real only if one admits at the outset that nothing in Judaism is irrefutable or, to put it positively, that everything in Judaism—every belief and practice—is historical and conditional; nothing is absolute. On the face of it, this looks like a commitment to some kind of relativism and historicism; if so, it is no wonder that so many thinkers, for example, Leo Strauss and Reinhold Niebuhr, resisted this view. But, and this is the second point noted earlier, Fackenheim often recalls that accepting it was the single most important development in his thought. His earlier view, expressed in his essays "On the Eclipse of God" and "Elijah and the Empiricists," was that experience and historical events could verify or confirm religious faith "but nothing empirical can possibly refute it."[81] The relation between God and persons and its implications for covenant, and so on, are both empirical and a priori; they are true in the sense that nothing in the world can possibly refute them, yet they are true about the world—more specifically, true about God's relation to persons in the world—so that events in the world and in history can confirm them. In chapter 1 of *Quest for Past and Future*, moreover, Fackenheim associates this view with the essence approach or essentialism of the nineteenth century and gives an existentialist critique of it.[82]

This general issue, whether philosophy and religious faith are or are not wholly historical—bound to the finite, limited perspective of the thinker and his or her context and lacking in transcendence and universality, was central to virtually all of Fackenheim's philosophical work in the fifties and sixties. It was the theme of both *Metaphysics and Historicity*, in which he tried to defend an existentialist conception of the self as self-constitution and the transcendence of metaphysical truth, and *The Religious Dimension of Hegel's Thought*.[83] Moreover, until this moment in 1967–68, Fackenheim had been convinced that at least the concept, the possibility of divine–human encounter, could not be refuted by history or human experience. But, in order to take history seriously, and that means specifically to take Auschwitz seriously, in order to accept it for all that it was, with its evil so radical and absolute, it was necessary to revise this commitment.[84] Part of Fackenheim's reason for adopting this new historicism was the existentialist protest against the old idealism; he, like others, as I have shown, worried about the risk of relativism when the older rational or naturalist views of religion were abandoned in favor of the existential approach. In a sense, part of his philosophical project, in *Metaphysics and Historicity* for example, was to show that existentialism did not necessarily lead to moral relativism. But his immersion in Hegel, for whom history and the perspectival, phenomenological account of human experience are central but ultimately overcome in detached, transcendent, absolute philosophical knowledge, showed him that the existential protest, if true, in principle makes all understanding and all belief conditional.[85] Indeed, only if this were so could Auschwitz be taken seriously or—as he was fond of putting it, if Hegel were alive today, he would feel compelled to take Auschwitz seriously and so would cease to be a Hegelian. If, then, Hegel is wrong and Judaism has not been superseded and indeed if there is no absolute standpoint that supersedes all historical religions, then each religion, and Judaism in particular, is historical through and through; each religion is autonomous and has status equal to all others. In *Quest for Past and Future* Fackenheim formulates this two ways: if God speaks to Israel in the historical moment and that means into any moment, then "Jewish theological thought, however firmly rooted in past revelatory events, has always remained open to present and future, and this openness includes vulnerability to radical surprise."[86] At the same time, Fackenheim here acknowledges the openness of traditional Jewish thought, the Midrashic Framework. "The Torah was given at Sinai, yet it is given whenever a man receives it, and a man must often hear the old commandments in new ways. There are times in history when evil can be explained as deserved punishment, others when no such explanation is possible. . . . Such openness is necessary if history is to be serious."[87] In part, then, Fackenheim reaches this new historicism via an existentialist critique of Hegel and idealism, in part through the Rosenzweigian view of revelation, as I will show, and in part out of a deeply felt need to take Auschwitz seriously.[88]

In the preface to the second edition of *To Mend the World*, Fackenheim recalls the events surrounding his participation in the *Judaism* symposium in 1967 and the problems that plagued him as he prepared his statement.[89] He recalls the worries that confronted him. One was the need to deal with Auschwitz in particular and not Nazism in general; the other—traumatic—was the possibility, the threat that after Auschwitz Jewish faith was destroyed and that all his efforts and those of others in the postwar years to engage in theological renewal were a failure, futile and vain.[90] What if Hitler had been unlike Haman and Pharaoh; what if he had succeeded where they had failed and no Judaism of any integrity was possible after him? This could not be, not if one were to remain loyal to the victims of Auschwitz and if one were to remain committed to the task of preventing Hitler's victory.

Hence, Fackenheim did two things: he sought a ground for an imperative for authentic Jewish life after Auschwitz, and he sought too a way of understanding that imperative. The first he found in the responses of Jews in terms especially of Jewish survival; what once might have seemed a response of nature—later he will add "mere nostalgia"—should be understood by the theologian as an act of faith. Then, as he puts it, what "emerges" from this is a 614th commandment. If authenticity requires a ground or imperative and the imperative is to be Jewish, then it must be a mitzvah, a commandment. A commandment, moreover, must have content, and, although the problems are obvious, Fackenheim gives the content in terms of opposition to Hitler's designs. He finds this unavoidable—mentioning Hitler and formulating the mitzvah negatively. I will discuss these and others problems later; for now it is sufficient to understand his thinking—the need to face Auschwitz and yet to retain Jewish commitment.

There are numerous problems with all of this: why turn to contemporary Jewish life? Why see it as a response to Auschwitz? How does the 614th commandment "emerge" and from where does it emerge? And more. These can be deferred. For the moment I will turn to the question, why call this imperative a commandment? And what does this imply for the hearer, for the post-Holocaust Jew? This brings me back to my first point.

In *To Mend the World*, Fackenheim admits that "a commitment to Sinai and Revelation has been first in [his] Jewish thought, and will . . . remain with [him] to the end."[91] This commitment is expressed in two places in the line of thinking in the *Judaism* statement. First, it is present in step 5, where he calls the imperative a mitzvah, thereby implying that it is the content of a divine revelation. Second, it is present in step 6, when he distinguishes between the reception of such a commandment by a believer and by a nonbeliever. Over the years Fackenheim had appropriated for himself the concept of revelation developed by Buber and Rosenzweig and had interpreted it in his own way. The gist of this of course was that divine revelation is an event of encounter between a divine present in history and a human recipient; all verbal traces and human action constitute a human response to this event and a human interpretation of it and the world in terms of it.[92] Moreover, according to Rosenzweig, one could perform ritual acts and study texts in order to facilitate an openness to new revelations. As he put it, in a famous recommendation, the Jew's task is to perform the law, turning a *Gesetz* into a *Gebot*, a law into a commandment. This of course only the believer will achieve; the skeptic can still perform the act, even as a necessity, but without a receptivity to bringing about a relation with the Commanding Presence itself.[93]

We can understand why Fackenheim might want to call the imperative to authentic Jewish response a mitzvah (commandment), but it is not clear what justifies his so doing.[94] Furthermore, we can appreciate why he distinguishes two types of recipients or hearers, and we can see that Fackenheim employs an explicitly Rosenzweigian strategy to distinguish features of their receptivity. It is against the background of Rosenzweig's conception of revelation that Fackenheim briefly describes the limitations of their respective hearing.[95] On the one hand, the agnostic or secularist hears *only* the commandment, that is, does not take it to be from God. But, unlike other agnostics or atheists, he or she does not take it to be an obligation grounded rationally or in nature. This nonbeliever is too honest for that; he or she sees in Auschwitz a reason to refuse any conception of rational progress. Hence "the 614th commandment must be, to him, an abrupt and absolute *given*, revealed in the midst of total catastrophe."[96] On the other hand, the believer may hear more than the commandment but only diffidently. "If a bond between Israel and the God of Israel can be experienced in the abyss, this can hardly be more than the *mitzvah* itself." Here are the echoes of the doubt, the uncertainty, and the contending with God that we saw in Buber's notion of openness after eclipse, in Fackenheim's early use of that doctrine, and throughout Wiesel's struggles with God. Fackenheim can say that the nonbeliever hears only the commandment but does hear it as a brute given, while the believer hears the voice of the commander but only dimly, uncertainly, and perhaps hopefully.

Within a year Fackenheim's more developed account of these thoughts would appear in two places, in *Commentary* and in the first chapter of *Quest for Past and Future*. Then, about the same time, a fuller version was presented at New York University in 1968 and published in 1970. In between, however, a momentous event occurred: the Six Day War.

Chapter Five

The Six Day War and American Jewish Life

For American Jewish life and for American Judaism, the Six Day War in May–June 1967 was a radically transforming event. Not only among scholars who have studied the event and its consequences but also among all those who lived in those days and remember them, there is complete agreement about the event's historical impact.[1] Institutionally, ideologically, ritually, educationally, psychologically—indeed in virtually every way that might come to mind, American Jewish life was dramatically altered. The impact was felt over a long period of time; the initial changes came in the relation to Israel itself, the sense of responsibility, commitment, and solidarity. But then, as the years passed, other developments occurred—in religious life, in institutional revisions, and in American Jews' sense of identity as Jews. Many changes were connected with Israel, but not all, or in many cases the connection to Israel was not direct or essential. What is undeniable, nonetheless, is that the War released and stimulated powerful emotions and energies in many different types of Jews that gave shape to extraordinary changes in American Jewish life and in American Judaism.

When news reports confirmed the military threat to Israel and then when, on Monday, June 5, the outbreak of war occurred, the response was intense, enormous, remarkably uniform, and largely political and psychological. Waxman notes that the war's impact on American Jews was "unanticipated" and that American Jewry was "panic stricken" and gave "overwhelming support" regardless of previous sentiments about Israel.[2] According to Arthur Hertzberg, "the immediate reaction of American Jewry to the crisis was far more intense and widespread than anyone could have foreseen. Many Jews would never have believed that the grave danger to Israel would dominate their thoughts and emotions to the exclusion of all else."[3] Reporting on the study of "Lakeville," after the war, Marshall Sklare points out that people were "unambiguously pro-Israel" and so deeply involved that "their appetite for news during the Crisis and the War was well-nigh insatiable."[4] In New

79

York the entire city was fixated on the news, people going nowhere without transistor radios pressed to their ears.[5] At the same time, personal involvement was dramatically expressed through fund-raising meetings and personal donations, generally in cash, that enabled American Jews to feel that they were somehow participating in the actual fighting and hence in the victory.[6] "Giving money was not simply an act of charity; it was a way of enlisting in Israel's struggle for survival, of becoming a participant instead of a passive spectator."[7] As Nathan Glazer notes, after the war in 1967, an "astonishing total of $432 million [was] raised voluntarily from the American Jewish community," as compared, for example, with $140 million in 1966.[8] Indeed, as Lucy Dawidowicz reported, $100 million was raised in less than a month, from the time the crisis began to the war's conclusion.[9] The mood in all of this, as Dawidowicz said, was at first anxious and tense; people waited and worried, irritable and nervous, and then, with the military victory, they felt "elation and pride, but, even more, release from tension, gratitude, a sense of deliverance."[10] Her overall impression was that of involvement: "American Jews, so frequently accused of indifference and passivity, turned into a passionate, turbulent, clamorous multitude, affirming in unprecedented fashion that they were part of the Jewish people and that Israel's survival was their survival."[11]

In the weeks and years after June 1967, the impact of this surprising but dramatic response and the sense of attachment to Israel was diverse and continuing.[12] It involved a higher rate of *aliyah* (emigration) to Israel, a dramatic increase in travel, flourishing exchange between Israeli and American scholars, greater commitment by the Conservative and Reform movements—for example, the CCAR convened in Jerusalem for the first time in March 1970, and that year the Hebrew Union College–Jewish Institute of Religion began its First-Year Israel program, an influx of Israeli music into Jewish summer camps and eventually into synagogue worship, and much more. Furthermore, "concern for Israel became one of the principal means by which American Jews express their identity."[13] As Lou Silberman commented, trips to Israel became virtually sacramental acts, acts of "religious and communal identification." To many, following Israel's political fortunes and expressing a fidelity to her became a central feature of their Jewish identity, to some in fact *the* central feature.

There were many reasons for both the immediate and continuing impact of the crisis and then the response to it. Some acted out of a sense of responsibility. Fellow Jews were threatened with annihilation; their situation called for vocal support, concern, personal sacrifice, and ongoing allegiance to their cause, their survival. The Eichmann trial and the Arendt controversy had publicized the question of Jewish cooperation during the Holocaust, and, among others, Wiesel had openly reminded American Jews of the failure of the United States to come to the aid of the camp victims.[14] Indeed, in 1966 Wiesel had published a report on his trip to the Soviet Union to visit the oppressed Soviet Jews, and in that work, *The Jews of Silence*, he had criticized the Jews of America for their silence regarding the Russian

Jewish problem.[15] Hence, in 1967 and thereafter, a number of dimensions of responsibility intersected to form a powerful motivation for many Jews: a sense of guilt or at least regret about America's failures during the Holocaust, of solidarity with the threat to Jewish survival in Israel, and of opportunity in view of the Soviet persecution of Russian Jews.

Others, moreover, doubtless acted out of a commitment to Zionism and to fighting anti-Semitism. The Arab radio reports during May 1967 were studded with traditional anti-Semitic slogans and threats; in an American environment in which anti-Semitism was less visible than in the past and in which the civil rights movement had made prejudice and bias publicly unacceptable, Jews could respond to the need to oppose it in the Middle East;[16] indeed, some had all along supported Zionism as a weapon against the hatred and persecution of Jews. These and other reasons, then, encouraged vigorous support for Israel, but more than this was involved.

Commentators often make a special point of the response of Jewish students, some members of the New Left, others activists of a general kind; what applies to them also applies to many Jewish intellectuals and liberals.[17] Silberman helps us to appreciate this type of response with a half-truth: "Thus the Six-Day War was a watershed between two eras—one in which American Jews had tried to persuade themselves, as well as Gentiles, that they were just like everybody else, only more so, and a period in which they acknowledged, even celebrated, their distinctiveness."[18] Silberman is right that for many youth and many intellectuals and Jewish leaders, the Six Day War contributed to their turn to Jewish distinctiveness. Not all, however, turned away from some significant universalist sentiment; not all turned from a kind of apologetic stance to greater self-assertion; not all, moreover, conceived of their response to the war as a rejection of some kind of universalism. It was not that simple. It is not true, as Silberman argues, that all "Jews became particularists because so many of the universalists to whom they had looked for support turned out to be particularists themselves—only on the opposite side."[19] *All* Jews did not become anything, and the particularism of the black separatists and the black power movement had a complex and not a simple impact on student activists and Jewish intellectuals in the late sixties.

In an essay on the Jewish counterculture, William Novak, editor of *Response*, called the transformation of the civil rights movement to black separatism and the Six Day War "the two key events . . . that radically transformed the lives of young Jews in this country."[20] How? Because black separatism said to Jews, Be Jewish; study, explore, recover your own culture and your own tradition. The Six Day War showed how Jews could unite in common cause and, to Novak, made one think about genuine Jewish community. In short, for Novak, it was not Israel as much as the idea of community, an idea that was part of the Student Nonviolent Coordinating Committee (SNCC), Students for a Democratic Society (SDS), and the New Left from the early sixties, that became the focus of attention for Jewish youth. Perhaps for some. But for others, a commitment to Israel was one step on the journey to a renewal of a Jewishly committed life. The key for some was a powerful sense of involvement, of being a part of the Jewish people, of being Jewish as one threatened, liberated, and somehow justified. There were those, then, who already felt committed to Judaism, were alienated by the exclusion from the black movement, could not however accept the commitment to Jewish particularism, and saw the War and the Jewish response to it as a spur to realize real Jewish community. Others had not, before the War, felt attached to Judaism, but the intense experience of the War and the mortal threat to Israel's existence drew them into commitment and a feeling of intense involvement.[21]

There is another side to the situation of young Jews at the moment of crisis. Not only had they been excluded by black nationalists and implicitly urged to retrieve their own culture and identity; in addition, both the New Left and the black militants, at least since 1965, had become increasingly aligned with Third World liberation movements and opposed to American imperialism, and this allegiance included the movement for Palestinian liberation and the Arab states in general.[22] Jewish students found that many of their old associates were anti-Israel and even anti-Semitic. By 1967, the year of the march on the Pentagon, the New Left was primarily focused on Vietnam and the issues of war and peace, American imperialism, national self-determination, and so forth. The crisis in Israel and the War perplexed many young Jews who had claimed pacifism and had given their support to local or national liberation movements. As their compatriots remained consistent and attacked Israel, many young Jewish radicals felt isolated, betrayed, and confused.[23] Clearly, one strategy was to maintain solidarity with other young Jewish activists and to incorporate their commitment to Israel into a larger goal or set of goals concerning Jewish community, authentic religious experience, and their identity as radicals and as Jews. The radical Jews emerged from this crisis in a variety of shapes, some eschewing universalism altogether, others seeking to find ways to coordinate Jewish particularity with universal moral principles, and some, like Arthur Waskow, seeking a Jewish orientation within the New Left.[24]

The *havurah*, first organized in 1968, was both a reaction to the War and one expression of the discontent of Jewish youth with the synagogue and ritual life of the fifties.[25] The new organization, its structure and character, and the style of their worship incorporated their sense of protest against American society, its nondemocratic spirit and gender relations, but did so as an expression of their Jewish commitment.[26] The synagogue was rejected in favor of a countercultural alternative, which coordinated Jewish life and student protest. If, moreover, the protest was an expression of moral principle, then the Jewish revisionism would have seemed to integrate universality and particula-ity, the past and the present, tradition and community and individual autonomy. Or so it might have seemed.

The founders of the early *havurot* had been student radicals, often members of the New Left.[27] They had rejected social organizations that emphasized conformity and utility, that were traditional and bureaucratic. They sought instead authenticity in new kinds of association—free clinics, community welfare organizations, and communes. At a certain point their interests came to encompass Judaism and a desire to vitalize Jewish life for themselves. In the late sixties, as one Jewish radical put it, "desperation" set in with senseless violence and conflict; people sought "new directions" in their quest for genuine community, an affirmation of something positive as well as a protest against the past.[28] The separatist trend in SNCC, and in the civil rights movement generally, eventually led to several interest-group movements. Jewish radicalism and the havurah movement were among them. And like the activists of the women's liberation movement, the environmental movement, and so many other causes, these Jewish activists borrowed language and strategy from the civil rights struggle and from the movement for black self-assertion. They sought community, mutual concern, dignity, and distinctiveness within the voluntaristic context of American society and yet with respect for tradition.[29] They had been transformed, as one person put it, from Jewish radicals to radical Jews.[30]

What did these radical Jews create? As Winnie Breines showed, in SDS and the New Left from the beginning there was a strong commitment to participatory democracy and genuine community. At the same time, there was a need to engage in public action, to demonstrate, to organize, and so forth. The young radical Jews were drawn to the project of creating ideal community and tying this community to an authentic mode of Jewish self-expression. To do the latter, however, involved confronting the Jewish past and the resources of traditional texts and conduct and recovering them for the present.[31] But this task of course stimulated the tension between traditional authority and freedom that I have shown was one of the central themes of Jewish theology in the fifties and sixties. What resulted for some radical Jews was an open, communal, ritually rich organization; the Havurat Shalom, the first of them, was founded by Rabbi Arthur Green and others in 1968 in Somerville, Massachusetts, near Cambridge;[32] in 1969 another was founded in New York City. These and other *havurot* emphasized egalitarianism, study, prayer, and integration of all concerns; they were small and family-like, and the interaction was often intense, because debates over change and experiment meant so much to each of the members. In terms of worship, there was an emphasis on mood and the aesthetics of prayer, and services were participatory; the members were opposed to the performance and presentation model of most Reform and Conservative worship. Here, too, as in almost all areas, the *havurot* "operated within the tension of 'tradition' and 'innovation'!"[33]

Alienation from the New Left affected primarily the young and those Jewish intellectuals who saw New Left anti-Zionism as confirmation of their criticisms of the counterculture and the student rebellions.[34] "After the New Politics debacle of August 1967, *Commentary* became the strongest critic of the New Left within the intellectual community in the United States."[35] But the attacks on Israel after the War by the SNCC leadership, Stokely Carmichael and others, embittered not only students; they also enraged many ordinary Jews, who had invested themselves throughout the sixties and even back in the fifties in the cause of civil rights and the struggle against discrimination and segregation. They too felt betrayed, and in the wake of various crises in northern cities, they also felt victimized by a coalition of liberal leadership and blacks. One incident was the Ocean Hill–Brownsville school crisis in 1968, but there was much more conflict to come. The upshot was a faultline of issues—from school integration to public subsidies for private schools to quotas and affirmative action programs—that pulled apart many Jews and blacks and alienated others from traditional liberalism.[36] In a sense, the problem of many ordinary Jews and some Jewish intellectuals was how to create a Judaism that was both liberal and ethnic-national, to use Nathan Glazer's expressions.[37]

The response of some black power advocates and much of the New Left to Israel after the Six Day War, then, created a dilemma for young radical Jews and for many Jewish intellectuals. It also was one factor, along with local issues, like schools, quotas, and housing, that galvanized ordinary Jews into the core of the so-called new Jewish right. Jonathan Rieder's important ethnographic study *Canarsie: The Jews and Italians of Brooklyn against Liberalism*, is an account of how this crisis was actually lived by ordinary people in the 1970s.[38] Rieder is careful to warn us that we should not simplify; the sources of discontent in Middle America, among ordinary people, were numerous and complex: "the civil rights revolution, the problems of the cities, black power, the war in Vietnam, the disaffection of the young, stagflation, the revolution in morals, [all] bedeviled them."[39] Rieder's study focuses on two such groups in Brooklyn, Jews and Italians, and their conflict with liberalism arising out of local political and economic issues. The issues had to do with school desegregation, safety, violence, and property values and put them in a position of conflict on the busing issue with the blacks and Hispanics of the contiguous neighborhoods, Brownsville and East New York. The Jews and Italians of Canarsie "viewed the shifts in Brooklyn's racial complexion as an invasion by a hostile army."[40] In 1972, worried about crime, violence, and property values and faced with the prospect of forced busing, one Jewish community leader compared their neighborhood to a menaced Israel, surrounded by enemies and with its back to the sea.[41] After 1967, ordinary Jews could and did conceive of themselves as under attack, and, like Jean Améry, many came to believe that resistance, even militant, violent resistance, was the only authentic response.

In the 1970s, some of these positions became polarized, and as events and issues arose, conflicts became more and more common—over affirmative action, Israeli policy concerning Palestinians and the territories (West Bank and Gaza), housing, and government aid to private schools. In the fifties and sixties Israel had not played a major or primary role in American Jewish life. There was, to be sure, strong attachment to Israel by many, a sense of identification, but it was abstract and theoretical rather than concrete and personal. Most American Jews were not Zionists and would never prefer Israel's economic needs to domestic, American ones. There

was little travel to Israel, few sermons on Israel's problems, and in general little interaction with Israeli culture, music, and art.[42] There were lingering remnants of
Reform Judaism's pre–World War II anti-Zionism, but once the state had been established and defended in 1948, more American Jews ignored Israel than attacked
it. American Jews did pay attention to events in Israel—the Arab-Israeli War and
the Suez Crisis in 1956 and the capture and trial of Adolf Eichmann—but the effects on American Jewish life were minimal. At the theological and intellectual levels, Israel played only a very small role; Rubenstein's essay "The Significance of
Zionism" appeared in the *Reconstructionist* in 1960 and was reprinted in *After
Auschwitz* in 1966, retitled "The Rebirth of Israel in Contemporary Jewish Theology."[43] *Midstream*, a journal devoted to Zionism, was founded in the fall of 1955; it
of course regularly discussed Israel and its importance for American Jewish life, but
few articles were theological.[44] In the *Yearbook* for its convention in 1950, the
CCAR reports on a symposium on "Israel and the American Jew," and the *CCAR
Journal* for October 1958 is devoted to Israel. In 1961, Ely Pilchik and Jakob Petuchowski debate the relationship between Israel and Reform Judaism.[45] Over the
span of nearly two decades, this is relatively little activity; the interest of Israel for
American Jews was limited and marginal. This attitude had changed with the Six
Day War, however, and in the late seventies, an angry public dispute broke out
about the relationship between American Jews and Israeli governmental policy on
the Palestinian issue; a broad coalition, organized as *Breira*, was energetically criticized and even vilified. All of this involved, in large part, variations on post-1967
themes.[46]

These are many of the issues and positions that were prominent in American
Jewish life before and after the Six Day War; they constitute the complex ethos of
American Judaism in the late sixties. The variety warns us against simplification.
During this period, in terms both of visible, public issues like black nationalism,
student campus rebellions, Jewish ritual experience, busing, and affirmative action
and of deeper, more theoretical issues, often not brought to consciousness but
present as foundational assumptions—like one's conception of morality as either
historical and contextual or rational and universal—some people changed their
views; others did not.

At any time, coalitions formed, and in the eyes of opponents, groupings were
formed that on reflection may now seem bizarre. A good example of this phenomenon occurs in an article by Rabbi Harold Schulweis in which he develops criticisms of the "new Jewish right."[47] Among his opponents, who all argue for the priority of Jewish self-interest over liberal universalism, he claims, are Seymour Siegel,
Jakob Petuchowski, Eliezer Berkovits, Michael Wyschogrod, Nathan Glazer, and
Milton Himmelfarb. The positions that they take on affirmative action, housing,
and Jewish–Christian dialogue are all elements in the whole he calls the "new Jewish conservatism." But, of course, not all of these people hold the same position on
all of these kinds of issues; Schulweis does not claim explicitly that they do. But he

does claim that the position—which they are all taken to share—does have a single underpinning: "While the motivations for Jewish self-interest are varied, one event haunts them all. One single event colors their perception of reality: the Holocaust."[48] But even without a detailed analysis of what Schulweis might mean by this, it should strike any reader as an exaggeration and a strange one at that. Not only is it obvious that Petuchowski, Wyschogrod, Fackenheim, and Berkovits, for example, do not treat the Holocaust in the same way; it is also not true that all feel or understand the Holocaust's impact in the same way. But this observation, which warns us against facile classifications, points us to a fundamental issue, the relation between the Six Day War and the role of the Holocaust in American Jewish self-understanding.

Nathan Glazer asks why the Six Day War had the impact it did on American Jews; along with the black and New Left criticism of Israel and Russia's support of the Arab nations, Glazer cites as a reason "the growing emotional response among American Jews to the Holocaust of 1939–1945."[49] Both young and old could feel threatened, their survival in jeopardy. Glazer, then, suggests one view on the role of people's awareness of and response to the Holocaust in the Six Day War's impact on American Jewry: sensitivity to Auschwitz enabled or even encouraged that impact. Glazer calls it a "reason," but it was no one's reason, nor a cause really; rather, if he is right, it was a condition that made the response of many Jews possible and perhaps even likely. It was therefore an enabling condition. But this is only one view; there are others.

The Six Day War of course was something that in a sense happened to American Jews, although it was really the reports or news of it that happened to them. And *how* it happened to them or affected them depended as much on their receptivity and the character of that receptivity as it did on what that news was; even less, in a sense, did it depend on what actually occurred in Israel and the Middle East. Each person who clung to the radio, hungered for news reports, felt threatened, wanted to participate in the fighting or at least to provide support for Israel's defense, and more—each had a reason or had reasons for wanting and doing these things. Glazer's suggestion is that for many the Holocaust had something to do with those reasons. Like a spectator who watches a basketball game and, as things progress, becomes involved, even passionately so, the Jews in America heard of the threat of war, of its outbreak, and its progress, and they—at least some—sought to be involved. If Glazer is right, part of their commitment had to do with the Holocaust, the sense of threat and insecurity that it engendered.[50] And in America of the late sixties, with its sense of disorder, violence, and dismay, this sense of threat and insecurity was doubtless appropriate and realistic.

Another possibility is this: some Jews may never have felt comfortable or able to deal with the gas chambers and the destruction of Jews. Perhaps it was too repelling or too horrifying or too close or too distant. They had, like Alfred Kazin and many others, seen the photographs and the films; they knew about Eichmann and the trial, but they could not do more than assimilate it to murder in general and suffering in general. They could not face it, this event, Auschwitz and the other camps; the sense of awe, of atrocity, of profound shame and embarrassment was simply too much to bear. But, then, as the Six Day War proceeded to unfold and as victory was won, there appeared a way of working through that evil and that darkness and transcending it, in a sense; at least there was a way of being involved in and even reenacting the historical process that did not stop with the abyss but went on beyond it. Some, that is, were initially involved in a powerful form of denial or setting aside of the camps; when the War came, they were uncertain, but as it proceeded, they came to see the pattern of Auschwitz and the pattern of the War coalesce. One was superimposed on the other, until the victory reinforced that understanding and encouraged them thereafter, again and again, to associate the two events, the destruction and the victory. To some, then, the Six Day War enabled the Holocaust to move to a central, focal location in the Jewish people's identity; hence the War somehow led to the Holocaust's primacy for many Jews. By the midseventies, as Rieder observed, the Holocaust and the Israeli victory in 1967 were intertwined with each other and with Jewish pride and the sense of responsibility to respond to threat with strength and self-confidence.[51]

If some felt that fear and the feeling of being threatened was what drew the Holocaust and the War together, others thought that it was guilt. When the crisis broke, "American Jews . . . experienced a trauma, perhaps best diagnosed as a reliving of the Holocaust in an eerie awareness of once again being put to the ultimate test." But what kind of test? As Dawidowicz describes it, "the Holocaust was the underlying catalyst. American Jews [were] afflicted with a deep sense of guilt. With the passage of time, their very survival when millions of other Jews were murdered and, even worse, their failure to rescue more than a minuscule number of European Jews have increasingly tormented them." The Eichmann trial stimulated these feelings, the controversy over Arendt's book even more so. American Jews felt guilty over Jewish passivity in Europe and in America; the whole question of "obedience to superior orders," which was applied to Vietnam by the young, deepened their own sense of guilt.[52] Some, then, felt endangered and isolated; others felt guilt and a need to atone, to rectify a flaw, a need for catharsis, first through recognition of the trauma, then through compensation—this time there would be no failure, no passivity, no abandonment.

On the one hand, then, the Six Day War allowed a release of tension, of repressed emotion, or stimulated a dormant sense of threat. To many, it fixed the Holocaust in the center of Jewish consciousness as a sign of the value of survival; but was such an intense commitment to survival admirable? Was it consistent with Judaism? Did it obscure or displace too much? Clearly questions like these were on the minds of many. On the other hand, the Six Day War, some thought, provided new vehicles for legitimizing Jewish distinctiveness. Waxman calls the Holocaust "the symbol and legitimating myth" of the unity and uniqueness of Judaism for many American Jews, who seek to cling to Jewish identity but feel alienated from traditional concepts like covenant and *halakhah*.[53] As a result of the War, Israel, the Holocaust, and survival became a symbolic nexus that grounded allegiance to Jewish history and Jewish self-identification. For many Jews in the late sixties and seventies, whose lives were endangered by public policies and political coalitions, this nexus would have had—and did have—a powerful appeal. Others, however, would have—and did—find it narrow and even false.

In 1970 *Response*, probably the most influential journal of the young radical Jews, published a symposium, its response to the famous *Commentary* symposium of 1966. Unlike the earlier project, however, the *Response* symposium was open not to a select few but rather to all who wanted to respond to the questions, was oriented to action as well as belief, and included a question about "the destruction of European Jewry and the re-establishment of the Jewish state."[54] This question, which was recommended to Bill Novak by Emil Fackenheim, yielded diverse responses, and they show that by 1970 the central importance of the Holocaust in particular in the beliefs and lives of North American Jews was not universal. Fackenheim was not alone in claiming that Auschwitz was unique and transforming and that there should be both negative and positive responses to it, political and religious.[55] But many disagreed. Arthur Green, for example, admitted that the Holocaust and Israel are "backdrop events to all of our lives," but he also claimed that the Holocaust is distant from him, pushed into the background by the sixties—civil rights, black nationalism, the peace movement, drugs, and the counterculture. The young Jews around *Response* and the *havurot*, he said, are "almost pure products of the American sixties. The Holocaust and Zionism are not the real issues that brought such groups together.... [T]hese are not the events that have most deeply shaped us." According to Green, the *havurot* have to do with conformity, mass society, a search for new community, alienation, and the search for religious learning and experience, and he even admitted to "resisting the influences of both the Holocaust and Zionism."[56] Arthur Waskow linked the Holocaust and Hiroshima, spoke of them together as a Sinai-event, the combination of world-destructive technology and the ability to mobilize an entire society to use it, attacked the established Jewish community as insensitive, pandering authoritarians, and called for a new Jewish coalition of prophetic Judaism, socialist Bundists, neo-Hasidim, communitarians, libertarians, and more.[57] By linking Auschwitz and nuclear weapons, Waskow was less focused than Green and Mintz on Jewish life; there is a sense that his response, radical and antiestablishment, is within the tradition of Spinoza, Mendelssohn, Cohen, and classical Reform. For Waskow, the Six Day War could hardly have made a difference; the issues of nuclear threat and peace were already on the table. He even alluded to the way that the American Jewish community supported Israel, calling it "bond-drive Zionism," and, like Green, claimed that real Zionism is not physical and geographical but rather symbolic. Green was committed to community and personal authenticity, Waskow to political radicalism; both eulogized *galut* Judaism. Nor were they alone; in the seventies, as the impact of the Six Day War became a matter of settled sensibility and as the Holocaust had become a central feature of the American Jewish psyche, there were those—young experimental Jews, Jewish radicals, and continuing liberals—who did not agree.[58]

After 1967, as most commentators point out, the Holocaust became central to Jewish identity for many American Jews and, to a certain degree, to American Jewry as a whole. Eventually Yom Ha-Shoah became a fixture of the cycle of annual holy days and commemorations for the community; courses on the Holocaust proliferated in colleges and universities; publishing about the Holocaust—memoirs, fiction, historical studies, psychological works, and poetry—flourished; memorials and museums were planned and constructed, and this is only a small indication of the prominence of the Holocaust in American Jewish life and consciousness.[59] Surely the War contributed to this efflorescence; at least it enabled feelings to be expressed and coped with that had, prior to 1967, disposed of Auschwitz by restricting it to a dark, secluded corner of American Jewish consciousness. In this way the War provided a vehicle for coming to terms with the horrors, the fears, and the guilt. But Jews in America were, in 1967, beset by many problems, concerns, needs, and ideas; many were receptive, if not eager, to express their Jewish commitment; many were already doing so in a variety of ways. Others, ordinary Jews with differing degrees of association and observance, experienced the War as a means to become deeply and publicly involved in Jewish life, and they did so, finding within themselves resources and needs for intense identification with Israel, the victims of Nazism, and the demands of Jewish survival.

The War functioned for American Jews to release a set of beliefs, commitments, and feelings. It did so, however, because there had grown in America after the mid-sixties a sentiment toward group solidarity and group identification. The themes of the War—group-relatedness, fidelity, mortality, historicity—were consonant with this mood. In short, there was an affinity between the character of American life and the themes of the War that created a very important and transforming moment for American Judaism, American Jews, and Jewish thinking about both. It was a historical moment of what might be called "internal nationalism," and for the American Jewish community that lived in that world the availability of an external nationalist sentiment was profoundly opportune and effective.

The past is inescapable but, at the same time, easy to ignore; we do and we must approach it selectively. The main categories of the sixties—alienation, self-fulfillment, community, authority, conformity, liberation, universalism, distinctiveness, pluralism—may appear to function without any attention to the vocabulary of the past, memory, and history. This was no longer so in the eighties and nineties. But we should not be confused or misled as we look back at that earlier period, its conflicts, debates, and struggles. The relation of today's present to the past is deeply implicated in the lives and thought of those years. The various types of Jews I have identified did think about the past; indeed, they meant different things by it and by history. Many assumed that their situation, with its problems and alternatives, was the product of history; they saw history as determinative, a trap to be escaped, chains to be broken. They wanted freedom, hungered for discontinuity, novelty, spontaneity; they preferred rock and improvisational jazz to opera and symphony. Others felt imprisoned by history and yet sought resources in it for renewal; one needed to learn more history and understand what could be valuably appropriated. There were those too who doubtless saw history as a turbulent river stretching beyond the horizon in both directions; they were immersed in that river, part of something that had gone on for centuries and would, if all went well, continue to go on after them. For them, history was certainly inescapable; it was the stage for their performance and the script too, or at least the plot. But there were those who placed such views in doubt, who stimulated new kinds of thinking about understanding the past and about recovering it for Jewish life and Western culture. These are the main authors of post-Holocaust Jewish thought.

Richard Rubenstein and the New Paganism

In Rubenstein's essays of the late fifties and early sixties, Tillich and Kaplan had influenced his early thinking about God and the Jewish people; by 1965, his response to Auschwitz had enabled him to coordinate his rejections of the God of history and the doctrine of chosenness into a systematic whole.[1] In 1965 Rubenstein wrote an autobiographical piece for Ira Eisenstein's volume *The Varieties of Jewish Belief*. His reflections are revealing, even if they do seem overly constructed and refashioned. In them, for example, he recalls that the revelations of the death camps and in particular the camp at Majdanek, during the early fall of 1944, "caused [him] to reject the whole optimistic theology of liberal religion" and to appreciate the human potential for evil.[2] Two years as a rabbinic student at the Hebrew Union College in Cincinnati, he reports, could not equip him to deny the force of the demonic in human life; liberal optimism gave way to pessimism and even nihilism and a recognition of the social ties that enable us to deal with nature and human frailty. Rubenstein also records his fascination with the notion of *golah*, or exile, and with the Kabbalistic imagination of Isaac Luria with its speculations about creation, *tsimtsum*, and God as a Holy Nothingness. He had, as he put it, "exchanged [his] atheistic nihilism for a mystic nihilism," in which God was conceived as absolutely nothing but nonetheless the ground of all being.[3]

What of religion in a world without God, hope, and transcendence? Rubenstein identifies himself as one who "regard[s] withdrawal from the religious community as unthinkable." In America, he notes, religious affiliation is an ineradicable part of one's identity. But there is more than inertia and conformity here. Rubenstein takes religion to be a set of strategies for dealing with the traumas and anxieties of human existence: the synagogue is "the institution through which I can dramatize, make meaningful, and share the decisive moments of my life," he says. These moments include birth, puberty, marriage, illness, and death, and the synagogue or religious community becomes, for him, a natural mechanism for survival. Here is social scientific explanation and naturalism applied to religious institutions and practices and a kind of nonrational justification of religion.[4] The heritage of Spinoza and Durkheim had come to save Rubenstein's Judaism from utter deterioration in the face of Camus, Kafka, and mystical nihilism.

Still, if his recollections are accurate, it was Majdanek and the death camps that were determinative from 1944 and throughout his years in seminary and graduate school.[5] As he puts it, "the problem of God and the death camps is the central problem for Jewish theology in the twentieth century."[6] Indeed, Rubenstein goes so far as to call this problem "the one pre-eminent measure of the adequacy of all contemporary Jewish theologies."[7] By 1965, then, Rubenstein had come to see how his attractions to Kabbalah, existentialism, Freud, Tillich,[8] and more could be coordinated with the realism and depth of Auschwitz as a revelation of human evil and frailty. He could say that the theological question was central because he could see how it was tied to issues about human nature, religion, community, and psychology. He had come to see the alienation of Jewish youth from traditional Jewish life and conventional institutions, the birth of the new Jewish state, and Jewish radicalism in general as elements of this posture, this strategy for coping with the Holocaust by rejecting authority and returning to the past as revised and reinterpreted.[9] Judaism is treated as a given; authenticity comes with understanding its natural— that is, social scientific—and therapeutic roles and purposes. The best life, then, has this stoic dimension; once we understand life and nature, we can live genuinely, as unperturbed as one can be in a world of death, anxiety, fear, frustration, joy, exuberance, and the like.

Rubenstein's recollections portray a journey of self-discovery and self-fulfillment; they are very much literature of the sixties. At the same time, they express a certain consolidation and self-recognition in his thinking, with the problem of God and the death camps emerging as a central feature. At the conclusion of this self-portrait, Rubenstein articulates this centrality well:

> God really died at Auschwitz. This does not mean that God is not the beginning and will not be the end. It does mean that nothing in human choice, decision, value, or meaning can any longer have vertical reference to transcendent standards. We are alone in a silent, unfeeling cosmos. . . . What then of Judaism? It is the way we Jews share our lives in an unfeeling and silent cosmos. It is the flickering candle we have lighted in the dark to enlighten and to warm us.[10]

By the end of 1965, this constellation of ideas—the centrality of Auschwitz, the rejection of the traditional conception of the God of history, the reinterpretation of election, Torah, and more as religious strategies for coping with human existence, and the psychoanalytic-existential understanding of the human condition—was fixed in Rubenstein's mind. It was realism, naturalism, and pessimism, fashioned into a rather novel theological position. The position is succinctly stated in the essay I just examined and in Rubenstein's contribution to the *Commentary* symposium in

1966. The opportunity that gave rise to the consolidation and articulation of the position occurred in 1965. Rubenstein, in his autobiographical *Power Struggle*,[11] reported that in November 1965 he was invited to respond to a presentation by Thomas J. J. Altizer at a conference in Atlanta, at Emory University, entitled "America and the Future of Theology." Altizer, well known as a "Death of God" theologian and author of *The Gospel of Christian Atheism*, gave a powerful talk to a full house, expounding his view that the "death of God" liberated people to a fully autonomous Christian life. In his comments Rubenstein added a cluster of ideas he had come to see as central: a focus on Auschwitz and the death camps, a denial of atheism, naturalism about the human situation—the belief that "men are irretrievably locked in the biological world of growth, decay, and mortality with no hope of escape," his pessimism and anguish about this situation, and his paganism, a Judaism of "earthly joys and celebrations."[12] One of the results of that conference and Rubenstein's response, if we are to accept his account, was some notoriety for him. Another was his eventual turn to the academic life and separation from Jewish institutional affiliation. A third was the publication of *After Auschwitz* in 1966.

Rubenstein's contribution to the *Commentary* symposium on Jewish belief, together with the essay that emerged from the encounter with Altizer over the meaning of "death of God" theology for Judaism,[13] are the best places to see this position formulated and stated clearly. Many of the issues Rubenstein discusses express the individualism, alienation, and antitraditionalism of the sixties. Auschwitz had a grip on Rubenstein, to be sure, but its role and how he came to deal with it are couched in a discourse that pervaded the decade. He himself notices this when he remarks that "the 'death-of-God' is a theological code word for *the collapse of authority*, political authority, moral authority, social authority and religious authority. . . . [All people] cannot do without social structures and their legitimating ideologies, yet these structures have had an increasingly pathogenic effect upon them as individuals."[14] Auschwitz is an especially powerful indication of how modern life and institutions have deteriorated and how confidence in science, government, family, religions, and Western culture has crumbled. Rubenstein's understanding of Auschwitz, God, and Judaism unfolded in this context.

Rubenstein pointed out that his own theological reflections are both like and unlike those of William Hamilton and Thomas Altizer. As Christian theologians, they can speak with propriety of God's dying and also with the optimism that looks forward to better times ahead. Rubenstein cannot. But he can share with them the recognition that in our world—with its barbarism, its alienation, its domination, its violence—the divine–human encounter no longer exists. This is part of what Rubenstein means when he says that "*we live in the time of the death of God*";[15] it is, he says, a cultural fact, a claim about human living and its severance from transcendence, its loneliness, and its isolation. But, although Rubenstein acknowledges this situation, he is less optimistic about it than Altizer and Hamilton, whom he associates with popular American culture with its "rejection of history and tradition," of tragedy and the tragic sense.[16] He scorns their "rejection of the past" as wholly unacceptable to Judaism, and he doubts that their conception of unbounded freedom is a realistic, accurate result in a world in which our existence is grounded in finitude and frustration.

In place of their optimism, Rubenstein recommends honest realism, what he calls "paganism," "a wise intuition of man's place in the order of things."[17] He encourages us to listen to Camus, not to Dostoyevsky. And in the place of unbridled self-expression, Rubenstein recommends ritual and myth, strategies for survival in a lonely cosmos, therapy for a life fraught with fear, danger, and anxiety—with "pain, suffering, alienation, and ultimate defeat," a life in which death alone is the Messiah.[18] "What about religion in the time of the death of God? It is the way in which we share and celebrate, both consciously and unconsciously, through the inherited myths, rituals, and traditions of our communities the dilemmas and the crises of life and death, good and evil. Religion is the way in which we share our predicament."[19] For Jews, religion is Torah. In essence, this is the same existential, social-psychological justification of religious symbols and ritual, of Torah, that Rubenstein had learned from Tillich and appropriated for Judaism as early as 1955. In 1965–66, however, it has been elaborated and coordinated with the problem of God and the death camps.

In his *Commentary* contribution, Rubenstein makes the connection explicit: "When I say we live in the time of the death of God, I mean that the thread uniting God and man, heaven and earth, has been broken. We stand in a cold, silent, unfeeling cosmos, unaided by any purposeful power beyond our own resources. After Auschwitz, what else can a Jew say about God?"[20] A God of history, a creator-revealer-redeemer God, a God of providential concern, a God who is our partner in history, our ideal and standard—such a God is inconceivable, or, more precisely, such a conception of God is no longer meaningful. Why? Here Rubenstein coopts the vocabulary of natural theology and the traditional problem of evil in order to dispose of it. He appropriates the Jewish version of these ideas, that God as omnipotent must be "the ultimate . . . actor in the historical drama" and that catastrophes in Jewish history must be "God's punishment of a sinful Israel."[21] This is not a simple, uncomplicated set of premises for setting out the problem of evil. For the problem as traditionally formulated shows either that the premises are coherent when properly interpreted or that they are not coherent and that some are to be accepted, some not. Rubenstein's goal, on the other hand, is to reject the entire vocabulary with which the problem is formulated. His point is that if we accept this framework, then we must treat "Hitler and the SS as instruments of God's will." As he puts it, "to see any purpose in the death camps, the traditional believer is forced to regard the most demonic, antihuman explosion in all history as a meaningful expression of God's purposes. The idea is simply too obscene for me to accept." His goal is to jettison the entire vocabulary of an active, historical God and all that such a vocabulary implies for Judaism, Torah, Israel, and covenant. In a sense, Rubenstein uses the traditional problem of evil to expose what is at issue, the way Auschwitz, a wholly negative event, forces the believer to abandon one religious vocabulary in favor of another, one set of symbols or mode of discourse for another. Auschwitz is a dissonance within a particular religious framework; to expose oneself to it is to see the problems with adhering to that framework. For this reason, it is not really an issue whether Rubenstein's argument works or not, whether the believer *must* use the doctrine of divine retribution to infer that Hitler was a divine device. For Rubenstein is saying all this just to indicate what is at stake here, that if, after Auschwitz, one persists in adopting the vocabulary of the chosen people and the God of history, then at some point or other one will be led to say, believe, and act in ways that will be deeply dissonant, indeed disgusting or repulsive — obscene, as he puts it.[22] Hence, one should dispose of that vocabulary, or, in other terms, one should respond to this concrete, historical encounter by returning to tradition, revising or rejecting what is unacceptable, and recovering what is appropriate and enriching. Hence the Jew retrieves ritual with a "theistic God," community and celebration "in an age of no God," that is, no God of history. Does this mean the rejection of God, that Rubenstein is or advocates atheism? Hardly. Indeed, he clearly rejects atheism for himself and advocates what he calls paganism.[23] This view, a combination of naturalism and mysticism, may not be wholly clear, but it is certainly not atheism. Rubenstein is no more an atheist than Hobbes or Spinoza was. But of course they were both maligned for being atheists, and so has he been.[24]

Rubenstein's paganism is not hard to understand. It involves a respect for all that is left once one has removed God or transcendence, and that means nature and the human condition, biologically, psychologically, and socially. Paganism involves the acceptance of human existence as part of the natural order, admitting our limitations, finitude, and mortality, and also accepting its contingency. There is a God that is distinct from this natural order, the being in which existence is grounded. But that God has no ongoing or occasional influence on how things go in nature, so far as we can tell. Hence Rubenstein is a naturalist without Spinoza's sense of how divinity permeates and orders nature and without Spinoza's optimism. Instead we have an earthly existence that is purposeless and without order, existential in its brute givenness and in our sense of despair, anxiety, and isolation as we face it. This is Rubenstein's amalgamated paganism, the home of resignation and not hope, of realism and threat and worry.[25]

There is a distinctly pragmatic dimension to Rubenstein's account of Judaism, Western culture and society, and the lapse of transcendence.[26] What justifies religion — ritual, celebration, myth — and indeed morality in our world, he argues, is utility or therapeutic effectiveness. In the late sixties, this pragmatism expressed itself in two articles that Rubenstein wrote about Jews, blacks, and politics.[27] Both appeared in the *Reconstructionist* during the year after the Six Day War, an event that exacerbated, we should recall, the growing rifts between Jews and blacks in America and between young Jewish radicals and the New Left.[28] These articles reveal

Rubenstein's thoughts about the situation of Jews in America during the period immediately after the Six Day War, although, as he makes clear, some of his thoughts
date from 1965.

Rubenstein, in the first of these articles, tries to reveal and clarify his sense of
betrayal as the civil rights movement became polarized, militant, and anti-
Semitic. I have shown that this theme is important to understanding Jewish life
in the seventies; it is central, for example, to Jonathan Rieder's ethnography of the
Jews and Italians in Canarsie in the early seventies. Rubenstein's reversal, from
standard liberal support for the civil rights struggle to a split with SNCC, occurred in Montgomery, Alabama, in March 1965, when Rubenstein had accompanied a group of 135 college students from the Pittsburgh area to a demonstration at the State House. He reports his impression of the rift developing between
Martin Luther King's Southern Christian Leadership Conference (SCLC) and
SNCC. The latter organization was represented by James Foreman, who, in
Rubenstein's eyes, sought a direct confrontation with the police regardless of the
risks or casualties to the students. As he puts it, Foreman orchestrated a bloody
police attack "with a full understanding of what the media would do with it."[29]
It was street theater.

Rubenstein was approached by a student leader of the Pittsburgh group, a "new
Left" supporter, who feared for the group. SNCC members were inciting the hundreds there with antiwhite, racial harangues, and the feeling was that Foreman had
lied when he said that there were permits for the demonstration. Later, the Pittsburgh group voted to leave, but before their buses arrived, they heard speeches by
King and by Foreman, who denounced white America and "mainstream Negro
leadership," King included.[30] Foreman fulminated against Lyndon Johnson and
cried for a radical revolution. Rubenstein recalls an oft-quoted statement: "If I can't
sit at the table, I'm going to knock the f...ing legs off."[31] It was a "call to a nihilistic
revolution without meaningful goal." Clearly, King's moderation, his nonviolent
strategy and goal of integration, were being superseded by something "more violent and radical" and frightening. To Rubenstein, equality was no longer the aim;
deep irrational forces, resentment and rage and bitterness, were at work that "economic advances" could not address.

The tone of the civil rights struggle, the goals and the strategies, all have
changed, Rubenstein argued. Leaders like Foreman and Stokely Carmichael were
aligned with Havana, Hanoi, and Algiers and with Maoist revolutionaries. The
question was: could the old, liberal, white supporters say anything? At a rally in
Pittsburgh, Rubenstein was asked to speak, and despite the pleas of several students
not to "voice objections," he did not refrain, charging Foreman with deception, manipulation, and racial violence. The result was that Rubenstein was lauded by the
right and denounced by the left, especially by liberal Jews. Eventually, he writes,
SNCC would become anti-Semitic, and the more radical and violent SNCC became, the more King and the SCLC could hold whites and Jews hostage to that

threat of violence. But, Rubenstein notes, this does not mean that SCLC and the moderates can function as they want. In Chicago, at the National Conference of the New Politics in September 1967, SCLC voted with the majority to condemn "Zionist aggression" against the Arab nations.[32] In Chicago, blacks saw themselves as part of a worldwide revolutionary movement; in August 1967 an Arab guide told Rubenstein that "he and his fellow Arabs saw the American Negro as their ally in the common struggle against America and Israel."[33] Rubenstein had come to realize that the victims of American injustice had become the enemies of his people; victims do not seek justice, he wrote; they seek victims of their own.

What conclusions did Rubenstein draw? "The Jewish community can no longer remain true to its own fundamental aspirations in America or its deep commitment to the safety and prosperity of Israel and, at the same time, support the Negro revolution." This does not mean a withdrawal from political action, but it does mean a change, from supporting revolutionary violence to engaging in establishment politics. This change is the subject of Rubenstein's second article, "The Politics of Powerlessness." Here he gives a social-scientific account of power in America, of white Protestant dominance, the Jewish use of moral rhetoric, the shift in the civil rights movement to Black Power and revolutionary violence, and the victimization of Jewish businesses as a by-product of ghetto violence.[34] His analysis is in the style of realpolitik and of Nietzsche: a naturalist account of power relations among groups and of morality as an ideological device for disposing and dealing with power. Rubenstein also elaborates on the American support for the Arab nations, especially among blacks, those on the left, and Christian denominations with interests in the Middle East, often missionary interests, and recommends greater political realism and less moral indignation.[35] "Jews must replace the rhetoric of morality, the language of powerlessness, with the responsible and insightful wisdom of political realism if they are to make a significant contribution to the goal of a decent America for all."[36]

Politically, Rubenstein's assessment and proposals should be associated with conservative or neoconservative developments in America in this period.[37] At the same time, his perception of America, the crisis in American social and political life, and Jews in America helps us to understand Rubenstein's theology. For he believed that Western culture had lost its sense of transcendence and was riddled with conflict, anxiety, and violence. The shift from moderation, nonviolence, and religious discourse in the civil rights struggle to Black Power, revolutionary rhetoric, and the militancy of power and violence exemplified this situation. Moreover, like his theology, Rubenstein's social and political interpretation had become naturalist and realist. Religion is possible and even useful in the age of the "death of God" as a set of practices, beliefs, and institutions for coping with our biological and historical situation; similarly, morality and moral rhetoric involve strategies for dealing with matters like power, love, and conflict.[38] At times acting in terms of moral principles is effective and propitious, but at other times it is useful to recognize and admit the

political and social-psychological forces that direct events and that need to be cultivated if one is going to succeed or even to survive.

Rubenstein's understanding of the civil rights struggle and the radicalization of
blacks and its implications for American Jews developed from 1965 to 1967. The
Six Day War and the alignment of blacks and the New Left with the Arab nations
only served to confirm his suspicions, his worries, and his reaction. But there is a
sense in which the events of 1965, 1967, and 1968 were assimilated in his mind to
patterns and strategies, his overall naturalistic pessimism and realism, that were in
place by 1965–66. The last chapter of *Morality and Eros*, a book that develops his
view of how religion and morality serve important social and psychological functions in a world without the God of history, gives the same sort of mystical account
of God that we found, for example, in the *Commentary* contribution of 1966.[39]
There is good reason to think, then, that the Six Day War led to no new thinking
about God and Torah and that it only confirmed Rubenstein's realism, his pragmatism, and his naturalist understanding of social and political phenomena. But
what about Israel, the land and the state? How was Israel conceived as part of
Rubenstein's paganism, and did the War and its aftermath lead to any changes or
developments in his view?

"The Rebirth of Israel in Contemporary Jewish Theology," which originally appeared in 1960, is included in *After Auschwitz*.[40] In that volume, commenting on
this early piece, Rubenstein notes that its main theme, the pagan aspects of the rebirth of the state and possession of the land, was still fundamental for him in 1966
but that he no longer took Israel to have a messianic dimension. In this article
Rubenstein focuses not on the historical aspects of Zionism, the founding of a
homeland and the response to anti-Semitism, as much as on the character of Zionism as a liberation movement that enables people to live freely, with emotional and
cultural vitality, indeed exuberance.[41] In Rubenstein's view, Zionism is antihistori-
cal and oriented to space, to finding "a creative union with earth and earth's powers."[42] It engages in this liberating, vital experience by rejecting the notion of exile as
divine punishment and replacing self-blame and self-distortion with emotional
self-expression. In Israel, Jews have begun a "post-historical existence," a return to
the earth, an acceptance of the joys and sorrows of our natural existence with no
false historical hopes or purposes.[43] Rubenstein calls this a religion of nature, in
which people enjoy and suffer what nature has to offer; it replaces a religion of history in which nature is the matter on which human beings work but has no intrin-
sic value. Religions of history, like Aristotelian physics, invoke form and matter
while privileging form; religions of nature, like materialisms of all kinds, accept
matter for what it is, ultimate and basic. With this change from time — linear and
progressive — to space, from history to nature, from reason to emotion, comes release, a disposal of bourgeois values, and even a theological shift. Following Tillich,
Rubenstein calls for the death of the God of theism, the God of history, and the
birth or rebirth of God "as the source and life of nature," the ground of all of na-

ture's expressions, indeed the ground of being.[44] Zionism is the return to body and earth, the casting off of repressions, and the exuberant advocacy of a new paganism.

This is an early essay, of course, but it does exhibit clearly Rubenstein's naturalism and his rejection of Judaism as a religion of history and purpose. In tone and spirit, it is a post-Hegelian, Rousseauian reading of the vitality of Zionism and its contribution to Judaism. Paganism incorporates reverence for nature and one's own natural, biological being; it is associated with cycles, emotion, growth, illness, death, and the sense of communion with the divine through natural functions and relations. Later Rubenstein's paganism will still be divorced from linear history; it will still focus on the natural, biological features of our condition. But it will be more resolute, resigned and even pessimistic rather than joyful and exuberant. And the divine will be shunted aside, the ground of nature but no longer present in or through it. By 1966, for Rubenstein, "Death is the Messiah" and "omnipotent Nothingness is the Lord of all Creation."[45]

After the Six Day War Rubenstein returned to think about the state and land of Israel but now in terms of its relation to Auschwitz. His important essay "Homeland and Holocaust: Issues in the Jewish Religious Situation" appeared in 1968.[46] The reestablishment of the state of Israel, as a secular state, poses a difficult challenge to traditional Jewish categories; diaspora Judaism will find it a problem to assimilate Israel in a serious religious way. For in Israel Judaism has become pagan and ceased to be historical;[47] it has become, that is, emotional, vital, and exuberant but especially political, "with effective political and military power."[48] Hence whatever Judaism becomes in Israel, it will be different from diaspora Judaism. "The religious values of a community destined to live by its military cunning cannot be the same as those of the middle class business and professional communities of the diaspora."[49] Yet there is a unity between diaspora Jews and Israel, a sense of kinship and ethnic-religious community. This was expressed, Rubenstein recalls, by the strong identification with Israel during the Six Day War. If theology tries to understand Judaism and Jewish unity and that unity was powerfully expressed in diaspora identification with Israel, then "no Jewish theology will be adequate which fails to take account of the response of the world's Jews to Israel's recent struggle."[50]

What Rubenstein then proposes is a reinterpretation of Jewish history in terms of the ancient Roman defeat; exile, powerlessness, and degradation; normative Judaism as a strategy of survival; the need for a "psychological and sociological analysis of ritual as a system of self-expression"; the rejection of religious explanation in terms of a divine–human encounter and the God of history; the failure of the strategy of compliance and appeasement against the Nazis, "a technologically competent enemy determined to annihilate"; the renunciation by Israelis of prophetic conciliation in favor of a commitment to "fight to the last man should an enemy seek to annihilate them"; and the Israeli use of power and terror in behalf of survival in an age when God is dead.[51] It is a reading of the past based on notions of political power and social psychology, not on theological categories such as providence, salvation, trust, and covenant. These, he points out, are concepts rooted in God and faith, and he charges with being unrealistic and deceived those theologians, indebted to Martin Buber and Franz Rosenzweig, figures like Arthur Cohen, Will Herberg, and Eugene Borowitz, who continue to interpret Judaism in terms of God, faith, covenant, and such notions. "They refuse to acknowledge that issues of power and worldliness must be faced in any realistic philosophy of religion."[52] What Rubenstein invokes is a new, realistic, and pagan theology, an interpretation of Judaism and the Jewish past that is "relevan[t] to human self-understanding," that serves the individual's life and needs.[53] Current Jewish theology fails to accomplish this task, he argues, because it fails to "face the reality of modern Jewish history in both its agony and its triumph."[54]

Often Rubenstein's writing speaks at too high a pitch, and here, where he is so critical, even belligerent, that pitch may repel. But behind the invective is a genuine attempt to relate Auschwitz and Israel to the tasks of Jewish theology. Rubenstein argues that Auschwitz cannot be thought and discussed with traditional Jewish vocabulary. Once we realize this, we can encounter Jewish history again, a history that extends through the Holocaust, the establishment of the Jewish state, to our own day, and reinterpret it without using that old language.[55] Rather, the mode of discourse that we use, social and political and psychological—in short, naturalist— will reveal a repressed tradition of pagan notions, power, violence, struggle, joy, and self-reliance.[56] In the end, this process is one of self-discovery and indeed self-recovery, for the central ideas and themes are found to be there, in our tradition, all along. They were, however, hidden from us until the darkness and the light led us to seek and expose them. In one sense, then, Judaism after Auschwitz is no longer a religion of history; in another, it still remains a religion of history and tradition, albeit with new content or old content reinterpreted in accordance with a naturalist hermeneutic.

In "Homeland and Holocaust" Rubenstein, writing shortly after the Six Day War, charges the Jewish theological establishment, even the young new theologians, with neglecting or ignoring Auschwitz and Israel and hence with refusing to face history. Only Emil Fackenheim receives some positive comment, and then it is slim. Within two years or at least six, Rubenstein could not make this charge in quite the same way, and in the eighties several of his subjects could no longer at all be chastised for denying the relevance of history, suffering, power, and politics to Jewish identity.

In 1973–75 Rubenstein published a book and articles that extend some of the themes I have been discussing, in particular how we should and can understand the death camps and what they indicate about our world.[57] Commenting on Emil Fackenheim's claim, made in 1967, that the Holocaust had *as yet* not been assimilated within the framework of normative Jewish thought, Rubenstein adds that the phrase "as yet" expresses "an understandable but pathetic hope destined never to be realized."[58] Rubenstein believes that traditional Jewish theological categories "have been exploded by Auschwitz." I have already looked at why Rubenstein thinks that this incommensurability exists and why he thinks that it would be *obscene* to doubt it, that is, why the results of doubting it would themselves be *obscene*. His point is not just that Jewish theology has not assimilated Auschwitz—or Israel; it is also that they cannot do so. Does this mean, then, that Auschwitz cannot be understood, that it does not fit any of our categories of analysis, explanation, or clarification? Clearly, Rubenstein need not mean anything so radical, and indeed he does not. Much of his work in the seventies was in fact devoted to just this task, how to understand Auschwitz and its implication for understanding our current historical situation.[59]

As early as 1960 Rubenstein had tried to understand the origin and nature of the death camps, especially the relationship between the Final Solution and Christianity.[60] In 1973 he returned to this theme and made three points.[61] The first two are indebted to Hannah Arendt's analysis in *The Origins of Totalitarianism*.[62] First, "Auschwitz was in reality the first triumph of technological civilization in dealing with what may become a persistent human problem, the problem of the waste disposal of superfluous human beings in an overpopulated world."[63] The proper way to understand the camps and the extermination process, that is, invokes social-psychological terminology and not moral or theological terminology. In a world without God, a "cold unfeeling cosmos," the proper modes of understanding are naturalist and social scientific. There is much to object to here. Rubenstein diminishes Arendt's rich notion of superfluity and the camp's production of superfluous human beings. To him, overpopulation is what makes the Jews and others superfluous and disposable; indeed it is what motivates the project of disposal. But for Arendt, the camps were the Nazi device or "laboratory" for totalitarian domination, which expressed itself as the destruction of individuality and the creation of anonymity and superfluity. Moreover, Rubenstein makes the Final Solution look like a political, economic project rather than the ideological one that it was.[64] Nonetheless, his point is that the camps can be understood as the products of a new intersection of need and means, the need for "human waste disposal" in an overpopulated world and the means of an advanced, "technological civilization."[65]

Second, in a post-Auschwitz world, "there is today no longer any credible intellectual basis for affirming the existence of *human rights*. . . . The only rights an individual has are those he possesses by virtue of his membership in a concrete community which has the power to guarantee him those rights."[66] The Nazi extermination and disposal process demonstrated the meaninglessness of the discourse of natural law, divine law, and natural rights. The language of rights, obligations, and moral and legal limits must be tied to concrete groups and their power relations. Morality is a function of politics and nature. Here Rubenstein's naturalism and his Nietzscheanism once again express themselves. The Holocaust exposes the truth about morality and religion. "The possession of power is indispensable for human dignity."[67] With this point, Rubenstein aligns himself with tendencies in intellectual culture that are expressed in Foucault and other post-Marxist and post-Nietzschean thinkers—the favoring of power and domination over theory and ideology as the basic structure of human relationships.

Finally, Nazism was not an expression of paganism. For, in essence, totalitarianism, the desire for the expansion of power without limit, is incompatible with paganism—at least Greek paganism—which abhors *polypragmosune*, or doing too much, and respects the limits of human power.[68] According to Rubenstein, "Nazism cannot be seen as neo-paganism, as it has been by one well-known Jewish theologian . . . but a kind of Judeo-Christian heresy . . . a dialectically negated heretical Christianity."[69] In *The Cunning of History* Rubenstein identifies this theologian as Emil Fackenheim and elaborates his point: Nazism is an expression of "bureaucratic objectivity" that itself derived from the secularization that emerged from Protestant Christianity.[70] It will not do, he warns, to think that a return to Judeo-Christian values will prevent a repetition of Nazi barbarism. Christianity is not the antidote to Nazism but its origin.

The gist of these three observations about Auschwitz is that Nazism and the death camps can be understood within the normal categories of social scientific explanation. Moreover, once one encounters Auschwitz theologically and sees that it leads to the disposal of normative theological terminology, the social scientific understanding of Auschwitz, which places it within modern history, can appropriately have theological implications and moral and political implications as well. In a paper delivered at the annual convention of the Rabbinical Assembly on May 6, 1974, Rubenstein calls this posture a "post-apocalyptic Jewish sensibility" and claims that the separation between it and preapocalyptic Jewish thinking is radical.[71] Paradoxically, by confronting Auschwitz seriously, and by placing it *in* history, one comes to realize that *"there can be little or no continuity between the pre- and post-apocalyptic world."*[72]

In this speech, Rubenstein weaves together his commitment to the determinative character of Auschwitz, his social scientific understanding of it, and the view of Jewish history that he sketched in "Homeland and Holocaust," a sketch that appears very similar to Hannah Arendt's account of Jewish passivity and collaborationism and to standard Zionist interpretations of Jewish history as exile, submissiveness, and powerlessness.[73] According to his interpretation of Jewish history and apocalyptic messianism, "the birth of the State of Israel is undeniably the most profound response of the Jewish people to the Holocaust."[74] It is the rejection of Rabbinic Judaism's "servile submission" and cooperation with non-Jewish governments in favor of a "new Torah of combat" and self-reliance. Such a change, moreover, arises only after "overwhelming catastrophe." Auschwitz "exploded" one conception of Judaism and Jewish history and pointed to another; Israel manifested that alternative conception. Rubenstein's account is secular and functionalist. Israel adopted a policy and a style that would serve her political situation; "compliant, submissive behavior" would be "absolutely dysfunctional in meeting Israel's need to survive."[75]

In addition, Rubenstein defends his view that Auschwitz has really changed everything and that the Pharisaic bargain with the Romans, the established power, can no longer be negotiated. There is no bargaining with the Nazis; "no submission would have altered the Nazi determination to annihilate" the Jews.[76] They exhibit the apocalyptic character of the threats that plague us, overpopulation, scarcity, and extermination as a bureaucratic strategy to reduce population surplus. In such a world, only power will count, and the traditional Jewish categories of providence, righteousness, and holiness will have no credibility, Rubenstein claims;[77] nor would the institutions, the leaders, and the traditional practices of Jewish life in America as they are. All have been discredited and deserve skepticism, not support, although they are needed and in need of revision.[78] That revision, however, must be grounded in a recovery of the past: "we are all of us thousands of years old the day we are born. None of us can know our present or project a viable future without knowledge of our past." No new self-interpretation of Jewish life can occur without recovery of the past. This is a persistent theme in Rubenstein's paganism, a careful, constructive "uncovering [of] the underlying social, economic, and political factors that led Jews in earlier times to formulate their religious universes in the mythic images they did" that will serve us in constructing new identities for ourselves.[79] In a sense, Rubenstein rejects his own claim for discontinuity; more precisely, he qualifies it. Because of Auschwitz and the world of crisis in which we live, our Judaism and our understanding of its history are radically different from what they have been. But at the same time, our Judaism is continuous with the past, a newly constructed identity built out of the resources of a reinterpretation of the Jewish past.

For Rubenstein, the Holocaust is a watershed event, a radical separation in our world that fractures history, but there is no need for it to be incomprehensible, somehow incommensurable with normal, rational categories of explanation and understanding. In fact, he would argue, it is a rupture only insofar as we *do* understand it. Since it will distinguish Rubenstein from others like Greenberg, Fackenheim, and Cohen, this point needs further clarification.

In the essays in *After Auschwitz* (1966), Rubenstein had said that modern culture and Auschwitz showed us that we live in a cold, unfeeling cosmos. In part, this means that the dominance of modern science has shown us that nature functions without any "sensitivity" to human concerns, but in part it means that history has revealed distinctly anti-human capacities. In the essays of 1973–74, he argued that scarcity, overpopulation, and the bureaucratic demands that did and could lead to extermination as a strategy for human waste disposal were part of what make the cosmos "cold and unfeeling." In *The Cunning of History: The Holocaust and the American Future*, published in 1975, Rubenstein elaborates this account.[80] The Nazis crossed a line or barrier; after them, governmental use of violence and organization can be employed in any way to handle any political, social, or economic problem.[81] Nazism extended the tradition of Machiavellianism and political realism or reason of state, and it did so in a radical way. But to understand what occurred, one must, he argues, use social scientific categories and place Auschwitz within the context of human manipulation, exploitation, and slavery in modern culture.[82] Most of all, appropriating a category from Hannah Arendt, Rubenstein places Auschwitz in the context of modern bureaucratic policies regarding superfluous, disposable people, human surplus, like refugees and the mentally incompetent. Like Arendt, Rubenstein takes the extermination process to be the work not of fanatics or maniacs but rather of normal bureaucrats. It is not "at odds with the great traditions of Western civilization"; it is "the expression of some of the most profound tendencies of Western civilization in the twentieth century."[83]

The Cunning of History is a gloss on the final pages of Arendt's Origins of Totalitarianism. It uses, but reinterprets, her vocabulary of superfluity and redundancy. It places the death camps in the traditions of slavery and exile and bureaucracy. Nonetheless, it is a book that shows how unprecedented and unique Auschwitz was. The camps expressed a certain attitude about social problems, government, politics, and human life, an attitude deeply embedded in Western civilization and one to be watched and feared.[84]

At least from his essays of 1967 and 1968 concerning Jews and blacks in America through the paper on Jewish theology and the world situation, The Cunning of History, and The Age of Triage (1983), Rubenstein's thinking focused on an interpretation of Auschwitz within Western culture and society and its implications for a naturalist, realist, social scientific recovery of Jewish history. It is thinking that is self-consciously historical and that acknowledges the centrality of historical memory to present identity. Moreover, Rubenstein does not simply try to solve the traditional problem of evil so much as use the problem and its structure to exhibit how Auschwitz compels Jews to abandon the normative concepts of covenant, redemption, providence, and the entire vocabulary of a religion of history. Influenced by Camus, he concludes that our situation and its history are best encountered and dealt with by a realistic, political reading that will facilitate conduct appropriate to survival and personal flourishing. For Rubenstein, then, Auschwitz is itself continuous with history, with past and present; it is an episode within Western culture and civilization and extends themes and developments within that world. Simultaneously, it marks a chasm between the religiously permeated past and a secular, political present. For all its derivativeness, its brashness, and its overstatement, this is an important view, and the fact that Rubenstein was for many years the only Jewish theological voice that dared to speak out about the centrality of Auschwitz only underscores his importance.

As one can easily understand, however, Rubenstein and his work were controversial; many Jewish leaders, intellectuals, and theologians criticized him, rejecting what he said, sometimes aided by inadequate understanding of the real point of his work. Many ignored him, and he has expressed the view that the establishment Jewish community either paid no attention to his work or utterly opposed it.[85]

Rubenstein owes a debt to the Reconstructionist naturalism of Mordecai Kaplan.[86] His rejection of divine transcendence, of providence, miracle, the God of history, chosenness, and his social scientific understanding of Jewish beliefs, institutions, and rituals—all this echoes Reconstructionism in very definite ways, and indeed Rubenstein himself makes clear his allegiance to features of Kaplan's thought.[87] But one difference he has with Reconstructionism is his assessment of nature and his pessimism; for Kaplan nature is either indifferent to human purposes or benign. Indeed, God is identical with just those natural forces and processes that contribute to salvation, to the flourishing of human life. For Rubenstein, on the other hand, once we learn that God, the ground of being, is nonetheless wholly separated from natural and historical life and that we are on our own as biological and social animals, alone in a "cold, silent, unfeeling cosmos," our appropriate reaction should be grim and unsettled. We should realize that values and morality, like religion, have no secure ground; they too are natural, or at least social, phenomena, strategies for coping with the human predicament and hence for survival. Hobbes was right; Nietzsche was right.[88] In his review of *After Auschwitz*, Alan Miller charged Rubenstein with too much despair, with unwarranted pessimism, with "overpowering morbidity."[89] He also charged Rubenstein with giving Auschwitz too much significance and noted that the two commitments, to the special importance of the death camps and to a tragic vision of contemporary existence, are linked. Writing in 1967, Miller may have had a right to demur and to argue that Rubenstein's pessimism is inadequately grounded. The Reconstructionist idea of God as the "Force, Power, or Process, making for salvation"[90] accommodates Auschwitz as absence, and Rubenstein then had no account sufficiently compelling to recommend against such an idea of God. By the seventies and eighties he did. We might not agree with it, but there is in his account of Auschwitz, slavery, the treatment of surplus human beings, bureaucratic extermination, and overpopulation a case for the special role of Auschwitz and for realism and worry, even for despair, for a sense of living after the apocalypse. In his paper to the Rabbinical Assembly, he makes this point most powerfully: "The scenario I suggest points to the possibility, if not the probability, of a world-wide social catastrophe," he says.[91] The "socio-political meaning of the Holocaust experience" is the realization of a modern, bureaucratically sophisticated "experiment in the elimination of a surplus population."[92] He calls his attitude "apocalyptic pessimism."[93]

If one is to confront Auschwitz and to take it seriously, one might say, then what is the outcome? How can one do so and yet go on? Miller argued: things are better than they look. Auschwitz is bad, but there is human progress, "despite setbacks such as Auschwitz."[94] Rubenstein's response would be that Miller has not looked at

Auschwitz deeply and carefully enough. Read Hilberg, Arendt, Steiner, Levi, Wiesel, and others; Auschwitz indicates something catastrophic, apocalyptic about our religion, our culture, and our world. It is not a mere "setback" on the progressive journey toward increasing goodness and achievement. But there is another alternative: admit the basic thrust of Rubenstein's pessimism and yet find some ground for a positive response, for a type of recovery rather than fighting back with power and violence. As Rubenstein himself puts it, his own is a conservative voice, politically speaking.

But there could be a liberal or even a radical voice, that accepted his dissatisfaction with American and Western society in the late sixties and seventies, that opposed corruption, government and military power, dishonesty, the threat of authority, and such things but sought a different way of responding to the "petty exploits of the cheap crooks in Washington" and to the "increasing moral irrelevance" of academics and clergy. This alternative could be the way of the *havurot*, of religious sensibility, and of principled spirituality. In his comments on Rubenstein, Arthur Green, a founder of the Boston havurah and a scholar of Hasidism and Jewish mysticism, articulated this kind of response. It does not focus on Auschwitz but accepts, as it were, Rubenstein's assessment of the world that Auschwitz exemplifies. It too demands a response, but it is one of finding significant expressions of traditional spirituality that can be recovered in opposition to the failures of Western civilization.[95] Green, then, avoids the centrality of Auschwitz and yet seeks a religious and moral, rather than a political, almost Nietzschean response to the crisis of American and Western culture.

All of these possibilities, however, leave open a further alternative. This would be one that includes a sensitivity and seriousness about Auschwitz, a mixture of realism with hope, and a response that is both political and religious. The post-Holocaust Jewish thinkers to whom I will turn shortly all move in the direction of this more complex, more nuanced option.

In reading Rubenstein, it is important to realize that he does not confront and employ the traditional problem of evil in any conventional sense. Rather Auschwitz is indicative of something about the traditional religious vocabulary we use and the world we live in. The vocabulary or discourse misconstrues, and the world is a place without purpose or plan. Human life has no meaning or design other than what we give to it. Reviewing Rubenstein's early work in *Commentary* in 1969, Marvin Fox comes near to appreciating this: "Auschwitz refutes God not by adding one more decisive step to the classical theological debate, but by making clear the meaninglessness and the hopelessness of human existence."[96] Fox "comes near to appreciating" how Rubenstein's thinking works, because he sees the connection between Rubenstein's understanding of Auschwitz and his interpretation of our historical crisis and the human condition but still speaks as if this is a refutation of God. It is not. Rather it is the abandonment of one mode of religious discourse for another, and this is an interpretive shift, like Thomas Kuhn's paradigm shifts or Alasdair MacIntyre's change in traditions, or it is a process whereby an exposure to Auschwitz leads to a retrieval through suspicion, as David Tracy recommends for Christian theology. This is not to say that Rubenstein is completely clear about what the status of Auschwitz is or ought to be or about what encounter with the camps is to yield. But with regard to theology, he is clear: Auschwitz does not refute God's existence, but it does call forth a revised conception of God and nature.

Perhaps this is an account Rubenstein would accept: encounter with Auschwitz through the testimony of witnesses, interviews with survivors, reading historical reconstructions, and more shocks and horrifies; it moves us to try to understand what the event means, how it might be assimilated to religious categories and to sociopolitical, historical frameworks. When we do this, we find that the religious terms are repulsive, while the naturalist accounts reveal something useful and informative about our world and our religious life in it. In this way, Auschwitz reveals itself as an occasion — a stimulus — for interpretive revision, and while not a necessary object of examination, it becomes an especially valuable object that can change our way of coping with the crises of our lives, with preparing for and dealing with the present and the future. The Holocaust, then, does not demand anything; nor does it merely psychologically motivate response. Rather it can play a central role in the interpretive revision that will enable us to deal most effectively with our historical situation.

In the end, of course, this response to Auschwitz, like Rubenstein's recovery of Torah, national and political allegiance, and ritual, is voluntaristic. One could still find modern society and culture in crisis and bankrupt, even without attending to Auschwitz at all. It is a particularly useful, salutary occasion for such an interpretive shift, but it is not necessary, theologically, morally, politically, or psychologically. Fox makes this point about Rubenstein's return to Torah; it is all too voluntaristic and hence, like liberal Judaism and Reconstructionism in general, lacking in a binding, authoritative character.[97] Fox's point is a good one, albeit not an especially revealing one about Rubenstein. For it is no different from a standard criticism of any Jewish view too deeply wedded to will and autonomy. Fox's point is that without the traditional God of history, revelation, and Torah, "we not only lose the foundations of morality, we also lose the possibility of seeing human life as meaningful."[98] Surely Rubenstein would have no trouble responding to such a charge, just as any constructionist or sociobiologist would not. The pressing issue, for Rubenstein, must be that his naturalism weakens even the role of Auschwitz to the point where it is hardly clear why it *must* be the watershed event that Rubenstein takes it to be. For, if we are right, the most he can say is that it is an especially vivid, prominent, and informative occasion for stimulating the interpretive shift to realist social science as the core of Jewish self-understanding. On his terms, it is comprehensible in social scientific categories and does not yield any special obligations or psychological motivations, like guilt or anger.

In 1968, "Homeland and Holocaust" was published with responses by Milton

Himmelfarb, Zalman Schachter, Irving Greenberg, and Arthur Cohen. Himmelfarb's is a hostile attack filled with narrow readings and bad argument.[99] He takes
Rubenstein to conclude from Auschwitz that God is not good, which, as I have
shown, poorly represents how Rubenstein approaches Auschwitz and why.[100] It is
clear that Rubenstein takes Auschwitz to be a distinctive, watershed event in ways
that Himmelfarb does not. Nor does he try to understand Rubenstein's paganism
or his tragic realism.[101] He dislikes Rubenstein's tone, his apparent arrogance and
rhetoric, which is understandable but hardly constitutes a serious objection. Himmelfarb clearly finds value in the fideism of Cohen, Herberg, and Borowitz and is
angered by Rubenstein's dismissal of it.[102] All this is understandable but not really
illuminating. The comments of Greenberg and Cohen are more helpful, together
with Rubenstein's responses. But it will be more appropriate to consider these ex-
changes later, in the course of discussing the post-Holocaust reflections of Greenberg and Cohen.

Chapter Seven

Eliezer Berkovits and the Tenacity of Faith

One of the most important features of the Holocaust's impact on Germans, Christians, and Jews was the problem it raised about the relation between history and self-understanding or memory and identity. For Germans, from the sixties through the eighties, the problem perplexed artists, politicians, historians, and social theorists who were concerned not about the epistemological status of national identity—for they all agreed on its historical situatedness—but about the role of the Nazi era and the ways it threatened the project of national recovery, of constructing an acceptable national character. Guilt and negativity were the issues, and the threat was that Nazi criminality might prevent national recovery and occlude German character.

For Christians and for Jews, the problem concerned the negativity of Auschwitz and the recovery of specific traditions and traditional beliefs, about God, providence, election, mission, and redemption. But for them the central problem is the historicity of self-understanding and its relation to tradition and the past. Auschwitz raises the question whether religious self-understanding is *not* wholly historical. And it is a radical question, for it seems to fly in the face of the traditionalism of Western religions, their rootedness in transcendence and aspiration for a transhistorical objectivity. Moreover, I have shown that Rubenstein seemed to accept such a view about Judaism; he appreciated the central role of historical interpretation in the construction of Jewish identity and the capacity of a historical event to generate a radical revision in religious, historical life and thinking. For Rubenstein, it is not rational argument that leads to abandoning one vocabulary, one discourse, for another; it is life that does so—life, in the West, in America, at a moment of crisis and threat.

Eliezer Berkovits, an orthodox Jewish theologian and philosopher, once chairperson of the Department of Philosophy at the Hebrew Theological College in Skokie, Illinois, who moved to Israel in 1975, examines the same phenomena that occupy Rubenstein. He explores Western civilization and its history; he confronts the Holocaust, how and why it occurred, its victims, its criminals, and the bystanders; and he reflects on classic Jewish texts and ideas and Jewish history. But his results differ dramatically from those of Rubenstein and not only in detail. The two thinkers differ fundamentally. For Berkovits is as opposed to the historicity of Jewish belief and practice as Rubenstein is committed to it. Both seek guidance in a time of crisis for Judaism and for Western civilization. For Rubenstein the guidance is prudential and pragmatic; in a sense, he abandons the aspiration to standards beyond ourselves, history, and nature. He achieves no principled situatedness in history because principles beyond our own resources are an illusion. Berkovits, on the other hand, finds guidance in the past, in tradition and the truths of tradition, but he denies the historicity of Jewish faith. Himmelfarb, in his own way, challenged Rubenstein from a similar perspective, but he did so while denying the distinctive importance of Auschwitz. At just this point, where the search for guidance in a world of crisis and a commitment to the ahistorical character of Judaism join with a sensitivity to the unique efficacy of the Holocaust, of history, Berkovits's thinking achieves something important. For it exemplifies a traditionalism that nonetheless respects the power of history, that exposes itself to Auschwitz and yet survives.[1]

In the first sentence of *Faith after the Holocaust*, published in 1973, Berkovits tells us that "the main thesis of [the book] was worked out during the critical weeks that led up to the Six Day War between Israel and the Arab nations, and was completed during those drama-filled six days. . . . It was written under almost unbearable tension, and against darkest fears and anxieties."[2] Between 1967 and 1973, a few parts of the book appeared in *Judaism*, *Tradition*, and elsewhere, but the book provides the most coherent, systematic account of Berkovits's conception of Judaism, the Holocaust, and Israel. In 1979, Berkovits further developed his account in his book *With God in Hell: Judaism in the Ghettos and Death Camps*.[3] These are his major post-Holocaust works and the ones on which I will focus.

Berkovits begins by discussing the Holocaust as a human and historical event and by examining its relation to Christian anti-Semitism and the integrity of the victims. As he puts it, "even more important than the question, Where was God? is, Where was Man?"[4] Berkovits does not focus on the immediate criminals but rather on the supporters and bystanders, "the free world, the Allies, the churches, and some of the neutral nations,"[5] and the moral "consequences for the present human predicament," "the collapse of man as a moral being."[6] Relying on the famous works of Arthur Morse and Guenter Lewy,[7] Berkovits bitterly paints a picture of moral turpitude: "In essence there was no difference between the murderers of these children and those who refused to save them."[8] He calls America and the Allies "active accomplices in the greatest crime in history"[9] and "the Hitlerite demoralization of the West" and charges the Catholic Church with a distorted appeal to impartiality,[10] deeply embedded, he argues, in Christian anti-Semitism.[11] The consequence for the West is extreme: "in [the holocaust] Western civilization lost its every claim to dignity and respect."[12] On the one hand, then, the Shoah points to the moral collapse of Western civilization as the criminals and accomplices of atrocity. On the other, it does so by the attempt of many to implicate the victims themselves in their own destruction.[13] The charge of cooperation indicts those who make it.[14] In fact, Berkovits argues, the Jews of Europe acted more heroically than the Poles, Russians, and others who were imprisoned, tortured, and killed by the Nazis.[15] And when they accepted their fate and did not resist, there were good political, moral, and psychological reasons why they did so.

A careful analysis of Auschwitz shows that "it was a world catastrophe on the widest possible scale." As Berkovits sees it, the real issues raised by Auschwitz are moral ones about human nature. "Auschwitz ushered in the final phase in the moral disintegration of Western civilization."[16] It is a "final warning to the human race." In this regard, Berkovits's conclusion bears some similarity to Rubenstein's, for both see Western society at a moment of crisis. Where they differ concerns the role of Judaism in the crisis and its theological implications for Jewish belief.[17]

Berkovits frequently calls attention to the rather extreme differences between Judaism and Christianity. Some features of Christianity are historical and accidental, for example, the position of power that Christianity occupied from Constantine to the nineteenth century. But some are integral to Christianity: its spiritualism, understanding of salvation, otherworldliness, and doctrine of original sin.[18] Radical theology is radical precisely because it opposes much of this and affirms a new, positive attitude toward the world, human freedom, and human capability. Clinging to history rather than a denial of it, its symbol is the death of God, that is, the death of the God that cursed history and superseded it.[19] The death of God, then, reveals the crisis of Christianity in the contemporary world; it is the same moment in which the Jewish people has experienced catastrophe and hope, but Berkovits needs to explain how.

The first point that Berkovits makes about the Holocaust and the death camps, then, is that they indicate the crisis or bankruptcy of Western, Christian or post-Christian civilization. The second is that the Jews, who were its victims, responded in different ways. Some succumbed but some did not, and among the latter were many whose faith was confirmed in acts of religious and moral heroism. For religious persons, it was appropriate for them to ask for God's aid and to challenge him, but many still performed acts of kindness and friendship and refrained from killing, even in the ghettos and the camps, under extraordinary conditions. Berkovits sees the camps as threatening to this faith in the "promise of existence." Some then and after were so overwhelmed that they would come to treat human existence as a tragedy, absurd; Berkovits uses Camus as an example. But this was not the only alternative; he finds too "affirmations of faith . . . made meaningfully notwithstanding God's terrible silence during the Holocaust."[20]

Berkovits notes that different questions and options are appropriate for different people. We, who come after and were not victims, are neither participants nor bystanders. We are, he says, "Job's brothers."[21] Our problem is situational, and while it is not that of Job, the victim, it is guided or at least shaped by our relation to him.[22] According to Berkovits, "those of us who were not there must, before anything else, heed the responses of those who were, for theirs alone are the authentic ones."[23] Berkovits argues that the victims faced a uniquely powerful, threatening, oppressive, and painful situation. We really cannot judge their conduct, for it is itself the standard for judging responses to the camps and the atrocities. This is what Berkovits means when he says that their conduct alone is authentic as a response and that we must "heed" their actions. Moreover, when we apply the victims' conduct as a standard for authentic religious response, we realize, Berkovits argues, that we ought not either reject faith or accept it; in either case, we would "desecrate" their conduct, belittling or demeaning the courageous faith of some and the angry but justified rejection of others. Berkovits claims that we should stand in awe of those who went to the gas chambers singing "Ani Maamin" and at the same time sympathize with those for whom the unendurable agony was too much.

> The faith affirmed was superhuman; the loss of faith—in the circumstances—human. . . . The faith is holy; but so, also, is the disbelief and the religious rebellion of the concentration camps holy . . . faith crushed, shattered, pulverized; and faith murdered a millionfold is holy disbelief. Those who were not there and, yet, readily accept the holocaust as the will of God that must not be questioned, desecrate the holy disbelief of those whose faith was murdered. And those who were not there, and yet join with self-assurance the rank of the disbelievers, desecrate the holy faith of the believers.[24]

According to Berkovits, then, the standard of authenticity for Jewish survivors, for Job's siblings, includes the holy belief and the holy disbelief of the victims. For us, both an unchallenged, simple or naive faith that Auschwitz is divine providence and a confident, self-assured denial of God because of Auschwitz are unacceptable. In this quotation, Berkovits gives one side of his argument: facile faith betrays the victims who abandoned faith in the face of incomparable suffering, and assured skepticism betrays those who clung to faith despite all their pain and misery. But there is more: facile faith betrays too the heroic faith of some victims, while assured skepticism betrays the victims who denied God but only when they experienced for themselves unspeakable horrors. Hence Berkovits applies as his standard of authenticity the varied responses of the victims: "in the presence of the holy faith of the crematoria, the ready faith of those who were not there, is vulgarity. But the disbelief of the sophisticated intellectual in the midst of an affluent society—in the light of the holy disbelief of the crematoria—is obscenity." The authentic response for Job's brother, Job's sibling, is a *questioning belief*; this, he says, "is our condition in this era after the holocaust."[25] This standard provides the religious imperative for post-Holocaust Jewish survivors. It mandates a fundamental Jewish posture—his or her "religious bearings"—and sets a standard of adequacy for response in act and in thought. In so doing, it rules out as inauthentic, Berkovits believes, radical theologians who abandon faith altogether and a kind of facile orthodoxy; it is not clear exactly whom, if anyone, Berkovits has in mind here, although it is very possible that the radical theologian he has in mind is Rubenstein as a disciple of Camus and compatriot of Thomas Altizer, Harvey Cox, and William Hamilton.[26]

It is very important to realize that for Berkovits faith after Auschwitz occurs at a moment of crisis for Western civilization that is also a moment of crisis for faith itself. As he puts it, faith cannot pass by the horror of the camps in silence.[27] But this sense of crisis is not new; it is a permanent feature of faith that the experience of agony and suffering registers in a questioning of divine justice and of God's involvement. In a sense, the standard for authentic response that arises out of Auschwitz recalls a *traditional pattern*: the experience of suffering regularly calls for a questioning or a rebellious faith. "The man of faith questions God because of his faith."[28] If Berkovits is right, the standard for post-Holocaust religious response arises out of the experiences in the camps, and these recover a traditional Jewish pattern: "the questioning of God's providence in the death camps was taking place within the classical tradition of Judaism."[29] To Rubenstein, Auschwitz discredits normative Jewish vocabulary and concepts; to Berkovits, it recalls precisely a feature of normative Jewish faith, the way that such faith responds to suffering and agony, challenges God but does not reject him. Berkovits puts the point in terms of a question: can one affirm one's faith meaningfully "notwithstanding God's terrible silence during the Holocaust?"[30]

The challenge that faces Job's brother or sibling, the post-Holocaust Jewish survivor, is one also faced by Abraham and Job. But Berkovits goes further: the outcome of one's questioning should still be faith, and this will be so because the Holocaust should be understood as part of Jewish and world history and ultimately in terms of traditional Jewish categories. In chapters 4 and 5 Berkovits sets out the main features of traditional Jewish theology, its conception of the task of the Jewish people, and its theory of history. Auschwitz requires not a rejection of traditional Jewish thought but rather its appropriation. It furthermore requires no theological revision at all. But if so, why is it still so tremendously important? Why is its impact so decisive? This, in a sense, is Berkovits's chief task: to show that our response to Auschwitz ought to be completely traditional but that it is also obligatory to take it with complete seriousness. In short, Auschwitz must be both continuous and discontinuous with Jewish tradition.

To meet the challenge of the world crisis, the Jew needs to understand his or her role in history and "to embrace" it, and this requires "placing the threefold experience of this generation—Auschwitz, Jerusalem, and the new threat to Jewish survival—in the comprehensive context of the world history of the Jewish people, of Jewish teaching, and of Jewish experience."[31] Berkovits refuses to treat these three in isolation from Jewish history, and this refusal reveals his commitment to find a continuous narrative for Jewish history and tradition that will give these events a special place but still a place. Moreover, since Auschwitz is, as he admits, an occasion of evil, that means the placing of evil in a history for which God is ultimately responsible; the evil must have "room in the scheme," he believes.[32] One must find a way to accept God's ultimate responsibility for Auschwitz. Berkovits's strategy will be to identify a theory of divine providence and history that incorporates a solution to the problem of evil—a completely general solution—and yet finds a *special* role for *this* evil.[33]

First, Berkovits incorporates Auschwitz into the framework of the traditional problem of evil: "the problem of faith presented by the holocaust is not unique in the context of the entirety of Jewish experience. From the point of view of the problem, we have had innumerable Auschwitzes."[34] What Judaism needs is a general doctrine of how a personal, providential God is related to a world in which suffering, pain, and agony exist.[35] This of course is the traditional problem of evil, and to find a solution for ourselves, Berkovits notes, we need to search the past.[36] We need not trace Berkovits's examination of the various theories of divine providence reflected in biblical and rabbinic texts.[37] It is sufficient to notice that these theories culminate in one that becomes normative and is most satisfactory. Berkovits associates the theory with the notion of *hester panim*, God's hiding of his face, when God is present but silent, and with texts in *Psalms, Jeremiah*, and *Isaiah*.[38] Alongside the accounts of such silence as punishment and indifference, Berkovits finds a different interpretation: hiding the face as a divine attribute, as an essential feature of God's permanent relation to human existence itself and to the world.[39] This is the traditional terminology that Berkovits uses; he fills it with a content that is also traditional. Evil, he argues, is innocent suffering, the result of human conduct, harm, injury, and injustice. But such action requires freedom on the part of human agents. Freedom, however, occurs only in virtue of divine self-restraint; human agents choose freely only because God allows such choices to occur and issue in actions. In short, Berkovits argues that the Bible and the Talmud articulate the traditional free will defense as a solution to the problem of evil.[40] The creation of humankind, which involves free will and the possibility of suffering, is a divine decision; to ask: why does God allow suffering is to ask: why did God create human life at all. God wants human goodness but only freely chosen; there is suffering but also hope. God is both present and absent at once.[41]

This present and absent God, moreover, with his unconvincing hiddenness, is verified in history by his people Israel. They manifest his desires and his guidance, but they do so voluntarily.[42] There are, Berkovits claims, two histories, that of the nations—what he calls "power history"—and that of Israel, "faith history." It is the task of the Jewish people to cultivate faith history, to teach and attempt to create a world of moral correctness and the good.[43] The history of the nations, Hobbesian history, is a history of politics and economics, of desire, power, and competition. The history of the Jewish people differs; "it testifies to a supra-natural dimension jutting into history."[44] It is the history of a people committed to justice, principle, right, and integrity. The conflict Berkovits portrays is between nature and morality, between is and ought, fact and value. This of course is an old distinction, now widely discredited and rejected.[45] But Berkovits finds it deep in Jewish texts and tradition, and his claim is that it is related to the notions of freedom, moral purpose, and divine providence. The result is a theory of God's relation to human experience and to history, a theory into which Auschwitz can be placed and a traditional theory grounded in the biblical and rabbinic texts.

How is that placement achieved? In the course of faith history and of power history, what does Auschwitz mean? As Berkovits points out, if we are concerned with Auschwitz in its particularity, the question should not be about God and evil. "The proper question is whether, after Auschwitz, the Jewish people may still be witnesses to God's elusive presence in history as we understand that concept."[46] The Holocaust and Nazism are powerful expressions of the "moral disintegration" of Western civilization.[47] They and other phenomena, including the use and threat of nuclear weapons, indicate how dominant have become the forces of power, brute conflict, cynicism, and competition. In such a climate, the commitment to moral purpose and faith in divine will could easily have been overwhelmed and destroyed. Berkovits calls this possibility "extinction through hopelessness" and an "hour of universal spiritual exhaustion."[48] The Holocaust, then, has no theological implications for Jewish faith; it is no greater a problem for Jewish thought about God, evil, and history than the death of one innocent child. "It does not," as Berkovits puts it, "preempt the entire course of Jewish history";[49] rather it fits it. In so doing, moreover, it does have nontheological implications; it does challenge Jewish faith not in content but in fact, as it were. In other words, the Holocaust could demoralize Jews so thoroughly that they would no longer witness to God's purposes, to faith history. The Holocaust, then, has psychological and historical implications for continued Jewish fidelity and survival at a moment of utter hopelessness. Jewish faith after Auschwitz is unchallenged in one sense and yet challenged in another; Auschwitz is both a link and a rupture, but unlike the way it is so for Rubenstein. Auschwitz is placed into the scheme of Jewish history two ways, as the ultimate manifestation of power history and as the agent for Israel's demoralization.

But, if Berkovits is right, the psychological impact, the exhaustion, was not terminal, for an event occurred that facilitated revival and rejuvenation. This was of course the reestablishment of the state of Israel. Psychologically and historically, it served to revive the people's commitment to their divine purpose, their sense of allegiance. Berkovits calls it a "vindication" of faith, an expression of divine providence, and a proclamation of "God's holy presence at the very heart of his inscrutable hiddenness."[50] If Auschwitz was a stimulus to psychological demoralization and hence if it was destructive, then the reestablishment of the Jewish state was a stimulus to psychological renewal. But how did it function and was it wholly accidental?

Israel served to invigorate Jewish faith by providing a framework or context in which Jews could create a culture and society founded on faith and moral principle, a moral polity.[51] By itself, political autonomy did nothing, but as a means to enable Jewish life, it was crucial, the reality in which the people could carry out its messianic task.[52] But was it fortuitous? Clearly not, but if not, why not? Recall the words that Berkovits uses to describe the state, an expression of divine providence and a proclamation of "God's holy presence."[53] Does this mean that the state, in a sense, is a product of divine intervention into the historical process, a miracle? And if God could intervene to enable the creation of the state and revive the Jewish people, why could he not intervene at Auschwitz to save them? The answers to these questions are that for Berkovits it is a miracle but not an act of divine intervention. As Berkovits puts it, the survival of this people and the persistence of faith history are the only historical miracle. "All God's miracles occur outside of history."[54] Only this one, performed by Jews freely in virtue of and in behalf of God's absence and His presence, occurs in history. The continued existence of the people of Israel as a people of faith *testifies* to "God's 'powerless' guidance in the affairs of men."[55] The state of Israel, a human creation, testifies to the same divine reality. Hence it is divine and human, a humanly constituted divine reality. This does not make it necessary in the sense of destined or determined, but it does make it necessary to history in the sense that without it history would be incomplete, not both divine and sacred. And this is consistent with the Jewish view of providence, whereby human moral conduct must be free and an expression of God's unconvincing presence, his hidden presence, and because without morality, nature is only partial and inadequate.

Berkovits notes that he began these reflections in the spring of 1967, prior to the Arab threat to Israel's existence and prior to the Six Day War. Once again, a threat was averted, and Israel was reprieved. But, he asks, was this too an act of divine providence? Was it an act of divine intervention? How, Berkovits asks, should the Six Day War be understood?[56] If it was experienced as a moment of revelation, what does the event and that experience mean?[57] Berkovits first registers the fact that "the majority [of the contemporary generation of Jews] experienced the recent confrontation between the state of Israel and the Arab nations as a moment of messianic history."[58] For the first time since antiquity, Jerusalem is the capital of a Jewish state, the result of events that were "unexpected" and "unwanted" yet "dramatically sudden."[59] Berkovits uses such language—"the transformation was rapid, radical, and unenvisaged"—to suggest why the events carried their "revelational impact."[60] The outcome, the reunification of Jerusalem and return of the old city, was unexpected yet longed for; the most unanticipated was the least anticipated.[61] There was, with the recovery of Jerusalem, a new sense of unity, with the past and among all Jews. Berkovits calls this not the Messiah but a "messianic moment, in which the unexpected fruits of human endeavor reveal themselves as the mysterious manifestation of divine guidance of whose coming the heart was forever sure."[62] It was a revelation of the direction of Jewish life and of history after Auschwitz, "a smile on the face of God."[63] A locale has been provided and now defended in which God's plan — the moral life — can be worked out; it is "the existential reality within which the deed of practical faith could flourish."[64] After centuries of shrinking domains of applicability, Berkovits claims, the Jewish people has been granted a venue for executing the Judaic deed, bringing faith to nature, morality to a Hobbesian world.[65] In short, the sudden victory, the unexpected return to Jerusalem, the moment of opportunity after utter destruction, all this is inexplicable without reference to God and the divine plan for the people of Israel in world history.[66]

For this reason, in Berkovits's view, the state of Israel is the primary venue, in a post-Holocaust world, for the working out of Jewish destiny. Hence, as he examines the attacks on Israel after the war in 1967, the negative world opinion, the silence, if not criticism of churches around the world, and more, Berkovits is defensive and angry. He is indeed in a difficult position, for he feels compelled to give Israel, the state, government, and society, a theologically preeminent position, while he knows full well the complications of social-political life. He wants to distinguish Israel's essence, as a bastion of moral probity, and her reality, as a participant in "power history."[67] Whether this can be achieved is doubtful, but Berkovits is committed to continuing his separation between fact and value, for his overall strategy is to distinguish the two, to separate history from faith, psychology and politics from faith and morality, and then to bring them together again.[68] But the categories are problematic and show the strain, as much as anywhere, when he seems forced to exaggerate Israel's political and social life in the aftermath of the Six Day War.[69] Perhaps his pessimism, his despair about Western society and civilization, are plausible, but his special pleading for Israel and the Jewish people has a rhetorical, homiletic, parochial tone that is deeply rooted in his own imperialism. All of this, however, to a certain extent instigated by his overall approach, is a by-product of his achievement, his attempt to give both historicity and religious principle their due, to find a way to take history and the Holocaust seriously while arguing that they do not alter the categories of traditional Jewish self-understanding.

The final pages of *Faith after the Holocaust* end on a note of hopefulness, an optimism that should not fade into despair and yet must avoid being easy or glib. Berkovits expresses his doubts and his hopes; by telling two tales of acts of genuineness and integrity by victims of Nazism he gives evidence in behalf of faith and moral dignity in the midst of human atrocity.[70] This should remind us that the word "after" in the title of Berkovits's book is extremely important. His task was to construct an adequate or authentic Jewish response to Auschwitz for those who did not experience the camps but live after them, for "Job's brother," as he puts it. The standard for such a response is the conduct of the victims, and in these last pages he reminds us of that. At the same time, he indirectly calls attention to a requirement yet to be satisfied: the questioning faith that he recommends to Job's brother or sister is grounded in two features of the experience of Auschwitz, the unspeakable horrors that the victims had to endure and the courageous faith of at least some of those victims. In 1979 Berkovits published a work that dealt with the second of these themes. In it he tries to clarify the faith of the victims as a standard for post-Holocaust Jewish faith.

With God in Hell: Judaism in the Ghettos and Deathcamps draws on memoirs, diaries, and other reports to try to understand what Jewish faith in the Nazi world amounted to.[71] It therefore serves to verify one dimension of the standard for the faith of Job's siblings and also to clarify what we mean by such faith.[72]

Berkovits records small acts of faithfulness and a host of *halakhic* cases concerning life and death, birth, and even suicide. In extraordinary conditions, people sought to live and practice as Jews, to pray, celebrate, and act according to custom and tradition. Berkovits sees this phenomenon as an act of nonsubmission: "Now while it is true to say that the authentic Jew also tried to adjust himself to the physical conditions of the ghettos and the death camps, the *raison d'être* of his entire existence became his heroic refusal to adopt the standards and values of the Holocaust world into which he had been thrown. . . . His inner center of gravity is not anchored in the outside world."[73] As Améry also noticed, this "inner center" enabled the authentic religious Jew to resist the degradation and to retain some element of dignity and hope. In the end, given the moral and political crisis of Western civilization, such resistance must be counted as a moral rebellion against evil, a rebellion grounded in this "inner center" and in a trust in God that supersedes the evil, the pain, and the suffering.[74] In their actions and in their words, victims of Nazism—not all but certainly some—exhibited this resistance and this faith, notwithstanding and indeed in spite of the extraordinary circumstances they endured. This, Berkovits claims, is authentic faith, a living trust that challenges and yet enables a life of principle and a life with God.

Berkovits's account of post-Holocaust Jewish faith involves three elements. First, he distinguishes the faith of the victims from the faith and the response of those who are the descendants of the victims, Job's brothers, as he calls them. This is a central distinction for Berkovits, and it leads him to two conclusions. One is that the faith and the disbelief of the victims becomes the standard for authentic post-Holocaust Jewish faith; it yields the notion of a questioning or doubting faith that serves as such a standard, a faith that lapses into neither a glib, easy piety nor a facile skepticism. The other, which Berkovits does not notice, is that there is a historical dimension to faith; it is situated and perspectival. It involves a response to one's circumstances and the events that shape one's situation. Faith, in short, is hermeneutical and historical.

The second feature of Berkovits's account is that the content of authentic Jewish faith contains a theory of providence and history, a solution to the problem of evil in terms of God's hiding his face, and a conception of the role of the Jewish people in history. These views arise out of biblical and rabbinic Judaism and are as viable now as at any moment in Jewish history. They are, in a sense, permanent features of Jewish self-understanding.

Finally, the Holocaust can be understood according to these conceptions of providence and evil. But, at the same time, the death camps and the Nazi atrocities, as historical events, mark a particular stage in history and have historical implications. They indicate a crisis in Western civilization when power and nature have become so dominant that there seems little hope for moral purpose and for limits on competition, acquisitiveness, and violence. They also, then, threaten to overwhelm the moral purposes of Jewish life, its spirituality and commitment to shaping life in terms of God's plan. Auschwitz threatens to demoralize the Jewish people and to destroy its will to bring moral character to history, politics, and nature. Israel, its reestablishment, its defense, and its reunification in 1967, provides the psychological renewal to offset this demoralization. Hence it is a historical miracle, a human event that exhibits and facilitates divine purposes in history.

Berkovits explicitly denies that Auschwitz transforms Jewish theological self-understanding. But he acknowledges the historicity, as well as the transcendence, of Jewish faith. He takes Auschwitz seriously at two points in this thinking, at its outset when the victims' faith is recognized as the standard of authenticity for post-Holocaust Jewish faith and later when Auschwitz is seen to play historical and psychological roles within history itself. Jewish faith, then, confronts Auschwitz externally and internally, as it were. Externally Auschwitz provides a historically particular standard for the character of faith; internally, it psychologically threatens the vitality and self-confidence of ongoing Jewish commitment. What Auschwitz does not do, however, is pose a new problem for Jewish theological self-understanding. Berkovits's conception of providence and his solution to the problem of evil are wholly traditional. Miracles are human actions that engage divine purposes; they are freedom manifest for moral purposes. God's presence and his absence coalesce to enable people to engage in voluntary, moral conduct. In effect, Berkovits's standard of authenticity serves to reject one set of responses to evil, those that treat evil as retribution. In this respect, Berkovits is akin to Rubenstein, for whom such a response would entail an obscene result. But whereas Rubenstein takes this rejection as telling against all traditional concepts of God, covenant, and providence, Berkovits does not. His version of the so-called free will defense, which he articulates in the biblical language of God's hiding his face, and in the vocabulary of faith and power history, is still available.[75] Whereas Rubenstein feels compelled to recover a naturalist, social scientific account of the Holocaust and of Jewish history, Berkovits finds his providential view of Judaism and faith history still available. It is even, in a sense, necessary, since the standard of the victims' response rules out a facile skepticism as much as an unquestioning faith. In this respect, Berkovits's discussion is more nuanced, more subtle than Rubenstein's global and undefended dismissal of all historical, providential conceptions of God, covenant, and history. Structurally, however, their accounts are very similar, for both recognize the historical situatedness of an authentic post-Holocaust response and both seek some recovery of Judaism within that situation.

Berkovits, however, does achieve something rather remarkable. As a traditional thinker, his conception of the content of Judaism and Jewish faith is unconditional and nonhistorical. The problem of evil is a perennial one; Judaism's understanding of God, history, miracle, revelation, and covenant is universal and absolute. Yet, given this commitment to a timeless conception of Judaism, Berkovits still feels compelled—morally bound—to appreciate the historical influence of Auschwitz. He is able to do this because for him faith involves life within the Jewish people; it is part of a nexus of relationship and response that is utterly historical. Here, at the psychological, historical, and political level, Auschwitz plays its decisive roles. In the end, for Berkovits, Auschwitz leaves faith untouched, at the same time that it decisively affects the life of faith. To have seen how this is so and to have articulated such realities is Berkovits's achievement. Too often his work is viewed simply as a traditional, uncomplicated treatment of Jewish faith and Auschwitz. This assessment is itself unsympathetic and certainly too superficial. Berkovits wrestles with a serious problem, his allegiance to an ahistorical set of Jewish beliefs and doctrines and his honest and deep sensitivity to the victims of Nazi criminality, and to a degree he solves it. He recognizes both the continuity and the discontinuity that Auschwitz registers between the post-Holocaust Jew and the Jewish past. He seeks to understand what it means to be "Job's brother," to accept the darkness for what it is and yet to transcend it while remaining true to his understanding of traditional Judaism.

Chapter Eight

Irving Greenberg and the Post-Holocaust Voluntary Covenant

L ike Eliezer Berkovits, Irving Greenberg is an orthodox rabbi and a deeply traditional Jewish figure. But he is also a bold and radical Jewish thinker and one for whom Auschwitz and Jerusalem represent transforming events in Judaism, Christianity, and the modern world. Greenberg was a member of the group of young Jewish theologians who met during the sixties to revive the notions of faith and covenant, struggled with revelation and *halakhah*, and sought a renewal of Judaism in America in the postwar period and the sixties. With other members of the group, in the years 1965–67, Greenberg began to think seriously about the transforming character of the Holocaust, and as a historian he studied the Nazi period. In the late sixties Greenberg was concerned about unity in American Judaism, pluralism, and the problems of Jewish practise and education.[1] By the early seventies, his thinking had become more focused on the Holocaust and its religious and moral implications. The first important result of this work and still his single most revealing account of these matters was "Cloud of Smoke, Pillar of Fire: Judaism, Christianity, and Modernity after the Holocaust," published in 1977. But before I turn to it and other essays of the same period,[2] I want to look first at Greenberg's essays from the late sixties in order to expose the roots of his interpretive openness and his receptivity to revision.

Greenberg's essays of the late sixties have common themes and a common strategy. They are largely historical and practical in spirit and attempt to articulate a platform for reform within Jewish Orthodoxy in America. Greenberg examines the American cultural and social situation in the late sixties, studies Jewish identity in America, and proposes various educational, ritual, and social strategies for dealing in the most authentic way with the American situation of Orthodox Judaism. In these essays, his goal is a pluralistic Judaism that seeks and finds ways of living authentically in the new situations in which it finds itself in twentieth-century American life and culture.[3] The Holocaust plays no explicit role in Greenberg's

thinking in these essays. His analysis is historical, contextual, and pragmatic; it is
not theoretical or theological in any detailed sense. It advocates an integration of authority and *halakhah* with individual choice, but it never tries to understand or defend such a unity.[4] It claims that Judaism must be particularist and universalist, but
it does not explore how this is possible. Above all, Greenberg is deeply concerned
about the survival of Judaism and the character of Jewish life, and the motivations
for his worries are the state of Jewish life in America and the failure of American
Jewish institutions to deal creatively and effectively with its problems. I will look
at some of the details of Greenberg's account; they will help, when I turn to his
writings about the post-Holocaust situation, to identify what his attentiveness to
Auschwitz contributes, whether it revises his assessment of the features and needs
of the Jewish situation or whether it dramatizes what he already, in these earlier essays, had identified as the central problems of American Jewish life.

Writing in 1965, Greenberg points out the affluence, the openness, and the he-
donistic ethos of American society and the massive way that Jews have, in the postwar years, become participants in the life of consumption, upward mobility, and
material success.[5] Greenberg's diagnosis of the Jewish situation, however, is that the
success has dramatically shattered genuine Jewish identity: "the [American Jew] is
a quintessential middle class American secularist in faith, culture, and practice."[6]
He draws an unremarkable conclusion, that Judaism in America is at risk, for it
lacks an authentic "group ethos" that maintains and justifies its distinctiveness.
Some are seeking such an ethos or identity;[7] many simply accept the secularism and
universalism that mark their lives, together with the intermarriage, the reduced
birth rate, and the other factors that threaten Jewish survival. With the high rate of
Jews entering universities, the college context is an especially powerful vehicle for
the erosion of Jewish identity and the promotion of American, Enlightenment secular humanism.[8] Hence, for Greenberg, a revival of Jewish life on college campuses
is a priority for the revitalization of a distinctive Jewish identity in the context of
this crisis of survival.[9]

As an orthodox rabbi and as someone immersed in orthodox Jewish life, Greenberg is especially troubled about the response of Orthodox Judaism to this situation
of crisis. His primary concern is the character of American society and its ethos:
"the new ethic is more universalist, relativist, self and pleasure oriented."[10] Affluence, productivity, availability of commodities, access to consumer goods, all of this
has permeated the Jewish community and eroded its sense of rule, obligation, and
obedience.[11] Greenberg argues against withdrawal and isolation as impractical, ineffective, and inappropriate.[12] His alternative is a modern orthodoxy that separates
the religious core of Judaism from its old cultural style and seeks to restore "the
Torah in the new emergent culture."[13] This process would require maintaining the
integrity and distinctiveness of Jewish life while situating it in the general culture
and society. Jews would become involved in issues of social justice as an expression
of their Judaism and not as a surrogate for it,[14] and they would find value in the joys

and resources available to them, while realizing the purpose and role of such op-portunities.[15]

The young Jewish theologians of the postwar period were preoccupied with the relationship between freedom and authority in Judaism and especially with issues concerning revelation, covenant, mitzvah, and *halakhah*. Fackenheim, Borowitz, and Petuchowski, for example, drew on the work of Franz Rosenzweig in order to articulate a plausible concept of revelation, interpretation, and mitzvah that incor-porated both divine command and human obedience, divine power and human freedom. Orthodox thinkers like Walter Wurzberger and Greenberg approached the same problem from a traditional rather than a liberal perspective. Greenberg's historical orientation already disposed him to some kind of pluralism and volun-tarism with regard to the traditions of Jewish belief and practice. Judaism, for him, changes as the historical situation changes, and it is self-constituting to the degree that it involves a selective, revisionary appropriation of the resources of Jewish texts, ideas, and practices.[16] To be sure, the Jew is bound to God through a vast array of interpretations of God's will, but that array has many strata, many levels and vari-ations, some dominant today, others subordinate or even repressed.[17] The challenge of constructing an authentic contemporary Jewish identity in America requires some selective appropriation and reconstruction from that array, some sense of obedience and obligation, but no particular one. Greenberg of course refused to succumb to the extreme voluntarism that he associates with the relativism and he-donism of American culture.[18] Nor, given his commitment to God, would he opt for a rational voluntarism, Kantian or otherwise. But he also opposed dogmatism and an "intellectual surrender of judgment" that registers in deference to absolute rabbinic authority.[19]

At the center of Greenberg's early thinking, then, is a new orthodox acceptance of human understanding and human decision. Greenberg puts it in terms that seem to echo Rosenzweig: "we need a greater recognition that God speaks in the *mitzvot* but that man, too, must be deeply involved in the response.... God's speech (or the *Gadol*'s in His name) should be the beginning and not the end of the re-sponse."[20] This compact, elliptical formulation does not address the issue: what *is* the content of revelation? Is revelation verbal and propositional or an event that is itself preverbal? Indeed, Greenberg seems to imply that the human response he has in mind involves reflecting on why and to what end the mitzvah is given and hence why and whether it should be performed; this is not yet radical enough for those in the Rosenzweigian tradition who would consider the human response as consti-tutive of the *content* of the revelation itself.[21] Alternatively, one might think this ac-count too radical, for it leaves open the possibility of an authority that is rational and pragmatic rather than divine in origin.[22] However we interpret it, Greenberg's ac-knowledgment of the role of human thought and choice within the *halakhic* process is a serious deflection away from standard orthodox thinking and indeed from any extreme traditionalism.

Greenberg's account of how free will and choice figure in a Judaism committed to norms and authority is not a theological or philosophical account. It occurs as part of a discussion of Jewish education and has a psychological, pragmatic character.[23] "Norms of behavior and value" are essential to Judaism, but why accept a determinative, central role for human freedom? Greenberg gives a pragmatic argument: we seek obedience to divine norms, to *mitzvot*; freely accepted laws are better supported and more obeyed than the laws of a despot—"our voluntaristic society has demonstrated an extraordinary capacity to elicit loyalty and sacrifice from its people. . . . Clearly people identify most strongly with laws which they feel they have voluntarily accepted";[24] therefore, we should educate Jews to accept the *mitzvot* freely. One purpose of Jewish education should be to help the student understand the purpose and significance of traditional norms in order to promote the "actual appropriation, analysis and voluntary acceptance of them" and "to appropriate restrictions as voluntary purposeful direction."[25] Hence free acceptance is not random or arbitrary; it is acceptance guided by rational deliberation based on an understanding of a practice's significance. Greenberg calls this a "restoration of the dialectic of freedom and authority."[26]

The result of Greenberg's new orthodoxy would be a greater attention to meaningful religious observance, a commitment to projects and causes that serve all people,[27] and an appreciation of genuine pluralism. I have pointed out that the fragmentation into specific group loyalties in the late sixties is an important setting for understanding Jewish life and thought in America during this period. Greenberg sees this too. His advocacy of a positive, ideological commitment to pluralism is, in part, a strategy for survival, rooted in his voluntarism and his historical sensibility. But it is grounded as well in his awareness that in America the tendency toward unity in virtue of commonality is "now being superceded [*sic*] by a search for a pluralism that respects differences. The new emphasis defends the Negro's right not to be just another white American in dark skin. . . . The will to encounter the other in his own terms opens up the possibility that Judaism can speak in its own authentic categories and yet be heard."[28] Here is an opportunity for a distinctiveness that moderates between abstract universalism and divisive ethnocentrism or crude parochialism. It is also a serious need; in a situation with increasing commitments to difference, groups seek a fuller expression of group ethos and identity. But, as Peter Berger would later put it in *The Heretical Imperative,* the content of that identity is chosen as well as received; in other words, it is an interpretive project grounded in individual spontaneity.[29]

By 1974 Greenberg's commitment to change within American Orthodoxy and to a more pluralistic appropriation of tradition had shifted to a preoccupation with the "religious and ethical implications of the Holocaust."[30] When a similar shift had occurred in Berkovits's thinking, the result was threefold: the recognition of the experience of the victims as a standard for authentic post-Holocaust faith; the comprehension of the theological meaning of Auschwitz within a traditional doctrine of providence and history; and the historical-psychological relevance of Auschwitz and Israel within an account of the crisis of Western civilization. In a sense, what enabled Berkovits to take Auschwitz seriously without giving it a special theological significance was the character of his theology, the distinction between the content as theory and its historical level of implementation. Berkovits's view of God, providence, and history, however, had already been worked out; he simply used it as the framework for dealing with Auschwitz.[31] On the face of it, Greenberg's approach to historical and theological issues seems more radical. He advocates dramatic changes in Orthodox practice and belief; he argues for a keen sense of universality through difference, a critical attitude toward the appropriation of *halakhah*, a revised program of education, changes in Jewish institutional life, and a "dialectic of freedom and authority" in our understanding of revelation and law. But, at the same time, Greenberg takes these changes to be results of detaching the Jewish religious tradition from its current cultural tradition and exposing the former to our new social and cultural world. Such an approach might be taken to imply that a religious core remains, untouched and unaltered, throughout this process. I doubt that it does, but Greenberg might not see it this way. He might think that there is in Judaism a detachable, transcendent core that is immune to history; when Judaism changes, this core remains the same. If Greenberg believed this, then he would be more like Berkovits than is first apparent.

Another way of formulating this issue is to ask whether, for Greenberg, Auschwitz has theological implications. Is it capable of altering the most central, deepest of Jewish beliefs about God, covenant, providence, redemption, and Jewish purpose? Whatever we might think about Greenberg's early essays and the relation between history and religious tradition articulated in them, the essays of the seventies tell a powerful and decisive story.

Greenberg begins by pointing out that both Judaism and Christianity are religions of redemption, that their conceptions of redemption are interpretations of human fate based on historical experiences, and that these conceptions affect people in history.[32] Central to both religions are views about history and its course. These views are responses to historical events, and their content influences conduct and life. Moreover, these views, as interpretive responses to events, are themselves historical events, both their articulation and their content. Hence, Greenberg concludes, both religions are open to historical modification: "implicit in both religions is the realization that events happen in history which change our perception of human fate" and "one such event is the Holocaust—the destruction of European Jewry from 1933 to 1945."[33] Judaism and Christianity, as views about redemption and hence about human history, change as a result of events in history.

To a historian and to common sense, this affirmation may sound like a truism. But to a theologian, especially a traditionalist, it is a momentous claim.[34] Is it a position that Greenberg comes to as a historian? Because of the crisis of Orthodoxy in America? As a result of reflection on the nature of Jewish and Christian theol-

ogy? Or as a response to something about Auschwitz? Greenberg's claim invokes
the recognition that Judaism is wholly historical, a hermeneutical enterprise grounded
in its historical situation. It is the recognition that I have shown Fackenheim to
make on philosophical grounds and that he called the most crucial change in his
thinking. Here we see Greenberg make it as well—and we see how much like
Rubenstein and Fackenheim it is and how much more radical than Berkovits's
more conditional appreciation of the historical situatedness of Jewish faith. What
are Greenberg's reasons for such a dramatically historicist position?

When read carefully, the early pages of Greenberg's essay reveal imprecision, if
not ambiguity, about this extremely important question. It is not clear whether
Greenberg arrived at his view about the historical character of religious belief independently of reflection on Auschwitz, whether reflection on Auschwitz occasioned such a conclusion, or whether it led to the conclusion or provided the primary reason for it. Indeed, there is evidence in the essay for all of these possibilities.
For example, the early paragraphs suggest the first one, and the line of thinking is
that which I sketched earlier.

But, two paragraphs later, Greenberg focuses on Auschwitz in a new way. He
argues that "the Holocaust is obviously central for Jews" because the level of destruction requires a "basic reorientation in light of [the Holocaust] by the surviving
Jewish community."[35] This reorientation would involve rethinking the meaning of
the covenant and the requirements for its survival and performance. Greenberg
even hints that the "magnitude of suffering" and the Nazi process of dehumanization are evils that cannot be dealt with by traditional categories and require revision
and absolute opposition.[36] "Judaism and Christianity . . . stand or fall on their fundamental claim that the human being is, therefore, of ultimate and absolute
value."[37] Greenberg then calls on the testimony of a Polish guard at Auschwitz,
S. Szmaglewska, concerning the burning alive of Jewish infants in order, she sur-
mises, to "economize on gas." He historically analyzes what that meant—"in the
summer of 1944, a Jewish child's life was not worth the two-fifths of a cent it would
have cost to put it to death rather than burn it alive"—in order to show vividly the
Nazi evil and its challenge to any confidence about God and the absolute value of
human life. One point of this argument is to demonstrate that reflection on the
Holocaust is at least an occasion for realizing that even the most central affirmations of Judaism and Christianity about human life can be altered. But another
might be that Auschwitz itself is *reason*—and perhaps the primary reason—for
doubting the immutability and transcendence of religious faith.[38]

Greenberg, then, has reasons for the unconditional historicity of Jewish religious
belief. Moreover, he realizes that the issue is one of self-understanding.[39] It concerns
the self-recognition of Jews and Jewish thinkers that Jewish belief is vulnerable to
historical influence and hence that Judaism is historically situated. Especially for an
Orthodox theologian, this is an utterly remarkable claim. For it is one thing to
admit that historians and sociologists take Jewish belief to be a historical phenom-

enon; it is another for a believing Jew to accept this about the content of Jewish belief and perhaps more. All would agree that Jewish believing is historical and changing; the issue concerns the status of the content of the beliefs themselves and whether they are conditional and relative. Rubenstein, Fackenheim, and Christian theologians like A. Roy Eckardt and David Tracy all accept this view, but Berkovits does not. That Greenberg does is extraordinary. I shall have to explore how, if at all, he lives up to its standards, for what it means is that nothing in Judaism is in principle immune to doubt, revision, rejection, or disposal, on the basis of historical experience.

In his essay, Greenberg speaks of three challenges posed by Auschwitz. The challenge to Judaism is to its beliefs in God, the covenant, redemption, and the value of human life. The challenge to Christianity concerns its doctrine of love, its anti-Judaism, and its triumphalism. And the challenge to modern Western culture concerns the human capacity for unlimited evil, the uses of technology and science for the performance of atrocities, the risks of morality grounded in power, and the weakness of universalism and liberalism.[40] Greenberg first articulates the ways that Judaism, Christianity, and the modern world have been tested by this event, how central ideas of each ought to be altered as a result of the death camps and the Nazi atrocities. How should each respond to Auschwitz in its historical situation? How should each come to grips with its plight, its failures, its beliefs, and its hopes, given its relationship to the event? How should each reinterpret itself, recover its past, and gain a sense of continuity with itself, once the horrifying rupture is grasped for what it is?

Rubenstein had set himself a standard for authentic Jewish response, what he called "obscenity." No view or approach that would lead to a sense of disgust or revulsion could be acceptable. Berkovits was more explicit: no Jewish faith could be authentic for those who survived, for Job's siblings, that does not do justice to Job's own experiences. No faith is authentic that is too facile or too easily rejected. Only a questioning faith is appropriate; only it does justice to the faith and the doubts of the victims themselves. Berkovits's standard is a standard for faith that concerns the nature of one's believing and not its content. What it requires is that one's believing be neither an unquestioning, overconfident act nor a glib, confident disbelieving or skepticism. Greenberg too recognizes a standard for post-Holocaust faith; to be more precise, he fixes at least two standards.

Greenberg begins by noticing an important feature of the historicity of Jewish existence. His point is a particular one, but it is really a special case of a more general point, that given the nature of time, human experience, and history, our actions unavoidably involve responses to the events and features that characterize our situation. Whether it is the execution of Charles I, the expulsion of Jews from Spain in 1492, the failure of Shabbatai Zvi's messianic movement in 1666, or the French Revolution, for those who lived after these events and especially for those who lived in places directly and powerfully affected by them at times just after them, response is necessary. Either one ignores the event, rejects it, resists it, denies it, accepts it, or praises it. What is impossible is to fail to respond, as long as the notion of response is conceived in broad enough terms. This is another way of saying that our histori-cal situation is marked by constituents that are proximate and distant, in time, place, and relevance. But given the character of history, once an event has occurred, it is impossible that its relevance or impact is totally nil. At any given moment, the entirety of what has occurred is relevant to each individual, to one degree or other, but never to no degree at all.

To be fair, Greenberg does not highlight this general point. Rather his attention is on the particular one, that with regard to an "unmitigated evil" like Auschwitz and the moral and religious views that facilitated it, "failure to radically criticize and restructure means collaboration with the possibility of a repetition. . . . The fact of the Holocaust makes a repetition more likely—a limit was broken, a control or awe is gone—and the murder procedure is no better laid out and understood. Fail-ure to confront it makes repetition all the more likely. . . . [N]ot to respond is to col-laborate in its repetition."[41] My point earlier is the conceptual one, that response is necessary once human existence is understood as hermeneutical, interpretive and historically situated. Greenberg's point is moral and historical, that once a moral limit has been crossed and a horrific act has been performed, then repetition is pos-sible and even likely; hence resistance is a moral imperative. The evidence shows that in the West, after Auschwitz, this has been so. Where resistance did not occur, there was a revival of Nazism or Nazi-like practices. Greenberg concludes for an imperative of resistance; this is acceptable, given certain conditions. We can ignore any problems or shortcomings with his account and turn directly to the key point, the *standard for the response*. If it involves faith, what kind of faith should it be? The general case yields a conceptual necessity, the particular one a moral necessity. What we now want to know is the shape the latter ought to take.

Greenberg proceeds to characterize, clarify, and defend what he calls post-Holo-caust dialectical faith.[42] What, however, does Greenberg mean by a response, belief, attitude, or view that is dialectical, and how is being dialectical related to the Holo-caust? To answer these questions, we must look at two principles that Greenberg formulates near the outset of his account:

1. "Living in the dialectic becomes one of the verification principles for alterna-tive theories after the Holocaust." (Dialectical Principle)
2. "Let us offer, then, as working principle the following: no statement, theolog-ical or otherwise, should be made that would not be credible in the presence of the burning children." (Working Principle)

What do these principles mean, and how are they related one to the other? In "Ju-daism and Christianity after the Holocaust," principle 2 occurs as the first sentence in a paragraph that explores what happens when it is applied; principle 1 is the last sentence in that paragraph. This appears to be the structure of Greenberg's think-

ing: he proposes the Working Principle, applies it and clarifies the results of applying it, and draws as a conclusion the Dialectical Principle. He calls the latter a principle of verification: not all dialectical theories or statements will be authentic post-
Holocaust theories or statements, clearly, but every genuine post-Holocaust theory
— belief, attitude, practice, view, or statement—will necessarily be dialectical. In
order to see why this must be so and what it means, we need to examine the Working Principle and its application. For Greenberg must show why applying the principle of the burning children will always yield a theory or statement or belief or
faith that is dialectical.

Greenberg's Working Principle is central to his theological enterprise; yet it is
imprecise and unclear. We need to clarify it by making at least some of its features
more precise. First, here is a paraphrase of principle 2:

(2*)   No statement, belief, action, and so on, that is now performed is acceptable
       if it were uttered, held, or performed in the presence of the burning chil-
       dren and were not acceptable in that situation.

Greenberg qualifies the types of statements, theories, and principles that he has in
mind; he calls them "theological or otherwise" and proceeds to say that "the Holocaust challenges the claims of all standards that compete for modern man's loyalties. . . . This surd will—and should—undercut the ultimate adequacy of any category, unless there were one (religious, political, intellectual) that consistently
produced the proper response of resistance and horror at the Holocaust. No such
category exists, to my knowledge."[43] Clearly, Greenberg is not thinking of mundane or trivial statements and beliefs. He has in mind religious or theological
claims, moral, political, and perhaps even historical, psychological, and sociological ones. But even this, of course, is still vague. Many statements, even religious and
political ones, are descriptive or factual; others are uncontroversial, even if evalua-
tive, normative, or explanatory. There probably is no easy way to classify or distinguish what Greenberg has in mind. Perhaps it is best to remember that the statements, theories, and beliefs in question, indeed the *responses* in question, are ones
that attempt to cope with the Holocaust in some significant way, to incorporate or
comprehend it into a practical or intellectual pattern, thereby defusing its potential
threat to our thinking and acting. Let us call this a "significant response." This
yields:

(2**) No significant response that is now performed is acceptable if it were per-
       formed in the presence of the burning children and were not acceptable in
       that situation.

Greenberg's reference to the burning children alludes to the Nuremberg testimony of the Polish guard at Auschwitz that he cited earlier. But does Greenberg
mean the event of the children being thrown into the burning pit near the crema-
torium or this event interpreted by the guard as a technique for economizing on gas

or the event as viewed by one of the mothers, or as viewed by a third party, or the entire event, together with Greenberg's historical reconstruction of the money saved and his moral outrage at the event? Moreover, does he mean that no significant response should be acceptable to *us now* if it would not have been acceptable to a *victim then*? Or, that it should not be acceptable to us now if it would not have been acceptable to *us* if we had been present *then*? Or does he mean something quite different, that no significant response is acceptable now that is dissonant with a serious sensitivity that we now feel toward the cruelty, the horror, and the atrocity of the death camps and the Nazi practices in general?

In principle 2 Greenberg says that "no statement . . . should be made," and this clearly means by us now; no response should be performed that fails a certain standard, a working standard that we can apply and employ. He then proposes a "thought-experiment," an imaginative projection for us, the respondents; imagine that you were there, that you saw the babies being torn from their mothers and hurled into the flaming pits, that you heard the cries, and that you were horrified, devastated, shattered. Could you, then, make the statement, respond as you proposed, believe what you supposed? This is what I think Greenberg means:

(2***) No significant response that you might now perform ought to be acceptable to you if you could not have performed it then, if you were present at the burning of those children.

Moreover, the point of this principle is that the test of authenticity for faith, morality, and so forth in our situation is a total, not merely cognitive, exposure to the Holocaust. The exposure must not be to an abstraction but rather to the particular horrors of Nazi criminality and to the pain, the atrocity, and the suffering, as experienced. The exposure too must be total, not merely a reflection on the event but a whole experiencing of it. The test, then, is whether you, the concrete particularity of the Nazi atrocities, and this belief or theory can *dwell* together; can they occupy the same existential space; can they be a whole? If not, then the response is unacceptable; it ought not be performed. Dissonance, existential impropriety, is a fault, and one sign of the fault is its failure to be dialectical.

Like the Working Principle, the notion of being dialectical and the Dialectical Principle are imprecise and vague. I think that Greenberg's understanding of the notion is not as radical as it could be. Still, he uses it everywhere, and one needs to make it somewhat clearer if one is to understand him at all.

In the paragraph I am discussing, after proposing the test of direct and total exposure to the horrors of Auschwitz, Greenberg identifies certain features of the results of such an exposure. As we try to understand or explain what happened and to draw some normative, theological, or political lessons from it, we fail. Our traditional categories, concepts, and standards do not apply to these events neatly; there are no "simple, clear answers or definitive solutions."[44] Our responses contain "irresolvable tensions"; as we confront the horrific events, we are thrown "from pole to pole in ceaseless tension."[45] To live, think, and respond dialectically is to do so without certainty, to recognize that there are no definitive solutions, that classical or traditional categories are inadequate until reconstructed, and that our responses must involve a ceaseless shifting from conviction to doubt and back again.[46]

"Dialectical," of course, is an expression with a long philosophical and theological history, from Socrates, Plato, and Aristotle to Hegel and Marx. Greenberg surely draws on the nineteenth-century tradition of its use, from Hegel to Marx and the younger Hegelians, but his own use is not precise or technical. To him, a belief, attitude, or response is dialectical if it is complex, unstable, shifting from one view at one time to another at another time, uncertain, and ambivalent. These features are reflected in his terminology of tension, a lack of definiteness, and the inadequacy of traditional categories. They are also revealed by his criticisms of Berkovits, Fackenheim, and Rubenstein, criticisms based on what he takes to be their use of conventional categories and sense of finality.[47] Finally, they are confirmed by his example of a dialectical response, drawn from Elie Wiesel's novel *The Accident*. In the novel, Wiesel portrays a survivor, Sarah, who is both a prostitute, used by the Nazi officers, and a "suffering saint" who gives herself to a shy survivor boy. She is, he suggests, pitiful at one moment yet noble at another. Here, as before, we have the lack of stability and precision of the old categories and a ceaseless shifting back and forth.[48]

But the dialectical character of faith could be even more radical than Greenberg believes. Drawing on Buber, who used the expression "moment Gods" when reflecting on the question of divine identity from one revelational encounter to another,[49] Greenberg refers to dialectical faith as momentary, "moments when Redeemer and vision of redemption are present, interspersed with times when the flames and smoke of the burning children blot out faith. . . . The difference between the skeptic and the believer is frequency of faith, and not certitude of position."[50] For Greenberg, faith and doubt occur at different times, so that for a person as a totality, faith is a matter of frequency or quantity of episodes of faith.[51] But this is a narrow interpretation. After Auschwitz, the polarities of existence not only shift over time; they also interpenetrate and occur simultaneously. The very same response, act, or belief can express self-confidence and self-doubt, joy and despair, sanity and madness, faith and doubt, religious purpose and secular self-reliance. What Greenberg calls for is a "troubled theism,"[52] but surely this response is not simply facile acceptance interspersed with moments of doubt. It must be a faithful trust that is itself riddled with uncertainty and worry, and a skeptical rebellion that is obedient and hopeful. As I have already shown, it is this kind of faith that Berkovits tries to characterize as the authentic response of Job's siblings, and in Fackenheim I will again identify it as characteristic of all authentic Jewish response. Later, in his effort to show the post-Holocaust interplay of the categories of secularity and religiosity, Greenberg appreciates the simultaneous interpenetration of polarities after Auschwitz, but he fails to acknowledge it earlier in the essay.[53]

Greenberg's failure to grasp with precision and adequacy the way that Auschwitz challenges traditional categories and yields dialectical results accounts in part for his mistaken understanding of the work of Rubenstein, Fackenheim, and even Berkovits.[54] Each in his own way calls for responses that are dialectical. Moreover, neither Rubenstein nor Fackenheim uses categories to grasp Auschwitz that are wholly traditional and unreconstructed. To call the former an atheist and the latter a classical theist, as Greenberg does, is certainly misleading and arguably false. Finally, Greenberg's dialectical or troubled faith is not unlike Berkovits's questioning faith. Berkovits's argument that Job's experience should be the standard for determining an authentic post-Holocaust faith certainly is similar to Greenberg's use of the Working Principle of the burning children. They differ, to be sure, but the core of both is that exposure to the horror of Auschwitz affects the response of survivors today. In Berkovits the exposure is mediated through the direct responses of the victims; in Greenberg it is immediate or imaginatively so. Later I will show how Fackenheim finds some truth in both strategies. For now one can appreciate what they share, the need of all contemporary theology and faith to confront Auschwitz in order to be at all authentic. Greenberg, then, does a poor job of characterizing the other post-Holocaust Jewish thinkers, and he fails to see clearly how his own views are like and unlike theirs. At least part of the problem is his impressionistic and incomplete account of the dialectical nature of responses to Auschwitz.

The account of these two principles and the character of post-Holocaust dialectical response and faith is the operative core of Greenberg's essay. In the remaining sections he defends and elaborates this account. First, he defends the dialectical character of faith by arguing that total skepticism is unacceptable.[55] Second, he calls the Holocaust a "new revelatory event," although he does not explain what he means by this or give grounds for saying it.[56] Clearly, Greenberg takes Auschwitz to threaten all faith and to mark a watershed. But why take it to incorporate a moment of Divine Presence? Third, the rupture threatens to cut the present off from the past, human beings from God, Jews from Judaism, but it does not succeed. A troubled faith returns for its theological models to the tradition and reinterprets the stories of Job, the suffering servant of Isaiah 53, and the portrait of Lamentations 3.[57] In the book of Job, for example, Greenberg finds a model of the "rejection of easy pieties or denials and the dialectical response of looking for, expecting, further revelations of the Presence."[58]

Finally, Greenberg distinguishes, although not in these terms, theoretical or theological from practical responses; he realizes that life must go on, even without waiting for articulation in thought. This realization leads him to set out three types of responses—moral, political, and ritual.[59]

Nazism was an assault on human dignity and human life. Hannah Arendt, Jean Améry, and Primo Levi gave vivid and evocative expression to this dimension of Nazi criminality, and Greenberg calls attention to its religious dimension. It was an attack on God as an attack on the image of God. In the face of "human worth-lessness and meaninglessness . . . there is one response . . . : the reaffirmation of meaningfulness, worth, and life—through acts of love and life-giving. The act of creating life or enhancing its dignity is the counter-testimony to Auschwitz."[60] Greenberg associates this religious—or moral—response with bearing and edu-cating children, the reaffirmation of life after tragedy, the rebirth of the state of Is-rael, love and community, world hunger, and Jewish survival. Here he ties together his earlier commitment to issues of universal moral concern, of justice, racism, women's rights, and care for the homeless and the hungry, with the authenticity of post-Holocaust religious life.[61] "The indivisibility of human dignity and equality becomes an essential bulwark against the repetition of another Holocaust. It is the command rising out of Auschwitz."[62] In earlier essays, Greenberg saw these issues as part of the modern situation and as morally compelling areas that were neglected by Orthodox Judaism. Now he ties them to the traditional notion of human dignity and human existence as a divine image and then to resistance, to authentic response to Auschwitz. This nexus provides these moral acts with a particular, historically distinctive ground and justification. In this way, Greenberg acknowledges the his-torical character of Jewish conduct, the way it involves an interpretive recovery of traditional themes, its contribution to Jewish identity, and its moral and religious commitment to the redemptive process. Greenberg's proposal is historically sensi-tive and worldly, morally responsible without being universalist.

In addition to this moral and religious response, there are political—and reli-gious—ones. One political response is support for the state of Israel, for "after Auschwitz the existence of the Jew is a great affirmation and an act of faith."[63] The state of Israel is committed to the survival of this people, to giving "life, health, en-ergy to the rehabilitation of the remnants of the covenant people."[64] It is commit-ted too to the covenantal responsibilities of admitting all Jews who seek citizenship, of being a homeland and a rescuer for those Jews in need, regardless of the politi-cal and diplomatic consequences of such a role.[65] "The lesson of Auschwitz is that no human being should lack a guaranteed place to flee again."[66] Another political response is based on the recognition that power controls our sense of human dig-nity, of our right to life and security, and involves the commitment to redistribute power so that each person has sufficient power "to assure one's dignity."[67]

Finally, Greenberg turns to ritual and liturgical responses, those forms of con-duct that support moral and political deeds "by reenacting constantly the event which is normative and revelatory," by memory through song, film, utterance, and act.[68] What Greenberg advocates here—the institution of new sacred forms—he later elaborates in the chapters on Yom Ha-Shoah and Yom Ha-Atzmauth in his book *The Jewish Way*. Ritual reenactment constitutes a process, perhaps painful and difficult, of "strengthen[ing] responsibility, will, and faith."[69] Response incorporates a reconstructed past into the present but only insofar as it is mediated to the present through an encounter with the event. That encounter, however, will yield a sense of imperative and an interpretive framework only if it is real and present; the latter, Greenberg argues, requires memory, reenactment, immediacy renewed and periodic. This is the purpose of ritual and liturgical recovery.

Earlier I asked whether Auschwitz, for Greenberg, has theological implications for Judaism. Clearly it does, and indeed its implications are very broad—moral, political, sociological, psychological, institutional, ritual, and more. For Greenberg, Judaism is a deeply historical phenomenon, influenced dramatically by the processes of modernization and emancipation and now by the Holocaust and the rebirth of the state of Israel.[70] And with historical situatedness comes the necessity of response, which is one way of indicating that all situated action is performed in a context constituted by discourse, memory, and attitudes already given to the agent. When Greenberg speaks of the inadequacy of the Reform, Conservative, and Orthodox movements to respond to Auschwitz and Jerusalem, he means that they did not "take the overwhelming events seriously."[71] They did not acknowledge that after these events, one could not go on as before; continuity with an institutionally constituted tradition of belief and conduct was simply assumed. To someone who appreciates the historicity of Jewish experience, this assumption must be suspended. To take Auschwitz seriously is to expose oneself to it wholly, to accept the threat of total discontinuity, and yet to see as well the imperative and the resources for continuity with and recovery of the past. Both the threat of discontinuity and the project of continuity, moreover, are inclusive. In this regard Greenberg is more like Rubenstein, Eckardt, and Tracy than he is like Berkovits, with whom he shares so much. Berkovits wants to save his traditionalism and hence refuses its historicity. Greenberg wants to save or renew some elements of tradition but only if they can survive the test of exposure to history; hence he in principle risks all, although it is very clear that he anticipates ab initio that authentic response to the Holocaust and history will involve Judaism's renewal and not its abandonment.[72]

As an element of authentic response to Auschwitz for Greenberg, the rebirth and defense of the state of Israel play a special role.[73] Writing in the midseventies, after the Six Day War and the Yom Kippur War, Greenberg claims that "fear of another Holocaust was dominant in American Jewry in May, 1967" and that the Six Day War "evoked the memory and ongoing spiritual force of the Holocaust in Jewish life."[74] He also argues that "the Holocaust has undoubtedly established Israel's centrality" vis à vis the diaspora, given questions of population density, intermarriage, assimilation, language, and culture.[75] For Greenberg, moreover, "the Holocaust did bring the end of *galut* Judaism: the Jewish way of life and meaning predicated on Jewish lack of power which accepted exile as normative even though it was not 'at home' in it."[76] As he argued elsewhere, modernity helped to erode the protected, insulated environment of Jewish values and practices;[77] it also promoted negative attitudes toward Zionism, until the Holocaust highlighted the awful capabilities of modern culture and technology.[78] The Six Day War confirmed the lesson of Auschwitz, that protection and security required secular power and could not count on the aid of others. After the War, and with the memory of the victimization and destruction of Auschwitz then revived, the Jewish community turned dramatically and vigorously Zionist. Greenberg warns against idealizing Israeli policy and practice, but at the same time he strongly defends its centrality to Judaism and Jewish survival in a post-Holocaust world, as a locus of Jewish self-defense and as a homeland, a refuge for Jews throughout the world.[79] In this case, ideological, social, and religious preeminence is confirmed by the conduct and words of everyday Jews, whose allegiance, financial commitment, and orientation to Israel demonstrate the real primacy of the state in contemporary Jewish identity.

Greenberg's views on Israel and its centrality for American Jewish life after the Holocaust are not without their difficulties. His arguments are historical and sociological more than theological, and many might doubt the reliability of his evidence and the uses to which he puts it. In addition, his assessment of the allegiance of America's Jews and of the role of Israel's political leaders is bound to be controversial. But my purpose here is not to evaluate Greenberg's interpretation or his reasons for it. He has been an iconoclast since the sixties, attacking American Orthodoxy and other entrenched Jewish institutions for failing to deal adequately with the resources and the problems of life in modern, postwar America. In his paper given to the Rabbinical Assembly in 1976, he makes the shortcomings of the denominations of American Judaism very clear.[80] He also shows that for him the Holocaust and the state of Israel add to the demands that modernity and the post-Enlightenment world already placed on Judaism and Jewish institutions. That all are failing he is convinced, and his life has been an active effort to meet the challenges he sees facing Jewish life in America.

At one time the nondenominational organization founded by Greenberg was called "The National Jewish Resource Center."[81] Its aims were to educate Jewish leadership, and it did this in part through publications series. In the early eighties, Greenberg issued three essays on post-Holocaust Jewish life in its historical and theological context. These dealt with what Greenberg called the Third Era in Jewish history and the age of the Voluntary Covenant.

Liberal Jewish theologians in the postwar period debated the problem of excessive freedom in Judaism; orthodox theologians, then and in subsequent years, had contrary worries about insufficient freedom. Both sides of course feared a slippery slope, but both—at least some on both sides—saw the necessity of arriving at a conception of covenant, revelation, and *halakhah* that joined the notions of authority, command, and obligation on the one hand and autonomy, creativity, and selectivity on the other. In his articles in the late sixties Greenberg, like Fackenheim, for example, did seek a strategy of mediation, but unlike Fackenheim, more deeply indebted to Rosenzweig, Greenberg's account made revelation more than an event and limited freedom to the acceptance or rejection of an already revealed content. The policy paper "Voluntary Covenant" builds on these foundations and extends them in a very historical way.[82]

In this essay Greenberg gives a theologico-historical sketch of Jewish faith and a homiletical exhortation to authentic post-Holocaust Jewish life. He begins with a traditional account of the covenant as a relationship grounded in divine purpose, the perfection of creation, divine restraint, human freedom, and a covenantal commitment to redemption. It is a covenantal relationship that unfolds in the biblical stories of Noah, Abraham, and the people of Israel, and because it is a relationship with people in history and about history, it is subject to change, to crisis, to divine mystery and human "moral fatigue." But in its biblical form, it is both voluntary to a degree and involuntary to a degree, with emphasis placed on God's governorship, his rule, his plan, and his control.[83]

Greenberg then traces the historical development of this covenantal way as it was challenged and then transformed by crisis—the destruction of the first Temple, of the second, and then the Holocaust.[84] After the first destruction, for example, the people's suffering is interpreted as punishment for sin, and God is shown to remain bound to his people even when they fail to serve their covenantal goals. After the second destruction, God becomes the teacher of a wayward Israel, and the rabbis conceive a new kind of authority that appreciates "both the continuity and the discontinuity in their role."[85] According to Greenberg, rabbinic law is even more authoritative than scripture. The later acceptance of the covenant, a reacceptance after destruction, is a renewed commitment to redemption and hence a confirmation that the way is binding. The more *halakhah* advances the cause of redemption, the more authoritative it is, and this is an insight of rabbinic Judaism.[86]

The Holocaust is the most recent and most devastating assault on the covenant, Greenberg claims, in part because it so dramatically diminished the number of Jews and in part because it assaulted the value of human life and exposed a divine absence that left the covenant with no justifiable authority.[87] Indeed, it is the latter point that reveals the crucial feature of a post-Holocaust covenant: Auschwitz showed that the covenant "can no longer be commanded."[88] But post-Holocaust Jewish life continued: "The overwhelming majority of survivors, far from yielding to despair, rebuilt Jewish lives and took part in the assumption of power by the Jewish people" by having and educating Jewish children, by supporting the state of Israel through settlement and charity, and by stimulating Jewish learning.[89] In short, the covenant became voluntary and hence authoritative through its voluntary assumption. In Greenberg's words, "[the covenant's] authority was broken, but the Jewish people, released from its obligations, chose voluntarily to take it on again. . . . God was no longer in a position to command, but the Jewish people was so in love with the dream of redemption that it volunteered to carry on its mission."[90] The Holocaust was "the shock that almost destroy[ed] the covenant" but did not.[91] Moreover, this responsibility expresses itself in opposition to the Nazi destruction and as a reaffirmation of life, human dignity, and redemptive values. These acts require a recovery of tradition that selects what is meaningful—consistent with the covenant, transmissible, and effective are the standards that Greenberg cites[92]—

and hence includes a "pluralist interpretation," a diversity of manifestations of adherence to the covenantal project of redemption.[93]

I need not review the details of Greenberg's own exhortation to novel modes of post-Holocaust covenantal existence. They are very much like the moral, ritual, and political responses that he sketched in his classic essay "Cloud of Smoke, Pillar of Fire." Indeed, much of "Voluntary Covenant" incorporates ideas from Greenberg's earlier work. The commitment to pluralism harks back to his essays of the late sixties, as does his emphasis on human freedom in the *halakhic* and covenantal process. The centrality of Israel is also a familiar motif, as is his caution that it not lead to chauvinism, idolatry, and such vices. In recognizing the importance and the opportunities of voluntarism beyond the scope of traditionalism, he even recalls his argument that democracies are more successful at eliciting commitment and obedience than tyrannies, although now this observation is not presented as a justification for freedom as much as an encouragement that post-Holocaust voluntarism can yield great successes.[94] These recollections of past themes might lead the reader to treat this essay as redundant and not at all novel. But this would be a mistake, for several reasons.

"Voluntary Covenant" raises and deals with the relation between authority and freedom in a way that is new for Greenberg, and it interprets the Holocaust as playing a crucial role in its current, post-Holocaust manifestation. His new way of treating these matters is tied to a close linking of God's role as commander and redeemer, as one who reveals his will and acts in history. The three great destructive events in Jewish history yield three different, historically cumulative understandings of God's role and the human role in the covenantal relationship. The nature of the destructions and the covenantal background against which they occur push Jews to new reinterpretations of their relation to God. Unlike Berkovits, Greenberg takes history to influence not just human morale or psychology; it also affects the content of Jewish beliefs and interpretations. It alters what they think as well as how they think it. And unlike Rubenstein, Greenberg takes the result to be not a wholesale abandonment of the covenant, the God of history, and redemption. Rather it is a revision and reclaiming of this language and its theological world. Indeed, Greenberg shows that the language and implications of a voluntary covenant are one strand of the covenant history and its tradition from the outset. We can see this, for example, if we focus on the relation between authority and freedom within that covenantal history.[95]

The covenant is grounded in creation and in God's creation of humankind. Life is grounded in God who desires its redemption, its perfection and ultimate realization, and who creates human beings to be his partner in bringing about this messianic goal. This requires human freedom: "although God yearns for this messianic consummation and promises that it will come to be, God will not force humans to be perfect. By a process of voluntary self-limitation (covenant), God allows humans to participate in the process of creating a perfect world."[96] This founding conception of divine purpose and human freedom is akin to Berkovits's conception of divine providence and faith history, but in Greenberg's view it is historical and undergoes revision.[97] Eventually, for Greenberg, this covenant with all humankind requires a special covenant with Abraham. But Israel, his descendants, are "erratic" and subject to "moral fatigue."[98] Hence the early covenant requires that the people be taught, directed, and sanctioned; in its early manifestation it is largely involuntary. Greenberg interprets the response to the destruction of the First Temple and the exile as a questioning of God's allegiance; was it a sign that he had had enough? No; "the prophetic answer [was] that God will not abandon the covenant no matter how many times the Jews break it."[99]

The novelty in Greenberg's account comes in his discussion of the rabbinic response to the second destruction and the impact of the Holocaust, the third destruction. The second destruction led some to seek a new covenant where the old one was broken. The rabbis differed; to them, the covenant now called for more human responsibility, for a learning that sought to understand his hidden presence and action that would bring his purposes to life.[100] Human freedom was then expanded in its scope; it was expressed through the rabbinic attempt to reveal God's will and the reacceptance of the covenant after the destruction. The authority of the covenantal obligations derives from the fact that they further the cause of redemption in a new context. Hence the authority is grounded in the covenant's purpose and the free reacceptance of that purpose after the destruction.[101]

Finally, the Holocaust; the covenant is assaulted and shattered. Greenberg takes this to mean, at least, that the Holocaust showed that the covenant cannot be commanded. Both God's credibility and the credibility of what he commands are put in doubt. If the Jews continue as Jews and remain loyal to the covenantal purposes, it is because they want to do so, because, despite God, the dream is so compelling.[102] Auschwitz extends the rabbinic emphasis on voluntary acceptance, human interpretation, and authority grounded in redemptive purpose. It reduces the sense of divine command, or what we might call *direct* divine command. God's presence has become more hidden, less direct and more indirect. There is freedom but also obligation, but now the two yield a plurality of paths to the same goal, a variety of interpretations of what the tradition takes to contribute to the redemptive achievement,[103] new responses to changing and challenging situations, and a new responsibility for judging what does and does not contribute to the covenantal project.[104] In short, for Greenberg freedom is not a requirement of Enlightenment liberalism or of modernity. It is a traditional strand that has always been present in covenantal existence but that has become a more central feature of the covenant after Auschwitz. Some will criticize this as too political and too secular a response, as evacuating God from history, as a "voluntarism [that] means liberation from duty,"[105] as a new chauvinism that admires voluntary acceptance over obedience. But this kind of criticism risks failing to appreciate that for Greenberg freedom as acceptance of the covenant *does* bring duty and that the challenge of human responsibility after Auschwitz is itself not chosen but rather is historically given. To believe otherwise is to diminish the events of Auschwitz, to believe that they make no difference to what one does as a Jew or why one does it.

Greenberg's essay does not make clear an issue of perspective that is critically important to understanding the status of his account. Who is the teller of Greenberg's tale? Who is its narrator? From what point of view is it carried out? What is its goal? Is it an *argument for* taking the Holocaust seriously? Or is it a *result of* taking it seriously? Or is it both?

Is Greenberg's account an argument for the necessity, at this historical moment, of taking the Holocaust seriously, of shaping one's understanding of Jewish belief and Jewish life in terms of it? If it is, then it is not a strong argument, for it assumes the historicity of Jewish life and it assumes too that Auschwitz requires a reevaluation and revision of traditional categories. We are more correct to treat this essay and Greenberg's other narratives about Jewish history and theology as *results* of exposing the tradition to Auschwitz, of the sort of historico-theological story that *can* be uttered and the kinds of practical recommendations that *can* be made in the presence of the burning children. The covenantal story that Greenberg tells shows how much can be retained and how much must be revised when exposing the traditional account to the Shoah. The key feature that remains is the human responsibility for God's redemptive goal; even if we are bewildered by God's role in the covenant now, we can still appreciate our own. And this means a voluntary assumption of obligations that we try to articulate in our world.

Here, then, we see Greenberg seeking the very same goal sought by philosophers such as Alasdair MacIntyre and Charles Taylor, as well as others. Some of them not only saw the need to accept the historical situatedness of human agency and to seek, within that context, transcendent standards or principles to guide human conduct and people's lives; they also sought to clarify and defend the coherence of this position. Greenberg does not attempt this philosophical task, but he does exemplify the framework of a principled and situated Jewish selfhood. He constructs a theological narrative for a post-Holocaust Jewish world and elicits the ground and direction of its authoritative source. The voluntary covenant is the expression of a situated Jewish commitment to the purposes of traditional Jewish existence, reinterpreted and conceived as the human articulation of the divine plan. After Auschwitz, Greenberg claims, this is the most authentic way of being Jewish and hence the most acceptable rereading of the Jewish past.

But if Greenberg's story of the emergence of the voluntary covenant is compelling, then one result is that the story is only one possible reinterpretation of Jewish life and history. Others are certainly possible, and if they too can be authentically responsive to Auschwitz, they will be plausible narratives for post-Holocaust Jewish existence. There is a circle here, but it is not a vicious one. For if one recognizes that all agency and all interpretation are historically situated, a dialectical and reciprocal relation to tradition and context is unavoidable. Greenberg's narrative has the virtues of being consistent with accounts of the Holocaust and with the experience of post-Holocaust Jews; it also supports the voluntarism of contemporary life and its pluralism. It is an open account that respects the threat of Auschwitz to cut Jews off from their past, to shatter the covenant, but also shows how a retrieval is possible that portrays post-Holocaust Jewish life as continuous with the pre-Holocaust Jewish past.

In the end, then, Greenberg tells a story that has integrity. Whether its integrity is bought at too high a price is another matter; later I will look at how his work was and has been received. For now, it is sufficient to have shown how Greenberg saw the historical exigency to articulate a responsible Jewish identity at a time of need, need for a renewed sense of attachment to the past and a responsible coping with the situation of American Jews.

Chapter Nine

Arthur Cohen and the
Holocaust as *Tremendum*

In 1984, Arthur Cohen wrote that both he and Richard Rubenstein were "outsiders to the Jewish establishment" and that it is "ironic that [they] . . . should be virtually the only Jewish thinkers who take each other's work seriously."[1] These statements are of course only partial truths. Since the fifties, both have been visible and prominent Jewish theologians, but neither has been institutionally tied to one of the denominations of American Judaism: Rubenstein was a Hillel rabbi and then an academic, Cohen an editor and novelist. In this regard, however, they do not differ from Berkovits, who was an academic, although closely tied to one strand of American Orthodoxy, Greenberg, who has been a radical among the Orthodox although he has had his own establishment among Federation leaders, and Fackenheim, who was an academic and whose appeal has certainly not been tied to denominational boundaries. Furthermore, they certainly have, in print, taken each other's work seriously: Rubenstein reviewed Cohen's book *The Natural and the Supernatural Jew* in 1963, and Cohen was a commentator on Rubenstein's "Homeland and Holocaust" in 1968.[2] But it is surely an exaggeration to claim that they are virtually alone in taking each other's work seriously; in *Judaism*, for example, Rubenstein's book *After Auschwitz* was favorably reviewed by Arnold Jacob Wolf and Cohen's early book by Will Herberg.[3] Perhaps Cohen's statement is best taken not as a historical one but rather as an expression of his own sense of alienation, his frustration and even anger that at least his recent book on the theological implications of the Holocaust, published in 1981, had been largely ignored by the Jewish world. Whether he was right is indeed a historical question, and probably his claim was made with some justification; its expression is a psychological one that is evident. In general, *The Tremendum: A Theological Interpretation of the Holocaust*[4] was ignored, perhaps for political reasons but also perhaps for its obscurity.

In this book and several articles Cohen seeks to give a theological interpretation of the Holocaust. But this work of the 1970s has a background. Cohen was a feature of the postwar Jewish theological landscape since the late fifties, a figure whose work, indebted to Buber and Rosenzweig, was akin to that of Herberg, Borowitz, Schwarzschild, and Fackenheim, and a thinker who should be counted among the existentialist, neoorthodox defenders of faith and transcendence in that restive period. An independent intellectual and theologian, he wrote on Buber, revelation, and Jewish–Christian dialogue. In 1962 he published an important work that examined modern Jewish thought and set out the framework for his own theological reflections. Cohen's later work on the Holocaust was rooted in this work, *The Natural and the Supernatural Jew*.[5]

The details of Cohen's theological history of Jewish reflection on Judaism and its historical task, from Solomon Ibn Verga and Moses Mendelssohn to Milton Steinberg, Abraham Joshua Heschel, and Will Herberg, can be set aside. What I want to identify is the framework for this historical exploration, Cohen's understanding of theology and Judaism, of the Jewish vocation in time and eternity. This account is set out largely in the volume's introduction and in parts of its final chapter.

Religious doctrine and theology concern God and man, eternity and time; "history is the medium through which God passes into human life" and the context in which religious beliefs arise.[6] History is inescapable for Judaism and Jewish life, even when Judaism attempts to sanctify it and give it a divine, eternal status. Cohen uses a Rosenzweigian language and model, in which the commandments point ahead to redemption and mandate a life that anticipates eternity.[7] Jewish theology reflects upon this life, the historical course of Jewish experience lived in relation to an ultimate reality and "a destiny which commands" the Jew.[8] This Jewish life is, therefore, both natural, that is, physical, social, political, and more, and supernatural—covenanted with God—but it is supernatural in terms of its goal and destiny.[9] As yet the Jew and history are unredeemed: "the Jew is a messianic being for whom there is *no* redemption until *all* history is redeemed."[10] Redemption is the covenantal task of the community of Jews; this people is charged to further the completion and the perfection of all peoples. The Jew's supernatural vocation gives the community direction; the Jew's natural situation, time and history, limit and condition how that direction is recognized, understood, and followed. This relation defines "the dialectical contrariety of divine prescription and historical freedom."[11] Cohen sets himself against an otherworldly spiritualism or mysticism, on the one hand, and a reductive naturalism, on the other; there is some truth in both[12] but not the whole truth. He calls the result a set of existential dogmas, an eschatological faith: "we may be assured of the beginning of history and we may demand its end, but all we have is the present and it is in the present, *the time between creation and redemption*, that we must live."[13] Cohen contends, moreover, that this perception of Jewish life is authentic, expressed by "the Jewish mind as it has thought and continues to think about its supernatural vocation."[14]

Judaism, according to Cohen, is the historical narrative of covenantal life, of a people, with all the frailties and finitude of natural, human existence, bound up with a transcendent task, for which it has been called and to which it has committed itself. In the fifties, this picture was part of a religious revival, associated with existentialism and the search for meaning, a turn to faith and relationship with the transcendent, covenant, and the tie between time and eternity. It was indebted to Buber and Rosenzweig and akin to the theological reflections of Fackenheim, Borowitz, and other of the new theologians. It is also a picture very much like that of Berkovits and Greenberg, like but unlike too, with more respect for nature than Berkovits shows and a greater allegiance to transcendence than Greenberg, a more ritual and even symbolic attunement to commandment, in the spirit of Rosenzweig, than Greenberg would ever accept. In short, Cohen defends a kind of covenantal fideism.[15]

In the last chapter of *The Natural and the Supernatural Jew* Cohen returns to this conception but in a more aggressive spirit. His theological picture is not only confirmed by history; it is also grounded in concern about the loss of transcendence in modern American culture. "The essential problem which underlies all our concerns is the evident withering of the Jewish vocation and the vanishing supernatural consciousness of the Jew."[16] To some, withering; to others, liberation. Cohen takes his stand with clarity and vigor; it is a stand based not on "kinship feeling and camaraderie" but rather on an "apodictic force."[17] It is, in other words, mandated, commanded. The Jewish vocation and belief in it are withering, vanishing, blowin' in the wind. History can help us recover what is being lost, if it is relevant history, which is the only kind of significance for the present.[18] That history tells us that Jewish survival has always been conceived in more than natural and historical terms: "the Jew considered his own history to be the central event of a divine drama."[19] This is "sacred history . . . a history according to God."[20] As Cohen reminds us, this means human history, fully human and natural, with a divine orientation, a destiny, nature attuned to the supernatural, history to transcendence.[21] "[W]e are committed to [God's] perfection, but pass our life in the shadow of *his* passion to consummation. We can know little or nothing of what God is in himself; we can only know what it is that God has made us and to what destiny we are appointed in the service of his freedom."[22] The loss of transcendence, then, is a lost sense of life's purpose and direction, a loss of meaning. Cohen is responding to Dostoyevsky and Camus, to that sense of chaos and meaninglessness that Americans associated with the European existentialists. He calls for faith, memory, and hope as bridges to meaning, a recovery of the past, and a meaningful future,[23] and he calls for the articulation of these in Jewish theology, the story of the Jewish people's historical relationship with God and "the history of God's presence to the Jew" and their recovery in the sense of the Jew's "supernatural vocation."[24]

For all his talk of history, particularity, and concreteness, Cohen's paean for the revival of this sense of transcendence has an airy abstractness about it.[25] Part of this abstractness arises because of Cohen's focus on the fact of divine election, purpose, and orientation but not on its content. For all his attentiveness to history as the locus of God's presence to the Jew, his recognition of human freedom and the reality of evil, Cohen remains detached from real everyday life, its moments of suffering, anxiety, despair, and even celebration. The most he can say about redemption is that bringing about justice and peace are insufficient.[26] Written in 1962 this is certainly a chilling comment. Cohen has a vivid appreciation of the historical situatedness of Jewish life and a very powerful sense that it has allowed its supernatural standards to "wither." But in his urgent desire to recover those standards, to restore foundations, that link to the divine, Cohen fails to honor the demands of history. His eschatology is vigorous but overly escapist, at least hollow, without the content that one might expect in an American context after the Holocaust, once the civil rights struggle had begun, and in a world with nuclear weapons and fears about communism, anticommunism, and government censorship. Moreover, at a time when Jewish theologians were concerned about *halakhah* and mitzvah, there is no sense in Cohen of the ritual and moral details of Jewish life.

Rubenstein, in his review of the book in 1963, sharply denounces it along these same lines. After the destruction of European Jewry and the dramatic rebirth of the state of Israel, how can Cohen claim that the central problem facing Jews in the modern period is the withering of their sense of transcendence and the need to rediscover their supernatural vocation? How can he ignore Auschwitz and refuse to take the messianic character of Israel seriously? How can he continue to theologize exile (*galut*) as the unredeemed character of historical existence?[27] How can he avoid dealing with ways that human beings must contribute to redemption in history, rather than focusing so exclusively on envisioning an eternity beyond time? Obviously Rubenstein has little sympathy for the Rosenzweigian character of Cohen's theology, for the centrality of covenant, divine providence, and such notions. Indeed, the very notion of transcendence is, for him, disqualified by exposure to Auschwitz. But he has seen correctly a shortcoming even more dramatic, what I have called Cohen's abstractness, his lack of sympathy for and attention to the historical sufferings, dangers, and troubles of Jews in a particular world.[28]

When, in the seventies and eighties, Cohen does turn to the Holocaust, given his respect for the historical contextuality of theology and his recognition of the plight of the Jewish supernatural vocation, as he calls it, how does he respond? How indeed might we expect him to respond? One option would be for him to see Auschwitz as the nemesis of history and as the most extreme manifestation of evil. It would express the total unredeemedness of history and stimulate faith, an otherworldly hope, and a continued despair about the capacity of history to transcend itself. Alternatively, Auschwitz might show that evil has become so dominating that it must be opposed; the redemption of history simply could not occur without human redeeming action *in* history. These options and others faced Cohen as he turned to the Holocaust and its role in continuing Jewish theological reflection.

In 1987, in a brief sketch of what theology means in contemporary Jewish thought, Cohen helps us to see the basic structure of his thinking about theology and the Holocaust.[29] In Cohen's view, theology arose in Jewish history only at times when "the bond of practice and obedience" had "eroded" to one degree or other. Theological beliefs were articulated in rabbinic texts but not with any systematic or intense commitment. In the early Christian period, the Middle Ages, and the modern period, the erosion proceeded apace, and so then did theological reflection but "always posterior to acts."[30] What, then, was the career of Jewish theology after the Holocaust? And what was Cohen's theological view after that event?

"Among young or postwar theologians, either the Holocaust is represented as such a great mystery that nothing theological can be said that is relevant, or else the Holocaust is treated as an historical *novum* from which we may derive moral imperatives and messianic hopes but hardly theological clarity."[31] Cohen presents these as alternatives, but we can see them as compatible and as one possible interpretation of what we find, say, in the responses of Greenberg and Fackenheim, responses that endure with less doubt than those of traditionalists and religious Zionists.[32] These theologians, then, denied that authentic responses to the atrocity and cruelty of Auschwitz included "theological clarity." Rather, the response was a matter of moral and even political action but without the traditional theological ground, the notion of a divine commander and redeemer.

To Cohen, however, this kind of response indicates that theology after Auschwitz is no longer secondary; it is primary. The Jewish religious vocation requires starting all over again, "addressing He Who Spoke and Created the Universe as though he were new to us, as though everything that had been thought about him was now demonstrably implausible or morally inadequate."[33] If we expose the old traditional categories to Auschwitz, either they become wholly unacceptable or we bypass the theological questions and derive practical results. Both routes lead to the need for theology. Berkovits does not see this; Greenberg does but is too quick to recover some sort of faith and the Jewish covenantal task; Rubenstein appreciates how total is the threat but is too hasty in discarding theology for sociology. With anything less than a new theological effort, faith and perhaps even a meaningful history—civilization—are lost.[34] Gone is the classical, medieval conception of God and gone the modern conception; gone is the God of nature and the God of history, God the creator and God the actor. All of this "must be explored again as if starting over." This is Cohen's commitment in this brief sketch. He argues that after Auschwitz, theology or thinking about God and confronting God is more central, more important than ever before in Jewish history. We cannot use the old categories to answer our questions, and we cannot simply act without any ground for our conduct. Theology is unavoidable if we are not to capitulate to nihilism.[35]

Hence Cohen shares something deep and important with Greenberg. Both, prior to confronting the Holocaust, believed that features of Judaism were being challenged. For one it was authority, for the other God and transcendence. Both took these features to be in need of serious rethinking. But then they accepted the challenge of the death camps, and the result was a recognition that Auschwitz undeniably called these features into question. For Greenberg, this led to a revised understanding of authority and freedom as he portrayed Judaism in the era of a voluntary covenant. For Cohen, this led to a recognition of the centrality of theology and the need for an utterly new set of theological reflections.

The Tremendum is a collection of four lectures, revised and published in 1981. The first was given at the Leo Baeck Institute in 1974, the other three at Brown University in 1979. The subtitle of the book is "A Theological Interpretation of the Holocaust." Rubenstein, Berkovits, and Greenberg were concerned with faith after Auschwitz, with the religious response of post-Holocaust Jews. Cohen is interested in interpreting the event theologically, and this must mean how Jews after the Holocaust think about God and the event. But this task may not really differ from theirs, for to determine how to speak of God and the atrocities of Auschwitz is after all to determine what belief in God could be like after that event. *The Tremendum* is about these matters.

Cohen begins by arguing that "thought and the death camps are incommensurable. . . . The death camps are unthinkable."[36] From this point he makes his way to a mandate, what I earlier called the primacy of the theological.[37] These are the order of Cohen's thoughts. First, rational analysis—historiographical, psychological, linguistic—"possesses a moral vector,"[38] and the death camps are "beyond the discourse of morality and rational condemnation." Rational and moral vocabulary, applied to the camps, is "inappropriate and unavailing."[39] Second, the death camps, then, are "a new event, one severed from connection with the traditional presuppositions of history, psychology, politics, and morality."[40] These camps, constructed to kill or liquidate all Jews in the most economical way, were unique in history, a caesura, a rupture, a break.[41] Third, Cohen calls the camps the *tremendum*, to represent the presence of an enormity of terror, an "unparalleled and unfathomable" celebration of murder, awful, chilling, overwhelming.[42] It is a caesura, "the discontinuity of the abyss," of the negative.[43] Finally, how ought we now respond to this *tremendum*? It cannot be "transcended," nor can we incorporate it in practice and text, "liturgy and midrash," before we enter it, try to grasp it, and then to address the theological question, who our God is after this event.[44] "We can ill afford to rush to prayer and midrash without first formulating the questions appropriately designated as theological."[45] No response has an appropriate grounding—moral, liturgical, religious—until our conception of God is examined, clarified, and revised.

Cohen does not make this reasoning easy to see, but I am confident that it is his.[46] The burden of the account falls on two points: the attempt to show that the death camps are unique, resist rational explanation, and are hence a caesura; and the argument for the primacy of theological reflection to subsequent response. In chapter 1, the argument for the former point is not compelling; the comments in behalf of the latter are more suggestive.[47] But I will return to both.

What is especially telling is that Cohen understands his strategy in a particularly illuminating way. It has two stages, first a serious, penetrating confrontation with "the *tremendum* of the abyss, a phenomenon without analogue, discontinuous from all that has been," that yields a "new language" and a destruction of the old and second, a reconnection to the past and then to the future.[48] Cohen perceives the process of dealing with the Holocaust as one that first recognizes the radical discontinuity, then reconstitutes continuity with the past, and finally unites the past, the event, and the present. The Holocaust is rupture, end point, and new beginning but only as one proceeds through the acts of encounter and recovery. Once again, as I have shown in others, the post-Holocaust thinker accepts the historicity of the religious situation, acknowledges the extreme threat of disconnectedness, and yet finds a way—or at least *seeks* a way—to continuity with tradition and its standards.

Three chapters of *The Tremendum* were first presented as a series of lectures at Brown University in 1979. They can be read as a deepening of the line of thinking that Cohen has already identified. The theme of the first lecture, "*Tremendum* as Caesura," then, is the relation between thinking and the Holocaust and the special character of the event. Cohen writes in a dense, obfuscating style, and it is hard to make out the structure of his thought. The central point of the chapter is that for Jewish life and thought the Holocaust is indeed a caesura, a break, a rupture, and that one needs to understand why this is so and what it means. This requires "separating the *tremendum* from all things and descending into the abyss."[49] Despite the abstraction, the lack of clear direction, and the heavy literariness, Cohen's chapter tries to accomplish this separation and this descent.

First, Cohen claims that the Holocaust as a specific, historical event, that begins and ends, can be understood in some ways but not in all. He calls it a *tremendum*, borrowing Rudolf Otto's term and using it for a negative event rather than for a divine or numinous presence. The Holocaust is a mysterious *tremendum* in this sense: "it is the immensity of the event that is mysterious but its nature is not mystery." What is "beyond comprehension" is not the details, features, or stages of the event but rather its dimension, which is not a matter of mere quantity. Like the notion of the sublime, it has to do with the experience of overwhelming immensity and its impact. That dimension registers in the observer as a sense of claim, awe, terror, "human debility, worthlessness, incapacity, and weakness." It "is mysterious because it exceeds the discernible causalities of history to which its apparent configuration refers." It is, then, its being a *tremendum*, an awe and dread yielding immensity, that is mysterious, incomprehensible, unexplainable, and this is so because the totality is also unexplainable and beyond an adequate grasp.[50] The immensity is somehow "alien," without "satisfactory analogue [or] historical model," and hence cut off from the past, but partially so.[51]

The Holocaust is "incommensurable with thought" in part because social, psychological, political, and historical judgments are unable to "compass" it; no final, comprehensive accounts are possible.[52] "The holocaust cannot be thought because it cannot be exhausted by historical narration. . . . The familiar disciplines of inter-pretation seem compromised or ineffective."[53] Frankly, Cohen's argument for this incomprehensibility is not perspicuous. He does not indicate what an "exhaustive" account would or should include, why it is desirable or even reasonable to expect, and if it is possible to provide such an account even for normal, mundane events. The best he does, perhaps, is to claim—not show—that the Holocaust eludes our *normal* categories, which seem "inadequate and trivial" when applied to it. Even this is not much help, but it gives the sense that traditional accounts miss some-thing.[54] In this regard, others do better.[55]

This appreciation of the Holocaust as both historical and yet distinctive and powerfully important marks a shift in Cohen's thinking since 1962 and his earlier work.[56] Then, as Cohen admits and Rubenstein saw, he had constructed a theology that avoided dealing with evil and especially with the evil of the Nazis.[57] Now, in the seventies, he had come to realize that escapism and avoidance were unaccept-able, that what was needed was a confrontation with the evil and a revised under-standing of God, man, and history in light of it.

One of Cohen's results, therefore, is that thinking has its limits when it seeks to comprehend Auschwitz. Another is that the event is "an evil portion of real his-tory," both a historical and a theological reality.[58] The Holocaust was in history, but its meaning is transcendent to history.[59] It is, in the latter respect, an "ultimate evil . . . a perfected figuration of the demonic,"[60] not to be incorporated into some plan or configuration that gives it purpose or goal or justification. In this respect, the Holocaust requires a reevaluation of Judaism and "inherited Jewish doctrine," which provides such a plan or framework. Cohen calls this a "normative decree," that Jews are "compelled by [the event] to recognize the respects in which the *tremendum* of this century resembles but is different from the catastrophes of old," the destruction of the second Temple and the expulsion from Spain.[61] The Holo-caust is two-dimensional, a historical and a theological event, and as theological it "insists upon a new reading."[62] It is a "metaphysical evidence that discloses some-thing new about our relation to God and God's relation to creation."[63]

This metaphysical or theological reality of the Holocaust is what Cohen means when he calls this mysterious *tremendum* a caesura or rupture. As he puts it, the Holocaust as historical reality involves "cruelties and murders"; the Holocaust as something "special, separable, ontic" and as a caesura "marks off and breaks."[64] The Holocaust challenges the belief in indestructibility, in election and trust; it is evidence that such confidence and such myth are false, and hence it is the "counter-event of Jewish history, the source of its revisionist reconsideration and self-appraisal."[65] Hence, if the Jew wants to go on, to take seriously his or her rabbinic past, the challenge of Christianity, and his or her confrontation with modern secu-larism, he or she must go on, but to go on means to deal with the Holocaust, to transform the caesura as end point and barrier into a new beginning.[66] The Holo-caust has theological implications because it raises the question, indeed forces the question whether God, the covenant, and redemption can be conceived now as they once were. Cohen shares this recognition with Rubenstein, Greenberg, and, as I will show, with Fackenheim too. Berkovits of course differs; for him, the event does not and cannot have a theological role to play.

In the second of his Brown lectures, Cohen engages in a historical survey of Jewish theology and begins this project of post-Holocaust theological renewal.[67] He confronts the challenge that "historical catastrophe ends certain intellectual options as surely and powerfully as it ends lives."[68] In the Middle Ages and for traditional Judaism, Jewish theology was subordinate to practice, law, and action, but Cohen notes that this primacy of action had been transformed long before the Holocaust so that theology was not a groundwork for law but the attempt to articulate "a schema of thought at once metaphysically sound and religiously authentic."[69]

Cohen, however, offers a new conception of Jewish theology, neither apologetic nor expository nor critical. It is "the struggle to take account of an obdurate and unyielding field of contrariety, where the content of revelation is at odds with the evidence of history, where historical reality raises a fist against faith and smashes it." This is, Cohen says, a new project for Jews as they seek to articulate what Judaism is after Auschwitz.[70] It is the project of dealing with Cohen's prior question: "if the *tremendum* marks off and separates; if it is caesura, how does one speak of God?"[71] It is the thinking that results when revelation and history, tradition and event, faith and experience engage each other, and in our case where a rupture threatens all continuity and yet calls for recovery. "[T]he *tremendum*, not alone as event of history, but as event that annihilates the past of hope and expectation confronts us as an abyss."[72] Like old-fashioned historicism but more radically, the abyss casts everything "into distance and remoteness."[73] Cohen's point is that to take Auschwitz seriously is to treat it as an immense chasm, a rupture, a break that radically separates us from our traditions, our modes of discourse, our conceptual resources, our world. Theology is part of the recovery, of the attempt to go on with God thereafter. Rubenstein had argued that no mode of covenantal recovery was acceptable. Greenberg demurred, as Cohen does, but Cohen's focus, more than Greenberg's or Fackenheim's, is on God.[74] Their responses are more political and active, his more intellectual and theoretical.

The language that Cohen uses—*tremendum*, caesura, abyss, rupture—makes it sound as if his respect for Auschwitz is extreme and fully serious. But it is not clear that it is. One criterion of such seriousness is the depth of one's historicism, as it were, the limit of immunity or vulnerability that marks one's categories and beliefs in their exposure to historical events and in particular to this event. Both Rubenstein and Greenberg can be read as extreme in this regard. For them there is no a priori boundary beyond which the horrors of Auschwitz cannot reach; every Jewish belief and practice is at risk; nothing is nonnegotiable, invulnerable, or fundamental. Like Fackenheim, both can be understood to reject an a priori essentialism. To be sure, they need not be read this way. One might contend that Ruben-

stein's naturalism and Greenberg's dialectical faith contain at least some nonnegotiable features. But this is an unfriendly way of understanding them and their general posture vis à vis Auschwitz. In both cases, the momentous burden of the death
camps is far greater than this. Both risk all and recover some; that is part of the pro-
fundity and the depth of their thinking.

Cohen can sound less radical about his historicism.

> The challenge of the *tremendum* to Judaism is . . . that its view of its own depths
> will be found shallow, insufficiently deep and flexible enough to compass and con-
> tain the *tremendum*. Jewish reality must account for the *tremendum* in its view of
> God, world, and man; it must constellate Jewish facts of practice and belief in such
> a way as to enable them to endure meaningfully in a universe that endures the
> *tremendum* and withstands it and a God who creates a universe in which such de-
> structiveness occurs. If either side goes, the whole collapses. If such a universe can-
> not withstand the *tremendum*, then it is not only ultimate but final. If God is cre-
> ator of the *tremendum* he cannot be accounted good as classical theism requires.[75]

Surely this passage assumes too much—that Jewish reality and belief must be comprehensive, that it must be a consistent whole, that there cannot be an unre-
deemable, final evil, and that natural theology and the traditional framework for
the problem of evil are standards for all, even post-Holocaust faith. At times Cohen
appears to want the threat to be total; at other times, as in this passage, he articulates
the threat as a challenge subject to pre-Holocaust standards.[76]

The challenge recognized and articulated by these post-Holocaust thinkers concerns the joint affirmation of continuity and discontinuity, of threat and recovery.
Cohen gives a vivid account of this challenge:

> It is time now to build a bridge over the abyss of the *tremendum*. It is a bridge that
> spans the abyss but does not obscure it. Wayfarers upon the bridge, however its
> moorings in the past of the Jewish people and its future in the prospect of its on-
> going life, cannot neglect the obligation to look over into the chasm beneath.
> They know the abyss but, since they pass along the bridge, they know equally
> that they do not have their being in its depths; however much the ineffaceable
> abyss informs them, their own being and proper life is elsewhere—on the
> bridge, in fact, over the abyss.[77]

There is no way from the present to the past, from Jewish life today to the traditions of
the past, other than by traversing the bridge that spans the abyss of Auschwitz. And
one must look into it but not be engulfed by it; remain on the bridge and live there,
with due respect for the chasm below and the transition between past and future. To
reach the past requires such a bridge, a strategy of recovery constructed in honest encounter with Auschwitz; it also requires finding a way over that abyss and not being
swallowed by it. That is the dialectic of authentic post-Holocaust Jewish existence.

In his final lecture, Cohen seeks to perform, if only schematically, that theological task, a post-Holocaust "redefinition of the reality of God and his relations to the

world and man."[78] Fulfilling the task will involve "account[ing] for the reality of God in the aftermath of the *tremendum* ... renew[ing] the meaning of creation and authenticat[ing] . . . the promise of redemption."[79] This means making sense of God's promise and plan, the world's receptivity, and human freedom in a post-Holocaust age — making sense of creation, redemption, and revelation.[80] Cohen sets standards for this theological task: that the evil must be accepted honestly and yet that God's relation to the created world must be made out.[81] His solution invokes the Lurianic notion of the divine as *ein sof*, nothingness, and creation as *tsimtsum*, contraction, executed through logos, divine speech.[82] Creation is an "event of speech and love," an act of divine overflowing out of God's abundance and generosity, and into this deaf and dumb world is placed man, whose essence is freedom ordered by reason.[83] Cohen rejects a religious naturalism, in which miracles are the remarkable orderliness of natural causation, and a traditional providentialism, in which a transcendent God intervenes in or interrupts the natural process.[84] He offers an alternative, that God is "in continuous community and nexus"[85] with history, and employs an image that is never really clarified. God is "a filament within the historical."[86] On this view, the *tremendum* as abyss does not alter the divine filament, but it does show how human beings have obscured, eclipsed, or burnt out that filament;[87] human freedom within history can extend or subvert revelation; and in the Holocaust, it subverted or opposed it — and threatened to extinguish it.

As a fact, "the Jew has returned out of the ashes of the *tremendum* to the historical *as an historical agent*."[88] Cohen points out how neither Rosenzweig nor Buber had anticipated or hoped for this return. Both venerated eternity as the core of Jewish life; Judaism had its locus "to the side of history" and not in it.[89] Cohen argues that this view, consistent with traditional Judaism, is no longer possible. After Auschwitz, the flesh and blood character of the Jewish people is undeniable, as victim and agent. "The Jew of today is not the same Jew as the Jew of yesterday or the Jew at Sinai. The Jew has a history even if [*sic*] it is an extraordinary history."[90] As a person, an individual, the Jew has a history; as a Jew, a member of the Jewish people, covenanted to God, the Jew has a goal. Historicity applies to the individual, eternity to the people.[91] The Holocaust calls forth the urgency, the need, the obligation for the redemptive project. Cohen notes that it is an abyss that inflicts not knowledge but memory: it tells us that "there is no portion of the human earth that does not need redemption in order that growth be renewed."[92]

Cohen carries out his project, obscurely to be sure, much as Greenberg, Berkovits, and Fackenheim had done. We cannot understand Auschwitz, nor can we ignore it. In some way or other, the redemptive vocabulary of the Jewish people must be carried on. In this way, a God totally absent in the abyss is present as support for the bridge over it. Cohen's retrieval is like Greenberg's voluntary covenant and Berkovits's questioning faith, an expression of continuity and hope after darkness.

In 1984 Rubenstein and Cohen engaged in a published dialogue about Cohen's work. We can learn something about both from this conversation and from one they had in 1968 in response to Rubenstein's "Homeland and Holocaust." Formally, these two events are mirror images, but it is crucial that Cohen's confrontation with Auschwitz separates them.

In 1968 Cohen thought little of Rubenstein's disposal of the God of history, covenantal Judaism, and transcendence. "What Rubenstein wants is force and potency, not faith and trust. And force and potency cannot, *ipso facto*, be wrung from the language of any theology of faith, covenant, and election."[93] It is no surprise that Rubenstein turns to naturalism, existentialism, and "the natural paganic optimism of the reborn folk." Rubenstein wears his Nietzscheanism on his sleeve but with too much boldness and too little compassion for Cohen.[94] Rubenstein admits that Cohen has read him correctly but objects to his assessment.[95] Rubenstein advocates dignity and self-respect; he does not find them in the death camps but does in post-1967 Israel.

By 1984, with the publication of Rubenstein's review of *The Tremendum* and Cohen's response, Cohen himself had come to an encounter with the death camps.[96] In his review, Rubenstein appreciates the turn in Cohen's thought but makes these charges. First, Cohen avoids the "crucial religious issue, which is not belief in God in the face of unspeakable evil but the credibility of God's covenant with Israel."[97] Cohen is obscure, allusive, and dense, but he deserves a more careful reading. He contends that to understand the post-Holocaust covenant and the Jewish commitment to and role in redemption, one needs a new conception of God and his relation to world and man. Rubenstein sees this, but he fails to recognize it as precisely an answer to the question of covenant.[98] He points to the language of divine presence not as intervention but as filament; this is akin to Berkovits's notion of an unconvincing presence or a hidden presence.[99] Rubenstein doubts that this succeeds at solving or dissolving the dilemma of a classical God of history or a God who is "functionally irrelevant," but he gives no reasons.[100] Clearly he finds the alternative too weak, but not all would agree.

Second, Cohen does not appreciate that the Jewish people's commitment to eternity or redemption might need to take "political form."[101] Where we might be forced to accept the role of nature and power in our lives, Cohen argues against any such capitulation. But, as Rubenstein points out, politics and statehood deserve more respect after Auschwitz. Surely, the Holocaust teaches the need for protection against the "obscenities a powerful aggressor can freely visit upon stateless victims."[102] There is nothing inauthentic about politicizing Jewish existence in order to save it; Greenberg and Fackenheim agree with Rubenstein in this regard, and even to a degree does Berkovits, although on this issue Cohen is closest to him.

Finally, Rubenstein criticizes Cohen for taking the Holocaust and the death camps to be incomprehensible "in terms of the normal categories of history, social science, demography, political theory, and economics."[103] This is a point of sharp difference. Rubenstein has always contended that the camps and Nazism can be rationally comprehended by social scientific means; this claim is already evident in the first edition of *After Auschwitz* and is also the foundation of *The Cunning of History* and the argument for extermination and population redundancy, based on Rubenstein's rather literalist reading of a notion used by Hannah Arendt in *The Origins of Totalitarianism*.[104] According to Rubenstein, he has always sought "*continuities* of seemingly disparate events and domains of reality, including that of God and humanity."[105] The issue, of course, is whether, after seeking such continuities, one finds them and indeed whether the threat of discontinuity is taken with complete seriousness. In this regard, ironically, Rubenstein fares better than Cohen.

How does Cohen respond? To begin, he seeks to locate and emphasize his task, to do theology after the Holocaust, and that means to think about "the nature and domain of God" after this event, monstrous, occluding, awesome, weighty, to fit God and the event into a seamless, coherent pattern of thought. It is, as he puts it, to tell the story of "God's involvement with Jewish history."[106] Cohen sees the theological response to Auschwitz as appropriate and even necessary; in an earlier place he argued for its primacy. He vigorously opposes Rubenstein's notion that theology should come after the fact and that it should serve social-psychological purposes: "dissonance reduction," as Rubenstein calls it.[107] To Cohen, there is a priority about theological thought, its complexity notwithstanding. It surely involves an act or process of thinking, but to Cohen the thought not the thinking is centrally important.

Finally, Cohen argues that Auschwitz is unique, a novum, not fully understood and yet theologically compelling even if it were. There is of course an important difference here, but it is not clear that Cohen makes his case. He says that "the Holocaust cannot be reduced to its rational causalities, precisely because — after all analysis is completed . . . the Holocaust remains a radical *novum*, a real novelty and therefore a conceptual conundrum."[108] There are two issues being conflated here: the event's being the first of its kind, unprecedented, and its being incomprehensible, which seems to mean not understood or not explained. Cohen then separates the two: even if a "totally satisfactory natural account of the event" were achieved, the systematic annihilation of a people is a novelty, and, at least in part because the people is God's people, it has theological implications. When, moreover, Cohen says that "the selection of the Jews to annihilation remains an *absurdum*, an *absurdum* that can be explained only in terms of fantastic unreason," does this mean that it can or cannot be explained, and if it can, of what relevance is this fact? In the end, I think that for Cohen the real issues are the Holocaust's unprecedented character and its nature as an evil, a result of "freedom no longer constrained by the check of death, of freedom infinitized."[109] For theology, any such episode of "unbounded freedom" yielding an unprecedented evil would lead to theological revision; since this event was the first to manifest such evil, it is a watershed. Cohen says this very clearly: an event that exhibits the human capacity for "systematic, radical evil" changes our theology, but only if it is the first such event, the one that gives rise to the concept of radical evil. From then on, any authentic theology will take it into account. If this correctly describes Cohen's views, then the issue of explanation or rational understanding can only have to do with the evil of the event, not its novelty. Even a novelty can be described and explained; indeed, all events, as novel, can be explained, or if they cannot, that surely does not distinguish one from the other. What makes the Holocaust an *absurdum* and a *tremendum* is not its being novel; it is rather that no social scientific account of its evil is without important shortcomings. The atrocity, the anguish, the pain, the negativity, and the degradation—all this is beyond our comprehension, whether we portray it from the victims' point of view or the investigators'. On this set of issues, then, Cohen and Rubenstein do differ, but their difference is less extraordinary than they think. When Rubenstein responds to Auschwitz by giving a naturalist account of it, modernity, religion, and so forth, the Holocaust becomes comprehensible. When Cohen responds by articulating a theodicy, then the Holocaust becomes theologically comprehensible. It is hardly surprising that they differ so vigorously and understand each other so well, for they are as similar as they are different.

Emil Fackenheim: Fidelity and Recovery
in the Post-Holocaust Epoch

In scope and depth, Emil Fackenheim's attempt to articulate an authentic response to Auschwitz and the post-Holocaust world is the richest and most developed. Since 1967 and the shift in his thinking Fackenheim has published nine books and about one hundred articles, chapters, and reviews relevant to post-Holocaust Jewish thought.[1] By any calculation, this is a monumental achievement, but quantity is not our only challenge. Another is subtlety and depth. Fackenheim is a professional philosopher, whose writing is tightly argued with precision and yet has impressive literary qualities. Furthermore, Fackenheim's articles are generally topical, incorporating discussion of current events and recent books, while at the same time extending and revising a general program, as it were, first sketched in 1967–68. One does not want to miss either the historical responsiveness of his writings or their overall systematic impulse.

My goal is to show how Fackenheim's post-Holocaust Jewish thought expresses that effort, prominent in the late sixties and seventies, to return to the past in order to reconstruct a Jewish identity that faces the Holocaust honestly and yet does not abandon God or Jewish tradition. How does Fackenheim confront the challenge of discontinuity and continuity, of history and identity?

As Fackenheim deepens, revises, and applies the framework he sets out in the late 1960s, his grasp of this problematic becomes increasingly self-conscious and nuanced. In this regard he exceeds all his peers. Nor is this surprising, for this theme — the relation between thought and life, between self-understanding and history — is central to the German philosophical tradition of which Fackenheim is a part and with which he has expert acquaintance. Although he only occasionally refers to or shows an awareness of postmodernist developments of the seventies and eighties and only once refers to the hermeneutical tradition of Gadamer and others, Fackenheim's thought is steeped in these issues. Indeed, one can read his work as a constituent of these developments, akin to but independent of them. Like

Gadamer, Charles Taylor, Alasdair MacIntyre, and others, Fackenheim acknowledges the primacy of the self, the central role of community and tradition, and the historical situatedness of all agency and all selfhood, and like them too he accepts the need for nonrelative, independent standards. What distinguishes his thinking is that the urgency underlying these needs and demands arises not primarily from intellectual pressures but rather from an ultimate religious and moral source, Auschwitz and the death camps. At the center of Fackenheim's thinking, then, is a sense of moral responsibility that distinguishes it from many of the secular modes of recent thought.[2]

I will deal with Fackenheim's writings in three stages. First, I will examine the essay "Jewish Faith and the Holocaust: A Fragment" that appeared almost simultaneously in 1968 as an article in *Commentary* and as part of the first chapter of the collection of essays *Quest for Past and Future*.[3] During the same period Fackenheim prepared the three lectures delivered at New York University as the Charles F. Deems Lectures in 1968 and published in 1970 as *God's Presence in History: Jewish Affirmations and Philosophical Reflections*.[4] In these works, he develops a framework for thinking about the Holocaust and a set of themes that are the foundation for his subsequent articles and books. Second, I will look at the role of the Holocaust in *Encounters between Judaism and Modern Philosophy*, published in 1973. As part of his attempt to examine critically the work of analytic philosophy of religion, Kant, Kierkegaard, Hegel, left-wing Hegelianism, Sartre, and Heidegger, Fackenheim exposes each to Auschwitz and exhibits shortcomings and distortions. Moreover, throughout the seventies, Fackenheim gave lectures and wrote articles that elaborated a response to Auschwitz vis à vis a variety of issues and the "constant tension" of current historical events. Many were collected in *The Jewish Return into History: Reflections in the Age of Auschwitz and a New Jerusalem*, published in 1978.[5] I will also examine various themes and developments that emerge from a reading of these essays. Finally, in the midseventies Fackenheim began a large project, a rethinking and elaboration of the impact of the Holocaust and authentic responses to it. The first result of that project was his extremely important work, in a sense his magnum opus, *To Mend the World*, published in 1982 and republished in 1987 and 1994, with new introductory material. I will complete my account of his work with comments on this book.

Confronting Auschwitz: The Late Sixties

Earlier I discussed the major shift in Fackenheim's thinking, the realization that nothing in Judaism is unconditional and a priori, that everything Jewish, all belief and all conduct, is historical, alterable, and possibly refutable. The very first sentences of "Jewish Faith and the Holocaust" announce that shift.[6] Jewish self-understanding is always contextual; it is a matter of identifying the major events that challenge Judaism, recognizing what the challenges are, and meeting them. For Jews living in the late sixties, they are three: the Emancipation, Auschwitz, and the rebirth of the state of Israel. Often, Fackenheim has addressed and will address the challenge of the Emancipation and the Enlightenment—in essays like "On the Eclipse of God" and in the second lecture of *God's Presence in History*. What is distinctive, he says, about Auschwitz is that it was an internal challenge to Judaism and yet wholly negative. How, he asks, can the Jew not avoid it and yet face it authentically, with honesty and integrity? Like Berkovits, who writes later, the victims provide some kind of standard, for unquestioning adherence to traditional doctrines would seem to slight them. The task of the Jewish religious thinker is somehow to face Auschwitz, to honor the victims, and still to retain some continuity with traditional Jewish faith.

Fackenheim's essay has two parts. The first deals with Jewish faith after Auschwitz, the second with the relation between Jews and Christians after Auschwitz and at that moment after the Six Day War. In the section on post-Holocaust Judaism,[7] Fackenheim elaborates his reasoning in the *Judaism* symposium of March 26, 1967, under the impact of the Six Day War and fixes the framework that persists through the subsequent two decades. Here is the structure of Fackenheim's thinking:

1. Both Jews and non-Jews, seeking to understand the Holocaust, have avoided the particularity or distinctiveness of the event, but it is distinctive, unprecedented, unique.
2. Auschwitz resists satisfying rational and religious explanations; it has no purpose or meaning.
3. Response is necessary.
4. There are no traditional, acceptable models for such response.
5. Jews after the destruction remained committed to Jewish survival.
6. Such a commitment to Jewish survival can be understood as a response of opposition to Nazi purposes, a "bearing witness" against the "demons of Auschwitz."
7. What accounts for this commitment to Jewish existence as an act of opposition is a "commanding Voice [that] speaks from Auschwitz."
8. This *commanding* but not *redeeming* voice is heard by religious Jews but not by secular Jews; the commandment to resist is heard by both. Buber's language of a divine eclipse is not applicable.
9. The content of this absolute commandment is: Jews are forbidden to grant posthumous victories to Hitler.
10. This commandment can be elaborated to mean: survive as Jews, remember the victims of Auschwitz, do not despair of humankind and the world, and do not despair of the God of Israel. Nor can there be any untroubled hope and joy, even after 1967; one must tremble and rejoice at once.

In this summary I have tried to use Fackenheim's own vocabulary and not yet to translate it or clarify it.[8] Even at this stage, however, one can see that this is a complex line of thought. Steps 1 to 3, for example, involve attempts at explaining and understanding Auschwitz in order to deal with it by cognitively or theoretically encompassing it. They announce a failure and yield a result: the event has no purpose or meaning but *requires* a response. But not all responses are acceptable, although all are actions of one kind or another. Steps 4 to 6 and 9 to 10 clarify a standard for authentic response, an imperative of opposition: how Fackenheim identifies it and interprets it. Finally, steps 7 to 8 say something about the ground of the imperative or obligation, the justification for it and how that justification applies to different agents.

It will be helpful if I condense and translate this line of thinking (with Roman numerals to distinguish these steps from Fackenheim's):

I. The Holocaust was unique, which means that no traditional religious or social scientific account comprehends it satisfactorily.

II. Although explanatory comprehension — meaning or purpose — is impossible, response is necessary.

III. There is no traditional model for authentic response today; there is no account of what a Jew living today must or ought to do.

IV. Actions after the event, by survivors and by Jews who lived after the event, can be interpreted by the religious thinker as responses to it.

V. Such actions or expressions of commitment to continued Jewish existence were unconditional.

VI. Such actions should be understood as responses to an unconditional imperative.

VII. Some responded to the imperative alone; others to the divine ground for it.

VIII. The imperative should be interpreted as requiring resistance to Nazi purposes and elaborated in terms of the variety of such purposes — the Nazi goal of destroying Judaism, the Jewish people, human dignity, and so forth.

This line of thinking is an attempt to answer the questions: how ought the Jew of today respond to Auschwitz? How can he or she take it seriously and yet go on as a Jew? In terms I used earlier, how can the Jew today, with regard to tradition and the past, respect both discontinuity and continuity, the threat of total rupture and the desire, as well as the need, for the recovery of the past? The answer is not without difficulties and weaknesses, some of which Fackenheim sees as time goes on and tries to address. But before I turn to them, it is necessary to examine this reasoning and these steps more carefully.

First, step I speaks of Auschwitz as unique and somehow incommensurable with traditional or conventional categories. "Auschwitz is a unique descent into hell. It is an unprecedented celebration of evil. It is evil for evil's sake."[9] Part of the "scandal of particularity" that people avoid is that the event was an unprecedented evil; moreover, it was evil done for no other purpose than to achieve and venerate evil, to perform atrocities in order to honor and esteem them. This was part of what made Nazi evil unprecedented, Fackenheim claims. Another part was its central focus on the Jews as victims, as the "prototype by which 'inferior race' was defined," as the initial and determinate target of the process of dehumanization and annihilation. Finally, it was unprecedented in the sense that "there is not, and never will be, an adequate explanation. . . . This is the rock on which throughout eternity all rational explanations will crash and break apart. . . . No purpose, religious or non-religious, will ever be found in Auschwitz."[10]

In these few pages, Fackenheim begins an account that he will return to again and again; it is an account of what it means to call Auschwitz unique or unprecedented, to call attention to its particularity or distinctiveness, and what reasons one might give in behalf of its uniqueness. He recognizes that it is tempting to assimilate it to standard categories—mass killing, anti-Semitism, innocent suffering, and genocide. But he argues against so doing, for two reasons. First, such classifications fail to attend to the distinctive features of the event—"where else has human skin ever been made into lampshades, and human body-fat into soap—not by isolated perverts but under the direction of ordinary bureaucrats?"[11] Second, such assimilation is evasive, a refuge, avoidance, and even itself a covert form of antisemitism. Normal as it may seem, to generalize is to encompass Auschwitz in conventional categories, to domesticate it, and thus to avoid its distinctiveness; to explain it is to place it into some scheme or pattern and thereby to give it a purpose, meaning, and justification. To be sure, social, economic, and political explanations do yield partially successful causal accounts, albeit not totally satisfying ones.[12] But religious explanations, as retribution for sin, for example, are impossible. The uniqueness of Auschwitz lies in the form of the atrocities, their victims, their goals, and their location in time; moreover, the uniqueness means conceptual, cognitive incommensurability. With sufficient attention to their details, the Nazi crimes are inassimilable to traditional and conventional thought.

Step II says: "Yet it is of the utmost importance to recognize that seeking a purpose is one thing, but seeking a response quite another. The first is wholly out of the question. The second is inescapable."[13] One might take this, as I suggested for Greenberg, as a conceptual truth, that once a historical event has occurred, response, that is, action in terms of it, is unavoidable, and Fackenheim's use of the unqualified word "response" recommends such a reading. In fact, however, this interpretation is incorrect; what he means is "authentic response," for he says: "But [the Jew's] faith, his destiny, his very survival will depend on whether, in the end, he will be able to respond," and surely "respond" here must mean "respond authentically."[14] Jewish faith and survival, even when no satisfactory or acceptable religious explanation is forthcoming, depends on how one ought to act, on what one ought to do. There is a need, then, for models of response, standards of authentic Jewish life and conduct, for those committed to continue as Jews and to keeping Judaism alive. The result is a conditional obligation: if one is committed to Jewish survival, then one ought to persevere as a Jew by responding to Auschwitz. But traditional responses to such a threat are unsatisfactory. Why? Because they presume that one is acting out of faith or despite it, but after Auschwitz one can be seen to act in behalf of others—future generations—and their faith. A response now could condemn future descendants; to abandon Judaism is both impossible and desirable, and there are no models for such a response.[15]

Fackenheim found himself at an impasse. The Holocaust requires for Jews a response and hence some guidance about how best to respond. The past provides no intellectual accounts that give the event meaning and no models for how to act after such an event and in terms of it. So, totally cut off from the past, how does one go on? And yet how does one not go on? Or, to put the matter in other terms, seeking guidance one turns to theologians and philosophers, but they are incapable of providing it. What, then, does one do? To whom does one turn? In the next paragraphs, among the most important in Fackenheim's literary corpus, he sketches an answer to these questions.[16] Here thought goes to school with life, as he later puts it. The thinker's understanding of what ought to be done finds its origins and development in the everyday Jew's doing of it. From actuality, one derives necessity, the necessity not of events but rather of obligation.[17]

"The scandal of the particularity of Auschwitz" is now the threat that the event is unique and so cut off from the Jewish past that faith is impossible after it. Fackenheim admits a "momentous discovery": "that while religious thinkers were vainly struggling for a response to Auschwitz, Jews throughout the world—rich and poor, learned and ignorant, religious and non-religious—had to some degree been responding all along . . . with an unexpected will to live—with, under the circumstances, an incredible commitment to Jewish group survival."[18] This is step IV. With thought at an impasse and no models of authentic response available, where does one turn? To life, to ordinary people whose lives and actions—bearing children whom they educate as Jews, celebrating *brit milah*, financially supporting religious institutions, and so forth—express a commitment to being Jewish and hence to the existence and survival of Judaism. In 1945, 1948, 1955, and 1963, the actions of ordinary Jews can be interpreted by the thinker as responses to Auschwitz and to an invitation to capitulate and abandon Judaism. Normal acts, then, whatever the intentions of their agents, can be understood as acts of resistance:

> In ordinary times, a commitment of this kind may be a mere mixture of nostalgia and vague loyalties not far removed from tribalism; and, unable to face Auschwitz, I had myself long viewed it as such, placing little value on a Jewish survival which was, or seemed to be, only survival for survival's sake. I was wrong, and even the shallowest Jewish survivalist philosophy of the postwar period was right by comparison. For in the age of Auschwitz a Jewish commitment to Jewish survival is in itself a monumental act of faithfulness, as well as a monumental, albeit as yet fragmentary, act of faith. Even to do no more than remain a Jew after Auschwitz is to confront the demons of Auschwitz in all their guises, and to bear witness against them. It is to believe that these demons cannot, will

not, and must not prevail, and to stake on that belief one's own life and the lives of one's children, and of one's children's children.[19]

The same action, performed at different times and in different contexts, can mean different things. Raising one's arm can be an act of stretching, reaching, or calling attention to oneself. And publicizing one's Jewishness, even in the most minimal way, can be an act of nostalgia or of fidelity or kindness to parents or, after Auschwitz, an act of courage, of faithfulness to Judaism and the Jewish people. In Hitler's shadow, a Sabbath candle casts a committed glow against the darkness.

Furthermore, the acts *are* committed acts; they are not instinctual or whimsical. They express allegiance and conviction and not a desire that seems strong now but might easily dissipate as circumstances change. There is an unconditionality about these responses, and that means that they are a response to a demand that comes from the outside, an imperative force, an obligation.[20] This is part of the answer to Fackenheim's question: "What accounts for this commitment to Jewish existence where there might have been, and by every rule of human logic should have been, a terrified and demoralized flight from Jewish existence?" What grounds the commitment? What distinguishes those who remain and those who flee? First, an imperative, a sense of obligation or duty. Second, an imperative from Auschwitz. Third, a divine imperative that speaks from Auschwitz. "Nothing less will do than to say that a commanding Voice speaks from Auschwitz, and that there are Jews who hear it and Jews who stop their ears."[21] Buber's image of an "eclipse of God" is unacceptable, for while God was absent at Auschwitz in one way, he was present in another. He was present in a commanding voice. Or, as Fackenheim puts it, an absolute commandment emerged from the event: "religious Jews hear it, and they identify its source. Secularist Jews hear it, even though perforce they leave it unidentified."[22]

Here, then, is Fackenheim's derivation, steps V to VIII: we begin with post-Holocaust Jewish action, interpreted as expressing a commitment to Jewish survival. Such action occurs as it does, absolute and performed out of conviction, and this requires as its ground an imperative or commandment. It is grounded in an obligation. Some respond only to it; others, in Rosenzweigian language, hear the voice of the *metzaveh* (commander) speaking through the *mitzvah* (commandment).[23] For these believers, there was a commanding voice present at Auschwitz; it was an occasion of revelation, issuing in a commandment—what he earlier called a "614th commandment," a supplement to the traditional 613. Finally, what was its content? How should the commanding presence be interpreted? What content clarifies the committed response in behalf of Jewish survival? Or—in other terms—when the presence of God is experienced within the context of the death camps, what does that mean to the Jew who survives? It is a response of opposition, of resistance, of maintaining Judaism, the Jewish people, and human dignity in the face of the Nazi threat and hence of whatever extreme threat may come. Fackenheim formulates it this way: Jews are forbidden to grant posthumous victories to Hitler;[24] and he elaborates it:

[Jews] are commanded to survive as Jews, lest the Jewish people perish. They are commanded to remember the victims of Auschwitz, lest their memory perish. They are forbidden to despair of man and his world, and to escape into either cynicism or otherworldliness, less [sic] they cooperate in delivering the world over to the forces of Auschwitz. Finally, they are forbidden to despair of the God of Israel, lest Judaism perish.[25]

As Fackenheim says, "the ultimate question is: where was God at Auschwitz?" —ultimate perhaps, but not central. The central question is: how ought the post-Holocaust Jew respond to the Holocaust? What is *authentic* Jewish existence after Auschwitz?[26] Ultimately one may need to ask about God; for the believer, that question may arise very quickly indeed. But, on the other hand, it may not arise so quickly; it may require a good deal to answer it. In the course of that struggle, there is still the imperative to oppose Nazi purposes and all that imperative can be understood to mean. Much can and should be done while the question about God still goes unanswered.

Out of Auschwitz itself and a wholly serious encounter with it arises, for Fackenheim, an obligation to "bridge the abyss" and recover the Jewish past for the purposes of recovering in the Jewish present. The rupture threatens all with total despair, but it is possible, indeed necessary to repudiate that despair and to recover hope. Here we have a self-conscious acceptance of the historicity of Jewish experience and at the same time a strategy for justifying and identifying an unconditional standard for authenticity.

Fackenheim's reflections in 1967 to 1968 and the line of thinking I have been tracing were formulated in part prior to the Six Day War.[27] But that event clearly advanced them.[28] The war—the response of Israeli soldiers, many not religious but rather wholly secular and without personal connection to the Holocaust, and of Jews around the world—strengthened his conviction that for Jews a commandment did arise out of Auschwitz and that for many it was divine. It also confirmed his sense that authentic response would be dialectical, involving both pain and joy; it would require facing the darkness and yet seeking light. The war made concrete the double, dialectical awareness of defeat and victory, of total annihilation and salvation. The events of May and June 1967, as Fackenheim himself puts it, created a bewildering situation, in which Jews could neither forget Auschwitz nor reject Jerusalem. The authentic Jew "must both tremble and rejoice. He must tremble lest he permit any light after Auschwitz to relieve the darkness of Auschwitz. He must rejoice, lest he add to the darkness of Auschwitz."[29] In the spirit of Hegel, Kierkegaard, Buber, and others, for Fackenheim religious experience is deeply dialectical and paradoxical. Auschwitz and then the Six Day War each reflect this understanding of the human condition. In that sense, these events only confirm Fackenheim's previous account of human experience and religious life.

From 1968 to 1970 and the publication of the Charles Deems Lectures, *God's Presence in History*, Fackenheim's thinking achieves a kind of consolidation and depth.[30] *God's Presence in History* is not a long book, but it is an extraordinary one, moving, terse in argument and formulation. It has three chapters. In the first Fackenheim gives an account of Jewish experience, its hermeneutical character, and its historicity. In the second, he engages in an encounter between modern philosophy and religious experience. Finally, in the third chapter, he exposes Jewish experience and modern, secular thought to Auschwitz. For my purposes, the most important chapter is the third. But one cannot totally ignore the first and second if one expects to understand the final chapter.

We should recall that Fackenheim's great shift came when he accepted the unconditional historicity of Jewish experience.[31] In "The Structure of Jewish Experience" he articulates the features and content of a hermeneutical recovery of classical Jewish religious experience. He clarifies what is required of a contemporary retrieval of biblical religious experience and its meaning, thereby exploring one dimension of the historicity of Jewish experience. He also identifies the classical content of the divine–human encounter, its reflective comprehension in Midrash, and its openness to historical recovery and reinterpretation. This can be put in a different way: today the Jew is informed by a certain conception of God, Torah, covenant, and such notions; it is the current understanding of these notions, the outcome of a current return to the past, that is challenged by recent events and intellectual developments. In this chapter, Fackenheim sketches how this return is possible and what it achieves; he seeks "a structured essence . . . [that] is vulnerable to epoch-making events."[32]

Fackenheim's lectures are about the God of history, the presence of God in history, and the human experience of that presence. Living today, however, we should be plagued by doubts, because of modern science, historiography, and other intellectual developments and because of events like Auschwitz. Yet the Jew should not despair, Fackenheim warns; there have been other evils, and faith has not been destroyed. We need to grasp that faith first before we expose it to new challenges.[33] This task, which takes up his first chapter, begins with an account of the hermeneutics of tradition. This is my term, not his, but it helps to indicate that what he sketches is about the reception of experiences, texts, accounts, and motifs by a process of interpretive recovery. He explores how Jewish interpretive reading of the past works; his account is as relevant, then, to his own recovery or reading and to ours, as it is to any other reading of the biblical text and its revelations. But here its purpose is local, to articulate the content of his own grasp of the divine–human encounter—in the manner of Buber and Rosenzweig—within Judaism, to understand the features of God's presence in history.

The interplay of history and thought in Judaism includes several components: root experiences, epoch-making events, subsequent interpreters, the divine presence, and Midrashic thought and literature. Drawing on a variety of sources and influences—from Buber and Kierkegaard to R. G. Collingwood and Irving Greenberg,[34] Fackenheim shapes these components into the following structure.

Jewish faith is a set of beliefs, practices, attitudes, and hopes that arose in history, as a response to historical events. The earliest responses to these original, determinative events Fackenheim calls "root experiences."[35] These experiences give shape to a world, a culture that later came to be called Judaism. In its history, this culture or way of life

> passed through many epoch-making events, such as the end of prophecy and the destruction of the first Temple, the Maccabean revolt, the destruction of the second Temple, and the expulsion from Spain. These events each made a new claim upon the Jewish faith . . . a confrontation in which the old faith was tested in the light of contemporary experience.[36]

Here, at the outset of Fackenheim's account, he expresses his commitment to the historicity of Judaism, embedded in history but not isolated or fragmented. Rather, Judaism and its reinterpretations are constituents of a tradition. Fackenheim's epoch-making events are like Alasdair MacIntyre's epistemological crises, moments when much is called into question and when the tradition takes a new direction.[37]

For Fackenheim, moreover, root experiences are not simply any experiences of or responses to an original event but only those that "continue to make a present claim—the claim that God is present in history."[38] Fackenheim specifies three conditions of root experiences; that is, features that enable those experiences to mean something to members of the subsequent tradition. In Judaism, these formative experiences testify to an encounter with God; they are authoritative to those who follow because those later adherents find the formative experiences meaningful and compelling. How is this possible? First, because the later recovery and the normative or root experience each has its own integrity; yet each depends on the other. They are distinct but related, independent yet interdependent. Fackenheim calls this a "dialectical relation between present and past" that enables "a past experience to legislate to the present."[39] The later interpreter does not have an original experience, but he or she is confident that original adherents did. Hence the original or root experience is both needed and relevant. The past can legislate; it can be authoritative, because it is not superseded by the present, gratuitous, or superfluous; nor is it cut off from the present or irrelevant. A root experience must be part of a continuum of epistemological possibilities. Second, root experiences are public events that are recalled by a community and contribute to the shaping of a community's tradition. Finally, root experiences exhibit an "accessibility of past to present" that is the critical condition of such experiences, that is, of their influence and their authority.[40] What does this mean? What, concerning the present grasp of the past, is at issue?

In Judaism, root experiences have as their object a natural event that is also a revelatory episode. At the Red Sea, the people experienced the Egyptian threat, the separating of the sea, and the sense of being saved from doom. "They also experienced the presence of God."[41] Members of the tradition can certainly recall the natural, historical events. They can remember them, use evidence to reconstruct them historically, and narrate them. But can they also "have access to the vision" of the people at the sea, that is, to the presence of God? Yes, Fackenheim answers, if they "reenact the past [event] as a present reality."[42] Fackenheim, in a highly condensed passage, then explains this reenactment or, to be more precise, clarifies that of which it is a reenactment. Using Martin Buber's account of the phenomenology of the experience of a miracle, a divine intervention, he distinguishes the natural-historical event, the "abiding astonishment" or sense of wonder in the witness, and the "sole Power" present in the event. For the one who experiences the miracle, the astonishment provides access to the reality of the divine presence in the event. Hence, for the later interpreter, the member of the tradition, the abiding astonishment provides access too but in an indirect way: "*In reenacting the natural-historical event, [the later believer] reenacts the abiding astonishment as well, and makes it his own.* Hence the 'sole Power' present then is present still. Hence memory turns into faith and hope. . . . Thus the reenacted past legislates to present and future. Thus, in Judaism, it is a root experience." By reenacting in memory—in words, performance, recollection—the Jew appropriates the subjective attitude of the original witness and actually has that experience of astonishment and wonder. The Jew is capable of encountering the divine presence, is open to it, receptive, and hence the old event, miracle, revelation is authoritative for him or her. Unless challenged or negated, its meaning for the original witness is his or her meaning.[43]

For Judaism, as Fackenheim explores through Bible and Midrash, the divine presence is both saving and commanding. And in the case of a commanding voice, as at Sinai, the encounter seems paradoxical: as divine, the command derives from a power that is unlimited and overwhelming; as commanding, it speaks to a human freedom, without which it cannot be heard. Fackenheim then gives an extraordinary—Hegelian and Rosenzweigian—interpretation of the complexity of the reception of the divine commanding presence:

> Hence the divine commanding Presence can be divine, commanding, and present only if it is *doubly* present; and the human astonishment must be a *double* astonishment. As *sole* Power, the divine commanding Presence *destroys* human freedom; as *gracious* Power, it *restores* that freedom, and indeed *exalts* it, for human freedom is made part of a covenant with divinity itself. And the human astonishment, which is *terror* at a Presence at once divine and commanding, turns into a *second* astonishment, which is *joy*, at a Grace which restores and exalts human freedom by its commanding Presence. . . . A man can receive [the Torah] only if he reenacts the double astonishment. . . . Only be reenacting both the terror and the joy can he participate in a life of the commandments which lives before the sole Power and yet is human.[44]

By performing a commandment today with a proper sense of utter subordination and yet self-determination, one can perform it as given by God and thereby recover a relationship with that God in history. At any moment, then, the Jew is related to the past and ultimately to the root experiences of Judaism and to God by means of contemporary reenactments—memory, recovery, retrieval—that are themselves historical events.

The notion of reenactment is an important one in Fackenheim's account.[45] He does not clarify it, but his use indicates what he has in mind. There are a variety of ways of reenacting the past—by carrying out acts of imaginative projection, by reading a narrative with a sense of participation in the events being narrated, by performing ritual acts that refer to past events and experiences, through song, performance, study, and more.[46] Reenactment, then, is not any interpretation of the past; it is a self-incorporating interpretation that provides access to the realities and experiences that gave rise to beliefs and practices that continue to be compelling for the current members of the tradition.

Reenactment, however, and the self-understanding grounded in it, are not without difficulties. Historical developments may threaten both the reenactments themselves and the appropriation of traditional interpretations of the root experiences and their meaning. Fackenheim associates these interpretations with the literature of Midrash and what he calls the Midrashic Framework.[47] Taken as a totality, the Midrashic way of thinking and the literature of Midrashic reflection have three features that are centrally important. First, they—the Midrashic Framework—are dialectical; they incorporate and do not dissipate the contradictions of Jewish existence and its root experiences,[48] contradictions like that of divine power and human freedom, divine immanence and transcendence. Second, Midrash is a whole, even while it admits its fragmentary contents. Finally, Midrash is open: "The Torah was given at Sinai, yet it is given whenever a man receives it, and a man must often hear the old commandments in new ways. . . . Such openness is necessary if history is to be serious."[49] Here we return to the commitment to historicity: for the Jew in the sixties in America, what is vulnerable to threat and open to history is the totality of his Jewish world and his understanding of God, covenant, people, and destiny; it is the tradition of Judaism—its root experiences, Midrashic thinking, and reinterpretations—as he reenacts and reappropriates them all. In the past, in the Roman Period and later after the expulsion from Spain, that tradition was called on to respond to challenge and yet to survive. So too was the Jewish faith in God's presence in history. Recalling these past challenges, Fackenheim turns to those of the present;[50] we are told by some, he notes, that "Auschwitz is punishment for Jewish sins" and by others that after Auschwitz "the God of history is impossible." Both responses should be rejected, and once they are, something must replace them.[51] In the third chapter of *God's Presence in History*, elaborating the thinking we have already met, he makes his proposal, his own "fragmentary attempts to cope with the Holocaust."

Having distinguished the believer from the Jewish secularist, Fackenheim has both figures confront Auschwitz, working toward the commanding voice of Auschwitz and the response to it. The basic structure of his thinking is the same: from the Holocaust's unprecedented, unique character to the impossibility of meaning, from response to an imposed imperative, from unconditional opposition to the divine commanding presence.[52] This enterprise has several features.

First, Fackenheim enriches his argument that the Holocaust is unique, unprecedented, and only inadequately understood and explained by traditional categories.[53] Auschwitz was an act of genocidal hatred, executed with care and sophistication. Its ends were not "rational," for often Jews were hunted down and exterminated when power, money, efficiency, and self-interest were at stake. "The Nazi murder of Jews was an 'ideological' project; it was annihilation for the sake of annihilation, murder for the sake of murder, evil for the sake of evil."[54] Here, as in "Jewish Faith and the Holocaust," Fackenheim notes the horrifying fact that Jews were killed because of the faith of their great-grandparents. There was no choice for the victims and an unknowing, irrevocable choice by their ancestors.[55]

Second, Fackenheim elaborates the exposure of Jewish tradition—the Midrashic Framework as he here calls it—to the atrocity.[56] Can we, three generations after, remain firm and not "abandon our millennial post as witnesses to the God of history?"[57] Or is Rubenstein correct in the confidence of his rejection?[58] One by one Fackenheim argues the inadequacy of traditional doctrines—the providential doctrine of retribution, that suffering is punishment for sins; the doctrine of martyrdom—"can there be martyrdom where there is no choice?";[59] the doctrine of a "protest which *stays within* the sphere of faith," which may result in a total indictment of God;[60] a conception of God as powerless, but radically so if we take seriously Wiesel's extraordinary portrait in *Night* of God hanging on the gallows;[61] and finally, the notion of a divine eclipse. Recall that earlier Fackenheim had used Buber's image of the eclipse of God to cope with Auschwitz.[62] Here he no longer finds satisfactory the view that God was temporarily absent.[63] It does not take seriously enough the horrifying possibility that the absent God may never return. After Auschwitz, a saving presence that can still come but was not present is impossible. As Fackenheim puts it, "what if our present is without hope?"[64] The traditional doctrine of the divine eclipse cannot endure this possibility, and yet no honest encounter with Auschwitz can a priori deny it.[65] The initial exposure of tradition and the God of history to the Nazi atrocities shows that Berkovits cannot be right but that Rubenstein might be.

Third, Fackenheim reiterates the line of reasoning from his earlier article:[66] after the Holocaust, both secular Jews and believers remain committed to Jewish existence; normal, social scientific explanations of this commitment are inadequate ("Humiliation causes pride in half-remembered loyalties");[67] we can interpret this commitment, under the special circumstances of Auschwitz, as an "absolute opposition" to the "demons of Auschwitz";[68] even the Jewish secularist "opposes the demons of Auschwitz absolutely by his mere commitment to Jewish survival";[69] the ground of this response is an absolute obligation against Nazi purposes; unlike the religious Jew, who hears the voice of God in the commandment to oppose, the secularist "bears witness by the mere affirmation of his Jewishness, against the devil";[70] this imperative "cannot be understood in terms of humanly created ideals," for example, reason, progress, or autonomous humanity: freedom.

In the earlier article, Fackenheim had *leaped* from positing an imperative of opposition to introducing God as its source. Here, in the course of arguing for the limitations of secularism, he shows that "Jewish opposition to Auschwitz"—the continuing commitment to Jewish existence—"cannot be grasped in terms of humanly created ideals but only as an imposed commandment." Once we recognize the response as unconditional and its basis as "an imperative which brooks no compromise," then we must *show* that such an imperative requires as its source more than principles like reason or progress, which are too abstract or too innocent of the real evil of Auschwitz. The outcome is that Fackenheim, the thinker, identifies the "imposed commandment" as the product of a divine commanding voice: "the Jewish secularist, no less than the believer, is absolutely singled out by a Voice as truly other than man-made ideals—an imperative as truly *given*—as was the Voice of Sinai."[71] The secularist only grasps the imperative; Fackenheim the Jewish thinker concludes that its source must be divine.

Fackenheim emphasizes that authenticity of response resides in adherence to this commandment of opposition. Authentic Jews affirm their Jewishness, whether they be religious or secularist. But we should appreciate three features of Fackenheim's argument. First, the believer and the secularist both oppose Nazi purposes unconditionally by affirming Jewish existence, but only the former witnesses to the divine. Fackenheim does not ignore or evade the secularist's rejection of God. He acknowledges it. Second, Fackenheim here *argues* for the rejection of grounds for the imperative of opposition that are human grounds. Finally, this is the crucial point where, within the context of historically situated agency, Fackenheim shows how a nonrelative principle and its foundation are grasped.[72] Here is the precise moment when the threat of discontinuity is overcome by the reality of continuity.[73]

Fourth, Fackenheim repeats his interpretation of the content of this "imposed commandment" of opposition; it is the 614th commandment, "Jews are forbidden to hand Hitler posthumous victories."[74] He elaborates each of its four fragments— not to abandon (1) the victims and the memory of the event, (2) the survival of the Jewish people, (3) hope for the world and human dignity, or (4) God.[75] Each picture is Fackenheim's interpretive account of what is required of the post-Holocaust Jew, of the believer who has heard the voice of Sinai and now hears the voice of Auschwitz and of the secular Jew who only hears the latter.[76] This is elliptical, of course; what it means is that the two both have post-Holocaust obligations concerning Judaism, the Jewish people, and humankind, whether or not those obligations involve a witness to God's presence in history. Moreover, as Fackenheim shows, if these are the imperatives, obedience to them is by no means easy, for they often come into conflict. This too is an expression of his opposition to a post-

Enlightenment conception of rational ideals, coordinated and compatible. History is the domain of moral and religious conflict, of no easy or glib adherence to ideals of progress or goodness but also of no easy disposal of hope and aspiration.[77] Both forgetting and despair are forbidden, Fackenheim argues, as are an unmitigated joy and expectation.

Finally, Fackenheim asks a probing question: if this is the commandment, the absolute imperative to oppose and to go on, how is it possible to perform it? How can one endure?[78] To the extent that we can, we understand the necessity of post-Holocaust Jewish existence, but can we understand its possibility? "We ask: whence has come our strength to endure even these twenty-five years—not to flee or disintegrate but rather to stay, however feebly, at our solitary post, to affirm, however weakly, our Jewishness, and to bear witness, if only by this affirmation, against the forces of hell itself?"[79] To this question he gives a strange and bewildering answer: "The Jew after Auschwitz is a witness to endurance. . . . He bears witness that without endurance we shall all perish. He bears witness that we *can* endure because we *must* endure; and that we must endure because we are commanded to endure."[80] It seems, then, that possibility is somehow grounded in necessity, that *can* is entailed by *ought*, a deep question but perhaps too glib an answer.

The general question, can the commandment be performed, cannot be divorced from the particular questions: "can the miracle at the Red Sea still be reenacted? Can the religious Jew still recall it twice daily in his prayers? After Auschwitz can we continue to celebrate the Passover Seder?"[81] In part, Fackenheim's book ends with the reminder that post-Holocaust Jewish thought is not merely about thought, belief, and principle; it is also about life—indeed about memory and life. It is about an authentic Jewish existence that seizes memory as it flashes up at a moment of danger, exposes itself to the abyss, and goes on. It is about celebrating the old Passover in new ways, retrieving and revising the past, and finding revolutionary relationships with one's people, one's God, and all others as well.[82]

As for Greenberg, unity of the Jewish people is one of Fackenheim's themes, especially the unity between religious and secular Jews.[83] Both hear the commandment of opposition to Nazi purposes; both are committed to Jewish survival. Indeed, this unity Fackenheim finds best expressed in the state of Israel and particularly in the young soldiers who defended her in the Six Day War. The unity of religious purpose and secular self-reliance embodied in these paradigmatic Israelis becomes, for Fackenheim, a model of post-Holocaust response and a way of understanding the link between Israel and the Holocaust. "Jerusalem, while no 'answer' to the Holocaust, is a response; and every Israeli lives that response. Israel is collectively what every survivor is individually: a No to the demons of Auschwitz, a Yes to Jewish survival and security—and thus a testimony to life against death *on behalf of all mankind.*"[84] Greenberg too had realized how Auschwitz altered our concepts and transformed categories and dichotomies into dialectical wholes; Fackenheim exhibits this in such a way that the intermingling of religious affirmation and purpose and individual autonomy and self-reliance becomes characteristic of authentic post-Holocaust Judaism and a way of understanding the connection between Israel and Auschwitz. Moreover, it was the Six Day War that called attention to that relation in part with its dialectic of threat and reprieve, despair and joy, and in part by exhibiting that model of response.[85] Fackenheim does not raise the political above the religious; nor does he denigrate secularism or faith. Rather he finds a way to draw them together into a complex whole that expresses the novel character of post-Holocaust Jewish life.

God's Presence in History and the essays written in the late sixties and early seventies express, I have argued, a framework for confronting the Holocaust and for articulating the fact and the content of an authentic Jewish response.[86] Even in the course of those years, however, Fackenheim was coming to appreciate difficulties and shortcomings in his thinking. As I proceed to look at his work in the seventies and early eighties, it will be valuable to have some of these problem areas in mind. The first is the uniqueness of the Holocaust. Fackenheim already has shown that what he has in mind is its unprecedented place in history and a constellation of distinctive features concerning the victims, the crimes, and the perpetrators. As the years go by, he continues to gather evidence and to formulate reasons why the event marks a rupture in history and thought, why it is incomprehensible by normal categories and conventional theories, and why it challenges all thought and all life.

Second, Fackenheim comes to recognize that the role of God at Auschwitz and the character of an authentic post-Holocaust faith are more complex and more disturbing than he had suggested in these early writings. Here he is too hasty to locate a divine commanding voice at Auschwitz and to incorporate it into the faith of the post-Holocaust believer. The Jew's relation to God after Auschwitz may be an object of a searching and a waiting that do not yield instant results or easy answers. And this means too that the ground of obligation that underlies the "imposed imperative" is less clear and less easy to define.

Third, the problem of obedience and its possibility, of endurance and the capacity for it, deeply concerns him, and only in *To Mend the World* does he reach a solution that is neither too easy nor too distant.[87] Indeed, the account of what makes post-Holocaust response possible is one of the work's central themes.

A fourth cluster of issues concerns the hermeneutical character of Jewish existence and hence of post-Holocaust Jewish life and thought. His understanding of the Midrashic Framework and the traditional faith in the divine presence in history is itself a hermeneutical one, shaped by intellectual and historical influences and then exposed to Auschwitz as he interprets and appropriates it. Eventually, Fackenheim realizes, these various understandings must be clarified, if only sketched, and the interpretive interplay between them identified and understood. This will involve a reading and critical encounter with influences such as Spinoza, Rosenzweig, Hegel, Heidegger, and others, and once again he undertakes this task in *To Mend the World*, insofar as he does so at all.

Finally, the framework of encounter and response as it appears in these early writings is a bridge, as it were, to a multifaceted retrieval of traditional Jewish beliefs, practices, texts, rituals, and more. Fackenheim shows how this is so in articles that respond to historical events and urgencies of the moment. Some of these discussions are abstract, but many are concrete, almost topical, focused on public explosions of anti-Semitism and anti-Zionism, on critiques of Western culture, and on moral questions. The interpretive process of spelling out what is demanded of post-Holocaust Jews is a controversial and sensitive one. The guidelines and directives for authentic response may be grounded in a source of obligation outside individuals and the community of Jews. But their content is articulated by such individuals and only as a result of their understanding of their past, their situation, and themselves. Fackenheim's interpretations, then, are persuasive or not, depending not on the framework itself but rather on his interpretive articulations and how compelling they are.

Judaism in the Epoch of Auschwitz and Jerusalem

As I now turn to *Encounters between Judaism and Modern Philosophy* and essays of the midseventies, I begin with the issue of uniqueness. Time and again, Fackenheim gives reasons why Auschwitz—the Nazi destruction of European Jewry— should be called unique, and just as often he warns that this claim does not belittle other events, such as Hiroshima, nor does it elevate Auschwitz alone. What we need to understand is how he argues for uniqueness, what he means by it, and what role or roles it plays.

In "Jewish Faith and the Holocaust," Fackenheim introduces this issue as follows:

> Men shun the scandal of the particularity of Auschwitz.[88] Germans link it with Dresden; American liberals, with Hiroshima. Christians deplore antisemitism-in-general, while Communists erect monuments to victims-of-Fascism-in-general, depriving the dead of Auschwitz of their Jewish identity even in death. Rather than face Auschwitz, men everywhere seek refuge in generalities, comfortable precisely because they are generalities.[89]

These are terms he will use often and in a context that begins to help us understand why uniqueness is so important. For Fackenheim, the issue includes a cluster of matters: that Auschwitz stands for a historical event, that such events are all concrete and real, that they are unique and distinctive, that they distinguish the times that precede and those that follow them, that some events do so importantly precisely because of their features, that Auschwitz is one of those significant events, and that this feature of Auschwitz is reflected in the fact that it is not easily described, explained, or understood. The old terms and theories are somehow inadequate; the event should cause a shift in our discourse. If it does not, then we are avoiding it, evading its special power, diminishing it. And our tendency may be to do this—to comprehend, generalize, "domesticate" the horrible, the terrifying, the beyond—but Fackenheim argues that morally and religiously we should not and that the event too should persuade us of this.[90] The crucial point here is that Auschwitz is not just one of a collection of bad events; its special features—the role of technology and bureaucracy, the motives of the agents, the victims, and more—single it out. And this singularity is not mundane; it is significant, a fact that is expressed in the way traditional discourse cannot adequately incorporate it. If we generalize, we do not encounter and deal with this event in and of itself; we avoid it, and this is inauthentic as a response.

In part, then, to urge and defend the uniqueness of Auschwitz is to call attention to its historical character, to its being a watershed, to its concreteness, and to the way in which it must be taken seriously as a singular historical event that should alter our thinking and our discourse—religious, moral, political, and more. These matters, moreover, involve coming to terms with this particular cataclysmic event in our past and not escaping or avoiding it; they also involve recognizing how historical our existence is and how some events threaten to seal us off from the past. Some events raise the specter of historicism, the almost hermetic isolation of historical events and moments, and all that it can mean for our identity and that of our communities and cultures. Auschwitz is such an event.

In arguing for the uniqueness of Auschwitz Fackenheim calls attention to episodes, features, and images that mark the event as unprecedented and hence as unassimilable to traditional discourse. Some of these concern the crimes themselves, others the criminals, the victims, and the survivors. There is no need to survey all of Fackenheim's reasons, but in order to appreciate his strategy and its goals, it will be helpful to look at a few examples.[91]

During the late sixties and early seventies Fackenheim used the following argument. Consider the children, one million, so cruelly killed. Why? Not because as martyrs they chose faith over apostasy or because they chose at all. But they "died neither because of their faith, nor in spite of their faith, nor for reasons unrelated to faith. They were murdered because of the faith of their great-grandparents."[92] Like Greenberg, Fackenheim here focuses on the children and on faith, but he argues that their murder is paradoxical—it is unrelated and yet related to faith. How? Because the faith in question was not theirs. Fackenheim compares these nineteenth-century Jews, their great-grandparents, to Abraham, but an Abraham who does not know what he is doing and for whom "there was no reprieve." What has happened is that the tie between faith and death is unmitigated by choice, heroism, indeed any goodness. In short, the Nazi crime succeeded as much as possible in making faith unconditionally bad.[93]

In 1976, writing on the work of Elie Wiesel, Fackenheim returns to this theme, the way that Nazism in a sense stripped the death of the victims of any mitigating goodness, of any nobility or dignity.[94] In order to grasp the horror, to gaze into the abyss, one must avoid abstractions and "take hold of individual examples which, at the same time, cannot be rejected by the mind as exceptions, aberrations, mistakes or excesses because they manifest altogether unmistakably the horror of the whole."[95] In this essay the example is a prisoner's identity card, which, Fackenheim shows, exposes the idea that Jewish existence itself was considered a crime, a central feature of the Nazi empire and of the death camps at its heart. "What made the murder camps into a kingdom not of this world—the Holocaust kingdom—was an unheard-of principle: that a whole people—Jews, half-Jews, quarter-Jews, honorary Jews—are guilty by dint not of actions but of existence itself."[96] By framing the assault on Jews and others in a legal-political terminology, the Nazis gave shape to an antistate, "a system of *absolutely* perverting *all* things human,"[97] for it severs the connection of crime, responsibility, and punishment with free will, rationality, and humanity. Hence the Nazi state surpassed a limit, and, as Fackenheim argues, if it had not been destroyed, we can hardly imagine what might have occurred.[98] In a passage very reminiscent of the last pages of Arendt's *Origins of Totalitarianism*, Fackenheim summons the language of hell and the diabolical only to admit even its inadequacy. The Holocaust was a kingdom of such unmitigated negativity—ruled by disgusting pornographic types, fanatics, and yet run by Arendt's "new philistines" —that it is beyond our imagination, beyond our conception of hell itself. It was a new, unprecedented depravity that outstrips our language, our thought, and our imagination.

At other times, the evidence Fackenheim cites is intended to show that the crimes exhibited an unprecedented kind of "human depravity," an unqualified disrespect for humanity itself. This assault on the dignity of their victims as human beings is reflected in the Nazis' separating "those to be murdered now from those to be murdered later to the strain of Viennese waltzes," in their making human skin into lampshades and human body-fat into soap, in their issuing two work permits to each able-bodied man—thus forcing him to decide who among his loved ones should die, who should live, and more.[99] Fackenheim's examples, like Greenberg's oft-repeated episode of the burning children and like the testimonies collected by Terence DesPres in his chapter in *The Survivor* entitled "Excremental Assault," are presented as evidence that the murder of Jews and non-Aryans incorporated strategies of dehumanization. The entire bureaucratic process that degraded the victims was essential to the destruction in various ways. It increased efficiency by educating the victims to see themselves as less than human, by enabling the murderers to carry out their tasks with as little regret and resistance as possible, and to maximize the sheer quantity of annihilation. But all of these features involved altering the understanding of humanity and human dignity. By all conventional standards, traditional moral perspectives, this enterprise exhibited a level of depravity and evil never before extant, and this is what Fackenheim seeks to point out and to persuade the reader to accept.

He also seeks to tie what happened to what the Nazis wanted to happen. These horrific, repulsive features of the system and indeed the entire system of destruction, with the death camps at the core, were not instrumental to some rational, political purpose. This question of intention or purpose is certainly a controversial one. Fackenheim takes the fact that at its center Nazism was an agency of evil for evil's sake as evidence for its uniqueness and unprecedented character, albeit not the sole evidence. I do not want to debate the facts but rather try to clarify what Fackenheim means by the claim of evil intention.[100] First, he cites evidence to show that the destruction and extermination process was not conceived by the Nazis themselves—at least some of them—as subordinate to goals or objectives like self-interest, gain, or victory; if it were and the two conflicted, then the extermination process would have been aborted.[101] It was not. Second, he also refers to the story of Hitler and Goebbels, in the Berlin bunker, "express[ing] ghoulish satisfaction at the prospect that their downfall might carry in train the doom, not only (or even at all) of their enemies, but rather of the 'master race'."[102] The ultimate goal of Nazism was murder and death, nothing more and nothing less. Indeed, for example, the tactic of issuing the two work permits, cited earlier, was not efficient; it was a way of elevating the torture, he claims, and making the murder more satisfying by implicating the victims in their own murder without any of the nobility of suicide or self-sacrifice.[103] In short, Nazism tortured and murdered because it loved to do both; Améry, in his brilliant account of torture, had come to the same conclusion. Finally, for Fackenheim, then, Nazism at its core sought unbounded murder and annihilation, what Arendt had called the essence of totalitarianism, a desire for unlimited expansiveness. *We* call that evil for evil's sake or unmitigated, unqualified evil; the religious tradition calls it "the demonic," although even here there are degrees of such conduct.[104] Presumably the Nazis themselves would not, but their actions and their utterances exhibit the fact that the depraved murder of all non-Aryans was their goal and that is sufficient to demand a serious, nonescapist response.[105]

A further reason for the uniqueness of Auschwitz concerns its victims. In part, the event is unique because its central target was a particular people and because it was a wholly distinctive assault on that people; as the ultimate form of anti-Semitism, the Holocaust set that phenomenon apart from others too often compared to it. But while Fackenheim does emphasize that the particularity of the central victims in part makes Auschwitz unique, there is something further about the victims that also distinguishes the Holocaust. Fackenheim finds a picture of the ideal victim of the death camps, drawn by Primo Levi in *Survival in Auschwitz* and cited by Terence Des Pres in his book *The Survivor*.[106] It is a picture of the *musselmanner*, the living dead, "the drowned . . . an anonymous mass, continuously renewed and always identical, of non-men who march and labor in silence, the divine spark dead within them. . . . One hesitates to call them living; one hesitates to call their death death."[107] The creation of this new mode of being Fackenheim calls an "unprecedented spiritual tragedy."[108] It is a challenge to Judaism and also the historical refutation of philosophical conceptions of human existence that orient the latter to its own human finitude, to a future but not a present death.[109] The reality of the *musselmanner*, then, takes its place alongside a host of other features, testimony, and episodes as a reason why the Holocaust ought to be encountered and responded to in novel ways, without assimilating it to traditional modes of discourse. As I will show, its most powerful use occurs in *To Mend the World*.

The account of authentic post-Holocaust Jewish existence is grounded in a serious encounter with the Holocaust, an exposure of Jewish history and tradition to that event, and a retrieval of the tradition for the contemporary historical situation. The demands of that situation—the world of Jewish life in the decades after the Six Day War—are moral, political, and religious. Often, as one might expect, they are the result of social and political events, but just as often they arise out of Fackenheim's sense of what Jewish life demands in terms of education and learning, ritual, Israel, social problems, and solidarity with world Jewry. Of special interest is the Jewish relationship to the state of Israel.[110]

Like Rubenstein, Berkovits, and Greenberg, Fackenheim's thinking about the Holocaust was stimulated and confirmed by the Six Day War and escalated in the wake of that event and subsequent events in Israel. Features of Israeli political and cultural life became, for him, emblems of authentic response to Auschwitz, and a commitment to Israel's existence and flourishing takes its place at the center of diaspora authenticity. Virtually every lecture or essay that Fackenheim composed after 1967 has a reference to Israel, and the centrality of the state of Israel is the theme of some of his most eloquent, powerful work.[111]

The relationship between Israel and the Holocaust and the role of the state of Israel in post-Holocaust Jewish life are complex matters in Fackenheim's work. The events of May and June 1967, a period of threat and danger, called forth for him the memory of the Nazi years, provided a background for understanding Christian response, and focused attention on the courageous, self-reliant defense of the state of Israel as a paradigmatic response to the threat to Jewish survival.[112] "These events cast into clear relief the whole as yet unassimilated fact of an embattled, endangered, but nevertheless free Jewish state, emerging from ashes and catastrophe. Solely because of the connection of the events of May and June with Auschwitz did a military victory (rarely applauded in Judaism, and never for its own sake) acquire an inescapable religious dimension."[113] Fackenheim avoids traditional techniques for joining the two events, the Holocaust and the rebirth and defense of the Jewish state, techniques such as the conjunction of destruction and salvation, in religious terms, or causal influence, in secular ones. Israel, for Fackenheim, cannot be the compensation for Auschwitz, nor can the death camps be somehow part of the explanation for Israel's rebirth. Rather the rebirth and defense of a Jewish homeland is a model of survivorship; *"the survivor is gradually becoming the paradigm for the entire Jewish people,"*[114] and "the state of Israel is collectively what the survivor is individually—

testimony on behalf of all mankind to life against death, to sanity against madness, to Jewish self-affirmation against every form of flight from it, and (though this is visible only to those who break through narrow theological categories) to the God of the ancient covenant against all lapses into paganism."[115] The state of Israel constitutes a mode, indeed a primary, exemplary mode of response to the atrocities and depravity of Nazism and the death camps. It opposes to the industry of death and anti-Judaism a corporate affirmation of life and Jewish renewal.

In "Moses and the Hegelians," the third chapter of *Encounters*, Fackenheim formulates this paradigm of response in terms of the old categories of the secular and the religious, and this account points to the relation in post-Holocaust Jewish life between self-reliant, heroic action and religious purpose in Israel and in general. Fackenheim begins by recalling his earlier reasoning: although thought has thus far proven incapable of encompassing Auschwitz, there has been "a radical normative Jewish response to the catastrophe . . . already actual . . . in the life-commitment of a people."[116] This response, "offered by every Jewish survivor by his mere decision to remain a Jew," is radical because it is an act of "uncompromising opposition." Moreover, "this decision is normative because, by virtue of it, the survivor has become the paradigm of the whole Jewish people."[117] Here is a compact version of Fackenheim's framework: the inadequacy of thought, the actuality of response, response as unconditional opposition, and the normative element, an imperative or model of authentic response. In earlier essays and in *God's Presence in History*, however, Fackenheim then turned to an interpretive articulation of this imperative or model. Here he does not, or at least the interpretation he gives is intended to clarify the nature of post-Holocaust Jewish life rather than to identify its constituent obligations. In other words, if it is an interpretation that he carries out, it is a different sort of clarification, one that exposes a central polarity in Jewish life and that shows how old categories, if applicable after Auschwitz, must be understood in new ways. This is what he means when he says that the survivor's decision to remain a Jew, in the face of Auschwitz, "requires philosophical thought to restructure the categories of religiosity and secularity." Fackenheim proceeds to do this, first for any survivor and then for Israel as the paradigm of survivorship.

Authentic Jewish response to Auschwitz incorporates both the religious and the secular; old exclusive categories are now combined in a dynamic, novel unity:

> Only by virtue of a radical "secular" self-reliance that acts as though the God who once saved could save no more can even the most "religious" survivor hold fast either to the Sinaitic past or to the Messianic future. And only by virtue of a radical "religious" memory and hope can even the most "secularist" survivor rally either the courage or the motivation to decide to remain a Jew, when every natural impulse tempts him to seek forgetfulness and even bare safety elsewhere.[118]

Before the Holocaust, the secular and the religious divided Jews into distinct categories, those who rejected divine transcendence, conceived of Judaism as a civilization or culture, and saw progress as a human product, and those who adhered to the covenant, felt bound to obey divine will, and took salvation to be ultimately in God's hands. After Auschwitz, the authentic religious Jew must engage in self-reliant action, faithfully pursuing old covenantal goals in new ways but without a trust in God's saving power. And the authentic secular Jew must exhibit a fidelity to old purposes and a confidence in their realization, even though abdication of one's covenantal post would be easy and even reasonable. As Fackenheim puts it, the secular Jew may not "submit to the commanding Voice of Sinai, which bids him witness to the one true God," but does "submit to a commanding Voice heard from Auschwitz that bids him testify *that some gods are false*."[119] One may not hear the voice of God, but one certainly recognizes who the devil is. And religious Jews may pursue God's purposes as they always have but not without accepting themselves the responsibility for the realization of those purposes.

What, then, makes Israel the paradigmatic response to Auschwitz and hence the ideal of survivorship? It is precisely the fact that "this commingling of religiosity and secularity has found historical embodiment in the rebirth of a Jewish state."[120] Israel, in short, is the ideal survivor, the model of authentic post-Holocaust Jewish existence:

> Except only for those who never became part of the modern world, all religious Israelis are willing, if required, to take up "secular" arms in defense of the state. And except for those who cannot extricate themselves from ideologies that do Jewish history no justice, all secular Israelis have the "religious" wish that the state be Jewish.[121]

Here, in a picture of Israeli personality that comes from the middle of the spectrum and excludes the all-too-real, all-too-inflammatory extremes, Fackenheim finds his union of the religious and the secular, of religious purpose and secular self-reliant action. To him, Israel is the model of authentic response; perhaps more accurately, more realistically, the paradigm lies within Israel as it does within diaspora Judaism as a particular combination of action and submission, of reverence for the past and responsibility for the future, of dependence and independence.[122] The old categories of secularity and religiosity, when treated as exhaustive and exclusive, no longer apply to the new reality. Genuine post-Holocaust existence requires their mingling in subtle and novel ways.

Thus far Fackenheim has recognized the way the Six Day War occasioned attention to Auschwitz, how Israel should be associated with authentic response to the Holocaust, and the mingling of the secular and the religious in paradigmatic Israeli action. Several tasks yet remain. How is Israeli action an "uncompromising opposition" to the demons of Auschwitz? And how is it associated with traditional Jewish hopes? In 1970, he could say briefly that Israel is a "hope and determination that there must be, shall be, will be no second Auschwitz."[123] In the diaspora, vis à vis Israel, there is an imperative, he writes, to complete the project of Emancipation, for Jews to seek "Jewish self-liberation" and to free Jewishness from the shack-les of anti-Semitism and indulgence. Here he says this but little more.[124] In 1974, in a moving essay entitled "Israel and the Diaspora: Political Contingencies and Moral Necessities; or, The Shofar of Rabbi Yitzhak Finkler of Piotrkov," he points to a "new moral necessity" that arises for Jews, Gentiles, for diaspora Jews and Israeli Jews, to prevent another Holocaust, so that no Jews will be "the helpless victims of the great hatred."[125] Moreover, he argues that this moral necessity crystallized in a Jewish state, as an act of refusal to "tolerate 'moral discrimination,'" a commitment of solidarity with the victims of Nazism and against the Nazi criminals.[126] Israel, support for Israel's survival and enrichment, authentic post-Holocaust Jewish ex-istence, the mingling of secular courage and religious purpose, all this is focused on an opposition to anti-Semitism and to powerlessness, to hatred and sufferance, con-ditions without which Auschwitz could not have taken place.[127]

For Fackenheim the relation between the Holocaust and Israel is one of event and authentic response, and the character of the response is that of an opposition to those conditions without which Auschwitz would have been impossible. In an extraordinary, powerful essay, published in 1974, Fackenheim ties these themes to-gether with the traditional idea of messianism and with his framework for ground-ing and articulating an authentic response.[128] Here he gives a sketch of the mes-sianic idea in Judaism and its relation to Zionism, a defense of the uniqueness of Auschwitz and the inadequacy of explanatory accounts of its relation to the rebirth of the state of Israel, and a portrayal of authentic response by means of the testi-mony of actual responses during the Holocaust and with reference to the creation of the Jewish state. Fackenheim begins by surveying rabbinic and medieval reflec-tions on the coming of the Messiah in order to depict "the inevitable tension be-tween contingent historical present and absolute messianic future in the Jewish re-ligious consciousness."[129] The modern world and especially Zionism try to dissolve that tension, but in fact it does not go away: Zionist secularism is still inspired by a messianic hope. As Fackenheim sees it, Zionism could not have succeeded against all historical odds without "a will in touch with an absolute dimension . . . and even those acting on this will may well be astonished by its accomplishments."[130] Once again, the categories of the secular and the religious are invoked but now as united in Zionist life—"if not when things appear normal, at any rate in those extreme moments when all appearances fall away and only truth remains."[131]

Recalling old arguments, Fackenheim claims that Auschwitz is a "celebration of degradation and death," an epoch-making event, and beyond theological and his-torical explanation.[132] He argues that explanation also fails concerning the connec-tion between the Holocaust and the state of Israel; "yet it is necessary not only to perceive a bond between the two events but also so to act as to make it unbreak-able."[133] Fackenheim then gives arguments why causal or historical and theological explanations are inadequate and concludes, as in earlier writings, that response is necessary, a moral obligation. So too is it necessary to see how Auschwitz and Israel are related. Why? Because if a "commitment to the autonomy and security of the state of Israel" is the core of every authentic response to Auschwitz, then it is necessary to see how this is so. The answer, for my purposes, is that Israeli self-defense exemplifies the union of secular action and religious purpose in behalf of Jewish survival, "a resistance to the climax of a millennial, unholy combination of hatred of Jews with Jewish powerlessness which we are bidden to end forever."[134] On the one hand, Israel is related to Auschwitz because it is a secular-religious assault against this "unholy combination." On the other, Israel is related to the Holocaust because the courageous resistance of victims like Itzhak Zuckerman and Mordecai Anielewicz of the Warsaw ghetto was carried on in Israel's battle for life itself. Anielewicz died in the ghetto in May 1943; the kibbutz named after him, Yad Mordekhai, was the site of a battle, during the war of independence, defending Tel Aviv from Egyptian troops. Thus the connection:

> The battle for Yad Mordekhai began in the streets of Warsaw. . . . [W]hat links [pious and secular resistance during the Holocaust and] the Ghetto fighters with Yad Mordekhai is neither a causal necessity nor a divine miracle, if these are thought of as divorced from human believing and acting. It is a fervent believing, turned by despair from patient waiting into heroic acting. It is an acting which through despair has recovered faith.[135]

It is, in our terms, a confrontation with discontinuity that has achieved continuity, a recognition of historicity that holds fast to an absolute standard that leads both to past and future.[136]

In the early seventies America had turned to a greater sense of ethnic, religious, or group commitment, to what Michael Novak called "the rise of the unmeltable ethnics."[137] These developments doubtless provided a context in which a Jewish search for grounds for distinctiveness took place. Some sought richer Jewish learning, more intimate communities, and deeper ritual involvement. Some too turned to Israel and to the memory of destruction, of Auschwitz. Others tried to balance these new tendencies to particular identification with liberal values, justice, equality, and a sense of commonality. Fackenheim participated in a conference on these themes at the Center for the Study of Democratic Institutions in Santa Barbara; his contribution, "Jewish 'Ethnicity' in 'Mature Democratic Societies': Ideology and Reality," was published in 1973.[138] Along with his references to political events of the seventies, especially concerning Israel, this essay reveals his impressions of the political-cultural climate of those years and articulates his dissatisfaction with the defenders of both ethnicity and general culture. It is a rare opportunity to see how Fackenheim views the very context that frames the reception of his work and that of post-Holocaust thinkers in general.[139]

Fackenheim appreciates the way that American life and culture was never in the fifties and certainly never became a homogeneous "melting pot." Blacks, Indians, and Puerto Ricans, as well as Jews and other groups of European heritage, rediscovered in an American setting a sense of identity and distinctiveness.[140] "Real tensions" existed in American life and flourished into "new particularisms" that belie any ideological camouflage. But, on the other hand, Fackenheim does not want Jewish uniqueness to be misunderstood as an ethnicity like all others, and here, as much as anywhere, is the focus of his critique. There is no universal culture and no civic unity, but neither are there only "ethnic subcultures" and "ethnic loyalty."[141] Some groups do not fit either category without distortion, and Judaism is one, certainly after the Holocaust and the rebirth of the Jewish state.[142]

Indeed, if the terms are accepted, then the Holocaust makes "the maintenance of a [Jewish] . . . subculture a genuine ideal"—that is, a moral and religious obligation and not "merely a temporary necessity."[143] For Fackenheim, the particularism in American life in the late sixties and seventies may have cultivated a receptivity to memory and to recovering the past for the present and future, but one should not reduce the relation between "ethnic loyalty" and Auschwitz to convenience or utility. Rather a proper, serious encounter with Auschwitz should lead to a sense of imperative, duty, and obligation—to keep alive Judaism, the Jewish people, and the memory of the victims.[144] Fackenheim's terms are religious and moral; sociology and history raise questions, but the answers, duty aimed at opportunities, run perpendicular to life. It is not surprising that he can call upon the "rise of the state of Israel from the ashes of Treblinka, Dachau, and Buchenwald" as testimony for that sense of duty, alongside "the rise of the nonwhite world against colonialism, intertwined with the demand of Black Americans for real, instead of merely ideological, liberation."[145] There is no narrow chauvinism here. The Jewish mandate to maintaining a distinctive heritage and destiny occurs alongside others. Just as every evil—Armenia, Auschwitz, Hiroshima, Vietnam—must be confronted in its uniqueness, so must each case of ethnic or group identification. There is escapism in avoiding any of these tasks.[146]

This essay can be read as Fackenheim's critique of the terminology and conceptualization of the new ethnicity, American pluralism, and general culture. Religions like Judaism may be cultural artifacts in one sense, but they are not wholly that, and after Auschwitz Judaism is not primarily an ethnic category. Ethnic groups and other such configurations do not generally cultivate conceptions of the good life and its demands; Judaism does. But the essay also is an expression of Fackenheim's appreciation of the tendencies toward diversity and pluralism in American culture. He argues that there are a variety of ways of distorting or escaping the challenges of such tendencies, especially if one is a Jew. But there are also ways of meeting them honestly. In part, it requires facing Auschwitz, Israel, and the tasks of Jewish survival; it also demands recognizing the risks of historicity and seeking to transcend them, to do justice to the faith and courage of the victims of Auschwitz and to find a way to bridge the abyss. But for him, as a thinker, while life may precede thought, it does not replace it. Sooner or later he had to show how recovery was possible and to make clear the role of God in that recovery.

The Necessity and Possibility of Being a Jew

To Mend the World is a classic of twentieth-century Jewish thought and philosophy. Published in 1982, it is the result of years of reflection on the foundations of Jewish thought after Auschwitz.[147] Fortunately my goals do not require that I examine all of its chapters in detail; I want to show how Fackenheim, extending his earlier work, develops his account of authentic Jewish response to Auschwitz, his understanding of its hermeneutical, historically situated character, and God's place in it. By exploring these themes, I will show that Fackenheim faces the challenge of discontinuity and strives as well to find a strategy of continuity with the Jewish past. He constructs a model for Jewish particularity and does so by articulating a relationship between history and Jewish identity. That relationship incorporates a sensitivity to historical situation, a serious engagement with Auschwitz, and a recovery of a normative past. At the same time, Fackenheim provides a focus and a direction for articulating Jewish identity in a pluralistic context; he draws on history and tradition to define Jewish selfhood. The intellectual response to his thinking has varied, but the response of ordinary Jews to the tendencies of his work and that of Greenberg, Wiesel, and others was overwhelmingly positive. In a sense, Fackenheim provided a deep, sophisticated formulation of the commitments of ordinary Jews.

For my purposes, three themes are central: the grounds of the possibility of authentic post-Holocaust Jewish existence, the hermeneutical character of that existence, and the character of the faith that occurs within it, that is, the role God plays. *To Mend the World* discusses much else that is exciting and important, but its central core concerns the very themes I have been highlighting: how to look into the abyss and yet go on, how to face Auschwitz honestly and seriously and yet continue life as a Jew.[148]

Writing in 1989, Fackenheim describes the central problem of the book as the attempt to show how the necessity of a post-Holocaust recovery is possible. For the Jew, on Fackenheim's view, that necessity is articulated in a moral-religious obligation, what he once called the 614th commandment and then the commanding voice of Auschwitz.[149] If the death camps altered human nature, how is obedience to such a commandment and opposition humanly possible?[150] If Auschwitz is a rupture, how can one still "mend the world?" This is the book's central, fundamental problem. It is the problem of discontinuity and continuity, of historical situatedness and nonrelative standards, of historicity and transcendence. In terms of Fackenheim's earlier framework, moreover, this problem is that of rethinking the relation between intellectual comprehension and uniqueness on the one hand and authentic response on the other, of thought's reaching an impasse and then, as he puts it, going to school with life.[151] Here the work of Wiesel, Levi, Améry, and other victims becomes decisive; it provides the personal perspective of the experiencing victim without which a genuine encounter with the Holocaust would not be possible. Fackenheim's encounter with Auschwitz and his understanding of responsiveness to it involve locating in the experience itself both confrontation and transcendence of a particular kind.[152]

In *God's Presence in History* Fackenheim had virtually taken for granted that Jewish existence after Auschwitz, since it was actual, was possible. One *could* respond; the question was how. Surely, if Jews survived as Jews and if they disarmed Jewish victimization and proclaimed "never again," then endurance, survival, and resistance were possible. But, as he notes, this confidence was glib and insensitive; it relied on an all-too-comfortable, Kantian inference from *ought* to *can* or a similarly facile "neo-orthodox (Jewish and Christian) answer, to the effect that a Grace that gives commandments also gives the freedom to obey them."[153] Here the language is that of moral obligation or divine power on the one hand and human freedom or autonomy on the other. In *To Mend the World*, however, Fackenheim calls on Levi's image of the *musselmanner*, the living dead, and asks: why did not all become such annihilated souls? Against Nazi criminality, how could some not be defeated? Even more, how could some resist? This is not merely a question about freedom; it is about the resources for dignity, a sense of selfhood, of value, of importance, of strength, and of courage. To this question Fackenheim came to give a remarkable, powerful answer; to find it one must look at chapter 4.

In a sense, the question of necessity or obligation, its source and content, is primarily a question about the aspiration to some principle or source beyond the individual or community in its historical being, while the question of possibility and its ground becomes a question about how seriously one accepts the historical situatedness of agency and human existence. Given the way Auschwitz occludes transcendence, to rely on it to account for the possibility of resistance would be facile and callous. In earlier works, from the statement of the 614th commandment through the treatments of Israel, Fackenheim's main concern was the fact and interpretation of the obligation to transcend the abyss. In *To Mend the World*, his attention is on the event itself and whether authentic response is at all possible. If the event is sufficiently unique and unprecedented, then it is possible that there could be no such thing as authentic response or indeed any response. The event could be wholly negative and destructive, an unqualified catastrophe. *To Mend the World*— its title is a bold commitment—seeks to open itself to this possibility and yet to overcome it, to find in the event itself a ground for authentic response by locating genuine self-conscious resistance. If such resistance was actual, then it was and is possible. For Fackenheim, then, both genuine post-Holocaust historicity, the recognition of one's historical situatedness and all it demands, and genuine post-Holocaust transcendence, the aspiration to bridge the abyss and recover from the past new, contemporary orientation and purpose, arise out of and within a confrontation with Auschwitz as a whole, a unique world of horror and depravity.

As Fackenheim tells us, his encounter is manifold, incorporating an attempt first to describe phenomenologically, through the work of the survivors, the "Holocaust world," focusing on its criminals and its victims,[154] and then to explain it; his goal is to expose the dark horrors and then to secure a route of resistance, a ground of the possibility of recovery, so that even the "total rupture" can be repaired.[155] Heidegger's philosophy emphasizes the historical character of human existence; Fackenheim contrasts the world of the death camps with the Heideggerian world of human existence, the Volk, leader, and purpose.[156] Setting aside the madmen and the ordinary people, the latter Arendt's favored group, Fackenheim turns to the idealists, whose "ideals were torture and murder," both the practitioners,[157] such as Rudolf Hoess, and the theorists, such as Johann von Leers. And he grounds their idealism and its goal, the elimination of the Jews as a whole, in Hitler's worldview since 1919 and finds in Heinrich Himmler its most characteristic adherent.[158] The destruction of world Jewry and the burning of Jewish children were at the core of Nazism, the Holocaust at the heart of the Nazi Reich. Confronted with this reality, which it ignores, Heidegger's world falls into inauthenticity and inadequacy.[159]

The confrontation with Heidegger's thought raises the general question: "perhaps *no* thought can exist in the same space as the Holocaust; perhaps *all* thought, to assure its own survival, must be elsewhere. This is the radical question."[160] Thought and discourse involve concepts, schemes, and patterns; perhaps Auschwitz, uniquely and historically, fits none with satisfaction. Perhaps it is an enigma, a caesura, to use Cohen's term, that threatens an isolating, immobilizing historicism. Fackenheim passes quickly over the evidence of the failure to confront the death camps directly or seriously—in the work of Heidegger, Karl Jaspers, Karl Barth, Paul Tillich, Rudolf Bultmann, Isaac Deutscher, Ernst Bloch, Abraham Joshua Heschel, and even Martin Buber.[161] The result seems clear, that "for thought vis à vis Auschwitz—philosophical, theological, other—unauthenticity [is] the price of survival." Or so it seems. In earlier work, Fackenheim had argued for uniqueness as incommensurability, on the grounds that old, traditional categories and theories could not incorporate Auschwitz with satisfaction. He then argued that lack of meaning or purpose was one thing, response another. For those living after the event, response is necessary, as is the search for standards of authentic response. But standards or models, to be emulated, must have both *obligatory force* and *enabling capacity*. Even if the turn to subsequent, postwar Jewish allegiance provided access for the former, it left the latter wholly unexplained. For that, the grounds of possibility for continued Jewish commitment, Fackenheim turns in a new direction, that of the victims and evidence of resistance among them.[162]

In earlier essays, especially after Fackenheim had read Terence Des Pres's book *The Survivor* in 1976, he had referred to episodes of resistance and asked why all the victims had not become *musselmanner*.[163] Here, in the two central sections of *To Mend the World*, he describes and analyzes the phenomenon of resistance and discovers in it the solution to the problem: how is obedience to the imperatives of opposition possible.[164] Moreover, in the course of his analysis of the resistance and its character, he gives his deepest account of what makes Auschwitz a unique evil, of "what was being resisted. . . . *The Nazi logic was irresistible, yet was being resisted*: this is the enormous fact that must be grasped."[165]

Calling on Des Pres's phrase "excremental assault," for example, and evidence that the camps were "designed to produce in the victim a 'self-disgust' to the point of wanting death,"[166] Fackenheim points out that "the Nazi logic of destruction was aimed, ultimately, at the victim's *self*-destruction."[167] Nazism and its racial doctrine portrayed the Jews as vermin and as disgusting subhuman creatures; it sought not only to eradicate them but also — indeed but *first* — to bring them to see themselves that way. The camps, that is, engaged in a process of self-dehumanization, self-abhorrence, and self-destruction. Indeed, Fackenheim claims, this attitude and this program were not accidental; they were grounded in Hitler's ideology and "set the tone for the world of Auschwitz."[168] The paradigmatic victim is the goal of this ideology; it is a person whose self-loathing anaesthetizes his or her sense of worth and vitality, whose life is death, the musselmann. Such a victim is "the most notable, if indeed not the sole, truly original contribution of the Third Reich to civilization."[169]

If this is the logic of destruction and the unique evil of Nazism, what is resistance to it? How indeed did some avoid becoming *musselmanner*? Fackenheim moves from one form of resistance to another. Of special importance is the testimony of Pelagia Lewinska:

> They had condemned us to die in our own filth, to drown in mud, in our own excrement. They wished to abase us, to destroy our human dignity, to efface every vestige of humanity, to return us to the level of wild animals, to fill us with horror and contempt toward ourselves and our fellows.
>
> But from the instant that I grasped the motivating principle . . . it was as if I had been awakened from a dream . . . I felt under orders to live. . . . I was not going to become the contemptible, disgusting brute my enemy wished me to be.[170]

Fackenheim calls this a witness by an ordinary person that exhibits a grasp of the "whole-of-horror," a confrontation with it, and resistance to it. It is, he says, a "monumental discovery."[171] Where, Fackenheim asks, does she get the strength? Not from "willpower" or "natural desire." There is no answer; the recognition and the commitment are ultimate, beyond explanation and further grounding. Furthermore, Lewinska speaks of orders, but whose orders are they?[172] For some, there is no giver. For others, it is divine. Both are ultimate. As I will show, both the orders and the capacity to obey them cannot be explained in ordinary terms. More — but an unexplainable more — is involved.

Fackenheim then turns to the indignant, armed resistance in the ghettos, what he calls a "unique affirmation . . . of Jewish self-respect" and "a unique celebration of Jewish life, and thus of life itself."[173] And once more, he seeks its causes, rejects mere "willpower" and "natural desire," and admits that here too is an ultimate. Like the "solitary struggle of Pelagia Lewinska," the armed Jewish resistance is an

unprecedented mode of opposition, a "way of being." Such resistance is characterized by the maintenance of human dignity in a world that sought to destroy it. "In
such a world . . . life does not need to be sanctified: it is already holy."

Here, then, Fackenheim claims, is the ultimate dimension needed to ground the
necessity and possibility of authentic post-Holocaust existence. Here is a mode of
being in which that being, life itself, is sacred, and its character is unexplainable in
further terms. One ought to resist because there is an imperative to resist, and one
can resist because in the Holocaust world resistance was actual and ultimate.

But is it ultimate? Fackenheim registers the criticism, or at least the doubt, and
then wonders whether any analysis used to defend the ultimacy of such resistance
would not, by reducing resistance to some other category, effectively negate it. In
short, Fackenheim formulates a dilemma: resistance by the victims cannot be
treated as ultimate, for without reasons, it is not taken to be ultimate, and with
them it is shown not to be ultimate. Fackenheim, in this the central section of the
book, must face this paradox of ultimacy; he must give reasons for treating the victims' resistance as ultimate, foundational, and basic that do not mitigate or under-
mine that ultimacy. In other words, the Holocaust threatens to be a total break, a
total rupture with our traditional categories and views. Authentic response to it
must be negative, but is it possible? If resistance was actual and yet analyzable in
terms of ordinary, standard motives or grounds, then the event is not as unprecedented as we once thought. The only way to save its uniqueness and yet find a way
to traverse its negativity is to justify a wholly novel form of resistance, that is, to find
in the event a form of life that is unconditionally threatened and yet exhibits a
wholly novel form of recovery. Here, if anywhere, is the bridge that will enable
later survivors to encounter the abyss and still go on. This is the goal of chapter 4,
section 9, the core of this chapter, indeed of the book, and perhaps of all of Fackenheim's later thought.[174]

He begins with a critique of psychological explanations of the conduct of the victims and of their resistance.[175] Such accounts, he argues, smack of escapism. To
avoid this escapism, Fackenheim claims, the "psychological critic . . . must abandon
his Archimedean standpoint outside and above it all and place himself *with* the resisting victims; and he must redirect his focus, away from their 'behavior' torn out
of context . . . onto their object, i.e., the Nazi assault in its unflattened-out uniqueness."[176] If properly conducted, then, psychological inquiry should recognize "that
the Holocaust transcends comprehension," and this means that no explanation of
the victim's conduct, the resistance, is fully adequate once one gives up a detached
perspective and accepts the victim's own perspective as reliable.

If we turn to the perpetrators, the criminals, and examine them, moreover, the
result is the same: historical explanations of why and how they did it are inadequate, Fackenheim argues.[177] Again and again, as history tries to explain all by
pointing to one goal, it fails, and as psychohistory tries to explain all by conjuring
up the psychopathic leader, it too fails. "The mystery remains." Reason and rational

explanation, he argues, aim at showing how an action or event was possible. With regard to Auschwitz, to recall Hans Jonas's statement, "more was real than was possible."[178] Reason, it seems, has confronted an obstacle, a reality that cannot be adequately encompassed. In Améry's words, in the camps reality was more real than at any point and place. Here, then, Fackenheim has systematized and developed his claim to the uniqueness of Auschwitz and to its conceptual distinctiveness.

But there is more. Vis à vis Auschwitz, psychology and historical explanation may be inadequate, but is philosophical understanding also limited? Here the problem is the particular evil of Auschwitz and the evildoer; philosophy at best has resorted to general categories, radical evil and the demonic. Fackenheim's point is that there is no easy fit between such general concepts and this particular evil. He sets out the problem as a dilemma or enigma: "while the doers of the deed were ordinary, the evil that they leapt into by doing the deed was absolute and unsurpassable."[179] One must beware not to mitigate either pole by somehow converting the agents into non–human beings, omnipotent demons or passive puppets, or by blurring the distinction between those who did it and those who did not. The agents were human beings and yet different from others, and what they did was evil but distinctive. Auschwitz involved ordinary persons doing extraordinary things; it involved individuals and a horrific "totalitarian" system in dialectical marriage: "just as the 'totalitarian' system produced the rulers and operators, so the rulers and operators produced the system."[180] Fackenheim contrasts this, the real enigma of the Holocaust, with Arendt's doctrine of the banality of evil. For Arendt, the doer and the deed, in Nazi Germany and in the camps, were separated, and hence the atrocities and the horrors were "thoughtless" in the sense that they were conducted without rational deliberation, choice, and rational motivation. But it is for just this connection that Fackenheim argues, the fact that horrific actions were performed willingly, knowingly, and intentionally by ordinary people.[181] It is this that "chills the marrow and numbs the mind."[182] Here is the nemesis that philosophical thought must confront.

What does this confrontation yield? In confronting this phenomenon in all its particularity, individuals choosing to perform acts of utter depravity, what does philosophy achieve? Fackenheim's answer is that philosophy grasps the whole and its horror, is itself horrified, resists or opposes what it grasps, and points to action and a life of resistance.[183] In doing this, philosophy follows at key points the path of the resisting victim's own thinking—Pelagia Lewinska's testimony provides the paradigm—and hence, in a sense, is grounded in that experience and that thinking. The turn from confrontation to authentic response, then, is made possible by the *actuality* of such resistance and its structure by the victims; they and their experience make possible the philosophical grasp of the horror, the horrified reaction, and the turn to action. Such resistance is a way of being; it is also an ontological ground that makes possible a deontological response.

To say this is one thing; to carry out the thinking is another. It is in fact the *analy-*

sis that Fackenheim had called for, the reasoning that would articulate the ultimacy of resistance as the ground for authentic response and show its connection with subsequent Jewish life without compromising the ultimacy of the victim's resistance. This analysis is also a demonstration—*another* demonstration—that the Holocaust is unique, that it cannot be adequately comprehended by traditional categories. In this case it is a way of showing how philosophical thought grasps but does not encompass the event. If, then, the possibility of authentic response requires some ground, some source that makes obedience possible, and if the resistance of some victims and their ability to avoid becoming *musselmanner* are Fackenheim's suggested grounds, then the ultimacy of that resistance as a nonreducible way of being is crucial for his account. Moreover, if the analysis or reasoning that is intended to show that ultimacy fails, then Fackenheim's project has failed. In other terms, if he cannot show that and how resistance is ultimate, then the discontinuity of Auschwitz, its role as total rupture, would have won its dark victory. The result would be a wholly unqualified separation between the pre-Holocaust past and the post-Holocaust present, a historicist isolation grounded in fact, not theory.

Furthermore, in his earlier thought, Fackenheim provides no justification for the turn from thought to life, from thinking to acting. Why, indeed, should the theologian, the philosopher, the thinker, when Auschwitz proves inassimilable, turn for guidance to actual responses to the event and in particular to the responses of those who live after the event? What is needed, as Fackenheim realizes, is a full-fledged justification of thought's going-to-school-with-life, as he calls it, and at least the first step in an account of what the outcome should be.[184] Perhaps the most important step in this process occurs here, with the analysis that takes philosophical thought to a grasping and recoiling from Auschwitz that points ahead to life lived in opposition to it. If Fackenheim is right, then thought itself, as it tracks a particular path, becomes oppositional and then ecstatic, pointing outside of itself to action that realizes opposition in the world, one reality resisting another. This is what Fackenheim sets out to achieve; I now will look at how he seeks to accomplish it.

Facing the ordinary agents and the "evil system," philosophical thought moves from one to the other, in a circle, and in so doing it grasps a whole, to the degree that this is possible, the "whole of horror." Unlike Hegel, however, there is no movement to a higher level, no transcendence, and no mitigation of its incomprehensibility. What thought grasps is that the death camps and the Nazi system were an integrated, organized totality and one without redeeming goodness, an unmitigated evil. But, as thought, seeking understanding, works at getting inside the agents and thinking their ideas, it becomes a kind of "surrender," as Fackenheim puts it, "for which the horror had vanished from the whole and the *Umwelt* has become a *Welt* like any other."[185] Philosophical thought, that is, resists one kind of satisfaction, by means of transcendence to a higher, detached standpoint, and yet succumbs to another. Slowly but surely, thought "surrenders" to its deepest native desire, to classify and to find meaning. But, then, Fackenheim notes, satisfaction yields to a "shudder," a fundamental, irresistible recognition that the evil, the horror cannot be comprehended or transcended. Using Hegelian language, Fackenheim asks: "what is the truth disclosed in that shudder?" He answers: "the truth . . . is that to grasp the Holocaust whole-of-horror is not to comprehend or transcend it, but rather *to say no to it, or resist it*. The Holocaust whole-of-horror *is* (for it *has* been); but it *ought* not to be (and *not* to have been). It *ought* not to be (and have been), but it *is* (for it has been)."[186] Thought confronts the enigma of ordinary, sometimes extremely educated and cultured people engaged in the most depraved, atrocious acts, and it moves back and forth, winning a moment of satisfaction that becomes self-critical. The "shudder" is the experience of that tension of self-satisfaction and self-critique, of comfort and discomfort, and it results in a transformation: "only by holding fast at once to the 'is' and 'ought not' can thought achieve an authentic survival. Thought, that is, must take the form of resistance."[187] But the subject of the "is" and "ought not" is a reality, the evil of the death camps; hence the resistance too must be a reality. So thought, even resisting thought, must point ahead, beyond itself, to action and, given the extent and persistence of the evil, to a life of resistance, a life that brings the truth of the shudder to its realization.[188] Still, the deepest questions remain: Fackenheim has proposed a strategy, a plot whereby philosophical thought engages Auschwitz, resists, and then points beyond itself. But this is form; we need content and more: "what is this thought? What is the reality it points to? And are both possible at all?"[189]

The thought is that which "follows, step by step, the circular movement by which [it] assumes its resisting stance."[190] It is a thought that begins with the torturers, murderers, and victims, moves to Rudolf Hoess, Commandant of Auschwitz, to Eichmann, Himmler, and finally Hitler himself.[191] In each case, thought struggles to take the agent as he takes himself, to understand and explain his beliefs, actions, and self-understanding, and then to resist being taken in by this. This is thought to assign responsibility, shift it from one to another, only in the end to find it nowhere. "This is the evil—the doers are inseparable from the deeds, and the deeds are inseparable from the doers—to be located wherever thought is not?"[192] In the face of thought, the deeds and the doers seek to flee each other, as it were. Fackenheim alludes to the thesis of David Irving, that Hitler never intended or commanded the extermination of the Jews. This is the thesis criticized by Martin Broszat, among others, and debated by Gerald Fleming, Hans Mommsen, Saul Friedlander, Christopher Browning, and others. To some, the death camps, associated with a focused murderous hatred of Jews, are the core of Nazism and Hitler's weltanschauung; to others, they are the systemic results of lower echelon decisions. In order to avoid a lack of seriousness and to overcome dishonesty, Fackenheim argues, thought must place itself and the evil together, and this can be done, as I have shown, by taking the Holocaust world as a whole, a whole-of-horror. Such thought is not an act of "comprehension" pure and simple. Rather, it is "at once a *surprised acceptance and a horrified resistance*." This is the surrender and the shudder, the tense realization of self-satisfaction and self-remonstrance; here Fackenheim calls it "horrified surprise" and a "surprised horror."[193] Moreover, as I have shown, this thought or horrified surprise cannot remain a "resistance-in-thought." The resistance, like the evil, must be a reality. Hence, "thought is required to become 'ecstatic,' such as to point beyond resistance within its own native sphere, to a resistance that is beyond the sphere of thought altogether, and in the sphere of life."[194]

From this result, Fackenheim draws two conclusions. First, this philosophical grasp of the evil of the Holocaust is the same sort of grasp that resisting victims like Pelagia Lewinska had during the event. She realized the "logic of destruction" and "felt under orders to live." Such a grasp—a recognition in thought that issues in a sense of being required to resist—is ultimate. "No deeper or more ultimate grasp than this is possible for philosophical thought that comes, or ever will come, after the event."[195] Second, the grasp of the victims that led to resistance was had in the midst of a terrible life and death struggle. Their grasp, then, as a way of being, is "ontologically" ultimate, more fundamental than that of later thinkers. In their case, the resisting thought and the life of resistance were united, and the ecstatic pointing of later thought points to their resistance at the same time that it points ahead to action in later life.[196]

Fackenheim sees this as the "monumental conclusion" of a "necessary excursus."[197] Here is the answer to the question, whether all thought after Auschwitz is paralyzed. His answer is that post-Holocaust thought and life are possible only because resistance during the Holocaust was actual.[198] The latter somehow provides a ground of possibility for the former. How is this so? Fackenheim puts it this way:

> [T]here arises for future thought . . . an imperative that brooks no compromise. Authentic thought was actual during the Holocaust among resisting victims: and, being possible, it is mandatory. Moreover, their resisting thought pointed to and helped make possible a resisting life; our post-Holocaust thought, however authentic in other respects, would still lapse into inauthenticity if it remained in an academically self-enclosed circle—if it failed to point to, and help make possible, a post-Holocaust life.[199]

In chapter 1 Fackenheim helps us to understand this important but ambiguous and condensed passage.[200] First, it marks the point at which Fackenheim recalls the earlier notion of the commanding voice of Auschwitz or at least of a sense of duty or commandment. In the works of 1967 to 1970, he had been concerned to establish that there was such a sense and such an imperative. Here he glosses over that issue: it "arises." Second, his central concern in *To Mend the World*, as I have explained, is the possibility of a post-Holocaust recovery: "how Jewish (and also Christian and philosophical) thought can both expose itself to the Holocaust and survive."[201] Here he gives the answer: post-Holocaust Jewish thought is authentic only if it is realized in post-Holocaust resistance to the horrors of Auschwitz, and this is possible only because both resisting thought and active resistance, as responses to a grasp of the event and to a sense of an imperative to resist, were actual in the midst of the event itself. "To hear and obey the commanding Voice of Auschwitz is an 'ontological' possibility, here and now, because the hearing and obeying was already an 'ontic' reality, then and there."[202] Different hearers will take the imperative to arise from different sources or possibly from no particular source. The issue at this point is not the ground of its necessity but rather the ground of the possibility of obedience to it. That obedience must be an obedience in action; moreover, it is possible now because it was actual then.

Fackenheim's analysis, then, has set the stage for establishing continuity while taking discontinuity seriously. One can survive as a Jew; the tradition can be recovered. How to accomplish this continuity, however, is another matter. Fackenheim appreciates the need when he asks: "but can this imperative be obeyed?"[203] What he means is this: Jewish thinking and historically situated philosophical thinking are both hermeneutical. They both involve recovery of the traditional past.[204] But has the exposure to Auschwitz shattered that "continuity between present and past?" If thought requires this continuity and if the latter is "broken," how can thought recover? Only if we locate a "new departure and a new category" that will enable us to bridge the abyss and return to the past "can the imperative that brooks no compromise be obeyed."[205] In other words, Fackenheim has argued for the uniqueness of Auschwitz and its character as wholly incommensurable with the past; he has also argued that the imperative to survive, to go on, and to resist is necessary and possible. This set of results suggests but does not demand that the going-on and the resistance be continuous with the past; nor does it show how this is possible. I now have to examine how Fackenheim solves these problems. If the hermeneutical character of all thought and all life requires some recovery of the past and yet if Auschwitz blocks such a recovery, how can one nonetheless go on at all? This is the second central theme of *To Mend the World*.

In Fackenheim's earlier work, from 1967 and indeed throughout the essays of the seventies, the interpretation of what the commanding voice of Auschwitz commanded, once it was established that there was indeed an imperative to resist Nazi purposes, was developed piecemeal. As I have pointed out, this process involved linking with Auschwitz such matters as Israel, anti-Semitism, the struggle for human dignity, ritual, learning, the interpretation of Bible and Midrash, all as modes or dimensions of authentic response.[206] But there is something ad hoc about this strategy, and the connection between the fact of an imperative and its content is weak. In "Jewish Faith and the Holocaust" and in *God's Presence in History*, the movement from the 614th commandment to the fourfold interpretation of it is certainly contextual and seems almost arbitrary. Here Fackenheim calls for a "new category" to bridge that gap and to reestablish the continuity between a post-Holocaust present and a pre-Holocaust past.[207] That category and its employment show how Fackenheim attempts to provide access to traditional standards in a historically defined post-Holocaust situation.

The new category, required as much by post-Holocaust philosophical and Christian thought as it is by Jewish thought, is not wholly new. It is not a neologism but rather a new, post-Holocaust retrieval of an old Jewish notion, that of *tikkun* (mending or repair) and specifically *tikkun ha-olam* (a mending of the world).[208] Fackenheim makes three points about this idea or category. First, it is a Jewish idea, and the retrieval requires a rereading of biblical, Midrashic, and Kabbalistic texts. Second, by employing it, we see how post-Holocaust authentic response is made possible by the response of the resisting victims and others. Third, the *tikkun* of the resisting victims and others, like that of all those who seek to obey the mandates of post- Holocaust existence, contains a duality: "both a recognition of the rupture and a mending of it."[209] Specifically, a genuine *tikkun* accepts the total, radical character of the rupture, of the rejection of the old, traditional beliefs, ideas, and principles, and yet simultaneously and in the very same act struggles to mend that rupture by recovering those beliefs, ideas, and principles in a new way. Fackenheim tries to show that such an act and such an idea are only available in Judaism, and that the themes and role of the Book of Lamentations show this, when reflected through the prism of the Midrash and the liturgy of the Ninth of Av (Tisha B'Av).[210] The rite of *Tikkun Hatzot*—the "midnight mending"—incorporates the rupture and the mending of it as Jews wake to weep with God and for God for the exile of Rachel's children and for him with them. As Fackenheim notes, the ritual begins with a weeping for exile, *Tikkun Rachel*, and continues with a rejoicing for redemption, *Tikkun Lea*; "but it *can* go on only because *Tikkun Rachel* is *already* a *Tikkun*."[211] That is, *tikkun* is an act that both recognizes the radical rupture and yet begins the process of recovery or repair, all at once. Moreover, in the Kabbalistic tradition of the Lurianic Kabbalah, rupture is treated as real and ontologically basic, for it occurs within God's very being.[212]

These three points allow Fackenheim to employ the notion of a radical but fragmentary *tikkun* in order to clarify how authentic post-Holocaust existence is possible and how it seeks continuity with a ruptured past. After Auschwitz, he argues, "no *Tikkun* is possible of *that* rupture, ever after. But the impossible *Tikkun* is also necessary."[213] Recall the acts of Pelagia Lewinska, of the Warsaw ghetto fighters, and of other resisting victims. For various reasons, their acts were conceived and should be understood as responses to an imperative, and what was imperative for them, a *tikkun* in the midst of rupture, is also a rupture for us today. "A *Tikkun*, here and now, is mandatory for a *Tikkun*, then and there, was actual. It is true that because a *Tikkun* of that rupture is impossible we cannot live, after the Holocaust, as men and women have lived before. However, if the impossible *Tikkun* were not also necessary, and hence possible, we could not live at all."[214] Recalling Fackenheim's previous argument for the necessity and possibility of resistance, one now can see that *tikkun* is the form that authentic resistance should take, an attempt to recover continuity with the past within the compass of a recognition of the utter discontinuity of Auschwitz. In each case, that of philosophical, Christian, and Jewish thought, he shows how a post-Holocaust *tikkun* is possible and what direction it should take by grounding it in a *tikkun* that took place during the event.[215]

Furthermore, post-Holocaust existence is hermeneutical and historically situated. Fackenheim notes this feature of human existence in order to show that human situatedness and the way that Auschwitz breaks the continuity of past and present limit the *tikkun*: "we must accept from the start that at most only a fragmentary *Tikkun* is possible."[216] The hermeneutical account he sketches is general, widely held, and indebted to Heidegger and Gadamer, among others.[217] Where he differs from others, however, is crucial. For him, the continuity between present and past and hence the accessibility of past to present are not unbroken. Others may believe that historicity does not isolate the present from the past, as long as both are historical and the present is constituted from the past.[218] But Fackenheim's historicism is more radical; events can occur that do cut us off from tradition and the past. There are no guarantees for continuity; it is not true that memory can grasp any piece of history, that all the past is available to us.[219] Retrieval, Paul Ricoeur's word, may need first to confront the challenge of total disruption and only then to seek to repair that breach. It must be *earned*, in more than one sense.

Like Alasdair MacIntyre, Charles Taylor, and others, moreover, Fackenheim's historicism denies the possibility of the present agent's transcendence of history, ascent to an impersonal, detached point of view. The agent or interpreter can alter his or her perspective, broaden it, but he cannot eschew it.[220] But this does not mean that one cannot also be receptive to another, both a human other and to a "reality-higher-than-human." Indeed, texts and testimony may provide just this access to the Other, to Being or God, as long as one is at least *open* to receive them.[221] This feature of the interpreter's situation, an aspiration and openness to the encounter with the Other, however, comes with a caution, for there are times when *suspicion* is in order, grounded in critical reflection or in events that mitigate, or at least qualify, such receptivity.

For Fackenheim and Jewish existence, this suspicion about a continued relation with God, about faith, should require some attention, and I can conclude my discussion of his work by considering what he has to say about it. In a sense, Rubenstein's post-Holocaust thought began by exposing a traditional conception of Judaism, God, covenant, and a religion of history to the Holocaust and by disposing of them all. A post-Holocaust traditional Jewish faith was deemed impossible. Both Berkovits and Greenberg defend forms of covenantal faith, as I have shown, while Cohen doubted that post-Holocaust Jewish thought had been sufficiently theological. Fackenheim's thinking on these matters is complex; it changes during the period between 1967 and 1982 and acquires at least subtlety, if not novelty.

It is safe to say that in his early statement in the *Judaism* symposium, in "Jewish Faith and the Holocaust," and in *God's Presence in History*, Fackenheim's thinking about God and faith after Auschwitz was influenced, on the one hand, by the Buber-Rosenzweig conception of faith or revelation as an event of divine–human encounter[222] and, on the other, by Elie Wiesel's account of post-Holocaust faith as involving doubt, rejection, and later a continuous divine–human struggle.[223] In the latter regard, his thinking was similar to Berkovits and Greenberg. As Fackenheim himself points out, the "return to revelation" as the core of Jewish faith did not provide "an all-at-once solution to theological and philosophical problems," and as he carried that view into an exposure to and encounter with Auschwitz, those problems, especially "how to move from the sheer event of divine Presence to any content at all," remained with him. In particular, Buber and Rosenzweig had in revelation found a way of reuniting the flesh-and-blood Jewish people with a conception of Jewish destiny. But both achieved this goal by sacrificing the centrality of historical existence to a kind of spiritualism. Their thinking, as Fackenheim puts it, "had to be liberated from what may be called a fideistic one-sidedness," and this was a chief task of postwar existential Jewish theology and Fackenheim's own encounter with Hegel. In 1967, however, he turned to Auschwitz and then to Jerusalem, two events that "called into question all things—God, man, the ancient revelation and the modern secular self-confidence, philosophic thought and indeed any kind of thought."[224] This is not the place to examine Fackenheim's understanding of God and revelation.[225] Instead I will look at the way God and revelation enter into his thinking in the early period, 1967–71, with regard to the 614th commandment and the commanding voice of Auschwitz, and then in later work, culminating in *To Mend the World* and *What Is Judaism?*

In the early period, once the Midrashic Framework is challenged with Auschwitz, how does God find a place in post-Holocaust Jewish existence? Recall that Fackenheim, in "Jewish Faith and the Holocaust," set aside Buber's image of an eclipse of God as inadequate.[226] No theological conception seemed acceptable, but the survival of Jews, when properly interpreted, was "a monumental act of faithfulness, as well as a monumental, albeit as yet fragmentary, act of faith."[227] What accounts for such an uncompromising commitment? An absolute commandment, which is heard by the believer as the words of a commanding divine voice and by the secularist without identifying its source.[228] Fackenheim alludes to a Rosenzweigian motif, that the believing Jew can, through hearing and acting, turn a *gesetz* (law) into a *gebot* (commandment), thereby drawing into relation with the commander. Here, then, is the first place where God enters into Fackenheim's post-Holocaust Jewish faith, as the divine commanding voice that grounds the obligation to resist Nazi purposes—for the believer. To be sure, as Fackenheim often says, not all hear this voice. Some ignore Auschwitz or seek to escape into abstractions. Others, however, hear the imperative but have no access to its divine source; as I have noted, he "had in mind Buber quoting Nietzsche to the effect that 'one takes and does not ask who gives.'"[229] Berkovits and Greenberg both tried to justify why a post-Holocaust faith ought to be questioning, risk-laden, and yet in some way present. Fackenheim's view here seems too facile and without adequate grounds, although elsewhere he admits Wiesel's doubts and his own.

Nor do things get dramatically better as he elaborates the four fragments of the 614th commandment in the final chapter of *God's Presence in History*. Faith is now itself, in a sense, mandated, a dimension of the content and not only the source of the imperative to resist Hitler's purposes. The imperative of course is heard by and applies differently to the believer and the secularist. "The Voice of Auschwitz commands the religious Jew after Auschwitz to wrestle with his God in however revolutionary ways; and it forbids the secularist Jew (who has already, and on other grounds, lost Him) to use Auschwitz as an additional weapon wherewith to deny Him."[230] The believer remains tied to God but in new ways, challenging his absence, his weakness, and his abandonment, while the secular Jew should not glibly appeal to Auschwitz as further evidence against God. Very much like Berkovits, who characterizes the faith of Job's brother as troubled and risk-laden, and like Greenberg, whose dialectical faith is complex and fragile, Fackenheim portrays a difficult faith filled with uncertainty, madness, and struggle.[231] Resistance to Nazism involves a contested covenantal commitment that seeks a new relationship with God and avoids lapsing into an easy idolatry. But Fackenheim's argument for this faith may not be compelling to all; honesty and fidelity may require more vigorous commitment or more demonstrative skepticism and opposition. Auschwitz may be ultimately incomprehensible, and our reaction to it ought perhaps to be troubled and uncertain. But opposition may require greater decisiveness.[232]

In *To Mend the World* Fackenheim returns to the problem of post-Holocaust Jewish faith in the final sections of the book. How, he asks, is a post-Holocaust Jewish fidelity—to God or at least to humanity—possible? "The *Tikkun* which for the post-Holocaust Jew is a moral necessity is a possibility because during the Holocaust itself a Jewish *Tikkun* was already actual."[233] Fackenheim focuses on the Jew's relation to "his own past history, past tradition, past God."[234] He raises, that is, just the question of continuity with tradition that is the core of identity and historical recovery in the seventies and eighties. I will focus on the issue of faith; how is the contemporary Jew, a member of the accidental remnant, as Fackenheim calls it, still related to the God of the past?[235] Post-Holocaust theology, Fackenheim points out, has moved toward the extremes of a "'God-is-dead' kind of despair" on the one hand and "a faith for which, having been 'with God in hell,' either nothing has happened or all is mended."[236] He appreciates that the faith in question is not all faith but rather the traditional, covenantal faith of divine providence, revelation, and more, and he cautions that Berkovits's views are more complicated than the second pole. But the polarity is helpful, for it provides the framework for understanding authentic post-Holocaust Jewish theology; it "must dwell, however painful and precariously, between the extremes, and seek a *Tikkun* as it endures the tension." What exactly does this mean? It means a *tikkun* that involves a recovery of tradition but is also fragmentary and at risk, a *tikkun* that is both an effort at mending and an act of *t'shuvah*, of return to the past that is also a return to the God of the past.[237] Fackenheim calls the needed *t'shuvah* a "quest for transcendence for our time," and he raises the question in a new way: "what is the fate of eternity in our time?" and turns to its final formulation: "after the Holocaust, can the Yom Kippur be what it was before? Is it still possible at all?"[238] Fackenheim's answer is that it cannot, that a genuine post-Holocaust Yom Kippur and its achievement of reconciliation must differ. It must involve a sense of recommitment to God and at the same time of human self-reliance; Yom Kippur is a re-turning to God and covenantal purposes that is grounded in human action and conviction.[239] After Auschwitz, moreover, unity is a special value; Fackenheim had said this as early as 1967. Hence, post-Holocaust *t'shuvah* cannot separate Jews or segregate God from Torah and Israel. The result for him is that some Jews, though not all, can return beyond a secular amazement to a religious faith, a bewildered anguish or despair at the question why all has not been destroyed and a joy that it has not been.[240] It is a faith in divine purposes that unites a realistic memory of the unprecedented destruction with the idealistic realization that God himself needs the Jewish people. *To Mend the World* concludes with this *groping, troubled affirmation of a post-Holocaust faith*.[241] That it ends on this precarious note and with as much of a theological encounter as Fackenheim thinks is possible, is not fortuitous. In a post-Holocaust world, as he suggests, the route to theology may be political and moral; the lack of a full-fledged post-Holocaust Jewish theology does not bespeak its impossibility. Rather it indicates that the time may not yet have arrived for its formulation.

Fackenheim appreciates the centrality of this issue, of God and Jewish existence. It is the question of how, in a post-Holocaust hermeneutical situation, cut off from the past and from the God of the past, the Jew can recover continuity and access to transcendence. All of Fackenheim's work since 1967, if not before, has been about these problems. Moreover, these problems and Fackenheim's strategies were shared by others in this period, by other Jewish thinkers, by philosophers and literary critics, by Christian theologians, and by German political thinkers. At the same time, however, not all agreed with the post-Holocaust Jewish thinkers, and it is important to turn to their reception and especially to some of the criticisms raised against them.

Chapter Eleven

The Reception of Post-Holocaust
Jewish Thought

Post-Holocaust Jewish thought was received in various ways, to different degrees at distinct times, by diverse Jewish and non-Jewish audiences. This multiplicity is hardly surprising, although it is indeed surprising how rarely they are read and how poorly the more subtle thinkers are understood. How well or how inadequately did their audience appreciate or reflect the way the post-Holocaust Jewish thinkers confronted the issues of historical situatedness, continuity with the past, and contemporary Jewish identity? What was most appealing about their thinking? What was most disturbing?

First came the popular reception of this work, the response of ordinary Jews. They do not, of course, constitute a homogeneous group. After the Six Day War, as I have discussed, American Jewry avidly committed itself to the defense of the state of Israel, and both the state and the Holocaust became central features of American Jewish identity and Jewish self-consciousness. Certainly, both meant different things to different people, and not all Jews incorporated the two into their sense of Jewish identity to the same degrees or in the same ways. In the early years, when euphoria undergirded a broad sense of allegiance to Israel, criticism of its centrality and of its character or policies was muted, if it existed at all. Later, especially after the Yom Kippur War, the increasing domination of the right in Israeli politics, and the Lebanon War, criticism of Israel became more vigorous and self-confident; along with it came criticism of the centrality and special importance of the Holocaust.[1] Some American Jews, staunchly liberal in their heritage and commitments, found much to doubt about the primacy of Israel and the focus on the Holocaust. The attention to a foreign national venue and to the past, with its European orientation, did not sit well with their interest in liberal issues that, they believed, were universal and nonpartisan, from issues of social justice to ecology, opposition to nuclear arms, world peace, hunger, homelessness, and antiimperialism and anticolonialism. Jewish national aspirations had never appealed to some, and the claims for a distinctive victimization smacked of the parochial and even the psychotic. All too often, the liberalism of many of these critics was stigmatized as escapism and even a mode of Jewish self-hatred, and they resented deeply such attacks.

To most American Jews, however, the Holocaust became a compelling, even central feature of Jewish self-understanding. It became the object of extensive and penetrating study and the subject of a tremendous number of widely marketed and read books—from memoirs and fiction to psychological and historical studies. Jewish education was redesigned to incorporate and even focus on it; adult education classes dealt with it, as did popular courses on college campuses; famous Holocaust authors spoke widely at congregations and in Jewish communities, and religious school education made a prominent place for study of the Holocaust. In effect, American Jewish self-consciousness underwent a revolution, with the historical events of destruction and renewal forming the polarities of a new Jewish discourse. To be sure, there was nothing subtle or nuanced about the ordinary Jew's grasp of these events, their meaning, and their role for contemporary Jewish life. What there was can be described as a massive group intuition that these events were undeniable and centrally important, indeed orienting. Some scholars and leaders, however, did not agree; to them, the overwhelming popular attention to Auschwitz and Jerusalem was excessive, misguided, and even harmful. Hence, insofar as the post-Holocaust thinkers, from Rubenstein to Fackenheim, Berkovits to Greenberg, articulated theoretically this general, popular intuition and the actions that followed from it, they became the object of all those who criticized those popular responses.[2] And the criticisms came from many directions.

As I mentioned earlier, *Response*, the foremost journal of the young Jewish radicals, published its symposium on Jewish life in the winter issue of 1970–71.[3] It was explicitly conceived as a reaction to the 1966 *Commentary* symposium on the state of Jewish belief. To the editors, Bill Novak reports, "the *Commentary* Symposium . . . somehow seemed to have come from another era."[4] The *Response* questionnaire, open to all readers and not to a restricted set of rabbinic leaders and intellectuals, differed in two ways. First, its questions concerned both the beliefs people held and how their beliefs influenced their lives. Second, it called on respondents to deal with "the destruction of European Jewry and the reestablishment of the Jewish state," neither of which had even been mentioned in the *Commentary* questions only four years before. As Novak points out, Emil Fackenheim had called Novak's attention to this fact in 1968 and was "thus the original spark behind [the] project."[5] As a whole, the *Response* symposium, with its questions about Jewish youth, the alleged hypocrisy of Jewish institutions, the influence of Jewish law and tradition, Zionism, and contemporary problems, expresses the agenda of discontented young Jews seeking new lifestyles and the need for Jewish revival. But its first question, about the epoch-making character of Auschwitz and Jerusalem, reflects Fackenheim's commitment to the centrality of these events for Jewish belief and life. His own answers indicate his thinking in this early period;[6] the responses of others give some indication of how his thinking was being received.

As one might expect, several of the responses reveal something about how the centrality of the Holocaust and post-Holocaust Jewish thought was understood by members of the Jewish New Left and by young Jewish radicals associated with the budding havurah movement. The answers by Arthur Green and Alan Mintz, for example, represent the latter type of reaction;[7] both were founding members and leading figures of the Boston and New York *havurot*, respectively. Green notes that the Holocaust and Israel, as "backdrop events," influenced American Jewry and his parents to return to the synagogue and develop a sense of Jewish commitment. But he feels distant from them; the forces and issues of American Judaism in the sixties "have pushed [these] great Jewish events into the background."[8] They affect his consciousness less than "civil rights, non-violence, riots, assassinations, black nationalism, the war and the peace movement, psychedelics, the rise and demise of hippie identity, the deepening alienation of sensitive American kids from the fifties lifestyle in which [they] were raised."[9] The *havurot*, for example, were not a reaction to the Holocaust and Israel; they were an expression of the "young American counterculture," a "search for new community," and a religious quest "in a generation that has read Hesse, Suzuki, and Tim Leary even more widely than it has read and been influenced by Wiesel."[10] To be sure, Green and others like him are moved by Wiesel's work and by memories of Auschwitz; they do think about Israel. "But these are not the events that have most deeply shaped [them]." This is not a proposal, a directive, or a choice; it is a "descriptive statement," Green says. But in this context, he also admits, "strangely, I find myself resisting the influences of both the holocaust and Zionism." He speaks of wanting to pray, to *daven*, to draw close to God in joy, and this involves bracketing Auschwitz, systematically setting it aside. It also means rejecting the idea that the Six Day War was a religious event, an episode of divine redemption, in part, he says, because of his opposition to war and violence.[11] Vietnam and Israel may differ, Green indicates, but it horrifies him to treat one as a divine event while opposing the other. He is opposed to religious nationalisms and takes the use of God's word as a "justification for our national/political ambitions" to be a "perversion of faith."[12] Jerusalem, for Green, is not the political reality that is part of a response to Auschwitz; it is a "symbol" of fulfillment and salvation. To Green, perhaps, it is also a symbol of true community and renewed spirituality. To Arthur Waskow, it is a symbol of victory over the forces of modern technology employed for destructive purposes, of a "resistance movement" against the superpowers and against the Jewish establishment's pandering to Israeli militarism.[13]

In short, Green, Mintz, and Waskow agree that the Holocaust is not the epoch-making event that needs to be encountered and bridged. Moreover, Israel, especially after the Six Day War, is not paradigmatic of authentic contemporary Jewish life. Rather, it is in many ways an obstacle to it, as are the American Jewish community and its institutions. The real demands of American Judaism concern piety, worship, community, and opposition to the establishment.[14] Just as women, alienated from SDS and SNCC, moved toward a sense of solidarity and common purpose, so these New Left Jews and young Jewish radicals, isolated by the polarization of the social movements of the sixties, consolidated around a sense of frustration, anger, and alienation from the established Jewish organizations and institutions.[15] It was a response in action to the shortcomings of American Judaism, akin in some ways to the attempt of the young theologians of the fifties who sought to recover the centrality of faith for American Jewish life. It was, too, a response to the pluralism of the day, but unlike that of the post-Holocaust thinkers, it sought a relation between history and identity that moved away from politics and the historical toward spirituality and transcendence, in the spirit, one might think, of a Rosenzweigian return to the eternity of the Jewish people.

Not all young Jewish radicals of the early seventies rejected the importance or the centrality of Auschwitz for Jewish life and Jewish identity. William Novak, once a student of Fackenheim in Toronto and editor of *Response*, certainly was sensitive to the Holocaust, as were Mintz and others.[16] But this sensitivity of course expressed itself in different ways. Not many agreed with Fackenheim and Greenberg that the Holocaust and the Nazi atrocities were a determinative feature of the historical situation and required special attention, that these events somehow transcended conventional concepts, categories, and theories. When read carefully, the works of the post-Holocaust thinkers reveal that they did not seek to elevate Auschwitz while diminishing the horrors of Hiroshima, Cambodia, or Biafra; nor did they ignore traditional Jewish texts and practices. Rather, they saw in Auschwitz a particular, unprecedented, and important event that needed to be confronted, grasped, and somehow bridged, since its occurrence marked off one epoch from another. Those whose immediate influences were the issues of the American sixties, as Green for example articulated them, generally did not accept this hermeneutical centrality for the Holocaust; they assimilated Auschwitz to a set of modern technological, bureaucratic atrocities, treated it as one Jewish tragedy alongside a history of others, and assumed that the most effective way of renewing Jewish faith and spiritual richness was to return directly to a lost world, to recover traditions from the past and shape institutions and life to incorporate them.[17] What did not seem to be recognized—something that was deeply appreciated by the post-Holocaust thinkers—was the claim that American Jewish existence was historical and hermeneutical and that working through the encounter with Auschwitz might be *necessary* for *any* authentic interpretive recovery of the Jewish past. In short, what was denied—implicitly if not explicitly—was that historically Auschwitz was undeniable, unavoidable, and hence momentous.

Nor was this claim accepted, if appreciated, by many Orthodox Jewish thinkers, for it requires a view of Judaism and Jewish self-understanding as historical and exposed to events, interpretations, new ideas, and political-social realities.[18] Among the most vigorous Orthodox critics of Fackenheim, Greenberg, and post-Holocaust thought in general was Michael Wyschogrod, professor of philosophy at the City University of New York and a prominent Jewish theologian. In 1968, Wyschogrod participated in a symposium entitled "The Religious Meaning of the Six Day War" convened by the Orthodox journal *Tradition;* the other participants were Rabbi Shear Yashuv Cohen, a deputy mayor of Jerusalem, and three prominent Orthodox philosophers and theologians, Norman Lamm, Pinchas Peli, and Walter Wurz-burger.[19] This cast of important Orthodox Jewish intellectuals can give us some insight into how modern American Orthodoxy viewed Israel and the Holocaust one year after the Six Day War and provide an introduction to Wyschogrod's later attacks on Fackenheim and Greenberg.

Wurzburger—rabbi, philosopher, and then editor of *Tradition*—introduced the symposium with a short statement and a set of six questions. Orthodoxy, he began, had largely ignored the great historic events of modern Jewish experience, and the Six Day War had raised this matter to a new level of controversy. Some argue that the Holocaust and Israel are evidence that God acts in history. Others disagree and hold that "as rational human beings we must interpret historical events in purely naturalistic categories . . . in the light of political and military realities."[20] The issues concern divine providence, miraculous intervention, the theological interpretation of historical events, and the practical implications of these theological matters for religious life.[21] The questions addressed to the participants reflected these concerns. Each of the four made a short statement, and discussion followed. The main issues were the theological and practical impact of Auschwitz and Jerusalem on American Orthodox Judaism.

Lamm, for example, did not speak of Auschwitz, but he argued vigorously, using the Biblical notion of hester panim, God's hiding his face, and the relief from that dark period, that "the Six Day War was certainly a case of 'revelation'" and a reinvigorating of the Jews' commitment to the "ideals of a full Torah life."[22] Perhaps it is hard to tell, given the brevity of Lamm's statement, but this view certainly sounds very similar to Berkovits's respect for the historical-psychological role of Auschwitz against the background of a traditional conception of history and divine providence. Moreover, while Lamm was reluctant to use, with regard to Israel and the war, the language of redemption and messianism,[23] neither Pinchas Peli nor Shear Yashuv Cohen were so cautious. Indeed, both claimed that the return to Israel, the reestablishment of the state, and its surprising defense in 1967 are all stages in the conclusion of exile and the advancement of the ultimate redemption.[24] All three, however, agreed that the Six Day War bespoke "the hand of God acting in history."

Wyschogrod differed. He warned that our gratitude and elation should not overwhelm us. Historical events are equivocal, ambiguous: some interpret them naturalistically, others theologically. Only when there is a clear, perspicuous divine word, or revelation, that indicates the "very meaning that God bestows on that

which transpires" should one view an event theologically.[25] "Jewish faith is therefore not based on events as such, be they events that appear redemptive or those,
such as the holocaust, that seem to point to God's powerful anger with the people
He loves above all other." Since there has been no clear divine word about either the
Holocaust or the Six Day War, these events remain ambiguous. Neither should orient Jewish belief or Jewish conduct.[26]

Wurzburger, Lamm, and Peli asked of Wyschogrod, why does the biblical
word and that of the tradition not serve "to decipher the meaning of the event," to
clarify what Auschwitz and Jerusalem mean? Indeed, why need one require an
independent revelation? Why can an event itself not *be* the revelation?[27] In short,
Wyschogrod reflected a desire, even more powerful than that of Lamm and
Berkovits, to adhere to a neo-Orthodox fideism, to a belief that what is true in Judaism comes from God, is permanent and universal, and applies to history but is
not altered by it. Like Joseph Soloveitchik, indeed, Wyschogrod endorsed a kind of
Jewish Platonism: individuals may suffer the pain and agony, the joy and surprise,
of historical events, but these events are not mediators between God and the
human. Rather, they are the recipients of divine direction; their meaning, theologically speaking, is determined wholly by how they fit a divine model or plot.

In 1975, Wyschogrod published a brief, personal reflection in which he acknowledged the importance for his personality of Nazism, the Holocaust, and his
own experiences as his family fled Poland and Germany in 1939.[28] He then set out
eight principles of faith. The first and foremost of these is that Judaism's basic message, which is self-evident and certain and is the teaching of the biblical prophets, is
that "God is a redeeming God." This commitment to trust in God, to his role and
power as redeemer, is fundamental. No historical event, nothing empirical, can
teach or advocate this message unequivocally; nor can it refute it unequivocally.
History is the recipient, the beneficiary of this teaching and of God's redemptive
acts. But it cannot refute the truth of this teaching, nor can it support it.

Furthermore, the Holocaust, although we should remember and study it,
should not be allowed to destroy or alter this basic message. Wyschogrod put this
several ways, and in so doing he opposed the reaction of Richard Rubenstein, who
exemplifies how "deeply destructive of faith" the Holocaust can be, and that of
Emil Fackenheim, whom Wyschogrod thinks "mute[s] or silence[s] this basic message": that God is a redeeming God. Specifically, Wyschogrod claimed that Fackenheim does this when he takes Judaism to be "based on the eleventh commandment: thou shalt not hand Hitler a posthumous victory."[29] By placing Hitler's evil
design at the center of Jewish faith, Wyschogrod argued, Fackenheim displaces the
true message of Judaism. This of course is to argue that no historical event can
influence that faith or that message. It is also to ignore Fackenheim's own caveats
about his formulation of the 614th commandment; surely it is unkind to chastise
him for using Hitler's name. The issue is that Fackenheim feels compelled to face
the event deeply and seriously, even at the theological level, and only to respond to

it once that encounter has been fully carried out and both the necessity and possibility of going on have been justified. Wyschogrod's commitment to transcendence and to the immutability of Jewish faith will not allow this kind of serious confrontation with a historical event. It is no wonder, then, that for him the only ground for going on as Jews is service to God, so that nonbelieving Jews who endure must be "in the service of God in spite of their convictions."[30] Indeed, without faith in God, one has no reason to go on as a Jew. "If I do not believe in the existence of God, either because of the holocaust or independently of it, I have no moral obligation to preserve Judaism because Hitler wished to destroy it. . . . In the absence of faith in the existence of God and the election of the people of Israel, the continuation of the Jewish people can reasonably be construed as a very expensive luxury."[31] Fackenheim of course wants such a rejoining of the divine–human covenant; he wants all Jews to hear the commanding voice. But he recognizes that both at Auschwitz and thereafter not *all* did, and there is nonetheless something genuine and dignified about their sense of duty and their responsiveness. With this Berkovits also agrees.

The essence of Wyschogrod's reaction to post-Holocaust Jewish thought is his commitment to the centrality of revelation, of the divine word, and of the a priori in Jewish life. To him, history and empirical contingencies are given meaning and are oriented by a divinely given, unconditional content, and that content at its core is the message of divine redemption and all it implies. The only meaning that the world can have is given to it not through human experience but rather by and through transcendence; there is, in Wyschogrod's thinking, an extreme denial of relativism and historicism but also of the hermeneutical, historically situated character of human existence. Hence, for him, thinkers like Rubenstein, Fackenheim, Greenberg, and Cohen, all of whom hold a different view of revelation and a more historicist belief about Jewish existence, radically misconceive what Judaism is.

This mode of Judaism, moreover, with its resonances of Soloveitchik and Heschel, of Kierkegaard and Luther, has serious political implications. It is realistic and pragmatic about the historical-political demands of the moment, for it disengages the worldly domain from salvation-history and yet places a premium on security and survival. Hence surrender can be as admissible as struggle, and a realistic attitude toward civil rights issues and the war in Vietnam might very well place Wyschogrod in differing company as circumstances change.[32]

Perhaps the most famous critique of Fackenheim's *God's Presence in History* was given in Wyschogrod's article "Faith and the Holocaust," published in 1971; he followed it in 1977 with a critical study of Greenberg's important essay.[33] This is not of course the occasion for a detailed response to Wyschogrod; instead I want to identify features of his critique that I have not yet considered in order to clarify one sort of Orthodox reaction to post-Holocaust Jewish thought.[34] First, Wyschogrod repeated his argument that no secular Jew, after Auschwitz, is obligated to preserve

Judaism; after Hitler was destroyed, the nonbelieving Jew is free to do whatever he or she wants or deems appropriate.[35] But Wyschogrod failed to appreciate the *structure* of Fackenheim's thinking, which, after exposing thought to the event, turns to victims and survivors who *do persist* in their Jewishness, believer and nonbeliever, and whose commitment Fackenheim understands as a response to an imperative. In *other* times, Fackenheim indicated, this could be ascribed to nostalgia and vague loyalties but not *at this time*. Wyschogrod's denial of this account forces him to ascribe this behavior, for the secularists, to just these motives or even to a subconscious commitment to God. This is to fail to take history seriously.

Second, Wyschogrod claimed that for Fackenheim "the sacred duty to preserve the Jewish people . . . becomes a total foundation for the continued existence of Judaism. . . . One is almost driven to the conclusion that in the absence of the Holocaust, given Fackenheim's profound understanding of the irreversibility [?] of the secular stance, no justification for the further survival of Judaism could have been found."[36] As I have shown, Wyschogrod's own view is that only commitment to the redeeming God justifies Jewish existence, and this requires receiving the word of God.[37] Wyschogrod, therefore, cannot allow ambiguous historical events to have revelatory or redemptive roles; nor can he think that secular Jews have any genuine reason to preserve Judaism. Here, then, he misinterprets how Fackenheim *arrives at* the imperative to resist Nazi purposes and *its status*. It is not a "total foundation" for Jewish survival; it is an imperative or duty that arises for Jews now, out of a confrontation with Auschwitz, and it incorporates several necessities, among them a recovery of the past. Indeed, it is clear that for Fackenheim, had the Holocaust not occurred, the situation of modern Jews would have involved a recovery of notions of faith and revelation, covenant and election, in the modern world. For Fackenheim, the "justification" for Judaism and Jewish survival is an historical matter; for Wyschogrod it is not.

Finally, Wyschogrod claimed that Fackenheim's argument for the uniqueness of the Holocaust is moral and not simply descriptive and that it is parochial. The event is one among many terrible occasions of suffering and atrocity.[38] The event is of special importance to Jews because of who was destroyed and because of Jewish theological commitments. Wyschogrod makes his perspective very clear: "we are fixated on the Holocaust to an extent quite unacceptable in a universalist framework." For the believer, the attack on the elect is also an attack on God; "for nonbelief Auschwitz is a member of a large and tragic class of human evil whose voice, if it commands anything, commands men to struggle against evil and injustice wherever perpetrated."[39] From an impersonal point of view, timeless and unsituated, the evils of Auschwitz are like any evils. From a similar but Jewish point of view, the evils are an affront to Jewish destiny. But Fackenheim argues that human existence and Jewish existence cannot be detached; the impersonal, abstract point of view is itself a strategy of avoidance. The Holocaust is unprecedented historically and incommensurable with all explanatory theories, not just Jewish ones. As a historical event that ruptures *all* history and *all* thought, none can simply ignore it or assimilate it honestly into convenient, traditional categories and schemes.

In 1977, when Wyschogrod turns to an exposition and critical assessment of Greenberg's "dialectical faith," his tone is more civil, his observations about difficulties in Greenberg's account more respectful, and his own views—on history, faith, revelation, and politics—more perspicuous. His grasp of Greenberg's article and the struggle to find a way between Rubenstein and Berkovits, disposal of traditional faith and adherence to it, is accurate, and he gives a clear account of his own Kierkegaardian conception of faith and the view of history and revelation that I have already discussed. Wyschogrod appreciates the psychological and historical roles of Auschwitz, while vigorously denying it any theological significance. In part, his view is grounded in his own conception of faith, revelation, and Judaism; in part, however, it involves a deep resistance to the historicity of Jewish existence and to its hermeneutical character. When he says that the central message of Jewish faith is that "God will fulfill his promise though no human being can see how He can do it" and when he claims that this means "believing that God will fulfill His promise to redeem Israel and the world in spite of Auschwitz,"[40] Wychogrod's attitude toward history is exposed as utterly subordinating. To him, certain truth about God's relation to humankind and historical destiny can only come from God. Events, by themselves, tell us nothing. It is clear how radically this view opposes in principle the historicism of recent thought as it does the post-Holocaust understanding of thinkers like Fackenheim and Greenberg.

The way the Six Day War both stimulated overwhelming public attention to Israel and the Holocaust together and occasioned the elaboration of post-Holocaust Jewish thought, especially by incorporating interpretations of the relation between Auschwitz and Jerusalem, had almost immediate political implications. Support for Israel, concern for her safety, and understanding Israeli life, politics, and its meaning all became increasingly entangled with the issues that had overwhelmed American Jews in the sixties and continued to influence Jewish thinking in the seventies.[41] In complex ways, ordinary Jews and Jewish intellectuals could not, and perhaps did not want to, separate their response to the Holocaust from their views about civil rights, black nationalism, Vietnam, American foreign policy, and nuclear disarmament, as well as the character and interests of American Jewish institutions and the needs of Judaism. Hence Israel and the Holocaust were drawn into the orbit of controversies like that over black–Jewish relations or that concerning Judaism and liberalism. Increasingly, in the seventies and the eighties, of course, with the rise of the right wing in Israeli politics and as the Palestinian problem and Israeli military actions raised issues that straddled the difficult border between public morality and realpolitik, the American Jewish community became more complicated and more polarized, all at once.[42] Insofar as thinkers like Fackenheim and Greenberg cultivated a very strong, unwavering commitment to Israel's survival, they were often viewed then—and continued to be viewed for many years—as extremists, and their post-Holocaust Jewish thought was taken to support well-defined political views. At the same time, Fackenheim's criticisms of those, both liberals and Orthodox, who classified the Holocaust among other acts of mass destruction as avoiding the particularity of the event may have conveyed to some that post-Holocaust thought was antiliberal and parochial. As so often happens, as intellectual and theoretical matters become intertwined with heated political debate, there was doubtless a great deal of misunderstanding and little interest in reading the theoretical writings with care. But there is no denying the result: that many liberals—as I call this heterogeneous group—in the seventies became more and more critical of the centrality of the Holocaust in Jewish identity and of the thinkers who defended that centrality.

In 1975, for example, in the first issue of *Moment* magazine, Harold Schulweis delivered a vigorous critique of the rise of Jewish self-interest and what he called "the New Jewish Right."[43] Six months later, he followed up his attack with a more focused one on what he called "the abuse of the Holocaust," to which Cynthia Ozick responded shortly thereafter.[44] Much of Schulweis's critique is beyond my concern, but it is revealing to look at how he views the issue of the centrality of the Holocaust and, in the course of his criticisms, how he understands the work of the post-Holocaust thinkers.

According to Schulweis, "the new Jewish conservatives . . . appear to favor private philanthropy over government welfare, favor an explanation of human behavior in terms of heredity and will, as opposed to environment, favor prayer in the public school systems and federal aid to parochial schools in opposition to the liberal's traditional insistence on separation of church and state."[45] They are against trying to solve, through welfare techniques, insoluble historical problems, and they advocate defending Jewish economic and social interests.[46] Moreover, "while the motivations for Jewish self-interest are varied, one event haunts them all. One single event colors their perception of reality: the Holocaust."[47] Continued attacks on Israel reopen the old wound again and again, reminding the new conservative Jews of their "abandonment and isolation."[48] Schulweis calls attention to Eliezer Berkovits's rejection of Jewish–Christian dialogue and Emil Fackenheim's "anger and despair" over the failure of respect for the Jewish victims of Nazism. In short, Auschwitz has cast a shadow of suspicion and paranoia over American Jewry, and the response has been an angry, often cool, defense of Jewish life and limb and Jewish interests.

The Holocaust, then, is a central target of Schulweis's attack on the new Jewish right of the seventies; he claims that it is misused as a ground of suspicion and pessimism. It is also, he says in his later article, a stimulus for "rage," precipitating a fear of others and angry challenge to them and leading to charges of blame and the cultivation of guilt.[49] All of this, Schulweis argues, is misguided, and he deplores too the sensationalist, shocking techniques used in summer camps and religious schools to teach the Shoah and the agony of the victims.

Schulweis then turns to the Jewish theologians, many of whom, he believes, "have generally kept their distance from the Holocaust, as if they sensed entrapment."[50] But not all. Emil Fackenheim is one who has not. Schulweis credits Fackenheim with good intentions, although he does not try to grasp what they are. Rather, he targets the "misuse" to which Fackenheim's reasoning is "vulnerable." That reasoning Schulweis calls "survivalism," the view that after Auschwitz, life is sacred: "Jews must not hand Hitler a posthumous victory. The commanding voice of Auschwitz demands a defiant spiting of the enemy; against Hitler's will to death, the Jewish will to life." The effect of this thinking is to keep the memory of Hitler alive and to convert Jewish self-definition into a "double negation: I am an anti-anti-Semite." It is an abandonment of some internal purpose for Jewish life in favor of response to an external threat. What should be done — the placing of some positive event and some positive content at the center of Jewish existence — is not done. What Schulweis does, of course, is to look at one stage in Fackenheim's thinking and to try to grasp it severed from how it arises and what follows from it. Fackenheim's argument for the unprecedented character of Auschwitz, his appreciation that as historically situated Jews we must face the dark abyss and rescue from that encounter both a recognition of its depth and means for continuing as Jews, and Fackenheim's way of identifying and interpreting the imperative to resist — all this is ignored by Schulweis. What he sees is the corruption and the misuse of the event as a device for diminishing the content of Jewish life. To Fackenheim, that content must be recovered and reinterpreted; to Schulweis, it is simply there to be grasped or ignored. Coupled with his earlier results, the final outcome of this essay yields an enraged dismissal: nothing beneficial for contemporary Judaism can be gained from the centrality of Auschwitz; Judaism is politically, morally, and religiously worse off for adopting that centrality.

To Schulweis, then, the contemporary Jew in the seventies can choose to situate Auschwitz among other catastrophes and to orient the response to it and to these other events by principles of goodness and holiness. Nature and history are not themselves sacred; "the Holocaust is our history but it is not our life."[51] Schulweis does not advocate ignoring Auschwitz. Rather, he wants Jews not to allow it to determine Jewish conduct and Jewish existence. For Wyschogrod, the prophetic message concerns God's redemption; for Schulweis, it is a moral message. In both cases, that message transcends history, helps Jews to understand its meaning, and then engages them in it. But the message is immune to history, and this is in part why neither can allow "history to address us," to use Cynthia Ozick's phrase.[52]

Clearly one target of Schulweis's concern is a vulgarization and misuse of Auschwitz, its trivialization and exploitation, and an inappropriate exaggeration of its role in Jewish life and consciousness.[53] There is no denying that such vulgarization and misuse occurred in the seventies and have occurred since, both in the United States and elsewhere. But Schulweis extends his attack on such vulgarization of Auschwitz to thinkers like Fackenheim, whose work is not a mere ration-

alization for popular beliefs and conduct but is, as I have shown, a sophisticated attempt to deal with Auschwitz, tradition, and the historical situatedness of Jewish
existence. Schulweis's critique is itself an alternative proposal that simply ignores
the subtleties of Fackenheim's work and assumes an alternative view of history and
religious life. It expresses, moreover, a view that Fackenheim himself often criticized as a form of escapism. The dispute was one that led to a growing antagonism
in the seventies between Fackenheim and many liberal Jewish intellectuals.[54] Much
of this dispute concerned Israel and its actions, on the one hand, and the survival
among Jewish leaders and intellectuals of a continuing commitment to a prophetic
ethics that had been the primary Jewish support for the liberalism of the sixties. It is
no surprise that Fackenheim himself could say in 1971 that "*the* major Jewish task
in America today is to reconcile, as far as possible, the tension between commitment
to Jewish survival and commitment to the ethical ideals of Judaism. That there *is* a
deep tension is manifest in the current mutual name-calling in which one Jew calls
another 'racist' only to be called 'self-hating' in turn."[55] Fackenheim did not call the
ethical ideals universal; indeed, the key to reconciling the polarity and resolving the
tension would be to admit that these ideals, like all Jewish imperatives, arise and
must be interpreted within historically distinctive situations. Still, such moral ideals
would arise and be held, alongside other principles, other necessities, political and
religious ones alike.[56]

As one might expect, there were more and less sympathetic versions of the liberal critique, versions that responded more or less positively to the significance of
the Holocaust and Israel.[57] Schulweis, in his two articles, certainly seemed to be
highly critical and unsympathetic; Leonard Fein, in his later book, sounds much
more receptive. In both, as elsewhere, one finds little reason to think that Fackenheim and the others were being read with care. The issues were being treated in
large, impressionistic ways, and the details and nuances of a thinker's work evaded
the grasp of most—or were simply being ignored. Superficial dismissal was as
much a price of relevance and political germaneness as superficial praise was of
popular recognition and endorsement. The movement of the Holocaust to the center of American Jewish identity and Jewish consciousness was treated largely as a
phenomenon of popular religious culture and political life. Its intellectual understanding was ignored, although it is clear that at the core of the dispute was an extreme disagreement about the historicity of religious belief and the relationship between historical recovery and religious identity.

Was this disagreement also to be found among historians? The American Jewish scholar and historian most critical of post-Holocaust Jewish thought was Jacob
Neusner. In an article published in 1973 and elsewhere, he severely challenged the
work of Emil Fackenheim and the priorities of post-Holocaust thinkers in general.[58] For Neusner, the myth of "Holocaust and redemption" is part of a strategy
of denial, by which American Judaism constructs a "barrier between direct and
personal participation in Judaism existence."[59] It is part of a response to "assimila-

tion and self-hatred," a response whereby "history" became "mythic theology."[60] This theology concerns destruction and redemption and has an "associated ritual [that] is bound up especially in various activities, mostly of a financial character, sometimes of a political one, in support of the State of Israel."[61] Regarding the Holocaust, Neusner claims that it raises no new theological questions but rather, as part of the myth of destruction and redemption available only after 1967, it is part of an American response to anti-Semitism and became a "pervasive theme of Judaic discourse."[62] For my purposes, the important stage in Neusner's thinking came early, in the essay "The Implications of 'The Holocaust,'" where he argues for the theological insignificance of the event.

As a historian, Neusner recognizes that the events of 1933–48 [note the assimilation of the Holocaust and the reestablishment of the Jewish state] are decisive for Judaism, as were the destructions of the two temples, the aftermath of the Black Plague, the expulsion from Spain, and the Chmelnicki massacres. But in this case, he argues, the response was largely secular and not religious in the narrow sense of writing new liturgy, creating new religious ideas, and so forth. What was done is to create a "new myth," the story of American anti-Semitism, destruction, suffering, and redemption.[63] But, Neusner argues, it is largely a myth for the older generation; the new generation, born after the war, do not have the same experiences, and what they seek in Judaism is "healthier" and "more affirmative."[64] As he then argues, the Holocaust has had no real implications; "nothing has changed. The tradition endures." But the language and symbols of Auschwitz do indicate a set of problems in American Jewish life and the articulation of a myth to cope with them.

In the course of his argument, Neusner engages in a critique of Richard Rubenstein and Emil Fackenheim.[65] He calls "Rubenstein's response to the Holocaust ... searching and courageous" and eulogizes him for the abuse he received by "established" Jewish leaders. Fackenheim, on the other hand, is the recipient of Neusner's venom: he charges him with mistreatment of Rubenstein and with "onomastic homicide."[66] He quotes Rubenstein but cites not Fackenheim but a summary of Fackenheim's thinking by Michael Wyschogrod from his critique "Faith and the Holocaust."[67] In the end it is hard to know what to make of a statement so uninformed as this: "Rubenstein tends, therefore, to center his interest on the tragic events themselves, while Fackenheim prefers to make those events speak to the contemporary situation of Jewry."[68] Moreover, Neusner claims—correctly—that for both Rubenstein and Fackenheim, Auschwitz marks a "radical" break with the past. He claims too that other theologians, including Abraham Joshua Heschel, Milton Steinberg, Mordecai Kaplan, and even Arthur Cohen (in his early period) treated the challenge of the destruction as a case of the problem of evil, which, he says, is correct. The Holocaust is not "unprecedented"; it does not "change everything." Wyschogrod's critique of Fackenheim, he says, "meets head-on the issue of 'radical evil' and ... demolishes the constructions of the whole 'after Auschwitz' school."[69] In fact, it is hard to find, in the passage Neusner quotes from Wyschogrod, an argument against the view that Auschwitz marks a rupture, or that it is a case of "radical evil." What does become clear is that Neusner sympathizes with Wyschogrod's critique and with his view of the redeeming God and the truth of a transcendent, permanent conception of God and Jewish history. In the end, Neusner agrees with Berkovits that there is no new theological problem here; the "classic tradition" continues unchanged. "Jewish public discourse has been ill-served by 'Auschwitz' without the eternity of Israel, misled by setting the response against Hitler in place of the answer to God who commands, and corrupted by sentimentality, emotionalism, and bathos."[70]

It is not necessary or even helpful to respond to Neusner's crescendo of anger and acrimony. From him we can learn about an attitude. He represents one way in which the post-Holocaust thinkers were received or rather not received. His view is that of a historian who believes that while catastrophe has often brought pain and suffering to the Jewish people, "in fact Judaic piety has all along known how to respond to disaster." To some, "the wisdom of the classic piety remains sound"; to others, "the Holocaust changes nothing" about their doubts. "Jews find in the Holocaust no new definition of Jewish identity because we need none."[71] The recovery of tradition through positive education and affirmation is what is needed, for history is the context in which "the tradition endures."

Clearly Neusner is indignant and defensive. He is committed to the richness of traditional Jewish piety, shaped in the rabbinic period, with its doctrines and forms of life. Auschwitz, to him, has not altered that tradition. American life and modernity, the customary villains of traditional piety, have posed a problem, and the Holocaust and Israel do not help American Jews meet these challenges as much as they divert attention from so doing. Neusner, then, allies himself with those who reject the historicity of Jewish destiny and purpose. Structurally, Neusner is a traditionalist; historical events do not alter the central teachings of Judaism, but they create obstacles to the adherence to or recovery of them. Holocaust consciousness and the post-Holocaust Jewish thought of the late sixties and seventies certainly, for him, have created such obstacles, and his critique is aimed at removing them and at enhancing the work of the havurah movement and those young Jews seeking a recovery of a mode of traditional Jewish piety.[72]

In the course of the seventies and the eighties, then, as ordinary Jews became increasingly sensitive to the centrality of Auschwitz and Israel to Jewish identity in America, as their self-understanding became complex and tangled with issues of morality, social relations, and politics, Jewish intellectuals split into various allegiances. Some intensified their interest in the Nazi period, the history of anti-Semitism, and the death camps;[73] some turned to a rich and exciting exploration of literary responses to the atrocities, to imagination, memory, and language as they have sought to cope with the dark events of those years.[74] Others have resisted any such focus and have even criticized it. Often issues of a political nature have been the engine of debate, and liberal values have seemed to be in tension with a sense of political urgency and realism. But the deep divide among commentators remains. It concerns their understanding of history and human existence, of the historicity of religious life, and of the compellingness of the Holocaust as a threat to the continuity between past and present, as both an object of and an obstacle to memory.

Post-Holocaust Jewish thought was and has been no isolated feature of American Jewish experience; nor has it been an intellectual anomaly. As we consider it juxtaposed with other phenomena of the postwar period, of the sixties and seventies, we see how it expresses deep worries about who we are, how we understand ourselves, and how we are related to the past. Post-Holocaust thinking has much in common with political thought, literary theory, philosophy, and other modes of thinking. What distinguishes it is its primary focus, its courageous but agonizing encounter with a particular historical reality that threatens all that has ensued, Auschwitz. Its importance lies in the honesty and seriousness, the tenacity and resignation, of this encounter and all that follows from it.

Chapter Twelve

Postmodernism, Tradition, Memory:
The Contemporary Legacy of Post-Holocaust
Jewish Thought

How might we understand the importance of post-Holocaust Jewish thought for contemporary Jewish self-understanding? What is its significance for recent reflection on Nazism, the death camps, and culture? What might its role be for those who study the impact of catastrophe on identity, community, tradition, and the past?

The situated self, objectivity, pluralism, the other, history and memory, the end of history, antihumanism—these are part of a litany of postmodernist themes that have pervaded American intellectual culture in the sixties and after. Only later of course were they united and called by this one name, but there is some value in seeing them as components of a single, global reaction to the past and its orthodoxies. The nineteenth century saw a flourishing of historical studies with a keen sense of realism, accuracy, and hence chronology. Broadly speaking, history was conceived as a set of events that were, having already taken place, fixed and precise; the task of historical inquiry and writing was, through the use of evidence, to determine exactly what had occurred and why and then to represent it accurately as part of a single pattern. Modernism is often thought to have broken with this tradition of realism and representational accuracy by repudiating altogether the value of the past. To an extent, this belief is correct, for there were modernist developments whose commitment to novelty, to a new understanding of subjectivity, to reflexivity, and to the autonomy of art did oppose the realist traditions of Western art and perhaps associated all attention to the past with conservatism and the status quo. In addition to realism, of course, the nineteenth century saw the growth of great, comprehensive historical systems, those of Hegel, Marx, and Comte for example. Within them history was viewed as a sequence of large patterns that were constructed by fundamental law-like principles or forces. While some modernists opposed history's conservatism, then, others opposed these large metahistorical theories as a burden, an obstacle to the novelty and creativity of the self, and hence as oppressive.[1] If history attended to the past, its natural adversary was a way of thinking that focused on the present, and modernity was certainly that. Paul de Man, in an essay on Nietzsche's views on history and modern literature, took history and modernity to be opposites and described modernity as "a desire to wipe out whatever came earlier, in the hope of reaching at last a point that could be called a true present, a point of origin that marks a new departure."[2] This attitude, expressed in Nietzsche, had its influence in religious thought as well, in the work of Karl Barth, Martin Buber, and Franz Rosenzweig, for example, and of all those who elevated the moment of religious encounter and the experience of transcendence beyond the natural, the mundane, and the historical.

While some modernists, then, were opposed to the historical and sought disengagement from it, others saw the present as deeply and inextricably tied up with the past. To them, the past became a challenge and a resource. The past was not dead and fixed; it was instead a constantly changing reservoir for the present and for the self, the poet situated in the present. In the words of Benedetto Croce, "every true history is contemporary history."[3] As James Longenbach has shown, the great modernist poets and novelists, among them Ezra Pound and T. S. Eliot, did not reject history and the great poetic voices of the past; rather they listened to those voices and appropriated them for themselves. In Pound's case, this recovery of the past was grounded in a "belief in a trans-historical spirit that unites all individuals," a neo-Pythagorean, neo-Platonic world soul to which all personal souls are related.[4] In a sense, some modernists achieved a receptivity to all history but only by denaturing that history, that is, by treating the totality of the past as a timeless present. The effect of this strategy, common to both Eliot and Pound, was to abandon "the pastness of the past" in favor of "its presence."[5] It was an antichronological conception in which the temporality of the past dissolved into present appropriation, and that appropriation, in someone like Pound, occurred in an act of "imaginative reconstruction," what Longenbach calls his "visionary sense of the past."[6] This historical program was codified by Eliot in his essay "Tradition and the Individual Talent," where he articulated his belief that all of history, past and present alike, was a single totality, one unified whole.[7] As he put it in his dissertation on F. H. Bradley, "and of course the only real truth is the whole truth."[8] In his own way, then, Eliot too sought to make the past present by nullifying temporality and chronology, by calling on a transcendent point of view from which the totality could be perceived, a perspective in which all disparate, finite points of view merged.[9] And Eliot is but one of many, from Nietzsche to Walter Benjamin.

In modernism, then, we find a rejection of history and an engulfing of it, both oriented around the unique capacities of the present and the self, although a self seeking visionary, transcendent comprehension of the whole of human, poetic experience. Postmodernism, as a changing phenomenon of the sixties, seventies, and beyond, calls for a return to the past, to history, and to tradition, but a return of a different sort.[10] Post-Holocaust Jewish thought, which responded to the historical and its problematic, was part of this shift; it sought to overcome the fideist dismissal of history in the fifties and sixties, an attitude entrenched in American postwar culture and indebted, as I have shown, to the theological inheritance of Buber and Rosenzweig.

In the sixties and especially in the seventies, there was widespread evidence of this renewed interest in recovering a sense of history and the past.[11] Andreas Huyssen has noticed, for example, the renewed interest in the avant-garde art of the early twentieth century—in futurism, surrealism, and Dada. Was this, Huyssen asks, a sign of decline or was it a search for tradition? And if it was the latter, does this signify a backlash or a new wave of conservatism?[12] In the sixties, both culture and counterculture sought relevance for art, fought the exclusivity and detachment of high culture, and worked to reunite life and art. The sixties found in the early avant-garde a precursor.[13] "For a moment in the 1960s it seemed the Phoenix avantgarde had arisen from the ashes fancying a flight toward the new frontier of the postmodern."[14] To be sure, Huyssen believes, postmodernism had to fight a very advanced culture industry that both institutionalized art and culture and was effective at diffusing challenges to it. One response was to seek a tradition for itself, "a viable modern tradition apart from . . . the canon of classical modernism."[15] In the case of recovery of the avant-garde, however, the result has this peculiarity: "the paradox of the 1970s is . . . that the postmodernist search for cultural tradition and continuity, which underlies all the radical rhetoric of rupture, discontinuity, and epistemological breaks, has turned to that tradition which fundamentally and on principle despised and denied all traditions."[16] In Jewish intellectual circles, one finds a similar phenomenon in Gershom Scholem's recovery of subterranean forces within Jewish history and in the return to Walter Benjamin's conception of history and redemptive critique.[17]

Huyssen associates "this intense [postmodernist] search for viable traditions in the 1970s" with the general "cultural and political identity crisis" of the 1970s and "the search for roots, for history and traditions" that arose from that crisis.[18] The crisis of identity grew out of a questioning of conventional or dominant traditions, and the search for history that followed was generally a search for alternative histories, for example, for a women's history or for a Native American history.[19] Huyssen notices that this need for alternative traditions, with attention to cultures not dominated by post-Enlightenment rationality, to new understandings of identity, to pluralism and difference, encourages a search for new cultural identities that supersedes or should supersede the older postmodern attack on history and historiography.[20] This old attack claimed that historical inquiry and writing was *constructive* and not representational; this left us with discontinuity and chaos and historical renderings that were in the end a matter of power. Huyssen finds this sixties stance unhelpful in the seventies, when an old realization of the importance of the past for the present was being seen in new ways.[21] In philosophy the work of Alasdair MacIntyre and Charles Taylor, and of all those who take the history of philosophy to be indispensable to contemporary philosophy, should be seen as part of this renewed commitment to history. The same can be said regarding political theory, literary theory, and much else.

This return to history and also the search for repressed, alternative histories had a distinctly populist side.[22] This was one of the legacies of the sixties and its attack on high modernism and elite culture. In historiography, it was expressed in the new interest in popular culture and in the work of Robert Darnton, Natalie Zemon Davis, and in Germany in the movement called *Alltagsgeschichte*.[23] Part of this shift in intellectual history, from classic documents of high culture to the worldviews of peasants and the lower classes, through the study of court records, rituals, and business documents, was a process of deflating the single center of interest, the intellectual perspective of science, philosophy, art, and politics, into multiple centers, many not reflected in the traditional texts of high culture. In Carlo Ginzburg's work, for example, the canon is set aside wholly in favor of court records that reveal the beliefs and attitudes of common people; in Quentin Skinner's study of Hobbes, it is a matter of using the pamphlets and sermons of seventeenth-century English religious and political life to determine the conventions of discourse within which Hobbes's work should be understood. At the same time, however, this shift carries us away from the elite to the culture and attitudes of the common people who in the seventies become more and more the focus of politics, art, culture, and religion. There was at once a sense of liberation in this change, of casting off the shackles of an oppressive cultural elite,[24] but there was also an antiintellectualism about it, a denigration of high rationality and an attraction to mass culture, nostalgia, and more intense, physical, even rhythmic public celebration.[25]

In some ways, then, the postmodernism of the seventies and beyond has been a continuation of the sixties with its confrontation of high modernism, its rebellion against rigid bureaucracies, its opposition to repressive institutions, and more. It has also involved, however, a rejection of the sixties, especially in its individualism and its neglect of tradition and the past, and perhaps, for some, its sense of political seriousness.[26] On this last matter, however, things are rather complex; for some but not for others, politics and political responsibility were at the core of their response to the sixties.[27] And this difference over the centrality of the political affected postmodernist views of authorship and the subject. After the attacks of Derrida and Foucault, extensions of the structuralist disposal of the subject, there has been a renewed interest in the author and the subject, and in part this interest is political. Huyssen emphasizes, from a Marxist perspective, how discussing subjectivity serves certain political views and makes a critique of the "ideology of the subject" all the more difficult. He compares the rejection with capitalism: both deny "subjectivity in the very process of its construction."[28] Postmodernists, however, appreciate the danger and "counter[ed] the modernist litany of the death of the subject by working toward new theories and practices of speaking, writing, and acting subjects. The question of how codes, texts, images, and other cultural artifacts constitute subjectivity is increasingly being raised as an always already historical question,"[29] and it is a question raised for moral and political purposes, as well as for cultural and religious ones, in America in the work of Michael Sandel and Michael Walzer, in Canada in that of Charles Taylor and James Tully, and in Germany within the debates concerning the Nazi past, historiography, and memory in postwar and now post–Cold War Germany.

The return to history, political seriousness, and a new understanding of the subject form a constellation, then, for some forms of postmodernism. Indeed, Huyssen argues that it is what distinguishes American postmodernism of the seventies from modernism and movements like the avant-garde: "the postmodern sensibility of our time . . . raises the question of cultural tradition and conservation in the most fundamental way as an aesthetic and a political issue."[30] Postmodernism rejects the polarities of the earlier movements and "operates in a field of tension between tradition and innovation, conservation and renewal, mass culture and high art."[31] It struggles, in other words, with the tensions between the past and the present, spontaneity and authority, continuity and discontinuity, and the self and the other.[32] These also mark central fields of tension for post-Holocaust religious thought. In some cases, these tensions could yield an intensity of purpose and a relatively homogeneous vision—for example, in the women's liberation movement; often, however, they did not. Rather the tensions led to discontinuous collections of old and new, bits and pieces, "cultural bricolage" or "juxtaposition," as Gitlin calls it, "the market-place jamboree, the divinely grotesque disorder . . . vulgarized pluralism," a sort of overextended democracy.[33]

There were of course many strands of postmodernism in the seventies, and while one prominent set of them emphasized textuality, pluralism, and lack of stability, others did not. Gitlin takes only the former to be postmodernist in a genuine sense, with its fondness for an "endless play of surfaces" that comes to no secure principles, no "ethical basis for politics."[34] The kind of view that I discussed in the post-Holocaust religious thinkers, with its joint commitment to the situated character of agency and the striving for principle, he recommends as a response to the unbounded relativism and the nihilism of extreme postmodernity. Gitlin calls it a "politics of limits" and describes it as a recognition of what limits are necessary in order to prevent "the atrocities to which our species is prone."[35] Given our historical situation, what kind of a politics can we construct that will protect us against destructive uses of human power, against nuclear threat, ecological irresponsibility, oppression of each other, and mutilation of our individuality and creativity? In this early essay Gitlin does not develop this hope, itself a desire that we solve the problem that Richard Rorty once proposed, to construct the conjunction of liberalism and irony that accepts historicity and yet finds for itself some kind of objectivity and conviction, except to say that it will call for "pluralist exuberance and critical intelligence." But this twin requirement is sufficient to tell us that his hopes are akin to some of the theory I have surveyed. Gitlin's "critical intelligence" points in the direction of some kind of rational inquiry and assessment, and his pluralism suggests his commitment to the multiplicity of historical contexts in which we live, think, and act. Whether we call this a form of postmodernism or an attempt to redeem ourselves from it is not important.[36]

Like Rorty and the others, Gitlin has a deep sense of distress about human capacities and inclinations, a concern nourished by current experience and an allegiance to the truths of the past, especially of the sixties. He is pessimistic and optimistic at once, fearful of the power that Foucault after Nietzsche exposed and that the death camps and the bomb expressed and yet confident in political renewal. In this regard, he is not alone. Realism goes back to Machiavelli and to Plato, at least; hope is a staple of rationalism and liberalism. But it was Kant who reminded us that hope is also central to religion. Kant of course was thinking of Christianity understood as a moral faith, but his reminder has wider impact than he intended. Judaism too is a religion of hope, of messianic expectation and confidence in an ultimate redemption. When wedded to catastrophe, however, that hope and realism form a volatile mix. Post-Holocaust Jewish thought is one manifestation of it and also, in a sense, of Gitlin's "politics of limit."[37]

Gitlin and Rorty portray our current crisis as a need for standards or limits in a highly pluralistic, relativist context. The crisis also involves a "massive disruption of traditional forms of memory" and a "sense of disconnection from the past."[38] But if we consider the sixties as the apogee of this crisis of historical memory and tradition, as the most extreme moment of rejection, opposition, and destruction of tradition, of "loss of connection with the past," it was also the time when popular culture and political fragmentation were seeking ways of reestablishing that connection, in part by discovering new techniques in music, dance, television, and public ritual and in part by excavating for previously suppressed or mutilated traditions. There was, then, a paradox at work that strained toward dialectical mutuality. The very same popular culture that had played such an important role in "creating the crisis of memory" was a "main vehicle for the expression of loss and the projection of hopes for reconnection to the past."[39] But that need for reconnection, for a renewal of memory, came in many forms. Some sought a history that would enrich their self-understanding or guide it as part of a process of liberation or genuine pluralism and a new recognition of distinctiveness. Others, however, saw the crisis as a failure to use the traditional past to ground old oppressions and old dominations. This neoconservative retrieval denies the pluralism of history for "a mythic construct invented to impose cultural unity and obedience to the present government." Lipsitz calls this an "uncritical glorification of the past and present . . . an institutionalized cheerleading for the victors of the past, no matter how villainous or immoral they may have been."[40] At the moment of crisis, then, when the past is conjured up as a palliative for current ills, the controversy becomes intense. For there is not only one past; nor is there only one way of understanding it or one reason for so doing. Rather, there are many histories to be written and many purposes to be served by them. These are themes clearly registered in American Jewish life, with its increasing populism, its spiritualism, its return to ritual and text, and its emphasis on diverse modes of religious expression. Indeed, when Nazism and the death camps are the subject of today's histories and today's memory, the controversy is especially threatening, for deep feelings of anger, fear, and guilt mingle with political motives to make a particularly volatile mixture. From the late sixties through the eighties, this was especially so in Germany, in America, and in Israel, places where a return to the past reached an ominous impasse in just these phenomena, Nazism and its horrifying legacy. It is a situation that persists to this day.

This postmodernist battlefield has been a central venue of post-Holocaust Jewish thought in postwar America. Another has been the world of contemporary American Jewish life and thought. What, then, is the legacy of post-Holocaust Jewish thought to American Jewish experience today?

Concerning the constellation of identity, memory, and tradition, post-Holocaust Jewish thought teaches three lessons. First, no recovery of the past can be taken for granted; one cannot simply leap into the past to retrieve what one will, what seems available and currently assimilable. All continuity must be earned, so to speak. Each piece of tradition—text, principle, belief, image, model, or practice—must be reclaimed from this side of Auschwitz and from a vantage point in part darkened by these events. Another way of putting this point is to note that all traditional narratives of Jewish life and Jewish history must be reevaluated, for any one might turn out on reflection to be a "tool of oppression" or a medium of distortion. Post-Holocaust Jewish thought provokes "suspicion"; in a very profound sense, it is subversive. It calls to mind Walter Benjamin's warning that any history may be a tool of the ruling class; even the dead, he says, will not be safe from the enemy if he wins.

This warning leads to a second lesson: after the death camps and Nazi totalitarianism, no beliefs, principles, and no world are immune from revision. No account of Jewish destiny is privileged, permanent, or eternal. If one were, then it would comprehend even Auschwitz, find a place for it, give it meaning and value, and hence mitigate its evil. Post-Holocaust Jewish thought—not every manifestation but overall—takes the Holocaust to be unavoidable and serious. No honest encounter with it can fail to discover its own limitations and remain honest—intellectually and existentially. This lesson, then, concerns the status of religious faith—beliefs, practices, and values; after Auschwitz thought and life are historical, revisable, and deeply contingent.

Historicity of this kind, however, does not require skepticism or relativism or nihilism. And this is the third lesson that this movement teaches: unconditional response to the horror, the inhumanity, and the trauma is both necessary and possible. At the theoretical level this means that there is still some sense in speaking about objective principles, models, beliefs, and values today, after the death camps. Different figures may understand what this objectivity amounts to in different ways, but in general they both acknowledge it and accept it. To be sure, it is possible—in some sense—that there is no such objectivity, that truth is a matter of power or might, that reason and humanity amount to no more than bestiality; it is possible, that is, that the musselman is the *only* paradigmatic product of the Nazi death camps. But post-Holocaust Jewish thought denies that this is so; it stands firm both on the obligation to hope and on the possibility of "going on" both as a Jew and as a humane person, and it believes that this is compatible with an honesty about the event, its criminality and its evil. In this sense, the challenge for those confronting the Holocaust is to grasp both horns of the apparent dilemma of discontinuity and rupture, on the one hand, and continuity and recovery, on the other.

Jewish thinking and Jewish life in America today are focused on Jewish renewal, spirituality, moral and social questions, political issues, the revival of ritual, and the return to texts. These matters—religious, ethical, and educational—are important, and Jews today are rightly concerned. But many do not seem aware of the lessons of post-Holocaust Jewish thought or, if they are, they ignore or reject them. The reaction to the post-Holocaust thinkers is part of a general rejection of the so-called centrality of the Holocaust to American Jewish identity. That rejection is by and large superficial and simplistic. Jewish life is charged with political conflicts and hostilities. It clings to a desire and perhaps a need for joy and celebration that is salutary, but it fails to appreciate the subtlety required to find joy after despair and to celebrate with the appropriate sense of uncertainty and doubt. In a post-Holocaust world, as long as we live in such a world, there are no facile, emotionally elevating ascents to the divine, no unproblematic returns to the sacred, no simple ways of rectifying social ills. Such attempts, whether through study, community, celebration, or quasi-mystical preparation, may very well promise authenticity and peace of mind to contemporary Jews in America, but their cultivation is not an alternative to a serious, honest, and responsible encounter with the Shoah. They and it may both, in their relationships, be the hallmarks of genuine Jewish life for Jews today. To warn against naive one-sidedness and simple goals may also be one of the rewards of studying carefully our recent intellectual past and the post-Holocaust thinkers who occupy its central venue. For today's American Jew, to paraphrase Kant, it is certainly true that trauma without Torah is empty, but it is equally true that Torah without trauma is blind.[41]

Preface

1. As Benedict Anderson puts it, a "characteristic device" in the process of constructing national identities is "to 'have already forgotten' tragedies of which one needs increasingly to be 'reminded'" (*Imagined Communities* [London: Verso, 1983; revised edition, 1991], 201).

Introduction

1. Throughout I use the expression "Jewish thought" as my shorthand for "Jewish self-understanding from a religious point of view," developed by Jewish theologians or others in North America for a North American situation.

2. For discussion, see James Young, *Writing and Rewriting the Holocaust*, and his second book, *The Texture of Memory: Holocaust Memories and Meaning* (New Haven, CT: Yale University Press, 1993); also, Lawrence Langer, *Holocaust Testimonies*; Geoffrey H. Hartmann (ed.), *Holocaust Remembrance: The Shapes of Memory* (Oxford: Basil Blackwell, 1994); Annette Insdorf, *Indelible Shadows: Film and the Holocaust*. 2nd ed. (Cambridge: Cambridge University Press, 1989); Ilan Avisar, *Screening the Holocaust: Cinema's Images of the Unimaginable* (Bloomington, IN: Indiana University Press, 1988); Yosefa Loshitzky (ed.), *Spielberg's Holocaust* (Bloomington, IN: Indiana University Press, 1997); Barbie Zelizer, *Remembering to Forget: Holocaust Memory Through the Camera's Eye* (Chicago: University of Chicago Press, 1998).

3. The thinkers we shall be discussing, together with a host of Jewish rabbis and leaders, have articulated the positive case. The negative case is prominent among many Jewish intellectuals, e.g., David Biale and Michael Lerner, and figures like Marc Ellis. It has also been given by Peter Novick in his book *The Holocaust in American Life* (New York: Houghton Mifflin Company, 1999); see also Hilene Flanzbaum (ed.), *The Americanization of the Holocaust* (Baltimore: The Johns Hopkins University Press, 1999), and Norman G. Finkelstein, *The Holocaust Industry: Reflections on the Exploitation of Jewish Suffering* (London: Verso, 2000).

4. To be precise, the first essay dealing with Auschwitz in the first edition of *After*

Auschwitz dates from 1960, after a visit to Germany but before Rubenstein's return to Germany and his visit with Heinrich Gruber, Dean of the Evangelical Church of East and West Berlin, in August of 1961.

5. I exclude the extreme orthodox; cf. Kaplan's paper in *Tradition* and Wychogrod's responses to Greenberg and Fackenheim. Also, for a modern orthodox perspective, albeit in an English context, see Jonathan Sacks, *Crisis and Covenant: Jewish Thought after the Holocaust* (Manchester: Manchester University Press, 1992), especially chapter 2.

6. See Neusner; also Michael Lerner, *Jewish Renewal* and the works of Mark H. Ellis.

Chapter 1

1. Raul Hilberg, *The Destruction of the European Jews* (Chicago: Quadrangle, 1961); also 3 vols. rev. ed. (New York, 1985). Two other surveys appeared in the early 1950s; Leon Poliakov, *Bréviaire de la haine* (Paris: Calmann-Lévy, 1951), and Gerald Rietlinger, *The Final Solution* (London: Vallentine, Mitchell, 1953). See Michael Marrus, *The Holocaust in History* (Hanover, NH: University Press of New England, 1987), 203. Also there is the work of the Frankfurt School; see Rolf Wiggershaus, *The Frankfurt School* (Cambridge: MIT Press, 1995). In addition see Victor E. Frankl, *Man's Search for Meaning* (New York: Pocket Books, 1963) (originally *From Death Camp to Existentialism*; German ed. *Ein Psycholog erlebt das Konzentrationlager*, 1947); Bruno Bettelheim, *The Informed Heart* (New York: Avon, 1960) and "Individual and Mass Behavior in Extreme Situations," *Journal of Abnormal and Social Psychology* 38 (1943), 417–452.

2. See Fackenheim, *To Mend the World*, 3rd ed. (Bloomington: Indiana University Press, 1994), 28, and index.

3. My account is based on Elizabeth Young-Bruehl, *Hannah Arendt* (New Haven: Yale University Press, 1982), 181–211, 241–242. See also Richard Bernstein, *Hannah Arendt and the Jewish Question* (Cambridge: MIT Press, 1996).

4. Quoted in Young-Bruehl, *Hannah Arendt*, 184–185, from an interview.

5. The account of the new criminal was repeated in OT and also in "Social Science Techniques and the Study of Concentration Camps," *Jewish Social Studies* 12, 1 (1950), 49–64 (reprinted in Alan Rosenberg and Gerald E. Myers (eds.), *Echoes from the Holocaust* [Philadelphia: Temple University Press, 1988]).

6. "Organized Guilt," 230–231 (in *The Jew as Pariah* [New York: Grove Press, 1978]).

7. By the time Arendt completed these sections of OT, her terminology had become refined; she distinguished between the mass man, the bourgeois, and the mob man. Here, in this early essay, her terminology is less precise.

8. Ibid., 229.

9. That is, the problem is a social, moral, and existential one and not an epistemological one. And insofar as it is about how one ought to respond to such a society, it is about shame, one's sense of self within such a society or in confronting it.

10. Ibid., 230.

11. Ibid., 230.

12. Ibid., 230.

13. Ibid., 231–234.

14. Ibid., 232.

15. This portrait also recalls Heidegger's account of "Das Man" in *Sein und Zeit*, the impersonal main character in modern technological society.

16. Ibid., 233.

17. Ibid., 234.

18. For discussion, see Margaret Canovan, *Hannah Arendt* (Cambridge, UK: Cambridge University Press, 1992); Maurizio Passerin D'Entreves, *The Political Philosophy of Hannah Arendt* (London: Routledge, 1994), and Seyla Benhabib, *The Reluctant Modernism of Hannah Arendt* (Thousand Oaks, CA: Sage, 1996).

19. Bernstein has a somewhat different and not sufficiently deep account that leads him to think that Arendt's later account, subsequent to *Eichmann in Jerusalem*, differs from this earlier one.

20. See Young-Breuhl, *Hannah Arendt,* 256, on Arendt's notion of the political.

21. OT, 337–339.

22. See Richard H. Pells, *The Liberal Mind in a Conservative Age* (New York: Harper and Row, 1985), 83–96.

23. Chapter 12, "Totalitarianism in Power." This last section, "Total Domination," includes large chunks from "The Concentration Camps," *Partisan Review* 15, 7 (July 1948), 743–763. The final three pages are new. See Young-Breuhl, *Hannah Arendt,* 204–206.

24. "The concentration and extermination camps of totalitarian regimes serve as laboratories in which the fundamental belief of totalitarianism that everything is possible is being verified" (OT, 437).

25. "[T]he appalling spectacle of the camps themselves is supposed to furnish the 'theoretical' verification of the ideology" (OT, 438).

26. OT, 438.

27. OT, 443.

28. OT, 437–443.

29. OT, 443.

30. OT, 440–441.

31. OT, 458; also 438.

32. See Wiesel, "A Plea for the Dead," in *Legends of Our Time* (New York: Avon Books, 1968), 230.

33. OT, 438. Arendt's theme should be compared to Levi's portrayal of the musselmänner as the drowned and Fackenheim's use of this notion in "The Holocaust and Philosophy" and *To Mend the World* as part of his attempt to show that even Heidegger's conception of human *Dasein* is challenged by Auschwitz.

34. OT, 441. It is the "reduction of man to a bundle of reactions." "The real horror of the concentration and extermination camps lies in the fact that the inmates, even if they happened to keep alive, are more effectively cut off from the world of the living than if they had died, because terror enforces oblivion. Here, murder is as impersonal as the squashing of a gnat" (OT, 443).

35. OT, 444–447.

36. OT, 444. Michael André Bernstein discusses this phenomenon, also explored by James Young, in *Foregone Conclusions* (Berkeley: University of California Press, 1994). Even the survivor's testimony is not unencumbered by conceptual and imaginative overlay; also, as Arendt emphasizes, it is unbelievable even to the survivor, once she has returned to the normal world, so great is the disparity, the dissonance.

37. OT, 444.

38. OT, 447.

39. For similar views, see the works of Améry and Des Pres and Emil Fackenheim, "Sachsenhausen, 1938: Groundwork for Auschwitz," in *The Jewish Return Into History* (New York: Schocken Books, 1978), ch. 5. As Arendt put it, "Seen through the eyes of the ideology, the trouble with the camps is almost that they make too much sense, that the execution of the doctrine is too consistent" (OT, 457).

40. Compare Fackenheim's essay "On the Life, Death, and Transfiguration of Martyrdom, in *The Jewish Return Into History* (New York: Schocken, 1978), chapter 15.

41. OT, 456.

42. OT, 457.

43. See Young-Bruehl, *Hannah Arendt,* 205.

44. OT, 459. I take the expressions "absolute evil" and "radical evil" to be synonymous. Some of this passage was added in the 1953 German edition, translated into English in 1958.

45. See Kant, *Religion within the Limits of Reason Alone* in Immanuel Kant, *Religion within the Boundaries of Mere Reason and Other Writings* (New York: Cambridge University Press, 1998) and Fackenheim, "Kant and Radical Evil," *University of Toronto Quarterly* 23 (1954), 339–353; also Allen W. Wood, *Kant's Moral Religion* (Ithaca, NY: Cornell University Press, 1970). Whitfield, *Into the Dark* (Philadelphia: Temple University Press, 1980), 102.

46. Allen W. Wood, *Kant's Moral Religion* (Ithaca, NY: Cornell University Press, 1970), 112–114, 210–219.

47. Hans Jonas's version of Arendt's point; in verbal communication with Ernst Simon, reported in Simon, "Revisionist History of the Jewish Catastrophe," *Judaism* 12,4 (summer 1963), 395.

48. For discussion of the book, Arendt's attitude toward Ben Gurion and Israeli policy, and the book's polemical purposes, see Jeff Isaac, *Arendt, Camus, and Modern Rebellion* (New Haven: Yale University Press, 1992). See also Bernstein, *Hannah Arendt and the Jewish Question* and Whitfield, *Into the Dark*.

49. Young-Bruehl, *Hannah Arendt,* 357; Lionel Abel, "The Aesthetics of Evil," *Partisan Review* 30, 2 (summer 1963), 210–230.

50. Compare Abel, "The Aesthetics of Evil," 219–220.

51. Young-Bruehl, *Hannah Arendt,* 567.

52. There is some evidence that she had used the notion of evil's banality in a letter to Karl Jaspers. In addition, in her report she emphasizes the legal and juridical issues, concerning where the trial should have been conducted and by whom. She therefore did not wholly ignore the uniqueness of the crimes, but her focus was on the legal and juridical context for considering them unique.

53. EJ (1965), 287–288; see also 276–277, 25–26.

54. See Whitfield, *Into the Dark,* 214–215, but especially Fackenheim, *To Mend the World* (hereafter TMW), 233–248; compare Young-Bruehl, *Hannah Arendt,* 370, and Christopher Browning, *Ordinary Men* (New York: HarperCollins, 1992). See also Daniel Goldhagen, *Hitler's Willing Executioners* (New York: Knopf, 1996); Browning, *Nazi Policy, Jewish Workers, German Killers* (Cambridge, UK: Cambridge University Press, 2000); Omer Bartov, "Inside, Outside" (review of Browning, *Nazi Policy*), *New Republic* (April 10, 2000), 41–45.

55. In a presentation at a conference on World War II and the Nazi Holocaust of European Jewry at Indiana University May 8, 1995, Jean Elshtain argued that the background of Arendt's conception is Augustinian. Eichmann's evil, that is, is a privation. Elshtain's analysis is illuminating, but my own interest is not in the metaphysical character of evil, for Arendt, but its moral and philosophical character. Nor am I concerned here with her rhetorical and political motives in using a term that suggests superficiality and insignificance and hence might be taken to demean the victims of such evil.

56. Young-Bruehl, *Hannah Arendt,* 369.

57. OT, 338, and "Organized Guilt."

58. My own view, that Arendt's account deepens her earlier one but is certainly a development of it, differs from that of Bernstein, who claims that her account changes or shifts its focus from superfluity to thoughtlessness. This must be wrong, since her earlier account of the new criminal articulates the same thoughtlessness.

59. OT, 443.

60. OT, 459.

61. *Jew as Pariah*, 250–51; originally in *Encounter* (January, 1964), 51–56.

62. Young-Bruehl, *Hannah Arendt,* 460–474; compare Mary McCarthy's Introduction in Hannah Arendt, *Thinking* (New York: Harcourt Brace, 1978).

63. See EJ, 124–134; also Young-Bruehl, *Hannah Arendt,* 337.

64. See Whitfield, *Into the Dark,* 237–247, 177–195; Young-Bruehl, *Hannah Arendt,* 337–378. In a sense, Arendt's criticism of Jewish leadership during the Holocaust was a very thinly disguised attack on David Ben Gurion and Israeli leadership during the 1950s and 1960s. Doubtless many participants in the debate saw this clearly and responded in terms of it.

65. Reprinted in *Jew as Pariah*, 164–177, especially 166.

66. This hostility was aimed especially at Ben Gurion and was later manifest as her opposition and belligerence toward him and his staging of the Eichmann trial as a show trial. See Marie Syrkin, "Hannah Arendt," *Dissent* 10, 4 (autumn 1963), 347; Young-Bruehl, *Hannah Arendt,* 340–342.

67. See Whitfield, *Into the Dark,* 177–179: on Eichmann as Zionist and Kantian. Also compare Young-Bruehl, *Hannah Arendt,* 362–366; Albert H. Friedlander, "The Arendt Report on Eichmann and the Jewish Community," *CCAR Journal* 11, 3 (October 1963), 51–52. Young-Bruehl's comments on the controversy are revealing: "Arendt's book did lend itself to misinterpretation more than any other she wrote: its conclusions were shocking, it contained numerous small errors of fact, it was often ironic in style and imperious in tone, and some of its most controversial passages were peculiarly insensitive" (338). "Her generalizations were, many felt, too sweeping; in the face of excruciating moral dilemmas sympathy was as important as frank acknowledgment of wrongdoing. Such sympathy seemed to be lacking in Arendt's account" (344).

68. For example, in the work of Yehuda Bauer. See Young-Bruehl, *Hannah Arendt,* 521 n. 40.

69. Among the participants were Harold Rosenberg, Bell, Podhoretz, Syrkin, Musamano, Simon, Abel, Lacquer, and Frachter.

70. For a general account, see Whitfield, *Into the Dark;* see, for example, Syrkin, "Hannah Arendt," 344–352.

71. *Partisan Review* 30, 2 (summer 1963), 211–230.

72. Abel, "The Aesthetics of Evil," 211.

73. Ibid., 219.

74. Ibid., 221.

75. Ibid., 221–223. But Arendt does judge him legally; see Norman Podhoretz, "Hannah Arendt on Eichmann," *Commentary* 36, 3 (September 1963), 205.

76. Ibid., 224–225.

77. Ibid., 219–220.

78. Ibid., 220, quoting de Beauvoir.

79. *Partisan Review* 30, 3 (fall 1963).

80. Bell, "Alphabet of Justice," 417–418, 428.

81. Ibid., 419.

82. Ibid., 427.

83. Ibid., 428.

84. Ibid., 428.

85. Compare 426–427: Bell's account of ideology and Eichmann is not exactly Arendt's account.

86. Contra Friedlander.

87. Podhoretz, "Hannah Arendt," 208.

88. Dwight Macdonald, *Partisan Review* (spring 1964), reprinted in Dwight Macdonald, *Discriminations* (New York: Grossmann Publishers, 1974), 308–317; Bruno Bettelheim, *New Republic* (June 15, 1963), 48–49.

Chapter 2

1. Alfred Kazin, *Starting Out in the Thirties* (Boston: Little, Brown, 1962), 166.

2. OT, 446 n. 138.

3. After Pells, in *The Liberal Mind in a Conservative Age* (New York: Harper and Row, 1985), I shall call these intellectuals liberals or liberal intellectuals, in a broad and loose sense. See Stephen J. Whitfield, *The Culture of the Cold War* (Baltimore: Johns Hopkins Press, 1996); Morris Dickstein, *Gates of Eden* (Harmondsworth: Penguin, 1989; orig. 1977); Howe, "The New York Intellectuals," in *Decline of the New* (New York: Harcourt Brace and World, 1970). For books on the New York intellectuals, see also Thomas Bender, *New York Intellect* (New York: Knopf, 1987), Alexander Bloom, *Prodigal Sons* (New York: Oxford University Press, 1986), and Alan M. Wald, *The New York Intellectuals* (Chapel Hill: University of North Carolina Press, 1987).

4. Theodor W. Adorno, *Negative Dialectics* (New York: Continuum, 1973), 361–408.

5. Trilling, "Art and Fortune," in *The Liberal Imagination* (New York: Viking Press, 1950), 247–271.

6. Ibid., 247.

7. One finds earlier incarnations of the same strategy in Georg Lukács, *The Theory of the Novel* (Cambridge: The MIT Press, 1971), and Lucien Goldmann, *Toward a Sociology of the Novel* (London: Tavistock, 1975).

8. Ian Watt, *The Rise of the Novel* (Berkeley: University of California Press, 1962).

9. Trilling, *The Liberal Imagination*, 248.

10. Ibid., 257–258.

11. Ibid., 256.

12. Ibid., 255.

13. Ibid., 256.

14. See Susan Sontag, *On Photography* (New York: Farrar, Straus and Giroux, 1977), 19–20, quoted in Whitfield, *Into the Dark*, 103–104.

15. Compare Irving Howe, "The New York Intellectuals," 244–245; Vivian Fry, "The Massacre of the Jews," *New Republic* (December 21, 1942), 816–818; "The Jews of Europe," *New Republic* (August 30, 1943), 304–305, 310–315.

16. Wiesel's *Night* actually first appeared in Yiddish in 1956.

17. See Alvin Rosenfeld, *A Double Dying* (Bloomington: Indiana University Press, 1980), 55–59.

18. Lawrence Langer, "The Dominion of Death," in *Responses to Elie Wiesel*, edited by Cargas (New York: Persea Books, 1978), 31; reprinted from *The Holocaust and the Literary Imagination* (New Haven: Yale University Press, 1975).

19. See Lawrence Cunningham, "Elie Wiesel's Anti-Education," in Cargas, *Responses to Elie Wiesel* (New York: Persea Books, 1978), 23–28; Langer, "Dominion of Death," 30.

20. See Irving Halperin, "From *Night* to *The Gates of the Forest*," in Cargas, 51–56.

21. See Robert Alter, *After the Tradition* (New York: Dutton, 1971), 155.

22. Especially on Fackenheim and Greenberg, as I will show.

23. Alter, *After the Tradition*, 153: "Wiesel's words . . . are more theological parable than realistic fiction."

24. Wiesel, *Night* (New York: Hill and Wang, 1960; orig. in French, 1958), 70–71.

25. Alter, *After the Tradition*, 156: "For Wiesel, however, Auschwitz was not just a personal trauma but a dark revelation of what man, God, and history were all about. . . . Wiesel's principal concern is to imagine a humanly possible aftermath, for himself, for all of us."

26. See Langer for a summary; also Rosenfeld, *A Double Dying*. Later the theme became central to a nonreligious, cultural encounter with the Final Solution. See Berel Lang, *Act and Idea in the Nazi Genocide* (Chicago: University of Chicago Press, 1990); Saul Friedlander (ed.), *Probing the Limits of Representation* (Cambridge: Harvard University Press, 1992); James Young, *Writing and Rewriting the Holocaust* (Bloomington: Indiana University Press, 1988); Michael André Bernstein, *Foregone Conclusions* (Berkeley: University of California Press, 1994).

27. Alter, *After the Tradition*, 151.

28. Ibid., 152.

29. *Night*, 40.

30. Ibid., 42–43.

31. Ibid., 43–44.

32. For discussion of Levi's art and his suicide, see Alvin H. Rosenfeld, "Primo Levi: The Survivor as Victim," in *Perspectives on the Holocaust*, edited by James S. Pacy and Alan P. Wertheimer (Boulder, CO: Westview Press, 1995), 123–144; Myriam Anissimov, *Primo Levi* (Woodstock, NY: Overlook Press, 1999), chapter 18.

33. Primo Levi, *The Drowned and the Saved* (New York: Summit, 1988), 145: "Like Améry, I too entered the Lager as a nonbeliever, and as a nonbeliever I was liberated and have lived to this day. Actually, the experience of the Lager with its frightful iniquity confirmed me in my non-belief."

34. Levi, *The Drowned and the Saved* (Italian, 1986; English, 1988), preface, 16–19, 36–42; compare *Survival in Auschwitz* (New York: Collier Books, 1961), 82–91.

35. *The Drowned and the Saved*, 16–17.

36. Ibid., 18.

37. *Survival in Auschwitz*, 84.

38. Ibid., 22–23, 79–82.

39. Ibid., 23.

40. Ibid., 81.

41. Levi calls this state a Hobbesian one because of the desire for survival and the constant competition; see *The Drowned and the Saved*, 134.

42. *Survival in Auschwitz*, 82.

43. Améry avoids the drowned. See Levi, *The Drowned and the Saved*, 142; Améry, *At the Mind's Limits* (Bloomington: Indiana University Press, 1980), 9. Fackenheim makes important use of Levi's portrayal in "The Holocaust and Philosophy," in Emil L. Fackenheim, *Jewish Philosophers and Jewish Philosophy*, ed. Michael L. Morgan (Bloomington: Indiana University Press, 1996), chap. 10, and in *To Mend the World*.

44. *Survival in Auschwitz*, 84.

45. Ibid., 78.

46. Ibid., 84.

47. Ibid., 35.

48. Ibid., 36.

49. Compare Des Pres, *The Survivor* (New York: Oxford University Press, 1976), 62–63, quoting Pelagia Lewinska: "I saw that it was not a question of disorder or lack of organization but that, on the contrary, a very thoroughly considered conscious idea was in the back of the camp's existence. They had condemned us to die in our own filth, to drown in mud, in our own excrement.... But from the instant when I grasped the motivating principle ... it was as if I had been awakened from a dream ... I felt under orders to live" (Lewinska, *Twenty Months at Auschwitz* [New York: Lyle Stuart, 1968], 41–42, 50).

50. Levi, *The Drowned and the Saved*, 127–148.

51. Levi, *The Drowned and the Saved*, 130; Améry, *At the Mind's Limits*, 3.

52. Levi, *The Drowned and the Saved*, 141.

53. Ibid., 139.

54. Ibid., 132.

55. Améry, *At the Mind's Limits*, 15–18.

56. Ibid., 10.

57. Ibid., 19. Compare 20: "We emerged from the camp stripped, robbed, emptied out, disoriented—and it was a long time before we were able even to learn the ordinary language of freedom. Still today, incidentally, we speak it with discomfort and without real trust in its validity." See also 27–28.

58. See the last essay in *At the Mind's Limits*, entitled "On the Necessity and Impossibility of Being a Jew," for the account of catastrophe Judaism.

59. Améry, *At the Mind's Limits*, 83.

60. Ibid., 83–86, 94; Sartre, *Anti-Semite and Jew*, chapter 3.

61. *At the Mind's Limits*, 89.

62. Ibid., 90.

63. Ibid., 91.

64. He also calls it Holocaust Judaism, 99. Many will later criticize the post-Holocaust Jewish theologians for developing a "Holocaust Judaism," but in their case the charge is not as appropriate as it might be in Améry's case. For a recent critique, see Michael André Bernstein, *Foregone Conclusions*.

65. Levi, *The Drowned and the Saved*, 139.

66. Améry, *At the Mind's Limits*, 96, 98.

67. Ibid., 97–100.

68. Ibid., 97.

69. Ibid., 98. He also calls this "solidarity of revolt" (99).

Chapter 3

1. Reinhold Niebuhr's major works include: *Moral Man and Immoral Society* (1932), *The Nature and Destiny of Man* (1941; 1943), *Faith and History* (1949), and *The Irony of American History* (1951).

2. English translations of the works of Kierkegaard date from the 1930s, many becoming available in America in the war years and afterward, e.g., *The Concept of Dread* (1944), *Fear and Trembling* (1941), *Concluding Unscientific Postscript* (1941), and *Sickness unto Death* (1941). Barth's works were available in English translations from the late 1920s and early 1930s, e.g., *Word of God and Word of Man* (1928) and *Epistle to the Romans* (1933). The postwar years saw a host of English editions of essays and works by Tillich

and Bultmann, including such central works as Tillich, *The Courage to Be* (1952), *The Protestant Era* (1948), and *Dynamics of Faith* (1956), and Bultmann, *Primitive Christianity* (1956) and *The Theology of the New Testament* (1951–55), as well as the influential collections of essays *Existence and Faith* (1960) and *Faith and Understanding* (1969).

3. For example, Ira Eisenstein, Roland Gittelson, and Jack Cohen.

4. See Bernard Martin (ed.), *Contemporary Reform Jewish Thought* (Chicago: Quadrangle Books, 1968), 180–183.

5. Herberg's first major theological work, *Judaism and Modern Man*, was published in 1951 (New York: Meridian Books), an outcome of discussions at the Jewish Theological Seminary. For a valuable collection of his essays, with an informative introduction, see David G. Dalin (ed.), *From Marxism to Judaism: The Collected Essays of Will Herberg* (New York: Markus Wiener, 1989).

6. See my later discussion of their influence.

7. See Edward K. Kaplan and Samuel H. Dresner, *Abraham Joshua Heschel* (New Haven: Yale University Press, 1998).

8. Eugene Borowitz called this a "theological seriousness . . . manifest in a minority of Jews in the American Jewish community," during the discussion following the symposium, "Toward Jewish Religious Unity," *Judaism* 15,2 (spring 1966), 159.

9. See Eugene B. Borowitz, "Existentialism's Meaning for Judaism," *Commentary* 28,5 (November 1959), 414–420.

10. See the debate between Zuckerman and Fackenheim in the *Reconstructionist,* May 7 and June 26, 1953.

11. See Fackenheim's response to the rationalists in Emil L. Fackenheim, "Some Recent 'Rationalistic' Reactions to the New Jewish Theology," *CCAR Journal* 26 (June 1959), 42–48; see also Levi Olan, "New Presences" in the *CCAR Yearbook* (1963) and in Martin, *Contemporary Reform Jewish Thought*; see also Robert G. Goldy, *The Emergence of Jewish Theology in America* (Bloomington: Indiana University Press, 1990), chapter 4.

12. Hence postwar existential theology is already a stage in the development of post-Holocaust Jewish thought. Later I will show that the accepted view, that post-Holocaust Jewish theology is a post-1967 phenomenon, released as it were by the Six Day War, is too simplistic in a number of ways. First, the key figures had already begun, prior to the war, to articulate their strategies for confronting Auschwitz. Second, the influence of existentialism on Jewish theology in the 1950s and the debate over its propriety already involves a sensitivity to the Holocaust and to the rise of totalitarianism. What *is* true, no doubt, is that the Six Day War altered the role of the Holocaust in the self-understanding of American Jews—people on the street as well as intellectuals, students, and so forth. Hence, that war decisively affected the reception of post-Holocaust theology and its continuation and development; it did not, however, give rise to it.

13. "Theological Conference," *Commentary* 9,6 (June 1950), 567–572; compare *American Jewish Yearbook* 52 (1951), 93–94.

14. Ibid., 567.

15. Ibid., 567–568.

16. Ibid., 570.

17. Ibid., 572.

18. Ibid., 569.

19. There were essays by Olan in 1956, Borowitz in 1957, Petuchowski in 1959, Fackenheim in 1961, Olan in 1962, and Silberman in 1963.

20. *CCAR Journal* 29 (April 1960), 11–33.

21. *CCAR Journal* 8,2 (June 1960), 51–56; 8,4 (January 1961), 39–42.

22. *CCAR Journal* 10,1 (April 1962), 23–25.

23. *CCAR Journal*15,1, 1 (January, 1968), 14–18; the colloquium was held at the Hebrew Union College – Jewish Institute of Religion in New York, April 17–19, 1967.

24. *CCAR Journal*, 25,4 (October 1968), based on a preconvention kallah, June 15–17, 1968.

25. For a lively report of these papers, see Ben Hamon, "The Reform Rabbis Debate Theology," *Judaism* 12,4 (fall 1963), 479–486.

26. For a survey of one dimension of the phenomenon, see Bernard Martin, "Reform Jewish Theology Today," in *Contemporary Reform Jewish Thought*, especially 182–183.

27. Lou Silberman, "Concerning Jewish Theology in North America," *American Jewish Yearbook* 70 (1969), 37–58.

28. In his concluding essay in *Contemporary Reform Jewish Thought*, "Reform Jewish Theology Today," Bernard Martin confirms this account as well. Reviewing the essays collected in the volume as well as Jewish theology in general in the postwar years, Martin points to a variety of issues that form the subject matter of Jewish theology. They include God; the problem of evil and God's nature; human nature, optimism, and realism; halakhah and revelation; election, covenant, and mission; and the influence of Rosenzweig on the understanding of the nature and task of the Jewish people and the church.

29. Note how different is Seymour Siegel's review in "The Current Theological Situation," *Conservative Judaism* 23,4 (summer 1969), 11–24.

30. Silberman, "Concerning Jewish Theology," 40.

31. The recovery of Buber and Rosenzweig was a major feature of theological discussion in this period, but a careful study of them in their own historical context shows how restricted and focused this recovery was. I have begun to carry out this task in "Redemption and Community: Reflections on Some European Jewish Intellectuals, 1900–1940," in David N. Meyers and William V. Rowe (eds.), *From Ghetto to Emancipation* (Scranton, PA: University of Scranton Press, 1997), 37–61; Paul W. Franks and Michael L. Morgan (trans. and ed.), *Franz Rosenzweig: Philosophical and Theological Writings* (Cambridge, MA: Hackett Publishing, 2000); and Morgan, *Interim Judaism* (Bloomington, IN: Indiana University Press, 2001).

32. Silberman, "Concerning Jewish Theology," 44.

33. Ibid., 47; compare Fackenheim, "More on Reconstructionist Theology," *CCAR Journal* (January 1961), 39–43.

34. As I will show when I come to examine Berkovits's work more fully, his thinking is wedded to this firm distinction between nature and morality, fact and value. One of the shifts that takes place in the 1960s and 1970s, with the rise of hermeneutical thinking and the attack on foundationalisms and realisms, is the revised interpretation of such a distinction.

35. Silberman, "Concerning Jewish Theology," 56–57.

36. Ibid., 56, 57.

37. The earliest essay, "Self-Realization and the Search for God," in *Quest for Past and Future* (Bloomington: Indiana University Press, 1968), essentially a critique of naturalism and Kaplan's Reconstructionism, originated as part of a project in Jewish theology that Fackenheim planned and partially executed in the mid- to late 1940s. It was also anthologized, as many of the essays were, in a set of readings for the adult education program of the Reform Jewish community in Toronto.

38. Fackenheim, *Quest for Past and Future*, chapter 1, 3–17.

39. Ibid., 3; compare Fackenheim's response to Agus in his letter to the editor, *Conservative Judaism* 16,1 (fall 1961), 4.

40. Fackenheim, *Quest for Past and Future,* 5.

41. All the religious existentialists saw this in their own way. A later and especially interesting account, from within the larger tradition of Anglo-American philosophy, comes from Charles Taylor in *Sources of the Self* (Cambridge: Harvard University Press, 1989). See Michael Morgan, "Religion, History, and Morality," in *Philosophy in the Age of Pluralism*, edited by James Tully (Cambridge, UK: Cambridge University Press, 1994), 49–66.

42. See, for example, the laudatory comments of Marvin Fox in his reviews of *Rediscovering Judaism* and *Quest for Past and Future* in Marvin Fox, "Naturalism, Rationalism and Jewish Faith," *Tradition II,* 1 (Fall 1970), 90–96 (review article on Emil L. Fackenheim, *Quest for Past and Future*).

43. Fackenheim, *Quest for Past and Future,* 10; compare 7–8. The shift he describes occurs between chapters 2–6 and chapter 7 in *Quest for Past and Future*.

44. Ibid., 8.

45. It gives rise to a genuine and honest mutual encounter between religion and philosophy and makes Jewish philosophy possible.

46. Fackenheim, *Quest for Past and Future,* 9–10.

47. Ibid., 11. Fackenheim develops this entire theme in his book *Encounters between Judaism and Modern Philosophy* (New York: Basic Books, 1972).

48. *Encounters between Judaism and Modern Philosophy*, chapter 1; *Quest for Past and Future*, chapter 15; and *God's Presence in History* (New York: New York University Press, 1970), chapter 2.

49. *Quest for Past and Future*, 12; compare 10. For Fackenheim's career-long encounter with these themes and the conception of a genuine Jewish philosophy, see Michael Morgan (ed.), *Jewish Philosophers and Jewish Philosophy* (Bloomington: Indiana University Press, 1996).

50. *Quest for Past and Future*, 12.

51. Ibid., 12 n.11 and chapter 14; see especially 204–208; also chapter 16.

52. Ibid., 205.

53. Ibid., 207.

54. Compare Alasdair MacIntyre's response to Peter Winch in their famous debate, reprinted in *Rationality*, edited by Bryan R. Wilson (Oxford: Blackwell, 1979), chapters 1, 4, 5, 6.

55. For example, see the essays by Unger, Silberman, and Cohen in *Arguments and Doctrines,* edited by Arthur Cohen (New York: Harper and Row, 1970).

56. See Fackenheim's review of Nahum Glatzer, *Franz Rosenzweig: His Life and Thought,* reprinted in *The Jewish Thought of Emil Fackenheim*, and my essay, "Philosophy, History and the Jewish Thinker," in *Dilemmas in Modern Jewish Thought* (Bloomington: Indiana University Press, 1992).

57. *Quest for Past and Future*, chapter 14; also in *Rediscovering Judaism*, edited by Arnold Jacob Wolf (Chicago: Quadrangle Press, 1965); a shorter version of the article appeared as "Kant and Judaism," *Commentary* 34 (December 1963), 460–467.

58. Fox appreciates the essay; Samuelson misunderstands it totally; Ellenson less so but still fails to grasp its special strategy. Marvin Fox, "Naturalism, Rationalism and Jewish Faith," *Tradition II*, 1 (fall 1970), 90–96; Norbert Samuelson, "Revealed Morality and Modern Thought," in Menachem Marc Kellner (ed.), *Contemporary Jewish Ethics* (New York: Sanhedrin Press, 1970), 84–99 [reprinted from D. J. Silver (ed.), *Judaism and Ethics* (New York: Ktav Publishing, 1970)]; David Ellenson, "Emil Fackenheim and the Revealed Morality of Judaism," *Judaism* 25,4 (Fall 1976), 402–413.

59. *Quest for Past and Future*, 12.

60. Ibid., 13.

61. Rosenzweig's comment occurs in his letter to Martin Buber of June 5, 1925; see Franz Rosenzweig, *Gesammelte Schriften: Briefe und Tagebucher,* vol. 2 (Hague: Martinus Nijhoff, 1979), 1040, translated in Franz Rosenzweig, *On Jewish Learning*, edited by N. N. Glatzer (New York: Schocken Books, 1955), 117–118. See *Quest for Past and Future*, chapter 4, 80 (from "Can There Be Judaism without Revelation?" *Commentary* 12, 1951]); chapter 8, 145–146 (from "The Dilemma of Liberal Judaism," *Commentary* 30, 1960]); chapter 19, 307–308 (from "A Response to Five Questions," *Commentary* 42, 1966]).

62. *Quest for Past and Future*, 13.

63. Ibid., 15–16.

64. For discussion of similar themes by another theologian of the period, see Eugene Borowitz, *A New Jewish Theology in the Making* (Philadelphia: Westminster Press, 1968), chapter 8, especially 192–194.

65. *Quest for Past and Future*, 16–17; see also 318 nn.16–17, especially n. 17.

66. Ibid., 17.

67. That is, the seriousness of history and respect for Auschwitz demand this openness.

68. This volume was Borowitz's first important theological statement, but it was not his first book. Earlier he had published the important and valuable book *A Layman's Introduction to Religious Existentialism* (Philadelphia, PA: The Westminster Press, 1965), based on a series of lectures he had given at the 92nd Street YMHA in New York City.

69. Irving Kristol, "How Basic Is 'Basic Judaism?': A Comfortable Religion for an Uncomfortable World," *Commentary* V (January 1947), 27–34 [review article on Milton Steinberg, *Basic Judaism* (New York: Harcourt Brace, 1947)].

70. Borowitz, *A New Jewish Theology*, 56.

71. Ibid., 59.

72. Ibid., 59–60.

73. Ibid., 60.

74. Ibid., 62–63. Borowitz notes the debt to Buber and Rosenzweig, 63. Compare Siegel, "The Current Theological Situation," *Conservative Judaism* 18, 4 (summer 1969), 17–18.

75. *A New Jewish Theology,* 63.

76. Ibid., 64.

77. Ibid., 65.

78. Ibid., 66. Compare chapter 9, "Autonomy versus Tradition," especially 207–213.

79. Ibid., 66.

80. Ibid., 67.

81. For a simplistic discussion of Herberg, Heschel, Fackenheim, and Soloveitchik, see Goldy, *Emergence of Jewish Theology,* chapters 6 and 7. I discuss Cohen's book briefly in chapter 9.

82. For example, see Borowitz, *A New Jewish Theology*, 15–17, 56–59.

83. In these years, even the opponents of existentialist Jewish theology claim this connection. See Judd Teller, "A Critique of the New Jewish Theology," *Commentary* 25,3 (March 1958), 251.

Chapter 4

1. For an entertaining and full portrait of the decade, see David Halberstram, *The Fifties* (New York: Ballantine Books, 1993).

2. I am not going to proceed chronologically in any strict sense. In part it is not necessary since I am interested in the character of post-Holocaust Jewish thought in the period from the mid-sixties through the seventies as a whole. Also, these thinkers' work does not change so much as it grows during this decade. We get a better picture if we worry less, in general, about change than we do about the development of a fuller and fuller account. Finally, we learn more by juxtaposing these figures and by saving Fackenheim for last. After Rubenstein, his work emerges earliest, as we have seen, and it continues to this very day. It is best to save him until last, since his views are the richest philosophically and the most developed, systematic, and subtle.

3. Rubenstein, *After Auschwitz* (Indianapolis: The Bobbs-Merrill Co., 1966), 226. For autobiographical information, see *After Auschwitz*, chapter 12, and Rubenstein, *Power Struggle*; also the introduction to the second edition of *After Auschwitz* (Baltimore: Johns Hopkins University Press, 1992).

4. 227–229. This edition cited hereafter.

5. Ibid., 227.

6. Ibid., 229.

7. Ibid., 233–235. Compare 210–212 and the Bar Mitzvah episode in Rubenstein's life.

8. Ibid., 235; compare 241 and 222 in "The Making of a Rabbi."

9. *After Auschwitz*, 236, 237.

10. Ibid., 237–240.

11. Ibid., 238.

12. Ibid., 239.

13. Ibid., 238.

14. See *After Auschwitz*, 87; this is still not a clear formulation of the problem of freedom.

15. As I will show, this role for Auschwitz should be compared with the much larger role it plays in "The Making of a Rabbi," 216–217, and elsewhere.

16. See "Reconstructionism and the Problem of Evil" (1959) in *After Auschwitz*.

17. *After Auschwitz*, "The Making of a Rabbi" (1965), 216.

18. Ibid., 89: "Reconstructionism and the Problem of Evil," *Reconstructionist* (Jan. 23, 1959).

19. Ibid., 90.

20. Ibid., 48; in August 1963 he recalls this, his third visit. Rubenstein recalls all the visits in his article "Some Perspectives on Religious Faith after Auschwitz," in *The German Church Struggle and the Holocaust*, edited by Franklin H. Littell and Hubert G. Locke (Detroit: Wayne State University Press, 1974), 256–260; he discusses the interview with Dean Gruber on 260–261 and in *Power Struggle*, 10–15.

21. "A Rabbi Visits Germany," *Reconstructionist* 27,1 (February 24, 1961), 6–13.

22. Ibid., 11.

23. Ibid., 12.

24. Ibid., 13.

25. "Religion and the Origins of the Death Camps" (1960–1961), chapter 1 in *After Auschwitz*.

26. Ibid., 2.

27. Ibid., 34, 39.

28. "The Dean and the Chosen People," chapter 2 in *After Auschwitz*, 46–58.

29. Ibid., 46.

30. Ibid., 86–87.

31. Ibid., 238.
32. Ibid., 85.
33. Ibid., 52.
34. Ibid., 52–53.
35. Ibid., 54. This entire account, of course, is given as Rubenstein remembers it and as he records it in his memoir. Whether Gruber said exactly these words is not really at issue, since my concern is how Rubenstein's experience and his memory shaped his thinking.
36. Ibid., 54–55.
37. Ibid., 57.
38. Ibid., 58. Mordecai Kaplan, in *The Future of the American Jew* (New York: Macmillan, 1948), rejects the chosen people doctrine with a functional argument based on Auschwitz and Nazism. See his comments in the discussion after the Symposium on Jewish Unity, "Toward Jewish Religious Unity," *Judaism* 15,2 (spring 1966), 155.
39. "Person and Myth in the Judeo-Christian Encounter," in *After Auschwitz*, 65.
40. Ibid.
41. Ibid.
42. See especially *After Auschwitz*, 68–70; 123–129.
43. Ibid., 76; compare 117–119.
44. *Commentary* 42,2 (August 1966), 71–160; reprinted as *The Condition of Jewish Belief* (New York: Macmillan, 1966).
45. "The State of Jewish Belief," 71. Like others, Himmelfarb bemoans the lack of a Jewish theology, but what of Fackenheim's articles, Herberg, and Heschel? It is likely that what Himmelfarb means is a lack of an orthodox Jewish theological response.
46. Ibid., 78; compare Fox, 89–90, Lamm, 110, and Lichtenstein, 112–113.
47. Ibid., 87; compare Petuchowski, 121, Schaalman, 135.
48. Ibid., Rubenstein, 132, Kaplan, 109, Schulweis, 139–140.
49. Ibid., 134; for Rubenstein's best account, see 134–135; *After Auschwitz*, 153–154 (see my discussion later).
50. "The State of Jewish Belief," Wolf, 158; Frimer, 97; Siegel, 143–144.
51. *Daedalus* 96 (1967), 193–219; reprinted in *Quest for Past and Future* (Bloomington: Indiana University Press, 1968), chapter 18 (also in Donald R. Cutler (ed.), *The Religious Situation: 1968* (Boston: Beacon Press, 1968). Fackenheim himself alludes to the connection between his answer to question 5 of the Symposium and the *Daedalus* essay; see *Quest for Past and Future*, 315 n. 3.
52. "The State of Jewish Belief," 89.
53. Ibid., 89; see also *Quest for Past and Future*, 315.
54. "The State of Jewish Belief," 89; see also *Quest for Past and Future*, 315.
55. Reprinted in Martin Buber, *On Judaism*, edited by Nahum Glatzer (New York: Schocken, 1967), 214–225, especially 224–225.
56. Ibid., 224–225.
57. *Quest for Past and Future*, 281.
58. Ibid., 307.
59. Ibid., 303.
60. In 1966 Fackenheim attended a meeting on Jewish–Christian dialogue at Harvard, convened by Krister Stendahl; the proceedings are recorded in a volume edited by Kaufman et al. Fackenheim reported that he was sixteen when the Nazis came to power; if I were German, he said, I don't know that I wouldn't have been one of them. In these years, there is this element of luck or contingency in Fackenheim's thinking, about having survived as well as about having been a victim rather than an agent.

61. Actually, Fackenheim's first public presentation concerning Auschwitz and Jewish faith was at the I. Meier Segals Center for the Study and Advancement of Judaism in Quebec during the summer of 1966; that presentation, to colleagues and theologians, became the foundation for the comments at the *Judaism* symposium, the introduction to *Quest for Past and Future*, and ultimately for the Deems lectures, *God's Presence in History* (New York: New York University Press, 1970). Fackenheim also gave a talk on hope at a conference entitled "Theology of Hope" held at Santa Cruz in 1968. The proceedings were later published as *The Future of Hope*, edited by Walter H. Capps (Philadelphia: Fortress Press, 1970); Fackenheim's piece is entitled "The Commandment to Hope: A Response to Contemporary Jewish Experience," 68–91.

62. The proceedings were published as "Towards Jewish Religious Unity," *Judaism* 15,2 (spring 1966), 131–163.

63. Ibid., 134. Compare 135: "this unity already exists. It is the unavoidable implication of the impact of the Holocaust." Compare too Jacob Taubes's reference to Auschwitz as "the crucial caesura" (155). In discussion Greenberg remarks: "I personally feel that after Auschwitz we should be embarrassed to use the words 'Orthodox,' 'Conservative,' or 'Reform'" (156).

64. Ibid., 156.

65. Note Michael Wyschogrod's response to this and his counterexample, the Nazi actions on the Sabbath (158). To abandon election or chosenness for this reason is inconceivable, he says, to him. Note also Greenberg's response: if we give it up, Hitler has won (161–162).

66. Ibid., 157.

67. Hershell Matt mentions this, ibid., 157–158.

68. Ibid., 157. Greenberg refers to the Segal Conference on 163; see Fackenheim's reference to this passage in *Quest for Past and Future*, 335 n. 48.

69. Published in *Judaism* 16,3 (summer 1967), 266–299.

70. George Steiner, *Language and Silence* (Forge Village, Mass.: Murray, 1967; New York: Atheneum, 1970).

71. As I mentioned in note 61, the first "public" event was the Segals Institute conference in the summer of 1966, but the group was relatively small and the event not as prominent as the symposium of 1967; nor were the proceedings ever published, as the symposium was in *Judaism* (summer, 1967).

72. "Jewish Values," 281; compare 298.

73. Ibid., 281.

74. Ibid., 284.

75. On the issue of the poverty of language, see Alvin Rosenfeld, *A Double Dying* (Bloomington: Indiana University Press, 1980); also, later, Berel Lang, *Act and Idea in the Nazi Genocide* (Chicago: University of Chicago Press, 1990).

76. *To Mend the World*, preface to 2nd ed. New York: Schocken, 1989 xvi–xx; *The Jewish Return into History* (New York: Schocken Books, 1978), introduction, xi; see also Michael Morgan (ed.), *The Jewish Thought of Emil Fackenheim* (Detroit: Wayne State University Press, 1987), 113.

77. "Jewish Values," 271.

78. Ibid., 272.

79. Ibid., 273.

80. For discussion of this reasoning, see Morgan, *The Jewish Thought of Emil Fackenheim*, 114–115, and "Jewish Ethics after the Holocaust," in *Dilemmas in Modern Jewish Thought* (Bloomington: Indiana University Press, 1992).

81. *Quest for Past and Future*, 231; *Encounters between Judaism and Modern Philosophy* (New York: Basic Books, 1973), chapter 1. See also "On the Eclipse of God," *Commentary* 37 (June 1964) and "Elijah and the Empiricists," in *The Religious Situation,* edited by Donald Cutler (1969).

82. *Quest for Past and Future*, 14–17.

83. *Metaphysics and Historicity* (Milwaukee: Marquette University Press, 1961); *The Religious Dimension of Hegel's Thought* (Bloomington: Indiana University Press, 1968).

84. See *Quest for Past and Future*, 17.

85. Ibid., 15–16; see also *Encounters between Judaism and Modern Philosophy*, chapter 3, and *The Religious Dimension in Hegel's Thought*.

86. *Quest for Past and Future*, 16.

87. Ibid., 17.

88. The hermeneutical context for the shift in American intellectual culture was the work of Gadamer, Kuhn, Taylor, Rorty, Putnam, Davidson, MacIntyre, and others. These remarks are intended as just a beginning, an initial display of this shift in Fackenheim's thinking that will turn out, I think, to be of tremendous importance for understanding the deepest themes of post-Holocaust Jewish thought. As Fackenheim puts it in *To Mend the World* (13), "what is the outcome once this admission is made?" This is the problem he has set for himself: how to accept this historicism and yet to locate a ground for the future, to find some direction that does not succumb to Auschwitz and therefore to discover how to go on.

89. As he prepared for the trip from Toronto to New York, Fackenheim was so nervous and anxious that he accidentally left his wife Rose's suitcase at home.

90. *To Mend the World*, xvii.

91. Ibid., xix.

92. It is important to contrast this notion of revelation as immediacy with the notion of revelation as essentially mediated, say by language. The contrast is between Kierkegaard and Hegel, or between Buber and Rosenzweig and Benjamin and Scholem. For some preliminary discussion, see David Biale, *Gershom Scholem: Kabbalah and Counter-history* (Cambridge: Harvard University Press, 1979). I have discussed this issue in chapter 2 of *Interim Judaism* (Bloomington: Indiana University Press, 2001).

93. See Franz Rosenzweig, *On Jewish Learning*, edited by N. N. Glatzer (New York: Schocken Books, 1955), 85.

94. I will return to this matter later.

95. This is elaborated in *God's Presence in History*, chapter 3.

96. "Jewish Values," 272.

Chapter 5

1. See Glazer, *American Judaism*, 2nd ed. (University of Chicago Press, 1989), 169–186; Chaim Waxman, *America's Jews in Transition* (Philadelphia: Temple University Press, 1983), chapter 5; Daniel Elazar, "The Rediscovered Polity: Selections from the Literature of Jewish Public Affairs," *American Jewish Yearbook* 70 (1969), 172–224; Lucy Dawidowicz, "American Public Opinion," *American Jewish Yearbook* 69 (1968), 198–229; Marshall Sklare, "Lakeville and Israel: The Six-Day War and Its Aftermath," *Midstream* 14,8 (October 1968), 3–21 (reprinted in *American Jews: A Reader*, edited by Marshall Sklare [New York: [Behrman House, 1983], 413–439); Daniel Elazar, *Community and Polity* (Philadelphia: Jewish Publication Society, 1976); Charles Silberman, *A Certain People* (New York: Summit Books, 1985), 181–185, 197–202, 205–207. This is not to say that

the impact of the war and the centrality of Israel and the Holocaust went uncriticized. For a severe indictment, see Jacob Neusner, *Stranger at Home* (Chicago: University of Chicago Press, 1981), which collects earlier material; I discuss Neusner briefly in chapter eleven.

2. Waxman, *America's Jews,* 112–113.

3. Lucy S. Dawidowicz, "American Public Opinion," in *American Jewish Yearbook* 69 (1968), quoted in Glazer, *American Judaism,* 170–171: from Hertzberg, "Israel and American Jewry," *Commentary* 44,2 (August 1967), 69–73.

4. Sklare, "Lakeville," 418.

5. Compare Silberman, *A Certain People,* 183; see the vivid account in Dawidowicz, "American Public Opinion," 204–206. I recall this from my own experience, living in New York at the time.

6. Sklare, "Lakeville," 421; Silberman, *A Certain People,* 185; Dawidowicz, "American Public Opinion," 206.

7. Silberman, *A Certain People,* 185.

8. Glazer, *American Judaism,* 178; Silberman, *A Certain People,* 185–199.

9. Dawidowicz, "American Public Opinion," 206; compare 206–209.

10. Ibid., 205.

11. Ibid., 204.

12. Glazer, *American Judaism,* 178–179.

13. Silberman, *A Certain People,* 199.

14. This was the point of Wiesel's hint, in *The Jews of Silence* (New York: Holt, Rinehart and Winston, 1966), that it was American Jews and not the Jews of the Soviet Union who were the real Jews of silence.

15. Wiesel, *The Jews of Silence,* 127; compare Glazer, *American Judaism,* 175–176.

16. See Silberman, *A Certain People,* 185. Movies like *Gentleman's Agreement* (1947) and *Crossfire* (1947) indicate the postwar public censorship of anti-Semitism.

17. Dawidowicz, "American Public Opinion," 211–218; Silberman, *A Certain People,* 204–207; Waxman, *America's Jews,* 114–116, 130–134; Glazer, *American Judaism,* 173–177.

18. Silberman, *A Certain People,* 201.

19. Ibid., 205.

20. William Novak, "The Making of a Jewish Counter Culture," *Response* 4, 1–2 (spring–summer 1970), 8. Novak in fact was from Canada. He has become a noted coauthor of famous autobiographies—of Lee Iacocca and other famous figures.

21. Some of these themes are expressed in Emil Fackenheim's essay, "From Bergen-Belsen to Jerusalem," originally delivered in Jerusalem at the President's Study Circle on Diaspora Jewry, in July 1970, as a lecture and then reprinted in *The Jewish Return into History* (Schocken Books, 1979). Fackenheim speaks about the way the Six Day War called forth a new sense of allegiance to Israel and strengthened the memory of Auschwitz, 130, 141. He also notes that the sense of self-liberation and Jewish liberation was akin to that felt by blacks, 141–143.

22. Glazer, *American Judaism,* 173–174.

23. Especially after the *SNCC Newsletter* article of 1967 defending the Palestinian Liberation cause; see Clayborne Carson, *In Struggle: SNCC and the Black Awakening of the 1960s* (Cambridge: Harvard University Press, 1981), 267–268, on the condemnation of Israel at the National Conference of the New Politics in Chicago, September 1967.

24. Glazer, *American Judaism,* 176–177.

25. There were other expressions of such discontent. In 1968 there was a confronta-

tion at the national meeting of the Federation of Jewish Philanthropies in Boston. For written expressions of the discontent of the young Jewish radicals, see the two anthologies *The New Jews*, edited by James A. Sleeper and Alan L. Mintz (New York: Vintage Books, 1971), and *Jewish Radicalism*, edited by Jack Nusan Porter and Peter Dreier (New York: Grove Press, 1973).

26. Novak, "The Making of a Jewish Counter Culture," 15, 18.

27. See Riv-Ellen Prell, *Prayer and Community* (Detroit: Wayne State University Press, 1989), chapter 3, especially 85–87.

28. Porter and Dreier, *Jewish Radicalism,* quoted by Prell, *Prayer and Community,* 76.

29. Prell, *Prayer and Community,* 70, 79, 84. See also Wini Breines, *Community and Organization in the New Left, 1962–1968* (New Brunswick: Rutgers University Press, 1989; orig. 1982).

30. Prell, *Prayer and Community,* 80, quoting Hillel Levine.

31. Prell, *Prayer and Community,* 90; compare Cowan, 214–215, quoted by Prell.

32. See Stephen Lerner, "The Havurot," *Conservative Judaism* 24,3 (spring 1970), 2–15; compare Prell, *Prayer and Community,* 92–101; Bill Novak, "The Havurah in New York City," *Response* 4,3 (fall 1970), 11–28.

33. Prell, *Prayer and Community,* 108; compare 101–109.

34. E.g., Norman Podhoretz. See Glazer, "Jewish Interests and the New Left," *Midstream* 17,1 (January 1971), 32–37.

35. Waxman, *America's Jews,* 115; see n. 23 above.

36. Glazer, *American Judaism,* 180–184; compare Steven M. Cohen, *American Modernity & Jewish Identity* (New York: Tavistock, 1985), 151; Waxman, *America's Jews,* 117; Leonard Fein, "Liberalism and American Jews," *Midstream* 19, 8 (October 1973), 12–18; Nathan Glazer, "Blacks, Jews, and Intellectuals," *Commentary* 47,4 (April 1969), 33–39; Earl Raab, "The Black Revolution and the Jewish Question," *Commentary* 47,1 (January 1969), 23–33; Ben Halpern, "The Jewish Liberal," *Midstream* 16,10 (December 1970), 32–49; Ben Halpern, "The Ethnic Revolt," *Midstream* 17,1 (January 1971), 3–16. See also Jonathan Kaufman, *Broken Alliance* (New York: Simon and Schuster, 1988; 1995).

37. Nathan Glazer, "The Crisis of American Jewry," *Midstream* 16,9 (November 1970), 3–11. For a theoretical account of such a blend, albeit in a general context not specifically tied to Judaism, see Charles Taylor, "The Politics of Recognition," in *Philosophical Arguments* (Cambridge, MA: Harvard University Press, 1995), originally in *Multiculturalism and the "Politics of Recognition"* (Princeton: Princeton University Press, 1992).

38. (Cambridge: Harvard University Press, 1985), 2; compare 96 on the importance of the shift among blacks.

39. Ibid., 3; compare 107–119 on affirmative action.

40. Ibid., 26.

41. Ibid., 26; compare 67–90, especially 79.

42. The general indifference of American Jews to Israel in this period was not absolute, of course. There were trips to Israel for youth, sponsored by United Synagogue Youth, for example, and there was interest among youth, in Young Judea for instance. But compared to the enormous involvement of the past decades, the neglect was significant.

43. *Reconstructionist* 26,6 (April 29, 1960), 6–13; *After Auschwitz* (Indianapolis: Bobbs-Merrill, 1966), chapter 7.

44. Will Herberg's article "Socialism, Zionism, and the Messianic Passion," *Midstream* 2,3 (summer 1956), 65–74, is not really about Israel.

45. *CCAR Journal* 14,3 (October 1961), 3–11.

46. See Jacques Kornberg, "Zionism and Ideology: The Breira Controversy," *Judaism* 27,1 (winter 1978), 103–114, and references therein to the work of Joseph Shatton in *Commentary* (1977) and elsewhere. See also Thomas Friedman, for example, *From Beirut to Jerusalem* (Farrar, Straus and Giroux, 1989).

47. Harold Schulweis, "The New Jewish Right," *Moment* 1,1 (May/June 1975), 55–61.

48. Ibid., 56. Schulweis attacks the tendency of the Holocaust to dominate Jewish consciousness, education, and so on, in "The Holocaust Dybbuk," *Moment* 1,7 (February 1976), 36–41; for Cynthia Ozick's criticism and Schulweis's response, see "Debate: Ozick vs. Schulweis," *Moment* 1,10 (May/June 1976), 77–80. This is just one episode in the two-decade-old debate over the centrality of the Holocaust to American Jewish identity and indeed to Jewish identity in general. For criticism of the general tendency to feature apocalyptic events in our historical memory, see Michael André Bernstein, *Foregone Conclusions* (Berkeley: University of California Press, 1994).

49. Glazer, *American Judaism*, 171.

50. Waxman agrees. He remarks that "there was an acute fear of another Holocaust" (*America's Jews*, 113). Also "the threat to Israel aroused the fear of another Holocaust in American Jewry and awakened a strong desire for survival within that community" (114). Compare 121–123.

51. Rieder, *Canarsie*, 47, 206; compare Jean Améry, *At the Mind's Limits* (Bloomington: Indiana University Press, 1980).

52. Lucy Dawidowicz, "American Public Opinion," 1968, 203–204.

53. Waxman, *America's Jews*, 122–123.

54. "The Response Symposium," *Response* 4,4 (winter 1970–71), 17–123.

55. Ibid., Fackenheim, 31–32.

56. Ibid., Green, 41–43; compare Alan Mintz, 103–104.

57. Ibid., Waskow, 119–123.

58. See Sleeper and Mintz, *The New Jews*, and Porter and Dreier, *Jewish Radicalism*. For a powerful statement for the centrality of the Holocaust and Israel by a young radical Jew, see Michael J. Rosenberg, "Israel without Apology," in Sleeper and Mintz, *The New Jews*, 79–88.

59. Of special interest are James Young, *Writing and Rewriting the Holocaust* (Bloomington: Indiana University Press, 1988), and, on the construction of the Holocaust Museum in Washington, Edward T. Linenthal, *Preserving Memory* (New York: Viking Press, 1995); see also Peter Novick, *The Holocaust in American Life* (New York: Houghton Mifflin, 1999); Hilene Flanzbaum (ed.), *The Americanization of the Holocaust* (Baltimore: Johns Hopkins University Press, 1999).

Chapter 6

1. His early writings reveal an indebtedness not only to Tillich and Kaplan but also to Mircea Eliade, Freud, and a host of others. His essays are eclectic and synthetic; their originality lies in the application of motifs from others to Jewish contexts and especially to the death camps. For Rubenstein's own review of post-Holocaust Jewish thought and especially his earlier work, see "The Silence of God: Philosophical and Religious Reflection on the Holocaust," in *Approaches to Auschwitz*, edited by Richard L. Rubenstein and John K. Roth (Atlanta: John Knox Press, 1987), reprinted as chapters 8 and 9 in Rubenstein, *After Auschwitz*, 2nd ed. (Johns Hopkins University Press, 1992).

2. Rubenstein, *After Auschwitz*, 1st ed. Indianapolis: Bobbs-Merrill, 1966, 216; see Ira Eisenstein, *The Varieties of Jewish Belief* (New York: Reconstructionist Press, 1966).

3. Ibid., 219.

4. Ibid., 221–222.

5. Ibid., 222–223.

6. Ibid., 223; see also 153.

7. Ibid., 223.

8. Ibid., 223: he refers to Tillich's phrase: the age of "broken symbols."

9. Ibid., 223.

10. Ibid., 224–225.

11. Rubenstein, *Power Stuggle* (New York: Scribner's, 1974).

12. *Power Struggle*, 2–3.

13. *After Auschwitz*, chapter 14, "Death of God Theology and Judaism."

14. *Power Struggle*, 8–9.

15. *After Auschwitz*, 245; see 243–247, 151–152. The affinity is with Nietzsche, Dostoyevsky, and existentialism and not with Heidegger and the conception of the "end of history."

16. Ibid., 250.

17. Ibid., 258–259; see "Some Perspectives," 262.

18. *After Auschwitz*, 260.

19. Ibid., 263; see also 152–153; *Morality and Eros* (New York: McGraw-Hill, 1970); also Peter Berger, *The Sacred Canopy* (Garden City, NJ: Doubleday Books, 1967), and Peter Berger and Thomas Luckmann, *The Social Construction of Reality* (Garden City, NJ: Doubleday Books, 1966).

20. *After Auschwitz*, 152; see "Some Perspectives," 260–262.

21. *After Auschwitz*, 153.

22. Ibid., "Some Perspectives," 262.

23. Ibid., 154; see also *Power Struggle*, 3.

24. See *Morality and Eros*, chapter 11 (reprinted in the second edition of *After Auschwitz*).

25. In the later essay in Rubenstein and Roth, *Approaches to Auschwitz*, Rubenstein acknowledges that one change in his thought had been the rejection of this early pessimism and despair in favor of optimism and joy.

26. There is a pragmatic element in much recent philosophy as well; compare Rorty and various interpretations of Heidegger.

27. "Jews, Negroes and the New Politics," *Reconstructionist* 33,14 (November 17, 1967), 7–16; "The Politics of Powerlessness," *Reconstructionist* 34,7 (May 17, 1968), 7–16. I remember hearing some of this material at a Hillel retreat in upstate New York in the spring of 1965.

28. See the articles in the two anthologies, *The New Jews*, edited by James A. Sleeper and Alan L. Mintz (New York: Vintage Books), and *Jewish Radicalism*, edited by Jack Nusan Porter and Peter Dreier (New York: Grove Press, 1973); see also Jonathan Rieder, *Canarsie* (Cambridge: Harvard University Press, 1985).

29. "Jews, Negroes and the New Politics," 9. See also Clayborne Carson, *In Struggle: SNCC and the Black Awakening of the 1960s* (Cambridge: Harvard University Press, 1981); Howard Zinn, *SNCC: The New Abolitionists* (Boston: Beacon Press, 1964).

30. "Jews, Negroes, and the New Politics," 10–11.

31. Ibid., 11.

32. Ibid., 14.

33. Ibid., 15.

34. "The Politics of Powerlessness," 7–13.

35. Ibid., 14.

36. Ibid., 15.

37. See Steinfels, *The Neoconservatives* (New York: Simon and Schuster, 1979); Jonathan Schell, *The Time of Illusion* (New York: Vintage Books, 1975); Irving Kristol, *Reflections of a Neoconservative* (New York: Basic Books, 1983).

38. See *Morality and Eros*, published in 1970.

39. "God after the Death of God" (reprinted in the second edition of *After Auschwitz*); also, "Symposium on Jewish Belief," *After Auschwitz*, 1st ed., chapter 8.

40. Originally "The Significance of Zionism," *Reconstructionist* 26,6 (April 29, 1960), 6–13.

41. *After Auschwitz*, 132–133.

42. Ibid., 134.

43. Ibid., 136.

44. Ibid., 139–142. In addition to Tillich, Mircea Eliade is a primary source for Rubenstein's conceptualization of religions and of God in this early period.

45. *After Auschwitz*, 154, 218–225; also *Morality and Eros*, chapter 11. See also "Some Perspectives on Religious Faith after Auschwitz," in *The German Church Struggle and the Holocaust*, edited by Franklin H. Littell and Hubert G. Locke (Detroit: Wayne State University Press, 1974), 256–268, especially on paganism, 267.

46. "Homeland and Holocaust," in *The Religious Situation: 1968*, edited by Donald R. Cutler (Boston: Beacon Press, 1968), 39–64 (with responses by Milton Himmelfarb, Zalman Schachter, Arthur Cohen, Irving Greenberg; response to them by Rubenstein).

47. "Homeland and Holocaust," 41.

48. Ibid., 42.

49. Ibid., 43.

50. Ibid., 44.

51. Ibid., 44–50.

52. Ibid., 53–54. See also, for an attack on Jewish theologians, 54–61.

53. Ibid., 61.

54. Ibid.

55. See "Some Perspectives," 263: the Six Day War is no royal road back to the God of history.

56. Rubenstein is indebted to Camus: "courage to live in a meaningless, purposeless cosmos," ibid., 262.

57. "Some Perspectives" (1974); "Jewish Theology and the Current World Situation," *Conservative Judaism* 28,4 (summer 1974), 3–25, with comments by Arthur Green and Elliott Dorff; *The Cunning of History* (New York: Harper and Row, 1975). For further discussion of his bibliography, see the second edition of *After Auschwitz*.

58. "Homeland and Holocaust," 39–40; see also *Morality and Eros*, chapter 11.

59. "Naming the Unnameable; Thinking the Unthinkable," *Journal of Reform Judaism* 31 (spring 1984), 43–55, especially 51–54.

60. See chapter 1 in *After Auschwitz*, "Religion and the Origins of the Death Camps."

61. "Some Perspectives," 264–267.

62. See my discussion in chapter 4.

63. "Some Perspectives," 264; see also "Jewish Theology." Notice how Rubenstein extends Arendt's use of the expression "superfluous."

64. See Eberhard Jäckel, *Hitler's Worldview: A Blueprint for Power* (Cambridge: Harvard University Press, 1981); Uriel Tal, "On Structures of Political Theology and Myth in Germany Prior to the Holocaust," in *The Holocaust as Historical Experience*, edited by

Yehuda Bauer and Nathan Rotenstreich (New York: Holmes and Meier, 1981), 43–74; and Saul Friedlander, *Nazi Germany and the Jews*, vol. 1, *The Years of Persecution, 1933–1939* (New York: HarperCollins, 1997). It may be that Rubenstein does not completely ignore the ideological dimension of the Final Solution. One might ask why the Jews and others were considered superfluous and why their existence constituted the problem of overpopulation, and the answer may have to do with anti-Semitism and the hatred of Jews, at least in part. But even if Rubenstein would defer to the ideological dimension in this way, clearly it plays a minor role for him.

65. "Some Perspectives," 264.

66. Ibid., 264–266; this point is credited to Hannah Arendt in *The Origins of Totalitarianism*.

67. "Some Perspectives," 266. Notice the connections between this point and the themes of the two articles "The Politics of Powerlessness" and "Homeland and Holocaust."

68. Recall the Delphic oracle's motto: "Nothing too much."

69. "Some Perspectives," 267.

70. *The Cunning of History* 30–31, 104 n. 24. See Emil L. Fackenheim, *Encounters between Judaism and Modern Philosophy* (New York: Basic Books, 1973), 157, 192–195. Rubenstein clearly owes a debt to Weber here.

71. "Jewish Theology," 4.

72. Ibid., 4.

73. Ibid., 4–14; notice too the debt expressed to the work of Jacob Neusner.

74. Ibid., 16.

75. Ibid., 17.

76. Ibid., 18.

77. Ibid., 19–20.

78. Ibid., 21–25.

79. Ibid., 23.

80. The same themes are further developed in *The Age of Triage: Fear and Hope in an Overcrowded World* (Boston: Beacon Press, 1983).

81. *The Cunning of History*, 2.

82. Ibid., 6–7.

83. Ibid., 21.

84. In the final pages, Rubenstein outlines the political philosophy—his conservatism—that underlies the essay. It is, he says, the result of a political conservative's reassessment of politics and society after Watergate and the Nixon presidency; see 95–97. The major problems in society, he believes, arise from increasing numbers of superfluous people.

85. By looking at some responses to *After Auschwitz* and Rubenstein's later articles, we can learn something about his thought, how others understood it, and the issues that have seemed most central. I want to examine first some early reviews of Rubenstein's work and then two sets of responses to later essays. In the first group are: Arnold Jacob Wolf, "Jewish Theology after the Death Camps," *Judaism* 16 (spring 1966), 233–236; Alan W. Miller, "How Radical Is Radical Theology?" *Reconstructionist* (June 9, 1967), 25–31; Marvin Fox, "Jewish Paganism," *Commentary* 47,6 (June 1969), 92–102. In the second group are the responses to "Homeland and Holocaust" and those to "Jewish Theology and the Current World Situation." There is also an interesting exchange between Rubenstein and Arthur Cohen that is best left until after I discuss Cohen's work. See "Naming the Unnameable; Thinking the Unthinkable," *Journal of Reform Judaism* 32,2 (spring 1984).

86. See Jacob Neusner, *American Judaism* (Englewood Cliffs, N.J.: Prentice-Hall, 1972), 130–132.

87. See "Reconstructionism and the Problem of Evil," *Reconstructionist* (January 23, 1959); reprinted as chapter 4 of *After Auschwitz*.

88. See Fox, "Jewish Paganism," 94.

89. Miller, "How Radical Is Radical Theology?" 27–30. Arthur Green accepts the account but also thinks that the pessimism is too extreme, in his comments on "Jewish Theology," "A Response to Richard Rubenstein," *Conservative Judaism* 28,4 (summer 1974), 26–28; see also Elliott Dorff, "A Response to Richard Rubenstein," *Conservative Judaism* 28,4 (summer 1974), 34–35.

90. Miller, "How Radical Is Radical Theology?" 28–29.

91. "Jewish Theology," 7.

92. Ibid., 8.

93. Ibid., 18.

94. Miller, "How Radical Is Radical Theology?" 29.

95. Green, "A Response," 26–32.

96. Fox, "Jewish Paganism," 94.

97. Ibid., 101–102.

98. Ibid., 102.

99. "Homeland and Holocaust," 64–79.

100. Ibid., 65.

101. Ibid., 66–67.

102. Ibid., 72–75, 77.

Chapter 7

1. Berkovits was a student and disciple of the great twentieth-century Halakhist Rabbi Jehiel Jacob Weinberg; see Marc B. Shapiro, *Between the Yeshiva World and Modern Orthodoxy: The Life and Works of Jehiel Jacob Weinberg 1884–1966* (Portland, OR: Littman Library of Jewish Civilization, 1999); Eliezer Berkovits, "Rabbi Yechiel Yakob Weinberg, My Teacher and Master," *Tradition* 8,2 (summer 1966), 5–14.

2. Eliezer Berkovits, *Faith after the Holocaust* (New York: Ktav, 1973), 1.

3. Eliezer Berkovits, *With God in Hell* (New York: Sanhedrin Press, 1979).

4. *Faith after the Holocaust*, 7; also 36.

5. Ibid., 7.

6. Ibid., 36.

7. Guenter Lewy, *The Catholic Church and Nazi Germany* (New York: McGraw-Hill, 1964); Arthur Morse, *While Six Million Died* (New York: Random House, 1967).

8. *Faith after the Holocaust*, 11–12. Claims like this, that identify the moral culpability of killing and letting die, are made of course without any argument or analysis. This particular distinction has been subject to extensive analysis especially within the context of the discussion of euthanasia.

9. Ibid., 13.

10. Ibid., 15–16.

11. Ibid., 16–17.

12. Ibid., 18; see also 18–26, 41–42.

13. Ibid., 27–36.

14. See especially ibid., 35, 36.

15. Ibid., 29–31.

16. Ibid., 36.

17. They also differ on their evaluation of Christian God-is-dead or radical theology; see 50–58.

18. Ibid., 52, 55, 64.

19. Ibid., 55–58.

20. Ibid., 85; see 67–85.

21. Ibid., 3–6. A version of this section was published as "Apprehending the Holocaust," *Judaism* 22,1 (winter 1973), 8–20. See also 67–70.

22. The experience of the victims will also play a central role for Greenberg and especially for Fackenheim, in his book *To Mend the World*. But that role is different for Berkovits from what it is, at least, for Fackenheim, as I will show.

23. *Faith after the Holocaust,* 4, 67.

24. Ibid., 4–5; see 69, where Berkovits calls these two responses authentic faith and authentic rebellion.

25. Ibid., 5, 69, where he calls it "believing rebellion and rebellious belief."

26. Ibid., 5, 70–76; see also 50–66, and especially 67: "For there is also an inauthentic quest. . . . [T]hey reject any faith in God or conceive God as an impersonal cosmic process that is by definition indifferent toward individual human existence." For Berkovits, this is too extreme; such a quest, to him, is a pretense.

27. Ibid., 68.

28. Ibid., 68.

29. Ibid., 69.

30. Ibid., 85.

31. Ibid., 87.

32. Ibid., 89.

33. Notice that both Rubenstein and Berkovits deal with Auschwitz in terms of the traditional problem of evil. But their responses are radically different, and they show precisely how divergent are their attitudes toward religious thought and history. For Rubenstein, Auschwitz so discredits the discourse of divine providence that we are led to dispose of the very notion of a God of history; for Berkovits, Auschwitz is like any example of innocent suffering and atrocity. It fits the understanding of God and history that is entrenched in the free will defense, as he understands it. To one, the emphasis is on discontinuity, to the other continuity. To one, the challenge is to find access to recovery; to the other, it is to find a way of acknowledging the decisive impact of the event.

34. Ibid., 90, 98: "each generation has its Auschwitz problem."

35. Ibid., 128, 130. See Berkovits, *God, Man, and History* (New York: Jonathan David, 1959).

36. *Faith after the Holocaust*, 91; specifically, for Berkovits, the Bible and rabbinic literature.

37. Ibid., 91–107.

38. Ibid., 99–107. E.g., Psalms 44, 13:2; Isaiah 45:15.

39. *Faith after the Holocaust*, 101.

40. Ibid., especially 105. The literature on the free will defense is extensive; see, for example, Nelson Pike (ed.), *God and Evil* (Englewood Cliffs, NJ: Prentice-Hall, 1964); John Hick, *Evil and the God of Love* (New York: Harper and Row, 1978); Alvin Plantinga, *God, Freedom, and Evil* (New York: Harper and Row, 1974); Marilyn McCord Adams and Robert Merihew Adams (eds.), *The Problem of Evil* (Oxford: Oxford University Press, 1991); Richard Swinburne, *Providence and the Problem of Evil* (Oxford: Oxford University Press, 1998).

41. *Faith after the Holocaust*, 107.

42. Ibid., 109–113; 114–116.

43. Ibid., 111–113; 122–123.

44. Ibid., 111; see also 119.

45. See, for example, the work of Charles Taylor. One mode of attack on the distinction is to argue that all descriptive claims are permeated with perspective, interest, and value. There are those who accept the distinction but deny that morality must be grounded in the divine. For discussion of the ground of obligation in early modern philosophy and its relation to divine voluntarism, see Stephen Darwall, *The British Moralist and the Internal "Ought"* (Cambridge, UK: Cambridge University Press, 1995).

46. *Faith after the Holocaust*, 131; 128.

47. Ibid., 132–133; 137–143.

48. Ibid., 134, 143; see also *With God in Hell*, 133–137.

49. *Faith after the Holocaust*, 134.

50. Ibid., 134.

51. There are obvious Kantian overtones here, as elsewhere, in Berkovits's thinking. For Kant's political theory, see Hans Saner, *Kant's Political Philosophy* (Chicago: University of Chicago Press, 1973); Hans Reiss (ed.), *Kant's Political Writings* (Cambridge, UK: Cambridge University Press, 1977).

52. *Faith after the Holocaust*, 143, 145–153, 157.

53. Ibid., 134; see also 66.

54. Ibid., 114.

55. Ibid., 115.

56. Ibid., 144–145.

57. Ibid., 145.

58. Ibid., 153.

59. Ibid., 154.

60. Ibid., 154.

61. Ibid., 155.

62. Ibid., 156.

63. Ibid., 156.

64. Ibid., 157.

65. See ibid., 158.

66. Ibid., 158.

67. Ibid., 165.

68. This is another occasion where Berkovits's Kantianism reveals itself and with it his deep rootedness in Stoic principles—about morality, virtue, intention, nature, and so forth.

69. See ibid. 158–169.

70. Ibid., 168–169.

71. *With God in Hell* (New York: Sanhedrin Press, 1979).

72. See especially ibid., 120–125.

73. Ibid., 54, 63, 79.

74. Ibid., 156–157.

75. See Marvin Fox, "Berkovits' Treatment of the Problem of Evil," *Tradition* 14,3 (spring 1974), 116–124, especially 122. Fox gives a nice exposition but only of Berkovits's solution to the problem of evil. He indicates no sense of the overall context of Berkovits's work. His criticisms are weak, and he does not adequately appreciate the role of his account of miracles.

Chapter 8

1. See Irving Greenberg, "Adventure in Freedom—Or Escape from Freedom? Jewish Identity in America," *American Jewish Historical Quarterly* 55,1 (September 1965), 5–21; "The Cultural Revolution and Religious Unity," *Religious Education* 62,2 (March–April 1967), 98–103; "Jewish Values and the Changing American Ethic," *Tradition* 10,1 (summer 1968), 42–74; "Change and the Orthodox Community," *Response* 7,1 (spring 1969), 14–21.

2. The essay appeared in *Auschwitz,* edited by Eva Fleishner (New York: Ktav, 1977), 7–55. A shorter version appeared as "Judaism and Christianity after the Holocaust," *Journal of Ecumenical Studies* 12,4 (fall 1975), 521–551. Other essays of importance are: "The Interaction of Israel and the Diaspora after the Holocaust," in *World Jewry and the State of Israel*, edited by Moshe Davis (New York: Arno Press, 1977), 259–282; "The End of Emancipation," *Conservative Judaism* 30,4 (summer 1976), 47–63; "Voluntary Covenant," in *Perspectives* (National Jewish Resource Center; 1982), 1–36.

3. See especially "Change and the Orthodox Community" and "Jewish Values and the Changing American Ethic."

4. As I indicated in chapter 3, the attempt to find a theoretical account of the reconciliation of authority and autonomy, of law and freedom, is one of the central theological problems of the postwar years for the young Jewish theologians.

5. "Adventure in Freedom," 5–12; "Jewish Values," 42– 50.

6. "Adventure in Freedom," 11.

7. Ibid., 19–20.

8. "Adventure in Freedom," 14–16; "Jewish Values," 48–50; "Jewish Survival and the College Campus," *Judaism* 17,3 (summer 1968), 259–281.

9. "Change and the Orthodox Community," 20.

10. "Jewish Values," 43.

11. Ibid., 44–48. This whole process has accelerated in subsequent decades, almost without any significant constraint and to unimaginable degrees, given the technological advances, especially in the computer industry. Greenberg's worries should be increased to the point of being overwhelming.

12. Ibid., 50–53.

13. Ibid., 50, 53–54; "Change and the Orthodox Community," 16.

14. Ibid., 57–59.

15. Ibid., 54–55.

16. Ibid., 50. E.g., it can choose isolation or an attempt to master the environment.

17. See "Change and the Orthodox Community," 19.

18. Ibid., 62.

19. Ibid., 61, 63.

20. Ibid., 61.

21. Ibid., 61; see also 62, 64.

22. See ibid., 64.

23. Ibid., 62–66. Greenberg is too casual. E.g., he says, "there is an obligation to take society seriously even if we do not accept its standards finally" (62). An obligation? Why?

24. Ibid., 62.

25. Ibid., 63, 64.

26. Ibid., 65.

27. Ibid., 59–60.

28. Ibid., 56; see also "The Cultural Revolution and Religious Unity," 103.

29. See Peter Berger, *The Heretical Imperative* (Garden City, NJ: Anchor Books,

1979). During the sixties and seventies Berger's work was widely read, especially *The Social Construction of Reality*, written with Thomas Luckmann (Garden City, NJ: Doubleday Books, 1966), *The Sacred Canopy* (Garden City, NJ: Doubleday Books, 1967), *Rumor of Angels* (Garden City, NJ: Doubleday Books, 1969), and then *The Heretical Imperative*. For a discussion of Berger, see Michael Morgan, "Judaism and the Heretical Imperative," in *Dilemmas in Modern Jewish Thought* (Bloomington: Indiana University Press, 1992).

30. "Judaism and Christianity after the Holocaust," *Journal of Ecumenical Studies* 12,4 (fall 1975), 521.

31. See *God, Man and History* (New York: Jonathan David, 1959).

32. "Cloud of Smoke," 7–8.

33. Ibid., 8.

34. For an important traditional encounter with this issue of historicity, see Jay Harris, *Nachman Krochmal* (New York: New York University Press, 1991).

35. "Cloud of Smoke," 8.

36. Ibid., 9.

37. Ibid., 9.

38. The argument is a fortiori: take the most fundamental belief of Judaism; note that Auschwitz requires revision even regarding such a central belief; hence, certainly, less central beliefs are historically revisable. In addition, of course, it is no accident that Greenberg cites the belief—the absolute value of human life—that he does.

39. "Cloud of Smoke," 8: "Both religions have sought to isolate their central events from further revelations."

40. Ibid., 7–20; "Judaism and Christianity," 522–528.

41. "Cloud of Smoke," 20; "Judaism and Christianity," 528–529.

42. "Cloud of Smoke," 22–55.

43. Ibid., 22; "Judaism and Christianity," 529–530.

44. "Cloud of Smoke," 22.

45. Ibid., 23; see also "The End of Emancipation," 55.

46. "Cloud of Smoke," 23–27.

47. For Greenberg's criticisms of these figures, see ibid., 26–27.

48. Greenberg also associates the notion of the dialectical and dialectical responses with the pluralism of his earlier writings; ibid., 27.

49. See Buber, "Who speaks?" in "Dialogue" in *Between Man and Man* (New York: Macmillan, 1965), 15.

50. "Cloud of Smoke," 27.

51. See ibid., 33.

52. Ibid., 33.

53. Ibid., 45–50, 43.

54. Ibid., 26–27.

55. Ibid., 27–34. That is, why did Auschwitz not destroy all faith? Greenberg gives four reasons: even real survivors have renewed their faith; modernity-rationalism and technology contributed to the Holocaust and do not warrant our loyalty, for making secular values absolute is a form of idolatry; the need for moral necessity and for hope *vis à vis* Enlightenment models; Israel as a sign of God's continuing presence.

56. Ibid., 24; see also 35: "It may be, in fact, that there is no revelation here. Those who deem it revelatory may be mistaken." See also 49.

57. Ibid., 34–41.

58. Ibid., 35.

59. These are my terms, not his, but they give some sense of the three types of deeds that Greenberg recommends. Ibid., 41–55; see also "The End of Emancipation," 59–63.

60. "Cloud of Smoke," 41; also 41–45. This theme is one of the reasons for Greenberg's report of the guard's testimony at the Nuremberg trial, to portray vividly the Nazi subversion of the value of human life.

61. Ibid., 44–45.

62. Ibid., 44.

63. Ibid., 48; also 48–50; "The End of Emancipation," 60–63.

64. "Cloud of Smoke," 48.

65. Ibid., 49. Compare the situation of Russian Jews, Ethiopian Jews, and Project Moses.

66. Ibid., 49.

67. Ibid., 54.

68. Ibid., 54–55; "The End of Emancipation," 60.

69. "Cloud of Smoke," 55; see *The Jewish Way* (New York: Summit Books, 1988).

70. See "The End of Emancipation."

71. "The End of Emancipation," 60; see also 58–61.

72. *In principle* Greenberg risks all, but not, I think, in fact. In his later writings Greenberg inclines less and less to a willingness to give up even central Jewish affirmations if they cannot survive the exposure to Auschwitz. Alternatively, one might see this as a realization that more and more must and can survive Auschwitz. In conversation, more than fifteen years ago, Greenberg balked at the extreme historicism that seemed to underlie his thinking.

73. See "Cloud of Smoke," 31–33 and 48–50; also "The Interaction," 259–282.

74. "The Interaction," 259.

75. Ibid., 260.

76. Ibid., 260–263, 264.

77. Ibid., 264–265; also "The End of Emancipation."

78. "The Interaction," 265–266.

79. Ibid., 266–271.

80. "The End of Emancipation."

81. It has since been renamed the National Jewish Center for Learning and Leadership (CLAL).

82. Greenberg, "Voluntary Covenant." Another Orthodox participant in the theological discussions of the sixties, and then a young rabbi in Montreal, David Hartman would later articulate his own liberal orthodoxy in *A Living Covenant* (New York, Free Press, 1985). But unlike Greenberg, Hartman's rethinking of covenant was never associated with a primary exposure to Auschwitz and the death camps.

83. "Voluntary Covenant," 2–5.

84. Ibid., 6–20.

85. Ibid., 10.

86. Ibid., 8–13.

87. Ibid., 14–17. Greenberg's attention to the threat of Auschwitz on the covenant recalls a similar attention on Wiesel's part in several places. One is in his short statement made at the *Judaism* symposium of March 26, 1967, "Jewish Values in the Post-Holocaust Future." See *Judaism* 16,3 (summer 1967), 281–284.

88. "Voluntary Covenant," 15.

89. Ibid., 16.

90. Ibid., 17.

91. Ibid., 20.

92. Ibid., 23.

93. Ibid., 22 and 21–28.

94. See ibid., 28.

95. The acknowledgment of the role of autonomy or voluntarism by Greenberg is remarkable in a traditional thinker and especially so since the motive for that acknowledgment in his case is the impact of Auschwitz on the covenantal relationship. This latter is what distinguishes Greenberg from earlier liberal or Reform theologians and from other Orthodox thinkers like Hartman.

96. "Voluntary Covenant," 2.

97. See ibid., 2–3.

98. Ibid., 4–5.

99. Ibid., 6.

100. Ibid., 7–8.

101. Ibid., 12–13.

102. Ibid., 16–19.

103. Ibid., 22–23.

104. Ibid., 24–25.

105. See Arnold Jacob Wolf, "The Revisionism of Irving Greenberg," *Sh'ma* 13/254 (May 13, 1983), 104–106, especially 105–106.

Chapter 9

1. Arthur Cohen, "On Theological Method: A Response on Behalf of *The Tremendum*," *Journal of Reform Judaism* 31,2 (spring 1984), 56–57; see also *The Tremendum* (New York: Crossroad, 1981), xvi.

2. Rubenstein, "The 'Supernatural Jew,'" *Reconstructionist* 29,6 (May 3, 1963), 13–20; reprinted as chapter 10 in the first edition of *After Auschwitz* (Indianapolis: Bobbs-Merrill, 1966); Cohen, commentary on "Homeland and Holocaust," in *Religious Situation: 1968*, edited by Donald R. Cutler (Boston: Beacon Press, 1968), 87–91.

3. Arnold Jacob Wolf, *Judaism* 16,2 (spring 1967), 233–236; Will Herberg, *Judaism* 12,3 (Summer 1963), 364–370.

4. Cohen, *The Tremendum*.

5. Cohen, *The Natural and the Supernatural Jew* (New York: Pantheon Books, 1962; reprint New York: McGraw-Hill, 1964). The best place to encounter Cohen is now David Stern and Paul Mendes-Flohr (eds.), *An Arthur A. Cohen Reader: Selected Fiction and Writings on Judaism, Theology, Literature, and Culture* (Detroit: Wayne State University Press, 1998).

6. *The Natural and the Supernatural Jew*, 4.

7. Ibid., 4–5.

8. Ibid., 5.

9. Ibid., 6.

10. Ibid., 7.

11. Ibid., 7.

12. See ibid., 309.

13. Ibid., 8.

14. Ibid., 9.

15. Cohen's work also calls to mind that of Herberg, Heschel, and certainly Borowitz. See especially ibid., 309–311. Also one might look at Cohen's articles in the resource

book he and Paul Mendes-Flohr edited, *Contemporary Jewish Religious Thought* (New York: Scribner's, 1987): "Eschatology," 183–188, and "Redemption," 761–765. By the time this dictionary appeared, Cohen had died.

16. *The Natural and the Supernatural Jew,* 287–288; also 312–314.

17. Ibid., 286.

18. Ibid., 288–290.

19. Ibid., 294.

20. See ibid., 301–305.

21. Ibid., 294.

22. Ibid., 298.

23. Ibid., 299.

24. Ibid., 302; also 304–305: "[Theology] sets itself but one task: to apprehend and interpret the presence of God in time and history" (304).

25. The same theme, the recovery of transcendence, was a central one in the late fifties and sixties. See the work of Peter Berger, Borowitz, and Samuel E. Karff, "Jewish Peoplehood—A Signal of Transcendence," in *New Theology No. 9,* edited by Martin E. Marty and Dean G. Deerman (New York: Macmillan, 1972). For Berger, see chapter 8, note 29.

26. *The Natural and the Supernatural Jew,* 310.

27. Rubenstein, *After Auschwitz,* 178–181.

28. Ibid., 187–188. Fackenheim charges Hermann Cohen with a similar abstractness in his essay on Cohen; see Michael L. Morgan (ed.), *Jewish Philosophers and Jewish Philosophy* (Bloomington: Indiana University Press, 1996), chapter 3.

29. Arthur Cohen, "Theology," in Cohen and Mendes-Flohr, *Contemporary Jewish Religious Thought*, 971–979, especially 976–978.

30. Ibid., 973.

31. Ibid., 976.

32. Ibid., 977.

33. Ibid., 977.

34. Ibid., 977–978.

35. Cohen is not alone in his conviction that after Auschwitz, theology or reflection about God is necessary. See Hans Jonas, "The Concept of God after Auschwitz: A Jewish Voice," *Journal of Religion* (January 1987), 1–13, also in *Out of the Whirlwind,* edited by Albert H. Friedlander (New York: Union of American Hebrew Congregations, 1968), 465–476; the essay incorporates parts of "Immortality and the Modern Temper," *Harvard Theological Review* 55 (1962), 1–20; also reprinted in Hans Jonas, *Mortality and Morality,* edited by Lawrence Vogel (Evanston, IL: Northwestern University Press, 1996), chapter 6; and *A Holocaust Reader*, edited by Michael L. Morgan (Oxford: Oxford University Press, 2000), 259–270. Jonas's notion of a finite God had virtually no impact on Jewish life or thinking. The anthology by Friedlander was one of the first, if not the very first, anthology of writings dedicated to intellectual responses to the Holocaust.

36. Cohen, *The Tremendum*, 1; see also 5.

37. Ibid., 24–26.

38. Ibid., 8.

39. Ibid., 8–10; also 16: "I have done everything I can to make the death camps not only unique, incomparable, *sui generis*, but, more to the point, beyond the deliberations of reason, beyond the discernments of moral judgment, beyond meaning itself" (16).

40. Ibid., 10.

41. Ibid., 12–16.

42. Ibid., 17–19.

43. See ibid., 19–21, especially 20.

44. Ibid., 21–26.

45. Ibid., 24.

46. A clearer, succinct formulation can be found in "In Our Terrible Age: The *Tremendum* of the Jews," in *The Holocaust as Interruption*, edited by Elisabeth Schussler Fiorenza and David Tracy (Edinburgh: T. and T. Clark, 1984), 11–16, especially 15–16: "is [God] the same as he was then?"

47. It should be mentioned that in *The Tremendum* Cohen argues neither clearly nor well. The book is at many points almost totally opaque, and it would not be surprising if its style is a prime factor for its relative lack of influence. Among the post-Holocaust theologians, writing is a serious problem. Berkovits is chauvinistic, Greenberg overly rhetorical. Rubenstein's early works are dilettantish and self-indulgent. Against this background, it is not puzzling that many prefer the lean, gripping prose of Levi and Appelfeld and the poetry of Celan, and not merely for aesthetic reasons.

48. Ibid., 25–26.

49. Ibid., 26.

50. Ibid., 28–32.

51. Ibid., 40–41.

52. Ibid., 39–45.

53. Ibid., 44–45.

54. Ibid., 45.

55. This issue, of the special significance of the Holocaust and the death camps, their so-called uniqueness, has been the subject of much discussion. See the article by Steven Katz, "The Unique Intentionality of the Holocaust," in *Post-Holocaust Dialogues* (New York: New York University Press, 1983), the work of Emil Fackenheim and Hannah Arendt, and the anthology edited by Alan S. Rosenberg, *Is the Holocaust Unique?* (Boulder, CO: Westview Press, 1996).

56. *The Tremendum,* 34–38.

57. Ibid., 35–36.

58. Ibid., 51–52.

59. Ibid., 43.

60. Ibid., 48.

61. Ibid., 50.

62. Ibid., 51–52.

63. Ibid., 52.

64. Ibid., 53.

65. Ibid., 53, 55. This is Cohen's best argument for the Holocaust's theological relevance.

66. *The Tremendum,* 55–58, especially 58; also 19–26 and "In Our Terrible Age," 15–16.

67. Ibid., 59–82.

68. Ibid., 61.

69. Ibid., 74.

70. Ibid., 76–77.

71. Ibid., 78; 51–58; "In Our Terrible Age," 15–16.

72. *The Tremendum,* 78.

73. Ibid., 78; see 80: "The one characteristic of the historical event as *tremendum* is that it annihilates for us the familiar categories by which we have read and decoded our past" (80).

74. Ibid., 81–82.

75. Ibid., 82.

76. See also ibid., 86.

77. Ibid., 82.

78. Ibid., 84.

79. Ibid., 84.

80. Although stated abstractly and broadly, this sounds very much like Berkovits and Greenberg.

81. Ibid., 86.

82. Ibid., 86–95.

83. Ibid., 90, 92. There are echoes of Hermann Cohen, Rosenzweig, Scholem, Walter Benjamin, and much else in this account.

84. Ibid., 95–97.

85. Ibid., 97.

86. Ibid., 97–98.

87. Ibid., 98.

88. Ibid., 102.

89. Ibid., 100–108, especially 103–104.

90. Ibid., 105.

91. Ibid., 108.

92. Ibid., 109.

93. Cohen, commentary on "Homeland and Holocaust," 90.

94. Ibid., 90–91.

95. Ibid., 102–105.

96. See "Naming the Unnameable; Thinking the Unthinkable," *Journal of Reform Judaism* 31,2 (spring 1984), 43–55; "On Theological Method: A Response in Behalf of *The Tremendum*," *Journal of Reform Judaism* 31,2 (spring 1984), 56–65.

97. Rubenstein, "Naming the Unnameable," 46.

98. See ibid., 46–49.

99. Ibid., 48–49.

100. Ibid., 49.

101. Ibid., 49–51.

102. Ibid., 50.

103. Ibid., 51, 51–54.

104. Ibid., 52–53.

105. Ibid., 54.

106. Cohen, "On Theological Method," 62.

107. Ibid., 64–65.

108. Ibid., 63.

109. Ibid., 64.

Chapter 10

1. For bibliography through 1987, see Michael L. Morgan, *The Jewish Thought of Emil Fackenheim* (Detroit: Wayne State University Press, 1987). For subsequent bibliography and essays, see Emil Fackenheim, *The Jewish Bible after the Holocaust* (Bloomington, IN: Indiana University Press, 1990) and Michael L. Morgan (ed.), *Jewish Philosophers and Jewish Philosophy* (Bloomington: Indiana University Press, 1996).

2. For this reason, as well as many others, Fackenheim's thinking is akin to that of

Emmanuel Levinas, who also sought to challenge the traditions of Western philosophy and religious thought out of a serious concern for Auschwitz and the encounter with it. Fackenheim met Levinas on two occasions but never either read or wrote about his work. Levinas does discuss Fackenheim, in "Useless Suffering," originally published in *Giornale di Metatisica* 4 (January–April 1982), 13–26, translated by Michael B. Smith and Barbara Harshav in *On Thinking-of-the-Other Entre Nous* (New York: Columbia University Press, 1998), 91–101, and by Richard A. Cohen in *The Provocation of Levinas: Rethinking the Other,* edited by Robert Bernasconi and David Wood (London: Routledge, 1988), 156–167. For brief discussion of Fackenheim and Levinas, see Tamra Wright, *The Twilight of Jewish Philosophy* (Netherlands: Harwood Academic, 1999), 97–109.

3. "Jewish Faith and the Holocaust: A Fragment," *Commentary* 46 (August 1968), 30–36; *Quest for Past and Future* (Bloomington: Indiana University Press, 1968), 17–26 (rev.); reprinted in *The Jewish Return into History* (New York: Schocken Books, 1978), 25–42, and in Morgan, *The Jewish Thought of Emil Fackenheim*, 161–164, 235–240. All references are to the version in *The Jewish Return into History* (hereafter JRH).

4. Hereafter GPH (New York: New York University Press, 1970; reprint, New York: Harper Torchbook, 1972). Another somewhat more informal piece of the same period was delivered as a lecture at the University of California, Santa Cruz, in 1968; it is reprinted in *The Future of Hope,* edited by Walter H. Capps (Philadelphia: Fortress Press, 1970), as "The Commandment to Hope: A Response to Contemporary Jewish Experience," 68–91, especially 83–91.

5. Seventeen essays; (New York: Schocken, 1978).

6. "Jewish Faith and the Holocaust," in JRH, 25–26.

7. Ibid., 26–32, 40–42.

8. See ibid., 26–32, 40–42.

9. Ibid., 27; compare 29.

10. Ibid., 28–29.

11. Ibid., 27; note Fackenheim's indebtedness to Arendt.

12. Ibid., 29.

13. Ibid., 29.

14. Ibid., 29. Eventually Fackenheim will regret the use of the term "authentic" for two reasons. One is because it is appropriated from Heidegger, who Fackenheim comes increasingly to see as a philosopher whose thinking is tied to his Nazism. Second is because Fackenheim comes to realize that many victims of Nazism did not live exemplary Jewish lives, but their suffering and their fate is to be respected and not in any way diminished. No standard so high that it would make them "inauthentic" is responsible.

15. Ibid., 30.

16. Ibid., 30–32.

17. This may look like the fallacy of inferring ought from is, of deriving moral obligations from facts of nature. But this is a mistaken understanding of what Fackenheim is doing; his thinking is more similar to Kant's transcendental deductions than to a simple inference of value from fact.

18. Ibid., 30.

19. Ibid., 30–31.

20. For an important recent study of the imperative force of moral duties, the authority of obligations, see Stephen Darwall, *The British Moralists and the Internal Ought* (Cambridge, UK: Cambridge University Press, 1995).

21. "Jewish Faith and the Holocaust," 31.

22. Ibid., 31–32.

23. Fackenheim uses virtually this exact language in the *Judaism* symposium. See JRH, 23.

24. "Jewish Faith and the Holocaust," 32; compare 22–24.

25. Ibid., 32; compare 23–24.

26. As I indicated earlier, Fackenheim would no longer use this term, for two reasons. One is that it was originally derived from Heidegger, who had used it in a very precise way; Fackenheim never really intended it in the strict Heideggarian sense and now has reservations about the implications of Heidegger's Nazi involvement for his philosophical views. Second, Fackenheim would not now want to diminish in any way the integrity and even heroism of many who were victims of Nazism yet whose conduct, by some "high" standard of authenticity, would be denigrated. These would include his own brothers.

27. The *Judaism* symposium took place on March 26, 1967, and the nucleus of that statement and the *Commentary* essay, "Jewish Faith and the Holocaust," were already delivered as a presentation to the meeting of theologians at the Segal Institute in Quebec during the summer of 1966.

28. See "Jewish Faith and the Holocaust," 40–42; *Quest for Past and Future*, 3–4, 24–26. The preface to *Quest* is dated October 4, 1967.

29. "Jewish Faith and the Holocaust," 42; see 40–42, also 32–40 on Christian–Jewish relations after the Six Day War.

30. In the preface to GPH, he points out that the lectures go back to a presentation given to the I. Meier Segals Center for the Study and Advancement of Judaism in 1967. Organized by David Hartmann, with Fackenheim's counsel, this group of theologians met during several summers in Quebec. The participants included Greenberg, Borowitz, Petuchowski, Lou Silberman, and others. See also JRH, chapters 4, 7–10.

31. He recalls this shift in "The People Israel Lives" (1970), reprinted in JRH, 43–44, 48, 52, as a form of escapism now overcome.

32. GPH, v.

33. Ibid., 3–7, especially 7.

34. Fackenheim acknowledges a debt to Greenberg for his notion of root experiences and his historical thinking; see GPH, v and 32 n.10. He is indebted to Buber for his theory of revelation and the experience of it; see GPH, 11–14, and "Martin Buber's Concept of Revelation," in Morgan (ed.), *Jewish Philosophers and Jewish Philosophy*, Chapter Four. His debt to Collingwood concerns his notion of reenacting the past; see GPH, 11–14. During the same period in the sixties, Fackenheim's colleague William Dray had been studying Collingwood's work on historical understanding, and Fackenheim recalls benefiting from discussions with Dray. See Dray, *Perspectives on History* (London: Routledge, 1980), chapter 1; and *History as Re-Enactment* (Oxford: Oxford University Press, 1995).

35. He points out that this is his reformulation of Greenberg's notion of an orienting event. Fackenheim, unlike Greenberg, then, distinguishes original or founding events from later ones, and he distinguishes the events from the experiencing of them, which shows his indebtedness to Rosenzweig's "new thinking," which is tantamount to the phenomenological dimension of thinking from Hegel and Kierkegaard to Buber, Rosenzweig, and other existentialists.

36. GPH, 8–9.

37. See MacIntyre, "Epistemological Crises, Dramatic Narrative, and the Philosophy of Science," *Monist* 60 (1977), 453–471; reprinted in *Paradigms and Revolutions*, edited by Gary Gutting (Notre Dame, IN: University of Notre Dame Press, 1980), 54–74.

38. GPH, 9.

39. Ibid., 9.

40. Ibid., 11; also 10–11.

41. Ibid., 10.

42. Ibid., 11.

43. Ibid., 11–14.

44. Ibid., 15–16.

45. See R. G. Collingwood, *The Idea of History* (Oxford: Oxford University Press, 1956), 205–249, 282–315; William Dray, *Perspectives in History*, chapter 1 ("R. G. Collingwood and the Understanding of Actions in History," originally *Dialogue* 17,4 [1978], 659–682). Both Dray and Lionel Rubinoff were colleagues and friends of Fackenheim at Toronto. Both wrote on Collingwood's philosophy of history. See also Dray, *Laws and Explanations in History* (Oxford: Oxford University Press, 1957); *Philosophy of History* (Englewood Cliffs, NJ: Prentice-Hall, 1964); *History as Re-Enactment*.

46. See GPH, 20; compare 47–49; 95–98; also *Encounters between Judaism and Modern Philosophy* (New York: Basic Books, 1973), 57–77.

47. GPH, 20–25; see also *Quest for Past and Future*, 16–17.

48. GPH, 16–20.

49. *Quest for Past and Future*, 17; GPH, 25–31.

50. In chapter 2, to the challenge of modern secular thought.

51. GPH, 30.

52. Ibid., 69–92.

53. See ibid., 100 n. 10, on the notion of uniqueness.

54. Ibid., 70.

55. See "Jewish Faith and the Holocaust," 30; "The People Israel Lives," in JRH, 47 and n.1; "From Bergen-Belsen to Jerusalem," in JRH, 136.

56. GPH, 71–79.

57. Ibid., 71.

58. Ibid., 71–72. Like Greenberg, Fackenheim is disturbed by Rubenstein's confidence, and his belief that we understand the camps—"the facts are in"—unsettles him. Will we *ever* know? (71–72). Compare "The People Israel Lives," 46.

59. GPH, 73–74.

60. Ibid., 76.

61. See *Quest for Past and Future*, 20.

62. Ibid., 300–303.

63. GPH, 78–79.

64. Ibid., 79.

65. Ibid., 79.

66. See also "The People Israel Lives," 53; "The Human Condition," in JRH, 93–95; "From Bergen-Belsen to Jerusalem," 137–138.

67. GPH, 81.

68. Ibid., 81.

69. Ibid., 82.

70. Ibid., 82.

71. Ibid., 83.

72. Fackenheim speaks of it in just these terms as a grasping of transcendence within a wholly historical context in "Transcendence in Contemporary Culture" (1969), in JRH, 102–111.

73. These pages, 81–83, are arguably the most central pages in GPH. See too 94–95: fear of being cut off from the present and the past.

74. GPH, 84.

75. Ibid., 85–89.

76. Ibid., 89.

77. The reality of conflict is an important theme of some recent moral philosophy; see, for example, the work of Bernard Williams and Stuart Hampshire, as well as MacIntyre and Taylor.

78. GPH, 92–93.

79. Ibid., 92–93.

80. Ibid., 95.

81. Ibid., 95.

82. "The unique crime of the Nazi Holocaust must never be forgotten. . . . [T]he rescuing for memory of even a single innocent tear is a holy task" ("From Bergen-Belsen to Jerusalem," 132).

83. GPH, 88–89; "The People Israel Lives," 53–54.

84. JRH, 54; see also *Encounters between Judaism and Modern Philosophy*, 166–167; "The Human Condition," 97; "Demythologizing and Remythologizing," in JRH, 113; "From Bergen-Belsen to Jerusalem," 139.

85. See also "From Bergen-Belsen to Jerusalem," 130: the Six Day War produced a "watershed in Jewish consciousness" (JRH, 130).

86. They also include favored evidence, arguments, images, and illustrations that remain central features of Fackenheim's thinking.

87. He has come to think that even this work's answer might be too easy; see his reference to the objection raised by Susan Shapiro in her review, in the preface to the second edition. See *To Mend the World*, 2nd ed. (New York: Schocken Books, 1989) (hereafter TMW), 336 n.13. See also Susan Shapiro, "For Thy Breach Is Great Like the Sea: Who Can Heal Thee," *Religious Studies Review* 13,3 (July 1987), 211.

88. See "From Bergen-Belsen to Jerusalem," 132–133.

89. JRH, 26; "The Human Condition," 89–95; "Transcendence," 107–108; "From Bergen-Belsen to Jerusalem," 132–134.

90. See also TMW, 10–13.

91. See foreword to Yehuda Bauer, *The Jewish Emergence from Powerlessness* (Toronto: 1975), vii–ix; Morgan, *The Jewish Thought of Emil Fackenheim*, chapters 10–16; TMW, 9–12.

92. "Jewish Faith and the Holocaust," 30; compare "The Jewish People Lives," 47, and "From Bergen-Belsen to Jerusalem," 136.

93. See also "Jewish Faith and the Holocaust," 28.

94. "Midrashic Existence after the Holocaust," in JRH (originally 1976), 252–272, especially 254–261.

95. Ibid., 254.

96. Ibid., 258; 254–258. Another example is the two work permits in "The People Israel Lives," 46; compare Oshry on forbidden pregnancies and my article "Jewish Ethics after the Holocaust," in *Dilemmas in Modern Jewish Thought* (Bloomington: Indiana University Press, 1992).

97. "On the Life, Death, and Transfiguration of Martyrdom," in JRH, 245.

98. "Midrashic Existence," 260.

99. "Jewish Faith," 27; "The People Israel Lives," 46. See also "Sachsenhausen 1938," (1975), in JRH, 59–64; "The Human Condition," 89–90, 94.

100. "Jewish Faith and the Holocaust," 27: "Auschwitz is a unique descent into hell. It is an unprecedented celebration of evil. It is evil for evil's sake"; see also 29.

101. JRH, 27, 45, 90, 133, and 107: "Nazi racism was not 'superstition,' but mass murder infused with infinite passion and elevated to pseudoreligious absoluteness, not the finite means to the winning of the war, but a boundless end in itself, pursued even at the risk of losing a war on account of it" ("Transcendence," 107).

102. "The Human Condition," 92–93.

103. Ibid., 94.

104. JRH, 46–47; compare *The Origins of Totalitarianism*, 459.

105. For an early examination of Nazism as a negative idolatry, see "Idolatry as a Modern Religious Possibility," chapter 4 in *Encounters between Judaism and Modern Philosophy*, originally published in *The Religious Situation: 1968*, edited by Donald R. Cutler (Boston: Beacon Press, 1968). This essay was originally delivered at one of the Segal Institute meetings in Quebec. For later accounts of why the Nazis did it, see TMW, 230–248, and "Holocaust and *Weltanschauung*: Philosophical Reflections on Why They Did It," *Holocaust and Genocide Studies* 3,2 (1988), 197–208 (reprinted in Morgan, *Jewish Philosophers and Jewish Philosophy*). On Nazism as celebration of evil, see "The Holocaust and the State of Israel," in JRH, 278–279.

106. Terence Des Pres, *The Survivor* (New York: Oxford University Press, 1976), 89, cited in "On the Life, Death, and Transfiguration of Martyrdom," in JRH, 246–249 (originally 1976).

107. Levi, *Survival in Auschwitz*, 82, quoted in JRH, 246.

108. JRH, 247.

109. The target here is Martin Heidegger. See "The Holocaust and Philosophy," *Journal of Philosophy* 82,10 (October 1985), 510–511, and TMW, chapter 4.

110. Prior to 1967 Fackenheim was far from Zionism. After the War, he took his first trip to Israel, and in the seventies he began to spend summers in Jerusalem. In 1982, he and his family made aliyah, moving from Toronto to Jerusalem. Increasingly, his topical writing has focused on Israel and the defense of Israel in the face of all that threatens her. Recently, he has turned to writing political essays on Zionism in the post-Holocaust era. So, beginning with 1967 and the early seventies, Israel has played a more and more prominent role in his thinking.

111. Especially, "Israel and the Diaspora," chapter 13 in JRH; "The Holocaust and the State of Israel: Their Relation," chapter 17; "Post-Holocaust Anti-Jewishness, Jewish Identity, and the Centrality of Israel," chapter 14. In the past decade or so, Fackenheim has written extensively about Israel and Israeli politics, both in essays and in the popular press, newspapers, magazines, and so on.

112. See "Jewish Faith and the Holocaust," 37–42; "The People Israel Lives," 54–57; "The Human Condition," 97–101; see also "Transcendence," 108–109; "Demythologizing and Remythologizing," 125–126.

113. JRH, 40–41.

114. See also *Encounters between Judaism and Modern Philosophy*, 166.

115. "The Human Condition," 97.

116. *Encounters between Judaism and Modern Philosophy*, 166 (words reordered).

117. Ibid., 166.

118. Ibid., 167.

119. Ibid., 167.

120. Ibid., 167.

121. Ibid., 167; compare "From Bergen-Belsen to Jerusalem," 139.

122. Fackenheim beautifully argues that Hegel would have appreciated this model of human courage with messianic hope — but not, as Hegel once put it, an ineffective hope

(*Encounters between Judaism and Modern Philosophy*, 168). See Hegel, On *Christianity.
Early Theological Writings* New York: Harper, 1961, 159. Fackenheim takes support for
Israel's existence as a core element of diaspora Jewish response: "From Bergen-Belsen to
Jerusalem," 140–143.

123. "From Bergen-Belsen to Jerusalem," 139; compare "Jewish 'Ethnicity' in 'Mature
Democratic Societies,'" 173–175.

124. "From Bergen-Belsen to Jerusalem," 141–143.

125. "Israel and the Diaspora," in JRH, 193.

126. Ibid., 197–198. Fackenheim wrote the essay shortly after Yassir Arafat's November 1974 address to the United Nations General Assembly, the approval of the delegates,
and Roy Eckardt's chilling indictment that the U.N. had become "the operative centre of
world antisemitism" (197–198, 201).

127. "Israel and the Diaspora," 207–209. See also "Post-Holocaust Anti-Jewishness,"
in JRH, 210–233. Fackenheim, like Arendt, accepts the view that Jewish powerlessness
historically contributed to the Holocaust as a persisting theme in the manner of Jewish
survival throughout history, as a diaspora people. Historically speaking, this is a view
that has come in for much serious criticism and one that is far too uniform and simple
to fit the evidence of Jewish conduct in the many venues of Jewish life for nearly two
millennia.

128. "The Holocaust and the State of Israel," 273–286 (originally 1974).

129. Ibid., 276.

130. Ibid., 277–278.

131. Ibid., 278.

132. Ibid., 278–279.

133. Ibid., 279.

134. Ibid., 284; see 282–286.

135. Ibid., 285.

136. In the 1980s and 1990s, having moved to Jerusalem, Fackenheim has written extensively about Israel. His articles, many written for newspapers and the popular press,
are often political, polemical commentary on current events. They are extremely protec-
tive of Israel's sovereignty and have generally been classified, both in Israel and in North
America, as right-wing and conservative, in one sense or another. I set these partisan issues aside and focus on foundations. What I have examined in the text are his central discussions of the foundations of his views about Israel and its relation to the Holocaust.

137. See Michael Novak, *The Rise of the Unmeltable Ethnics* (New York: Macmillan,
1971).

138. Entitled "The Survival of the Jews," *Centre Magazine* (November–December
1973), 15–28. Reprinted in JRH; all references are to the JRH version.

139. See also on these themes the essays in *New Theology No. 9*, "Theology in the context of the New Particularisms—nation, tribe, race, clan, ethnic group, gender and generation," edited by Martin E. Marty and Dean G. Peerman (New York: Macmillan,
1972).

140. See "Jewish 'Ethnicity' in 'Mature Democratic Societies'" 167–168.

141. Ibid., 144–149, 153–167.

142. Ibid., 156.

143. Ibid., 144, 162.

144. Ibid., 162.

145. Ibid., 162–163.

146. As there is in a spiritualizing of the American Jewish task—by havurots that

focus on prayer, meditation, and study but neglect or ignore the concerns of Jews in Iraq, Syria, Russia, and Israel; see 167 where Fackenheim says as much. See also Hannah Arendt, "On Humanity in Dark Times," in *Men in Dark Times* (New York: Harcourt Brace, 1968; originally 1959), 17–18, 23.

147. It was originally published by Schocken in 1982, republished by them with new introductory material in 1989 and then again by Indiana University Press, with additional introductory material, based on a lecture given in Halle, in 1994. In 1976, Fackenheim made a six-part proposal to the Killam Program of the Canada Council. TMW is the result of pursuing the proposal, of which it encompasses only part I. See TMW, 14–22, especially 21. The proposal is available in the Fackenheim section of the Canadian National Archives in Ottawa, Ontario, Canada. But TMW incorporates themes that go back to the fifties and Fackenheim's work on revelation, Hegel, German idealism, Heidegger, and more.

148. We do not have a comprehensive exposition of TMW. I discuss some of its central issues in an essay in *Dilemmas in Modern Jewish Thought* and in "The Central Themes of Fackenheim's *To Mend the World*," originally delivered as a presentation at a colloquium on Fackenheim's thought held in Toronto, at Holy Blossom Temple, on March 23, 1992; my essay was published in the *Journal of Jewish Thought and Philosophy* 5,2 (1996), 297–312. For his own overview of TMW, see Fackenheim's introduction, 3–30, and his preface, xi–xxv, to the second edition (1989). Other features include discussion of Spinoza, Rosenzweig, Hegel, and Heidegger; the content of authentic response by Christians, historians, and others; and the recovery of a notion of revelation in a post-Hegelian world.

149. The phrase "the 614th commandment" drops out of Fackenheim's work between 1970 and 1993, when he published a short piece, "The 614th Commandment Reconsidered," in *Reform Judaism* 22, 1 (1993), 18–20; reprinted in Morgan (ed.), *Jewish Philosophers and Jewish Philosophy*, chapter fifteen. But, I would argue, the idea of such an imperative with its content of opposition is present throughout his work of those two decades.

150. See TMW, xx, xxii.

151. See TMW, 13, 19–20, 23–24.

152. Ibid., 22–28.

153. Ibid., 24; see GPH, 92.

154. See chapter I, section 8 (26–28).

155. See 188 n; 230 n; and chapter IV, sections 6B, 8, 9; also 182 n, and 182–183.

156. See TMW, 182–190.

157. Ibid., 183–184.

158. On Hitler's worldview, or *Weltanschauung*, Fackenheim later wrote an important essay, reprinted in Morgan, *Jewish Philosophers and Jewish Philosophy*, chapter 12. See also Gerald Fleming, *Hitler and the Final Solution* (Berkeley: University of California Press, 1984) and Eberhard Jäckel, *Hitler's Weltanschauung: A Blueprint for Power* (Middletown, CT: Wesleyan University Press, 1972), whom Fackenheim does cite in TMW.

159. TMW, 189–191.

160. Ibid., 191.

161. On Buber's difficulty with radical evil, see TMW, 195–198, and Michael Morgan, "Martin Buber, Cooperation and Evil," *Journal of the American Academy of Religion* LVIII, 1 (1990), 99–109.

162. Arguably, as early as "Jewish Faith and the Holocaust," Fackenheim had included victims among those who were already responding, but not until TMW does he

take them seriously as "ontological paradigms" of a sort whose role is fundamental and determinative.

163. See especially "On the Life, Death, and Transfiguration of Martyrdom," in JRH, 249–251.

164. TMW, chapter IV, sections 8–9, 201–250.

165. Ibid., 201.

166. Ibid., 208–209.

167. Ibid., 208–209.

168. Ibid., 211; also 209–210, 214–215.

169. Ibid., 215.

170. Ibid., 217. Quoted by Des Pres, in *The Survivor* (New York: Oxford University Press, 1976), from Lewinska, *Twenty Months at Auschwitz* (New York: Lyle Stuart, 1968), 141–142, 150.

171. TMW, 218.

172. Once again, as he has done on many occasions, Fackenheim refers to Nietzsche's statement from *Ecce Homo* (*On the Genealogy of Morals and Ecce Homo,* translated by Walter Kaufmann [New York: Vintage Books, 1967], 300) so often cited by Buber (e.g., in *I and Thou* [New York: Scribner's, 1970], 158), that there are occasions when one receives and does not ask who gives. See TMW, 218.

173. Ibid., 222–223, 220–225.

174. Ibid., 225–250.

175. Ibid., 226–229.

176. Ibid., 229.

177. Ibid., 230–231. See also Fackenheim, "Holocaust and *Weltanschauung*."

178. In conversation with Ernst Simon, reported by Simon in "Revisionist History of the Jewish Catastrophe," *Judaism* 12,4 (summer 1963), 395.

179. TMW, 235–236.

180. Ibid., 237.

181. Ibid., 237–238; overall 236–240.

182. Ibid., 238.

183. Fackenheim's best formulation of the complex confrontation is on ibid., 238–240 and 247–250. Pages 238–250 are the core of the book.

184. Ibid., 14–30, especially 15, 19–20, 23–26.

185. Ibid., 239.

186. Ibid., 239.

187. Ibid., 239.

188. Ibid., 239. On p. 240 Fackenheim notes that this "pointing-by-thought-beyond-itself" is Schelling's motif in response to Hegel. It is exemplified in Kierkegaard's leap of faith and Marx's revolutionary action. The Holocaust poses a new problem and hence a new kind of pointing-beyond. It is the analogue of the absurdity that motivates Kierkegaard and the historical urgencies that motivate Marx. Here, at this precise moment in Fackenheim's thinking, our themes draw closest to Benjamin and the aphorism that is the epigraph of this book. Historical recovery involves seizing hold of a memory as it flashes up at a moment of danger.

189. Ibid., 240.

190. Ibid., 241.

191. Ibid., 241–244.

192. Ibid., 244.

193. Ibid., 247.

194. Ibid., 247.

195. Ibid., 248.

196. Ibid., 248.

197. Ibid., 249.

198. Ibid., 249.

199. Ibid., 249.

200. Ibid., 24–26.

201. Ibid., 24; see also 300.

202. Ibid., 25.

203. Ibid., 249.

204. Ibid., 249–250; 14–19 and 151–166, 256–259.

205. Ibid., 250.

206. See the essays in JRH, the selections in Morgan, *The Jewish Thought of Emil Fackenheim*, and later, *What Is Judaism?* (New York: Summit Books, 1987).

207. I am here interested in the basic strategy, not the application of it to philosophy, Christianity, and Judaism; see TMW, 262–313.

208. This is an expression that has become popular in Jewish circles during the past decades. It originates in the Talmud and is then appropriated in Kabbalistic literature. For clarification, see Gershom Scholem, *Major Trends in Jewish Mysticism* (New York: Schocken Books, 1941), and *On the Kabbalah and Its Symbolism* (New York: Schocken Books, 1969).

209. TMW, 261.

210. If Fackenheim succeeds, of course, he shows that within Judaism such a concept as this is present; he does not show that it is *only* available in Judaism, although I think that he challenges others to show how it is available elsewhere.

211. TMW, 252.

212. Ibid., 253–254.

213. Ibid., 254.

214. Ibid., 254.

215. Ibid., 262–313; see especially 266, 276–277, 280, 292–293, 299–301, 308–313.

216. Ibid., 256.

217. Ibid., 256–259.

218. Ibid., 257.

219. Ibid., 260–262.

220. Ibid., 257.

221. Ibid., 259.

222. Ibid., 6–8; see GPH, and *Quest for Past and Future*.

223. TMW, 2nd ed., xvi; *Quest for Past and Future*, 20, 303–305; GPH, 67–69, 72.

224. TMW, 6–9.

225. This would require studying his pre-1967 writings on the Buber-Rosenzweig conception, his book and articles on Hegel, the second chapter of GPH, the third chapter of TMW, and much else.

226. JRH, 31–32.

227. Ibid., 31.

228. Ibid., 31–32; GPH, 83–84.

229. TMW, 26.

230. GPH, 88.

231. See "Midrashic Existence After the Holocaust: Reflections Occasioned by the Work of Elie Wiesel," delivered as a lecture in September 1976; published in *Confronting*

the Holocaust: The Impact of Elie Wiesel, edited by Alvin H. Rosenfeld and Irving Green-berg (Bloomington: Indiana University Press, 1978); and reprinted in JRH, chapter 16, especially 263–267.

232. GPH, 88–89.

233. TMW, 300; 300–302.

234. Ibid., 308.

235. See ibid., 308, for the notion of an accidental remnant as a central feature of Jew-ish identity today.

236. Ibid., 309 and note.

237. Ibid., 310; see the whole of chapter 5, 317–331.

238. See ibid., 318, 320, 321.

239. Ibid., 324–325.

240. Ibid., 329–331.

241. So does *What Is Judaism?* chapter 14.

Chapter 11

1. This criticism manifested itself in different ways, e.g., in criticisms of the way the Holocaust was being promoted and fetishized in contemporary culture in "Holocaust kitsch." See the works of Friedlander, Novick, and Rosenfeld. This was noticed by intel-lectuals for different reasons and with different motives. Also, as time went on, criticism of the centrality of the Holocaust was often conducted by those also critical of right-wing politics in Israel, mistreatment of the Palestinians, and opposition to the peace process. The work of Marc Ellis and the Ruethers are examples.

2. See Fackenheim's own reflection on the widely quoted 614th commandment, *To Mend the World,* 2nd ed. (New York: Schocken Books, 1989), 299; see also xix ("subse-quently much quoted, but also misquoted, misunderstood and even distorted"). See Chaim I. Waxman, *America's Jews in Transition* (Philadelphia: Temple University Press, 1983), 121–123; Glazer, *American Judaism,* 2nd ed. (Chicago: University of Chicago Press, 1983), 184–186; Leonard Fein, *Where Are We?* (New York: Harper and Row, 1988), 69, 142.

3. *Response* 4,4 (winter 1970–1971) (hereafter *Response* symposium), 17–123. See my brief discussion in chapter 5.

4. *Response* symposium, 17.

5. Ibid., 17. Novak had known Fackenheim from Toronto. Later Novak conducted an interview with Fackenheim; see William Novak, "An Interview with Emil Facken-heim," *New Traditions* 3 (summer 1986), reprinted (in part) in *The Jewish Thought of Emil Fackenheim,* edited by Michael L. Morgan (Detroit: Wayne State University Press, 1987), 349–356.

6. *Response* symposium, 31–33; note his responses to liberals, the New Left, and so on.

7. For historical background on the havurot, see Stephen C. Lerner, "The Havurot," *Conservative Judaism* 24,3 (spring 1970), 2–15 (also in *Response* 4,3 (fall 1970), 15–28).

8. *Response* symposium, 41.

9. Ibid., 41.

10. Ibid., 42; see also Mintz, 103–104.

11. Ibid., 43.

12. Ibid., 43.

13. Waskow, *Response* symposium, 119–123.

14. See also Arthur Green's response to Rubenstein in *Conservative Judaism* 28,4 (summer 1974), 26–32.

15. On the situation of women in the civil rights movement and the rise of the new feminism, see Sara Evans, *Personal Politics* (New York: Random House, 1979).

16. See David G. Roskies, *Against the Apocalypse: Responses to Catastrophe in Modern Jewish Culture* (Cambridge: Harvard University Press, 1984); Alan Mintz, *Hurban: Responses to Catastrophe in Hebrew Literature* (New York: Columbia University Press, 1984).

17. For a response different from Green and others but also in the liberal spirit, see Eugene B. Borowitz, "Rethinking Our Holocaust Consciousness," *Judaism* 40,4 (fall 1991), 389–406. Although written much later, this rejection of post-Holocaust Jewish thought reflects the basic tendencies of Borowitz's thinking in the late sixties and early seventies.

18. For an excellent account of the relationship between Zionism and messianism, especially in Israeli Orthodox circles, with salient comments on the treatment of the Holocaust, see Aviezer Ravitsky, *Messianism, Zionism, and Jewish Religious Radicalism* (Chicago: University of Chicago Press, 1996), especially 63–66, 74–75, 126–128, 194–195.

19. "The Religious Meaning of the Six Day War: A Symposium," *Tradition* 10,1 (summer 1968) (hereafter *Tradition* symposium), 5–20.

20. Ibid., 6.

21. Ibid., 6–7.

22. Ibid., 7–8.

23. Ibid., 7; also 15–16.

24. Ibid., 12–13. See Fackenheim's eulogy to Peli, reprinted in *Jewish Philosophers and Jewish Philosophy,* edited by Michael L. Morgan (Bloomington: Indiana University Press, 1996).

25. For a clear account, see "Auschwitz," *Tradition* 17, 1 (fall 1977), 68–76: on revelation and a kind of Kierkegaardian faith.

26. *Tradition* symposium, 9–10.

27. Ibid., 13–14.

28. Michael Wyschogrod, "Some Theological Reflections on the Holocaust," *Response* 19,1 (spring 1975), 65–68.

29. Ibid., 67. Wyschogrod is not alone in confusing Fackenheim's 614th commandment. In a lecture delivered at the United States Holocaust Museum, Raul Hilberg called it the "366th commandment."

30. "Some Theological Reflections," 67; see also "Faith and the Holocaust," *Judaism* 20, 3 (summer 1971), 289.

31. "Some Theological Reflections," 67.

32. For these political implications, see the discussion following the *Tradition* symposium; also Michael Wyschogrod, "The Jewish Interest in Vietnam," *Tradition* 8,4 (winter 1966), 5–18; Charles S. Liebman, "Judaism and Vietnam: A Reply to Dr. Wyschogrod," *Tradition* 9, 1–2 (spring–summer 1967), 155–160; Wyschogrod, "Auschwitz," 76–78.

33. Michael Wyschogrod, "Faith and the Holocaust," *Judaism* 20,3 (Summer 1971), 286–294; review of Greenberg, "Auschwitz: Beginning of a New Era? Reflections on the Holocaust," *Tradition* 17,1 (fall 1977), 63–78.

34. I can, for example, omit discussion of Wyschogrod's gratuitous attack on his view of Fackenheim's treatment of Rubenstein, "Faith and the Holocaust," 287–288.

35. Ibid., 288–289.

36. Ibid., 290.

37. Ibid., 293–294.

38. Ibid., 291–293.

39. Ibid., 292, 293.

40. "Auschwitz," 69.

41. See Jacques Kornberg, "Zionism and Ideology: The Breira Controversy," *Judaism* 27,1 (winter 1978), 103–114, especially 105–109.

42. For one popular and representative example of this situation, see Thomas Friedman, *From Beirut to Jerusalem* (New York: Farrar, Straus and Giroux, 1989), not as an account of the situation as much as a reflection of the thinking the author goes through as he engages the issues in his personal way.

43. Harold Schulweis, "The New Jewish Right," *Moment* 1,1 (May/June 1975), 55–61.

44. Harold Schulweis, "The Holocaust Dybbuk," *Moment* 1,7 (February 1976), 34–41; "Debate: Ozick vs. Schulweis," *Moment* 1,10 (May/June 1976), 77–80.

45. "The New Jewish Right," 56. It should be clear that there is no necessary connection between post-Holocaust Jewish thought and political conservatism, but to some, in the seventies and thereafter, there has seemed to be such an alliance.

46. Ibid., 55–56.

47. Ibid., 56.

48. Ibid., 57. The Jews Schulweis is describing come from all economic classes. There is an excellent portrait of the middle-class variety in Jonathan Rieder, *Canarsie* (Cambridge: Harvard University Press, 1985).

49. "The Holocaust Dybbuk," 36–37.

50. Ibid., 40.

51. "Debate," 80.

52. Ibid., 77.

53. Many have been concerned with the trivialization and vulgarization of the Holocaust by the techniques of mass culture. See Saul Friedlander, *Reflections on Nazism: An Essay on Kitsch and Death* (New York: Harper and Row, 1984); Alvin H. Rosenfeld, *Imagining Hitler* (Bloomington: Indiana University Press, 1985), and "The Americanization of the Holocaust," *Commentary* 99,6 (June 1995), 35–40. The manipulation of the Holocaust as part of American Jewry's quest for identity and the role of competitive victimization in that quest are central themes of Peter Novick, *The Holocaust in American Life* (New York: Houghton Mifflin, 1999).

54. See, for example, *Sh'ma* 2,23 (December 31, 1971), 31–32 (a letter from Fackenheim); and the response by Steven S. Schwarzschild, *Sh'ma* 2,30 (April 7, 1972), 80: on *Commentary*; this led to a break with Borowitz as well. See also Schwarzschild, "On the Theology of Jewish Survival," *CCAR Journal* (October 1968), 2–21; reprinted in Schwarzschild, *The Pursuit of the Ideal* (Albany: SUNY Press, 1990), 83–98.

55. Fackenheim, "The Dangers of Name-Calling," *Sh'ma* 2,23 (December 31, 1971), 31–32.

56. For a broad view of the tension between liberal and ethnocentric Jewish interests, see Nathan Glazer, "The Crisis of American Jewry," *Midstream* 16,9 (November 1970), 3–11. There is excellent discussion of the historical rootedness of moral and ethical ideals in the work of Alasdair MacIntyre and Charles Taylor.

57. See, for example, Leonard Fein, *Where Are We?*; see also Fein, "Liberalism and American Jews," *Midstream* 19,8 (October 1973), 3–18; "Israel and the Universalist Ideal," *Midstream* 17,1 (January 1971). See also Michael Meyer, "Judaism after Auschwitz," (review of *God's Presence in History*), *Commentary*, 53,6 (June 1972), 55–62.

58. Jacob Neusner, "The Implications of the Holocaust," *Journal of Religion* 53,3 (1973), 293–308; see also its reprint and other essays in *Stranger at Home: "The Holocaust,"* *Zionism, and American Judaism* (Chicago: University of Chicago Press, 1981).

59. *Stranger at Home*, 5.

60. Ibid., 6; compare chapter 4.

61. Ibid., 7.

62. Ibid., 62–63.

63. Ibid., 66–67.

64. Ibid., 68–70.

65. Ibid., 70–77.

66. Ibid., 71.

67. Neusner refers to the 614th commandment as an "emotional claim" and as an "appeal—one can hardly dignify it as an 'argument'" (79). "The rest is either mere sentimentality or meretricious. It is an argument that cannot be examined, let alone criticized" (80).

68. Ibid., 74.

69. Ibid., 76.

70. Ibid., 80. See the whole page for Neusner's attack on the trivialization and vulgarization of the Holocaust.

71. Ibid., 81.

72. Neusner and Harold Schulweis were two of the earliest to write about and advocate Jewish fellowship in havurot, but there seems to be little connection between that dimension of their thinking and their opposition to the post-Holocaust thinkers.

73. The literature is vast, but for a good sample of issues, see Francois Furet (ed.), *Unanswered Questions* (Cambridge: Harvard University Press, 1989); see also Saul Friedlander (ed.), *Probing the Limits of Representation* (Cambridge: Harvard University Press, 1992).

74. See the works of Lawrence L. Langer; Rosenfeld, *A Double Dying* (Bloomington: Indiana University Press, 1980); Sidra Ezrahi, *By Words Alone* (Chicago: University of Chicago Press, 1980); James Young, *Writing and Rewriting the Holocaust* (Bloomington: Indiana University Press, 1988); also Friedlander, *Probing the Limits of Representation*.

Chapter 12

1. See James Longenbach, *Modernist Poetics of History* (Princeton: Princeton University Press, 1987).

2. Paul de Man, "Literary History and Literary Modernism," in *Blindness and Foresight*, 2nd ed. rev. (Minneapolis: University of Minnesota Press, 1983), 148.

3. Croce, *History: Its Theory and Practice* (New York: Russell and Russell, 1960), 12, quoted in Longenbach, *Modernist Poetics*, 27; compare 149.

4. Longenbach, *Modernist Poetics*, 31–44, 56–61.

5. Eliot, *The Sacred Wood* (London: Routledge, 1989), 49; quoted in Longenbach, *Modernist Poetics*, 62. One finds a similar strategy in Walter Benjamin's notion of dialectical images and the juxtaposition of present and past in an illuminating image; see Michael W. Jennings, *Dialectical Images: Walter Benjamin's Theory of Literary Criticism* (Ithaca: Cornell University Press, 1987), and especially Walter Benjamin's last fragments, "Theses on the Philosophy of History," in Benjamin, *Illuminations* (New York: Harcourt Brace and World, 1968), 255–266.

6. Longenbach, *Modernist Poetics*, 92; compare 94–95, 110–111.

7. "Tradition and the Individual Talent," in Frank Kermode (ed.), *Selected Prose of T. S. Eliot* (New York: Harcourt Brace Jovanovich, 1975), 38–39.

8. Quoted in Longenbach, *Modernist Poetics*, 200.

9. Longenbach, *Modernist Poetics,* 203, 204, 220, 226–237.

10. For a fascinating account of history and memory in postwar American popular culture, see George Lipsitz, *Time Passages: Collective Memory and American Popular Culture* (Minneapolis: University of Minnesota Press, 1990). The literature on memory has exploded.

11. See Andreas Huyssen, *After the Great Divide* (Bloomington: Indiana University Press, 1986), especially chapters 9–10.

12. Huyssen, *After the Great Divide*, 162; compare 188–195.

13. Ibid., 163–164, 165; compare 192–193.

14. Ibid., 165.

15. Ibid., 169; compare 185.

16. Ibid., 169.

17. See especially the work of Robert Alter, Susan Handelman, and David Stern, in addition of course to that of Gershom Scholem. See also Michael L. Morgan, *Interim Judaism* (Bloomington: Indiana University Press, 2001).

18. Huyssen, *After the Great Divide,* 171–172.

19. See James Tully, "Aboriginal Property and Western Theory," in *Property Rights*, edited by Ellen Frankel Paul, Fred D. Miller, Jr., and Jeffrey Paul (Cambridge, UK: Cambridge University Press, 1994), 153–180; Tully, *Strange Multiplicity* (Cambridge, UK: Cambridge University Press, 1995). Compare Huyssen, *After the Great Divide,* 194.

20. See Todd Gitlin, "Postmodernism: Roots and Politics," in *Cultural Politics in Contemporary America*, edited by Ian Argus and Suj Jhally (London: Routledge, 1989), 347–360.

21. Huyssen, *After the Great Divide,* 172, 174, 175; compare 185.

22. Lipsitz's discussion of the recovery of tradition in film, television, ritual, and the popular culture of native American and immigrant communities in inner cities underscores this point—and the dialectic between mass culture and technology and tradition. See Lipsitz, *Time Passages*.

23. This populism and pluralism, with its fear of oppression and its openness to the everyday, has influenced some responses to the Holocaust and Nazism. In his book *Foregone Conclusions* (Berkeley: University of California Press, 1994), Michael André Bernstein argues against the use of the Holocaust as part of a narrative that imposes constraints on reading and liberating the past. He opposes such "backshadowing" and favors what he calls "sideshadowing" and a "prosaics of the quotidian" in which the everyday is allowed to emerge in all its variety and richness. This leads him, at one point, to criticize Fackenheim's 614th commandment as a form of coercion and to challenge any attempt to generalize a set of principles for all responses to Nazi persecution (44). Bernstein is against privileging one standard not because he denies the importance of responding but rather, I think, because he wants to acknowledge the significance in a diversity of such responses.

Bernstein's challenge to Fackenheim is akin to the encounter between Saul Friedlander and Martin Broszat and their debate over the relativization or normalization of Nazism and German life under Nazism. In a certain sense, Fackenheim and Friedlander stand on the same side of the fence, although Bernstein's motives, unlike Brozsat's, are moral and normative and not simply academic. On the relativization debate and the role of Alltagsgeschichte, see, for example, Charles S. Maier, *The Unmasterable Past* (Cambridge: Harvard University Press, 1997).

24. Huyssen, *After the Great Divide*, 198: "the recuperation of buried and mutilated traditions."

25. Ibid., 196–199; compare Matei Calinescu, *Five Faces of Modernity* (Durham: Duke University Press, 1987), 276–277.

26. Gitlin, "Postmodernism," 353–354.

27. Compare ibid.; also Huyssen, *After the Great Divide*, 199–206, especially 219–221. See Gitlin, "Postmodernism," 348: "how to inhabit a drastically changed political space."

28. Huyssen, *After the Great Divide*, 213.

29. Ibid., 213; compare Gitlin, "Postmodernism," 357.

30. Huyssen, *After the Great Divide*, 216; compare Lipsitz, *Time Passages,* chapters 1–2.

31. Huyssen, *After the Great Divide.*

32. Compare Gitlin, "Postmodernism," 356–358.

33. Gitlin, "Postmodernism," 355; compare Calinescu, *Five Faces of Modernity,* 282–283.

34. Gitlin, "Postmodernism," 357, 358.

35. Ibid., 359.

36. See Todd Gitlin, *The Twilight of Common Dreams* (New York: Holt, 1995).

37. For Gitlin's account of the postwar period, the emergence of multiculturalism, and the need for a recovery of liberal values, see *The Twilight of Common Dreams*; for a similar set of themes, see also David Hollinger, *Postethnic America* (New York: Basic Books, 1995).

38. Lipsitz, *Time Passages,* 6.

39. Ibid., 12.

40. Ibid., 27; compare 22–28, 31, 36.

41. I have begun to sketch a strategy for Jewish self-understanding at the turn of the twenty-first century in *Interim Judaism*. There I try to show how Jewish thinking about objective principles, messianism and redemption, revelation, and politics has come to a point between a past of high theorizing and a future yet to be; Judaism at this moment should be pragmatic and provisional yet nonetheless committed and directive. It is a Judaism that takes seriously the lessons of post-Holocaust Jewish thought and post-Holocaust philosophy, as I have tried in part to expose those lessons in this book.

Abel, Lionel. "The Aesthetics of Evil: Hannah Arendt on Eichmann and the Jews." *Partisan Review* 30,2 (summer 1963), 210–230.

Alter, Robert. *After the Tradition*. New York: Dutton, 1971.

Altizer, Thomas J. J. *The Gospel of Christian Atheism*. Philadelphia, PA: The Westminster Press, 1966.

Altizer, Thomas J. J., and William Hamilton. *Radical Theology and the Death of God*. Indianapolis: Bobbs-Merrill, 1966.

Améry, Jean. *At the Mind's Limits: Contemplations by a Survivor on Auschwitz and Its Realities*. Bloomington: Indiana University Press, 1980.

Arendt, Hannah. *Between Past and Future*. Cleveland: Meridian Books, 1963.

———. "The Concentration Camps." *Partisan Review* 25,7 (July 1948), 743–763.

———. *Crises of the Republic*. New York: Harcourt Brace Jovanovich, 1972.

———. *Eichmann in Jerusalem: A Report on the Banality of Evil*. New York: Viking Press, 1963.

———. *The Human Condition*. Garden City, NY: Doubleday, 1959.

———. *The Jew as Pariah*. Edited by Ron H. Feldman. New York: Grove Press, 1978.

———. *Men in Dark Times*. New York: Harcourt, Brace and World, 1968.

———. *On Revolution*. Harmondsworth: Penguin Books, 1973; orig. 1963.

———. *On Violence*. New York: Harcourt, Brace and World, 1970.

———. *The Origins of Totalitarianism*. New York: Harcourt Brace & Company, 1979. Orig. 1950.

———. "Thinking and Moral Considerations: A Lecture." *Partisan Review* 38,3 (autumn 1971), 417–446.

———. "Understanding and Politics." *Partisan Review* 20,4 (July–August 1953), 377–392.

Arendt, Hannah, and Karl Jaspers. *Correspondence 1926–1969*. New York: Harcourt Brace, 1992.

Aschheim, Steven E. *Culture and Catastrophe: German and Jewish Confrontations with National Socialism and Other Crises* (New York: New York University Press, 1996).

———. *In Times of Crisis: Essays on European Culture, Germans, and Jews*. Madison, WI: The University of Wisconsin Press, 2001.

———. "Nazism, Culture and *The Origins of Totalitarianism*: Hannah Arendt and the Discourse of Evil." *New German Critique* 70 (winter 1997), 117–139.

Baldwin, Peter (ed.). *Reworking the Past: Hitler, the Holocaust, and the Historians' Debate*. Boston: Beacon Press, 1990.

Barnouw, Dagmar. *Visible Spaces: Hannah Arendt and the German-Jewish Experience*. Baltimore: Johns Hopkins University Press, 1990.

Bartov, Omer. *Mirrors of Destruction*. New York: Oxford University Press, 2000.

———. *Murder in Our Midst*. New York: Oxford University Press, 1996.

Bauer, Yehuda, and Nathan Rotenstreich (eds.). *The Holocaust as Historical Experience*. New York: Holmes and Meier, 1981.

Bell, Daniel. "The Alphabet of Justice: Reflections on 'Eichmann in Jerusalem.'" *Partisan Review* 30,3 (fall 1963), 417–429.

———. *The End of Ideology: On the Exhaustion of Political Ideas in the Fifties*. New York: Collier Books, 1961; orig. 1960.

Bell, Daniel (ed.). *The Radical Right*. New York: Doubleday, 1963; expanded version of *The New American Right*, 1955.

Bellah, Robert N. *Beyond Belief: Essays on Religion in a Post-Traditional World*. New York: Harper and Row, 1970.

Bellah, Robert, et al. *Habits of the Heart: Middle America Observed*. Berkeley: University of California Press, 1985.

Bender, Thomas. *New York Intellect*. New York: Knopf, 1987.

Benhabib, Seyla. *The Reluctant Modernism of Hannah Arendt*. London: Sage, 1996.

Berkovits, Eliezer. "Approaching the Holocaust." *Judaism* 22,1 (winter 1973), 18–20.

———. "Crisis and Faith." *Tradition* 14,4 (fall 1974), 5–19.

———. *Faith after the Holocaust*. New York: Ktav, 1973.

———. *God, Man and History*. New York: Jonathan David, 1959.

———. *Major Themes in Modern Philosophies of Judaism*. New York: Ktav, 1974.

———. *Man and God: Studies in Biblical Theology*. Detroit: Wayne State University Press, 1969.

———. *Not in Heaven: The Nature and Function of Halakha*. New York: Ktav, 1983.

———. "Rewriting the History of the Holocaust." *Sh'ma* 10/198 (October 3, 1980), 139–142.

———. *With God in Hell: Judaism in the Ghettos and Deathcamps*. New York: Sanhedrin Press, 1979.

Berman, Ronald. *America in the Sixties: An Intellectual History*. New York: Harper and Row, 1968.

Bernstein, Richard J. *Hannah Arendt and the Jewish Question*. Cambridge: MIT Press, 1996.

Bloom, Alexander. *Prodigal Sons: The New York Intellectuals and Their World*. New York: Oxford University Press, 1986.

Borowitz, Eugene B. "Emil Fackenheim as Lurianic Philosopher." *Sh'ma* 13, 254 (May 13, 1983), 109–111.

———. "Existentialism's Meaning for Judaism." *Commentary* 28,5 (November 1959), 414–420.

———. "God-Is-Dead Theology." In *The Meaning of the Death of God*, edited by Bernard Murchland. New York: Vintage Books, 1967, 92–107.

———. "Hope Jewish and Hope Secular." *Judaism* 17,2 (spring 1968), 131–147.

———. *How Can a Jew Speak of Faith Today?* Philadelphia: Westminster Press, 1969.

———. *The Mask Jews Wear: The Self-Deceptions of American Jewry*. New York: Simon and Schuster, 1973.

———. *A New Jewish Theology in the Making*. Philadelphia: Westminster Press, 1968.

———. "Theological Conference: Cincinnati, 1950: Reform Judaism's Fresh Awareness of Religious Problems." *Commentary* 9,6 (June 1950), 567–572.

Boyer, Paul. *By the Bomb's Early Light: American Thought and Culture at the Dawn of the Atomic Age*. New York: Pantheon Books, 1985.

Breines, Wini. *Community and Organization in the New Left, 1962–1968: The Great Refusal*. New Brunswick: Rutgers University Press, 1989; orig. 1982.

Brocke, Michael, Herbert Jochum (HG.). *Wolkensaule und Feuerschein*. Munich: Kaiser, 1982.

Brown, James. *Kierkegaard, Heidegger, Buber and Barth*. New York: Collier Books, 1955.

Browning, Christopher R. "The Decision Concerning the Final Solution." In *The Path to Genocide*, 96–118.

———. *Fateful Months: Essays on the Emergence of the Final Solution*. New York: Holmes and Meier, 1985.

———. *Ordinary Men: Reserve Police Battalion 101 and the Final Solution in Poland*. New York: HarperCollins, 1992.

———. *The Path to Genocide: Essays on Launching the Final Solution*. Cambridge, UK: Cambridge University Press, 1992.

Capps, Walter H. (ed.). *The Future of Hope*. Philadelphia: Fortress Press, 1970.

Cargas, Harry James (ed.). *Responses to Elie Wiesel*. New York: Persea Books, 1978.

Carson, Clayborne. *In Struggle: SNCC and the Black Awakening of the 1960s*. Cambridge: Harvard University Press, 1981.

Chafe, William H. *The Unfinished Journey: America since World War II*. 2nd ed. New York: Oxford University Press, 1991; orig. 1986.

Christian, C. W., and Glenn R. Wittig (eds.). *Radical Theology: Phase Two, Essays on the Current Debate*. Philadelphia: Lippincott, 1967.

Cohen, Arthur A. Commentary on Richard L. Rubenstein, "Homeland and Holocaust." In *The Religious Situation: 1968*, edited by Donald R. Cutler. Boston: Beacon Press, 1968, 87–91.

———. "In Our Terrible Age: The *Tremendum* of the Jews." In *The Holocaust as Interruption*, edited by Elisabeth Schlusser Fiorenza and David Tracy. Edinburgh: T. and T. Clark, 1984, 11–16.

———. *The Natural and the Supernatural Jew*. New York: McGraw-Hill, 1962.

———. "On Theological Method: A Response on Behalf of *The Tremendum*." *Journal of Reform Judaism* 31,2 (spring 1984), 56–65.

———. *The Tremendum: A Theological Interpretation of the Holocaust*. New York: Crossroad, 1981.

Cohen, Arthur A. (ed.). *Arguments and Doctrines: A Reader of Jewish Thinking in the Aftermath of the Holocaust*. New York: Harper and Row, 1970.

Cohen, Arthur A., and Paul Mendes-Flohr (eds.). *Contemporary Jewish Religious Thought*. New York: Scribner's, 1987.

Cohen, Steven. *American Assimilation and Jewish Revival*. Bloomington: Indiana University Press, 1988.

———. *American Modernity and Jewish Identity*. New York: Tavistock, 1983.

Coser, Lewis A., and Irving Howe (eds.). *The New Conservatives: A Critique from the Left*. Rev. ed. New York: New American Library, 1976.

Cutler, Donald R. (ed.). *The Religious Situation: 1968*. Boston: Beacon Press, 1968.

———. (ed.). *The Religious Situation: 1969*. Boston: Beacon Press, 1969.

Dalin, David G.(ed.). *From Marxism to Judaism: Collected Essays of Will Herberg*. New York: Markus Wiener, 1989.

Davis, Moshe (ed.). *World Jewry and the State of Israel*. New York: Arno Press, 1977.

Dawidowicz, Lucy. "American Public Opinion." *American Jewish Yearbook* 69 (1968), 198–229.

D'Entreves, Maurizio Passerin. *The Political Philosophy of Hannah Arendt*. London: Routledge, 1994.

Des Pres, Terrence. *The Survivor: An Anatomy of Life in the Death Camps*. New York: Oxford University Press, 1976.

Dickstein, Morris. *Gates of Eden: American Culture in the Sixties*. Harmondsworth: Penguin Books, 1989; orig. 1977.

Diggins, John Patrick. *The Proud Decades: America in War and Peace, 1941–1960*. New York: Norton, 1989.

Dorff, Elliot. "A Response to Richard Rubenstein." *Conservative Judaism* 28,4 (summer 1974), 33–36.

Edelheit, Joseph A. (ed.). *The Life of Covenant: The Challenge of Contemporary Judaism*. Chicago: Spertus College of Judaica Press, 1986.

Eisen, Arnold M. *The Chosen People in America: A Study in Jewish Religious Ideology*. Bloomington: Indiana University Press, 1983.

———. *Galut: Modern Jewish Reflection on Homelessness and Homecoming*. Bloomington: Indiana University Press, 1986.

———. "Jewish Theology in North America: Notes on Two Decades." *American Jewish Year Book* 91 (1991), 3–33.

Eisenstein, Ira. Review of Richard L. Rubenstein, *The Religious Imagination*. *Reconstructionist* (May 23, 1969), 9–11.

Elazar, Daniel J. *Community and Polity: The Organizational Dynamics of American Jewry*. Philadelphia: Jewish Publication Society, 1976.

———. "The Rediscovered Polity: Selections from the Literature of Jewish Public Affairs, 1967–1968." *American Jewish Yearbook* 70 (1969), 172–237.

Ellenson, David. "The Continued Renewal of North American Jewish Theology: Some Recent Works." *Journal of Reform Judaism* 39,1 (winter 1991), 1–16.

———. "Emil Fackenheim and the Revealed Morality of Judaism." *Judaism* 25,4 (fall 1976), 402–413.

Ellis, Marc H. *Beyond Innocence and Redemption: Confronting the Holocaust and Israeli Power*. New York: Harper and Row, 1990.

———. *Toward a Jewish Theology of Liberation*. Maryknoll, NY: Orbis Books, 1987.

Evans, Sara. *Personal Politics: The Roots of Women's Liberation in the Civil Rights Movement and the New Left*. New York: Random House, 1979.

Ezrahi, Sidra DeKoven. *By Words Alone: The Holocaust in Literature*. Chicago: University of Chicago Press, 1980.

Fackenheim, Emil L. "The Commandment to Hope: A Response to Contemporary Jewish Experience." In *The Future of Hope*, edited by Walter H. Capps. Philadelphia: Fortress Press, 1970, 68–91.

———. "Concerning Authentic and Unauthentic Responses to the Holocaust." *Holocaust and Genocide Studies* 1,1 (1986), 101–120.

———. "The Dangers of Name-Calling." *Sh'ma* 2,23 (December 31, 1971), 31–32.

———. *Encounters between Judaism and Modern Philosophy*. New York: Basic Books, 1973.

———. *God's Presence in History: Jewish Affirmations and Philosophical Reflections*. New York: New York University Press, 1970.

———. "Idolatry as a Modern Religious Possibility." In *The Religious Situation: 1968*, edited by Donald R. Cutler. Boston: Beacon Press, 1968, 254–287.

———. "Jewish Optimism and the Twentieth Century." *Reconstructionist* 19,10 (June 26, 1953), 22–25.

———. *The Jewish Return into History*. New York: Schocken Books, 1978.

———. Letter to the Editor. *Conservative Judaism* 16,1 (fall 1961), 59–60.

———. *Metaphysics and Historicity*. Milwaukee: Marquette University Press, 1961.

———. "On the Eclipse of God," *Commentary* 37 (June 1984), 55–67; reprinted in *Quest for Past and Future*, Ch. 15 and in *The Jewish Thought of Emil Fackenheim*, Ch. 9.

———. *Quest for Past and Future*. Bloomington: Indiana University Press, 1968.

———. *The Religious Dimension in Hegel's Thought*. Bloomington: Indiana University Press, 1967.

———. Review of Abraham Joshua Heschel, *God In Search of Man. Conservative Judaism* 15,1 (fall 1960), 50–53.

———. Review of Nahum N. Glatzer, *Franz Rosenzweig: His Life and Thought. Judaism* 2,4 (October 1953), 367–372.

———. Review of Will Herberg, *Judaism and Modern Man: An Interpretation of Jewish Religion." Judaism* 1,2 (April 1952), 172–175.

———. "Some Recent 'Rationalistic' Reactions to the 'New Jewish Theology.'" *CCAR Journal* 26 (June 1959), 42–48.

———. *To Mend the World*. 3rd ed. Bloomington: Indiana University Press, 1994.

———. *What Is Judaism?* New York: Summit Books, 1987.

Fein, Leonard J. "Liberalism and American Jews." *Midstream* 19,8 (October 1973), 3–18.

———. *Where Are We? The Inner Life of America's Jews*. New York: Harper and Row, 1988.

Fiorenza, Elisabeth Schussler, and David Tracy (eds.). *The Holocaust as Interruption*. Edinburgh: T. and T. Clark, 1984.

Flacks, Richard. *Making History: The American Left and the American Mind*. New York: Columbia University Press, 1988.

Fleischner, Eva (ed.). *Auschwitz: Beginning of a New Era?* New York: Ktav, 1977.

Fleming, Gerald. *Hitler and the Final Solution*. Berkeley: University of California Press, 1984; orig. 1982 in German.

Fox, Marvin. "Berkovits' Treatment of the Problem of Evil." *Tradition* 14,3 (spring 1974), 116–124.

———. "Naturalism, Rationalism and Jewish Faith." *Tradition* 11,1 (fall 1970), 90–96.

Frei, Hans W. "Niebuhr's Theological Background." In *Faith and Ethics: The Theology of H. Richard Niebuhr*, edited by Paul Ramsey. New York: Harper and Brothers, 1957, 9–64.

Friedlander, Albert H. "The Arendt Report on Eichmann and the Jewish Community: An Evaluation." *CCAR Journal* 11,3 (October 1963), 47–55.

Friedlander, Saul. "From Anti-Semitism to Extermination." In Furet *Unanswered Questions*, 3–32.

———. *Memory, History, and the Extermination of the Jews of Europe*. Bloomington: Indiana University Press, 1993.

———. *Reflections of Nazism: An Essay on Kitsch and Death*. New York: Harper and Row, 1984.

Friedlander, Saul (ed.). *Probing the Limits of Representation: Nazism and the "Final Solution."* Cambridge: Harvard University Press, 1992.

Funkenstein, Amos. "Theological Interpretations of the Holocaust." In *Unanswered Questions*, edited by Francois Furet. New York: Schocken Books, 1989, 275–303.

Furet, Francois (ed.). *Unanswered Questions: Nazi Germany and the Genocide of the Jews*. New York: Schocken Books, 1989.

Gershman, Carl. "Israel: The New Left Is Not the Enemy." *Sh'ma* 1,18 (October 22, 1971), 137–139.

Gilbert, James. *Another Chance: Postwar America, 1945–1985*. 2nd ed. Chicago: Dorsey Press, 1986.

Gitlin, Todd. "Postmodernism: Roots and Politics." In *Cultural Politics in Contemporary America*, edited by Ian Angus and Sut Jhally. London: Routledge, 1989, 347–360.

———. *The Sixties: Years of Hope, Days of Rage*. New York: Bantam Books, 1987.

———. *The Twilight of Common Dreams*. New York: Holt, 1995.

Glanz, David. "The Holocaust as a Question." *Worldview* (September 1974), 36–38.

Glazer, Nathan. *American Judaism*. 2nd ed. Chicago: University of Chicago Press, 1989; orig. 1972; 1st ed., 1957.

———. "Blacks, Jews and the Intellectuals." *Commentary* 47,4 (April 1969), 33–39.

———. "The Crisis of American Jewry." *Midstream* 16,9 (November 1970), 3–11.

———. *Ethnic Dilemmas 1964–1982*. Cambridge: Harvard University Press, 1983.

———. "Jewish Interests and the New Left." *Midstream* 27,1 (January 1971), 32–37.

———. "The Jewish Revival in America." Part I. *Commentary* 20,6 (December 1955), 493–499. Part II. *Commentary* 21,1 (January 1956), 17–24.

———. *Remembering the Answers: Essays on the American Student Revolt*. New York: Basic Books, 1970.

Goldscheider, Calvin. *Jewish Community and Change: Emerging Patterns in America*. Bloomington: Indiana University Press, 1986.

Goldy, Robert G. *The Emergence of Jewish Theology in America*. Bloomington: Indiana University Press, 1990.

Gordis, Robert. "Some Observations on Jewish Existentialism." *Conservative Judaism* 11,3 (spring 1957), 8–17.

Graubart, Judah L. "Perspectives of the Holocaust." *Midstream* 19,9 (November 1973), 53–64.

Green, Arthur E. "A Response to Richard Rubenstein." *Conservative Judaism* 28,4 (summer 1974), 26–32.

Greenberg, Irving. "Adventure in Freedom—Or Escape from Freedom? Jewish Identity in America." *American Jewish Historical Quarterly* 55,1 (September 1965), 5–21.

———. "Change and the Orthodox Community." *Response* 7,1 (spring 1969), 14–21.

———. "Cloud of Smoke, Pillar of Fire: Judaism, Christianity, and Modernity after the Holocaust." In *Auschwitz: Beginning of a New Era?* edited by Eva Fleischner. New York: Ktav, 1977, 7–55, 441–446.

———. Commentary on Rubenstein, "Homeland and Holocaust." In *The Religious Situation: 1968*, edited by Donald R. Cutler. Boston: Beacon Press, 1968, 91–102.

———. "The Cultural Revolution and Religious Unity." *Religious Education* 62,2 (March–April 1967), 98–103, 224.

———. "The End of Emancipation." *Conservative Judaism* 30,4 (summer 1976), 47–63.

———. "Jewish Values and the Changing American Ethic." *Tradition* 10,1 (summer 1968), 42–74.

———. *The Jewish Way: Living the Holidays*. New York: Summit Books, 1988.

———. "Judaism and Christianity after the Holocaust." *Journal of Ecumenical Studies* 12,4 (fall 1975), 521–551.

———. "Religious Values after the Holocaust: A Jewish View." In *Judaism and Christianity after the Holocaust*, edited by Abraham Peck. Philadelphia: Fortress Press, 1982, 63–86.

————. "Voluntary Covenant." In *Perspectives*. National Jewish Resource Center, 1982, 1–36.

————. "Will There Be One Jewish People by the Year 2000?" *CLAL Perspectives* (1985), 1–8.

Greenspan, Louis, and Graeme Nicholson (ed.). *Fackenheim: German Philosophy and Jewish Thought*. Toronto: University of Toronto Press, 1992.

Gross, John. "Arendt on Eichmann." *Encounter* 21 (November 1963), 65–74.

Gutting, Gary (ed.). *Paradigms and Revolutions: Applications and Appraisals of Thomas Kuhn's Philosophy of Science*. Notre Dame: University of Notre Dame Press, 1980.

Habermas, Jurgen. *The New Conservatism: Cultural Criticism and the Historians' Debate*. Cambridge: MIT Press, 1989.

Halberstam, David. *The Fifties*. New York: Ballantine Books, 1993.

Halpern, Ben. "The Ethnic Revolt." *Midstream* 27,1 (January 1971), 3–16.

————. "The Jewish Liberal." *Midstream* 16, 10 (December 1970), 32–49.

Hamon, Ben. "The Reform Rabbis Debate Theology: A Report on the 1963 Meeting of the CCAR." *Judaism* 12,4 (fall 1963), 479–486.

Handelman, Susan. *Fragments of Redemption*. Bloomington, IN: Indiana University Press, 1991.

Hartman, Geoffrey (ed.). *Bitburg in Moral and Political Perspective*. Bloomington: Indiana University Press, 1986.

Hayes, Peter (ed.). *Lessons and Legacies: The Meaning of the Holocaust in a Changing World*. Evanston, IL: Northwestern University Press, 1991.

Herberg, Will. "Jewish Existence and Survival: A Theological View." *Judaism* 1,1 (January 1952), 19–26.

————. *Judaism and Modern Man: An Interpretation of Jewish Religion*. New York: Meridian Books, 1951.

Heschel, Abraham Joshua. *God in Search of Man*. New York: Meridian Books, 1959.

————. *Israel: An Echo of Eternity*. New York: Farrar, Straus and Giroux, 1969.

————. *Man Is Not Alone*. New York: Harper and Row, 1951.

Hill, Melvyn A. (ed.). *Hannah Arendt: The Recovery of the Public World*. New York: St. Martin's Press, 1979.

Himmelfarb, Milton. Commentary on Richard L. Rubenstein, "Homeland and Holocaust." In *The Religious Situation: 1968*, edited by Donald R. Cutler. Boston: Beacon Press, 1968, 64–79.

Hodgson, Godfrey. *America in Our Time*. New York: Vintage Books, 1976.

Hollinger, David. *Postethnic America*. New York: Basic Books, 1995.

Howe, Irving. "The New York Intellectuals." In *Decline of the New*. New York: Harcourt, Brace and World, 1970, 211–265.

Huyssen, Andreas. *After the Great Divide: Modernism, Mass Culture, Postmodernism*. Bloomington: Indiana University Press, 1986.

————. *Twilight Memories: Marking Time in a Culture of Amnesia*. London: Routledge, 1995.

Isaac, Jeffrey C. *Arendt, Camus, and Modern Rebellion*. New Haven: Yale University Press, 1992.

Jacobs, Paul, and Saul Landau. *The New Radicals*. New York: Vintage Books, 1966.

Jay, Martin. "Force Fields, Songs of Experience: Reflections on the Debate over *Alltagsgeschichte*." *Salmagundi* 81 (winter 1989), 29–41.

Jens, Inge (ed.). *At the Heart of the White Rose: Letters and Diaries of Hans and Sophie Scholl*. New York: Harper and Row, 1987.

Jonas, Hans. "The Concept of God after Auschwitz: A Jewish Voice." *Journal of Religion* (January 1987), 1–13; originally 1961.

Kaes, Anton. *From Hitler to Heimat: The Return of History as Film*. Cambridge: Harvard University Press, 1989.

Kaplan, Lawrence. "Rabbi Isaac Hutner's 'Daat Torah Perspective' on the Holocaust: A Critical Analysis." *Tradition* 18,3 (fall 1980), 235–248.

Karff, Samuel E. "Jewish Peoplehood—A Signal of Transcendence." In *New Theology No. 9: Theology and the New Particularisms*, edited by Martin E. Marty and Dean G. Peerman. New York: Macmillan, 1972, 59–69.

Kateb, George. *Hannah Arendt: Politics, Conscience, Evil*. Totowa, NJ: Rowman and Allanheld, 1983.

Katz, Steven T. *Historicism, the Holocaust, and Zionism*. New York: New York University Press, 1992.

———. *Post-Holocaust Dialogues*. New York: New York University Press, 1983.

Katz, Steven T. (ed.). *Interpreters of Judaism in the Late Twentieth Century*. Washington: B'nai B'rith Books, 1993.

Kaufman, Jonathan. *Broken Alliance*. New York: Simon and Schuster, 1988; 1995.

Kazin, Alfred. *New York Jew*. New York: Knopf, 1978.

———. *Starting Out in the Thirties*. Boston: Little, Brown, 1965.

Kornberg, Jacques. "Zionism and Ideology: The Breira Controversy." *Judaism* 27,1 (winter 1978), 103–114.

Kristol, Irving. *Reflections of a Neoconservative*. New York: Basic Books, 1983.

LaCapra, Dominick. *Representing the Holocaust: History, Theory, Trauma*. Ithaca, NY: Cornell University Press, 1994.

Lacoue-Labarthe, Philippe. *Heidegger, Art and Politics*. Oxford: Blackwell, 1990.

Lamm, Norman. "Israel: Are There No Limits to Jewishness?" *Sh'ma* 1,18 (October 22, 1971), 139–140.

Lang, Berel. *Act and Idea in the Nazi Genocide*. Chicago: University of Chicago Press, 1990.

———. "Heidegger and the Jewish Question." Unpublished manuscript.

———. *Writing and the Moral Self*. New York: Routledge, 1991.

Lang, Berel (ed.). *Philosophy and the Holocaust. Philosophical Forum* 16, 1–2 (fall–winter 1984–85).

———. *Writing and the Holocaust*. New York: Holmes and Meier, 1988.

Langer, Lawrence L. *Admitting the Holocaust*. New York: Oxford University Press, 1995.

———. *The Holocaust and the Literary Imagination*. New Haven: Yale University Press, 1975.

———. *Holocaust Testimonies*. New Haven, CT: Yale University Press, 1991.

———. *Preempting the Holocaust*. New Haven, CT: Yale University Press, 1998.

———. *Versions of Survival: The Holocaust and the Human Spirit*. Albany: SUNY Press, 1982.

Lanzmann, Claude. *Shoah: An Oral History of the Holocaust*. New York: Pantheon Books, 1985.

Lasch, Christopher. *The Culture of Narcissism: American Life in an Age of Diminishing Expectations*. New York: Norton, 1979.

Lerner, Michael. *Jewish Renewal*. New York: Putnam, 1994.

Lerner, Stephen C. "The Havurot." *Conservative Judaism* 24,3 (spring 1970), 2–25; reprinted in *Response* 4,3 (fall 1970), 15–28, with comments by Jacob Neusner and Robert Goldman.

———. "Ramah and Its Critics." *Conservative Judaism* 25,4 (summer 1971), 1–28.

Levi, Primo. *The Drowned and the Saved*. New York: Summit Books, 1988.

———. *Moments of Reprieve*. New York: Penguin Books, 1987.

———. *The Periodic Table*. New York: Schocken Books, 1984.

———. *The Reawakening*. New York: Collier Books, 1965.

———. *Survival in Auschwitz*. New York: Collier Books, 1961.

Levkov, Ilya (ed.). *Bitburg and Beyond: Encounters in American, German and Jewish History*. New York: Shapolsky Books, 1987.

Lipsitz, George. *Class and Culture in Cold War America*. South Hadley, MA: Bergin, 1982.

———. *Time Passages: Collective Memory and American Popular Culture*. Minneapolis: University of Minnesota Press, 1990.

Madison, G. B. *The Hermeneutics of Postmodernity*. Bloomington: Indiana University Press, 1988.

Marrus, Michael R. *The Holocaust in History*. Hanover, NH: University Press of New England, 1987.

Martin, Bernard. "Reform Jewish Theology Today." In *Contemporary Reform Jewish Thought*, edited by Bernard Martin. Chicago: Quadrangle Books, 1968, 180–214.

Martin, Bernard (ed.). *Contemporary Reform Jewish Thought*. Chicago: Quadrangle Books, 1968.

Marty, Martin E., and Dean G. Peerman (eds.). *New Theology No. 6: On Revolution and Non-Revolution, Violence and Non-Violence, Peace and Power*. New York: Macmillan, 1969.

———. *New Theology No. 8: On the Cultural Revolution*. New York: Macmillan, 1971.

———. *New Theology No. 9: Theology in the Context of the New Particularisms*. New York: Macmillan, 1972.

Matusow, Allen J. *The Unraveling of America: A History of Liberalism in the 1960s*. New York: Harper and Row, 1984.

May, Elaine Tyler. "Cold War—Warm Hearth: Politics and the Family in Postwar America." In *The Rise and Fall of the New Deal Order*, edited by Steve Fraser and Gary Gerstle. Princeton: Princeton University Press, 1989, 153–181.

———. *Homeward Bound: American Families in the Cold War Era*. New York: Basic Books, 1988.

Mayer, Arno J. *Why Did the Heavens Not Darken? The "Final Solution" in History*. New York: Pantheon Books, 1988.

Metz, Johann Baptist. "Christians and Jews after Auschwitz." In *The Emergent Church: The Future of Christianity in a Postbourgeois World*. New York: Crossroad, 1981.

Meyer, Michael A. "Judaism after Auschwitz." *Commentary* 53,6 (June 1972), 55–62.

Mintz, Alan. *Hurban: Responses to Catastrophe in Hebrew Literature*. New York: Columbia University Press, 1984.

Morgan, Michael L. "The Central Problem of Fackenheim's *To Mend the World*," *Journal of Jewish Thought and Philosophy* 5 (1996), 297–312.

———. *Dilemmas in Modern Jewish Thought*. Bloomington: Indiana University Press, 1992.

———. *Interim Judaism*. Bloomington, IN: Indiana University Press, 2001.

———. "Reflections on Contemporary Jewish Thought." *CCAR Journal* 40,4 (fall 1993), 33–49.

Morgan, Michael L. (ed.) *Emil Fackenheim: Jewish Philosophers and Jewish Philosophy*. Bloomington, IN: Indiana University Press, 1996.

———. *The Jewish Thought of Emil Fackenheim*. Detroit: Wayne State University Press, 1987.

Murchland, Bernard (ed.). *The Meaning of the Death of God*. New York: Vintage Books, 1967.

Neusner, Jacob. "The Implications of the Holocaust." *Journal of Religion* 53,3 (July 1973), 293–308.

———. *Stranger at Home: "The Holocaust," Zionism, and American Judaism*. Chicago: University of Chicago Press, 1981.

Novak, Bill. "The Havurah in New York City: Some Notes on the First Year." *Response* IV,3 (fall 1970), 11–14.

———. "The Making of a Jewish Counter Culture." *Response* 4, 1–2 (spring–summer 1970), 5–10.

———. "The Response Symposium." *Response* 4,4 (winter 1970–71), 17–123.

Novak, Bill, and Robert Goldman. "The Rise of the Jewish Student Press." *Conservative Judaism* 25,2 (winter 1971), 5–19.

Novak, Michael. *The Rise of theUnmeltable Ethnics*. New York: Macmillan, 1971.

Novick, Peter. *The Holocaust in American Life*. New York: Houghton Mifflin Co., 1999.

Ozick, Cynthia, and Harold Schulweis. "The Holocaust Dybbuk Debate." *Moment* 1,10 (May/June 1976), 77–80.

Pells, Richard H. *The Liberal Mind in a Conservative Age: American Intellectuals in the 1940s and 1950s*. New York: Harper and Row, 1985.

Petuchowski, Jakob J. *Ever since Sinai: A Modern View of Torah*. New York: Scribe, 1961.

———. *Heirs of the Pharisees*. New York: Basic Books, 1970.

Podhoretz, Norman. "Hannah Arendt on Eichmann: A Study in the Perversity of Brilliance." *Commentary* 36,3 (September 1963), 201–208.

———. *Making It*. New York: Random House, 1967.

Podhoretz, Norman (ed.). *A Commentary Reader*. New York: Atheneum, 1966.

Polenberg, Richard. *One Nation Divisible: Class, Race, and Ethnicity in the United States since 1938*. New York: Viking Press, 1980.

Porter, Jack Nusan, and Peter Dreier (eds.). *Jewish Radicalism*. New York: Grove Press, 1973.

Prell, Riv-Ellen. *Prayer and Community: The Havurah in American Judaism*. Detroit: Wayne State University Press, 1989.

Raab, Earl. "The Black Revolution and the Jewish Question." *Commentary* 47,1 (January 1969), 23–33.

Reisman, Bernard. *The Chavurah: A Contemporary Jewish Experience*. New York: Union of American Hebrew Congregations, 1977.

"Religion and the Intellectuals." *Partisan Review* 17,2 (February 1950), 103–142; 17,3 (March 1950), 215–256; 17,4 (April 1950), 313–339; 17,5 (May–June 1950), 456–483.

"The Religious Meaning of the Six Day War: A Symposium." *Tradition* 10,1 (summer 1968), 5–20; participants: Shear Yashuv Cohen, Norman Lamm, Pinchas Peli, Michael Wyschogrod, Walter S. Wurzburger.

Rieder, Jonathan. *Canarsie: The Jews and Italians of Brooklyn against Liberalism*. Cambridge: Harvard University Press, 1985.

———. "The Rise of the 'Silent Majority.'" In *The Rise and Fall of the New Deal Order*, edited by Steve Fraser and Gary Gerstle. Princeton: Princeton University Press, 1989, 243–268.

Rieff, Philip. "The Theology of Politics: Reflections on Totalitarianism as the Burden of Our Time." *Journal of Religion* 32 (1952), 119–126.

Rosenbaum, Irving J. *The Holocaust and Halakhah*. New York: Ktav, 1976.

Rosenberg, Alan, and Gerald E. Myers (eds.). *Echoes from the Holocaust: Philosophical Reflections on a Dark Time*. Philadelphia: Temple University Press, 1988.

Rosenberg, Harold. *Discovering the Present*. Chicago: University of Chicago Press, 1973.

———. "The Trial and Eichmann." *Commentary* 32,5 (November 1961), 369–381.

Rosenfeld, Alvin H. *A Double Dying: Reflections on Holocaust Literature*. Bloomington: Indiana University Press, 1980.

———. *Imagining Hitler*. Bloomington: Indiana University Press, 1985.

Rosenfeld, Alvin, and Irving Greenberg (eds.). *Confronting the Holocaust: The Impact of Elie Wiesel*. Bloomington: Indiana University Press, 1978.

Roskies, David G. *Against the Apocalypse: Responses to Catastrophe in Modern Jewish Culture*. Cambridge: Harvard University Press, 1984.

Rubenstein, Richard. *After Auschwitz*. 1st ed. Indianapolis: Bobbs-Merrill, 1966; 2nd ed. Baltimore: The Johns Hopkins University Press, 1992.

———. *The Age of Triage*. Boston: Beacon Press, 1983.

———. *The Cunning of History: The Holocaust and the American Future*. New York: Harper and Row, 1978.

———. "Homeland and Holocaust: Issues in the Jewish Religious Situation." In *The Religious Situation: 1968*, edited by Donald R. Cutler. Boston: Beacon Press, 1968, 39–64; 102–111.

———. "Jewish Theology and the Current World Situation." *Conservative Judaism* 28,4 (summer 1974), 3–25.

———. "Job and Auschwitz." In *New Theology No. 8: On the Cultural Revolution*, edited by Martin E. Marty and Dean G. Peerman. New York: Macmillan, 1971, 270–290.

———. *Morality and Eros*. New York: McGraw-Hill, 1970.

———. "Naming the Unnameable; Thinking the Unthinkable: A Review Essay of Arthur Cohen's *The Tremendum*." *Journal of Reform Judaism* 32,2 (spring 1984), 43–55

———. *Power Struggle*. New York: Scribner's, 1974.

———. "A Rabbi Visits Germany." *Reconstructionist* 27,1 (February 24, 1961), 6–13.

———. "Some Perspectives on Religious Faith after Auschwitz." In *The German Church Struggle and the Holocaust*, edited by Franklin H. Littell and Hubert G. Locke. Detroit: Wayne State University Press, 1974, 250–260.

———. "The 'Supernatural' Jew." *Reconstructionist* 29,6 (May 3, 1963), 13–20.

Rubenstein, Richard L., and John K. Roth. *Approaches to Auschwitz: The Holocaust and Its Legacy*. Atlanta: John Knox Press, 1987.

Ruether, Rosemary Radford. "The *Faith and Fratricide* Discussion: Old Problems and New Dimensions." In *Anti-Semitism and the Foundations of Christianity*, edited by Alan T. Davies. New York: Paulist Press, 1979.

Sacks, Jonathan. *Crisis and Covenant*. Manchester: Manchester University Press, 1992.

Santner, Eric L. *Stranded Objects: Mourning, Memory, and Film in Postwar Germany*. Ithaca, NY: Cornell University Press, 1990.

Sartre, Jean Paul. *Anti-Semite and Jew*. New York: Schocken Books, 1948.

Schachter, Zalman M. Commentary on Rubenstein, "Homeland and Holocaust." In *The Religious Situation: 1968*, edited by Donald L. Cutler. Boston: Beacon Press, 1968, 79–86.

Schulwies, Harold. "The Holocaust Dybbuk." *Moment* 1,7 (February 1976), 34–41.

———. "The New Jewish Right." *Moment* 1,1 (May/June 1975), 55–61.

Schwarzschild, Henry. "Israel: Importing American Jewish Racism." *Sh'ma* 1,18 (October 22, 1971), 142–144.

Schwarzschild, Steven S. Letter in response to Emil Fackenheim. *Sh'ma* 2,30 (April 7, 1972), 80.

Schwarzschild, Steven S. (ed.). "Jewish Values in the Post-Holocaust Future: A Symposium." *Judaism* 16,3 (summer 1967), 266–299.

———. "Toward Jewish Religious Unity: A Symposium." *Judaism* 15,2 (spring 1966), 131–163; participants: Irving Greenberg, Mordecai M. Kaplan, Jakob J. Petuchowski, Seymour Siegel.

Seeskin, Kenneth. *Jewish Philosophy in a Secular Age*. Albany: SUNY Press, 1990.

———. "Jewish Philosophy in the 1980s." *Modern Judaism* 11 (1991), 157–172.

Shechner, Mark. *After the Revolution: Studies in the Contemporary Jewish-American Imagination*. Bloomington: Indiana University Press, 1987.

Siegel, Frederick F. *Troubled Journey: From Pearl Harbor to Ronald Reagan*. New York: Hill and Wang, 1984.

Siegel, Seymour. "The Current Theological Situation." *Conservative Judaism* 23,4 (summer 1969), 11–24.

———. "Theological Reflections on the Destruction of European Jewry." *Conservative Judaism* 18,4 (summer 1964), 2–10.

Silberman, Charles E. *A Certain People: American Jews and Their Lives Today*. New York: Summit Books, 1985.

Silberman, Lou H. "Concerning Jewish Theology in North America: Some Notes on a Decade." *American Jewish Year Book* 70 (1969), 37–58.

Singer, David. "The Case for an 'Irrelevant' Orthodoxy: An Open Letter to Yitzchak Greenberg." *Tradition* 11,2 (summer 1970), 74–81.

———. "Passed over Jewishness in the Radical Haggadah." *Reconstructionist* 36,13 (December 25, 1970), 23–26.

Sklare, Marshall (ed.). *American Jews: A Reader*. New York: Behrman House, 1983.

Sleeper, James A., and Alan L. Mintz (eds.). *The New Jews*. New York: Vintage Books, 1971.

Soloveitchik, Joseph B. *Halakhic Man*. Philadephia: Jewish Publication Society of America Press, 1983.

"The State of Jewish Belief: A Symposium." *Commentary* 42,2 (August 1966), 71–160.

Stein, Howard F., and Robert F. Hill. *The Ethnic Imperative*. University Park: Pennsylvania State University Press, 1977.

Steinberg, Stephen. *The Ethnic Myth: Race, Ethnicity, and Class in America*. Boston: Beacon Press, 1989; orig. 1981.

Steiner, George. *In Bluebeard's Castle: Some Notes towards the Redefinition of Culture*. New Haven: Yale University Press, 1971.

———. *Language and Silence: Essays on Language, Literature and the Inhuman*. New York: Atheneum, 1974.

Steinfels, Peter. *The Neoconservatives*. New York: Simon and Schuster, 1979.

Stern, David. Review of *The Correspondence of Walter Benjamin*. *New Republic* 212 (April 10, 1995), 34–37.

Stern, David, and Paul Mendes-Flohr (eds.). *An Arthur A. Cohen Reader*. Detroit, MI: Wayne State University Press, 1998.

Syrkin, Marie. "Hannah Arendt: The Clothes of the Empress." *Dissent* 10,4 (autumn 1963), 344–352.

Taylor, Charles. *The Malaise of Modernity*. Concord, Ontario: Anansi Press, 1991; reprint, *The Ethics of Authenticity*. Cambridge: Harvard University Press, 1992.

———. *Philosophical Papers 1 and 2*. Cambridge, UK: Cambridge University Press, 1985.

————. *Sources of the Self: The Making of the Modern Identity*. Cambridge: Harvard University Press, 1989.

Taylor, Charles, et al. *Multiculturalism and "The Politics of Recognition."* Princeton: Princeton University Press, 1992.

Teller, Judd L. "A Critique of the New Jewish Theology." *Commentary* 25,3 (March 1958), 243–252.

————. "Israel: Neither Surrogate Nor Inferior." *Sh'ma* 1,18 (October 22, 1971), 140–142.

Tiefel, Hans O. "Holocaust Interpretations and Religious Assumptions." *Judaism* 25,2 (1976), 135–149.

Trilling, Diana. *The Beginning of the Journey: The Marriage of Diana and Lionel Trilling*. New York: Harcourt Brace, 1993.

Trilling, Lionel. *The Liberal Imagination*. New York: Viking Press, 1950.

————. *Sincerity and Authenticity*. Cambridge: Harvard University Press, 1971.

Tully, James (ed.). *Philosophy in an Age of Pluralism: The Philosophy of Charles Taylor in Question*. Cambridge, UK: Cambridge University Press, 1994.

Unger, Irwin. *The Movement: A History of the American New Left 1959–1972*. New York: Harper and Row, 1974.

Unger, Irwin, and Debi Unger. *Postwar America: The United States since 1945*. New York: St. Martin's Press, 1990.

Wald, Alan M. *The New York Intellectuals: The Rise and Decline of the Anti-Stalinist Left from the 1930s to the 1980s*. Chapel Hill: University of North Carolina Press, 1987.

Walzer, Michael. "Liberalism and the Art of Separation." *Political Theory* 12,3 (August 1984), 315–330.

Waxman, Chaim I. *America's Jews in Transition*. Philadelphia: Temple University Press, 1983.

Wertheimer, Jack. *A People Divided: Judaism in Contemporary America*. New York: Basic Books, 1993.

Whitfield, Stephen J. "The Holocaust and the American Jewish Intellectual." *Judaism* 28,4 (fall 1979), 391–401.

————. *Into the Dark: Hannah Arendt and Totalitarianism*. Philadelphia: Temple University Press, 1980.

————. *Voices of Jacob, Hands of Esau: Jews in American Life and Thought*. Hamden, CT: Archon Books, 1984.

Wiesel, Elie. *The Gates of the Forest*. New York: Holt, Rinehart and Winston, 1966.

————. *The Jews of Silence*. New York: Holt, Rinehart and Winston, 1966.

————. *Legends of Our Time*. New York: Avon Books, 1968.

————. *Messengers of God*. New York: Random House, 1976.

————. *Night*. New York: Hill and Wang, 1960; orig. in French, 1958.

————. *Souls on Fire*. New York: Random House, 1972.

————. *The Town Beyond the Wall*. New York: Avon Books, 1964.

Wisse, Ruth R. "The New York (Jewish) Intellectuals." *Commentary* (November 1987), 28–38.

Wolf, Arnold Jacob. "The Revisionism of Irving Greenberg." *Sh'ma* 13,254 (May 13, 1983), 104–106.

Wolf, Arnold Jacob (ed.). *Rediscovering Judaism: Reflections on a New Theology*. Chicago: Quadrangle Press, 1965.

Woocher, Jonathan S. *Sacred Survival: The Civil Religion of American Jews*. Bloomington: Indiana University Press, 1986.

Wyschogrod, Edith. *Spirit in Ashes: Hegel, Heidegger, and Man-Made Mass Death*. New Haven: Yale University Press, 1985.

Wyschogrod, Michael. "Auschwitz: Beginning of a New Era? Reflections on the Holocaust." *Tradition* 17,1 (fall 1977), 63–78.

———. *The Body of Faith*. New York: Seabury Press, 1983.

———. "Some Theological Reflections on the Holocaust." *Response* 9,1 (spring 1975), 65–68.

Young, James E. *Writing and Rewriting the Holocaust: Narrative and the Consequences of Interpretation*. Bloomington: Indiana University Press, 1988.

Young-Bruehl, Elisabeth. *Hannah Arendt: For Love of the World*. New Haven: Yale University Press, 1982.

Zimmels, H. J. *The Echo of the Nazi Holocaust in Rabbinic Literature*. New York: Ktav, 1977.

Zinn, Howard. *Postwar America: 1945–1971*. Indianapolis: Bobbs-Merrill, 1973.

Zuckerman, Arthur J. "The Error of Absolutist Metaphysics." *Reconstructionist* 19,10 (June 26, 1953), 26–28.

———. "Judaism and the Age of Anxiety." *Reconstructionist* 19,7 (May 15, 1953), 9–16.

Name Index